Notable Comm...

Both Alexander Hamiltons share West Indian and Scottish heritage, and both stem from the first-named Hamilton, born in England in 1185, as I also do. The author writes absorbing stories of dozens of famous Hamiltons over eight centuries.

His Grace the Duke of Hamilton.
The 16th Duke of Hamilton and 13th of Brandon.

I loved reading of modern-day Alec Hamilton's great-Uncle meeting my great-Uncle, the Tsar of Russia. Alec and his Scottish and Jamaican ancestor's stories are essentially the histories of Jamaica itself. What an eye-opener when the author evidence that both Alexander Hamilton's of his book can trace their bloodline back to 880 A.D.

H.H. Princess Olga Andreevna Romanov, great-niece of the last
Tsar of Russia and President of the Romanov Family Association.

What a wonderfully serious, well-researched, and well-written book this is. The author's genealogical work deserves praise, and we did not previously realize that a Hamilton was once close to becoming the King of Scotland. The Author, both Hamilton's, Scotland, and the Caribbean are all entwined, a must-read book!

Celia & John Lee, Authors & Military Historians.

Spelling American Style:

The author has lived in the United States and worked for American companies for over twenty-one years and transitioned long ago to using Americanized English spelling rather than British English spelling. He begs his non-American English-language readers' understanding.

> *We have really everything in common with America nowadays, except, of course, language.*

By Oscar Wilde.

The playwright and wit was the first to write the phrase in his short story, The Canterville Ghost, 1887. Many others have paraphrased Wilde's words since, including George Bernard Shaw in 1942 in an interview, and it has erroneously been attributed to British Prime Minister Sir Winston Churchill.

THE LIFE & TIMES OF

ALEXANDER HAMILTON

TWO APPLES THAT FELL FROM THE SAME TREE

BY
ROBERT GARY DODDS-AUTHOR ™

 FriesenPress

One Printers Way
Altona, MB R0G 0B0
Canada

www.friesenpress.com

ISBN
978-1-03-912559-9 (Hardcover)
978-1-03-912558-2 (Paperback)
978-1-03-912560-5 (eBook)

1. HIS010000 HISTORY, EUROPE
2. HIS041000 HISTORY, CARIBBEAN & WEST INDIES
3. HIS036030 HISTORY, UNITED STATES, REVOLUTIONARY PERIOD (1775-1800)

Distributed to the trade by The Ingram Book Company

The author's website: **www.rgdodds-author.com**
Instagram: **@rgdoddsauthor**

Robert Gary Dodds – Author ™

It is a wholly-owned name and legal entity of MG Consulting (USA) LLC., Company registration No. C201433500625, North Carolina, USA.

Table of Contents

Foreword by

His Grace the Duke of Hamilton, and Brandon
Chief of Clan Hamilton and the Premier Peer of Scotland.

In this book, the author writes about two apples falling from the same family tree. Both Alexander Hamiltons share West Indian and Scottish heritage, and both stem from the first named Hamilton, born in England in 1185, as I also do.

He writes absorbing stories of dozens of famous Hamiltons over eight centuries, and we'll read an abridged journey of several of their lives and how many affected Scottish and British history. The author includes General Claude Hamilton, 1st Lord Paisley, and Abercorn, a supporter of Mary, Queen of Scots, whose heirs became the earls of Abercorn; two of his brother's heirs became the Earl of Arran and Duke of Hamilton. We'll read of Alec Hamilton's great-uncle, General Sir Ian Hamilton, who fought in both the Boer wars and World War One and was Rudyard Kipling's friend and Sir Winston Churchill's lifetime chum. Winston wrote a book on him entitled Ian Hamilton's March, published in 1900.

The author writes an excellent summary of his other Alexander Hamilton's life, a Founding Father of America born in 1757 on Nevis, in the West Indies. He also unearthed a high-ranking British Hamilton, who fought in the American Revolutionary War on opposite sides of the future Hamilton, Founding Father. Finally, he unfolds the "modern-day" Alexander Hamilton's life and times; born in Scotland in 1932, he served in The Gordon Highlanders regiment in Malaya and lived in Jamaica from 1954 until he sadly died Easter Sunday 2020. This Hamilton and his maternal ancestors' stories may well read as a history of Jamaica itself, in the same way, many often say, that the Hamilton family history is one of Scotland itself.

I am delighted to see this book published and hope you enjoy reading it.

His Grace Alexander Douglas Douglas-Hamilton.
The 16th Duke of Hamilton, and 13th of Brandon.

Introductory Summary

In 1066 William, The Duke of Normandy, successfully invaded England. He was accompanied by two de Beaumont brothers and from one of these siblings comes eleven centuries of de Beaumont and Hamilton descendants who have helped shape British and global history. These include both the Alexander Hamiltons in this book, the present Dukes of Hamilton and Abercorn, the Earl of Arran and all who bear the Hamilton name.

Historical, genealogical, and DNA research evidence that a Viking earl is the direct male bloodline ancestor to the de Beaumont brothers. Among their male bloodline descendants are the first to be named Hamilton, America's Founding Father, who helped create the future United States of America, and the "modern-day" Alexander Hamilton, his namesake. The latter Hamilton, in his way, helped shape the future of his adopted nation, too, Jamaica. Scottish, English, American, and Jamaican history were all shaped by Hamiltons and their forefathers. The book unearths another high-profile Hamilton in America's War of Independence, on the other side.

The following chapters introduce some fascinating Viking, de Beaumont, and Hamilton individuals and their stories from the ninth to the twenty-first centuries. We'll read of family forebears, including the Viking who helped settle the region in France known today as Normandy in the tenth century. We'll hear of the 1st Norman Earl of Leicester from the eleventh century and his descendant, the Hamilton in the sixteenth century, who spent his life defending Mary, Queen of Scots, and the Hamiltons fighting with William Wallace and Robert the Bruce. This Hamilton's father was at one time heir to the Scottish throne. His progeny became the earls of Arran, the "modern-day" Alexander Hamilton, and heirs to two of his brothers became the dukes of Hamilton and Abercorn.

Then there's the nineteenth-century Hamilton, whose Gordon Highlanders' officer record none may ever match with its volume of significant theaters of war in which he served across the globe over forty-five years. This book shares the terror of ninth to twentieth-century war, battles, betrayal, intrigue, failure, and inhumanity. It is also a book with tales of humanity, utter splendor, wealth, royalty, and power—stories of integrity, benevolence, loyalty, determination, and duty.

The Elusive Family Tree

One of the first questions the author planned when arriving in Scotland was to enquire if the modern-day Alexander Hamilton had a family tree, which would save much research time. Alec recalled somewhat ominously that he had seen it many years ago (past tense) but presumed it was lost.

The author was permitted to wander about the endless, closed-off wing rooms, and he gently pushed open doors and swished cobwebs away. One of the bedrooms seemed frozen in time. Old white cloths covered everything in the room, strewn around under layers of dust. The paintings on the walls had not escaped the passage of time, their glass dulled by blankets of past isolation. The author could not help thinking that the windows would have quivered with excitement and squeaked with joy if a window cleaner had appeared. Old mahogany furniture included a baby's rocking bassinet, likewise, draped in dust-covered white cloth.

The author's eye caught something hanging from the back of the room door. He could hardly believe it: a very grimy, glass-framed Hamilton of Westport and Elrick family tree going back to AD 1274. Not many families can evidence that their male bloodline goes back 747 years. That framed copy of the family tree, hanging out of sight for goodness knows how many decades, ended with Alec's great-grandfather, born in 1825.

The author would eventually break through somewhat of a genealogical barrier by cross-referencing evidence to show that the first Hamilton's male bloodline went back 837-years. Evidencing the first-named Hamilton was one success, but who were his parents, if not Hamiltons? How far back could his lineage be proven and evidenced by historical records, genealogy, and DNA data? As far back as could be reliably validated, a new and complete family tree would also show Alec's grandchildren and their descendants where they fit, going right back to AD 880. By 2022, that would be 1,142 years ago. Now that's a family tree!

When in-depth research appeared to suggest that Alec shared the same Hamilton ancestor as one of America's Founding Fathers, another Alexander Hamilton, the author thought it unlikely and too good to be true. But after discovering three diverse, reliable genealogical and DNA project sources that confirm the shared ancestor, he was delighted. If you like, two apples fell from the same branch of an ancient and noble Hamilton family tree, hence the book's sub-title.

What's in a Family Name

After unearthing the first-named Hamilton (William de Hameldone, born 1185 as William de Beaumont), the author drafted a new family tree for Alec's Westport and Elrick branch of the Hamiltons. It took months of research, checking, and counterchecking each family link by genealogical, DNA, and local historical records to be 100% sure of lineage. This was incredibly complicated, as so many male Hamiltons carried the same first names for generations. Just as you think you have found fascinating facts or the next-generation ancestor's link, you spot a mismatch, and it's not the Hamilton you thought it was. Back to the drawing board, you go.

When did the family name become Hamilton? Surnames, as such, did not exist much before the late-fourteenth century and became more common in the early fifteenth century. The word "surname" is derived from the Anglo-Norman French *sornoum*, which most likely arrived in England with its conquering in 1066. Sometimes a person's surname was taken from the trade they practiced, so John, the carpenter, became John Carpenter. Similarly, Sir David, known as from or of (de) Hameldone, became known as Sir David Hameldone.

The Book Evolved from Writing One Story to a Work of Three Parts

First, it covers ancient times and selected ancestor stories of multiple Hamiltons and earlier bloodlines who impacted history. This book's Alexander Hamiltons share the same direct ancestor, and many of their forefathers were legends in their own time. Some remain so in history; others we'll look at have been forgotten by the passage of time. This book then traces the founding father of America, Alexander Hamilton, and a summary of his life and times, and the modern-day Alexander Hamilton's life and times too. The book created is a biographic and historical work, covering a period spanning from the ninth century to the present-day family, history, and roots.

Alec and Erica Hamilton permitted the author to use Erica's notes from a handful of Alec's dictated stories made some years ago about his early years in Jamaica before they one day slipped from his consciousness. She wished to ensure that Alec's remarkable life in Jamaica was captured for his descendants so that they might know what momentous times and events he lived through on the island and how unique he was in his own right. These notes formed part of the author's research in writing about Alec's life and times.

Two Quotes That Resonate With The Author Regarding This Book

First, the exceptional film director Sir Richard Attenborough, speaking about the Mahatma in his film, *Gandhi,* summed up how the author feels about the writing of this or any biographic and historical work (which can be applied to any individual regardless of gender):

"No man's life can be encompassed in one telling. There is no way to give each year its allotted weight, to include each event, each person who helped shape a lifetime. What can be done is to be faithful in spirit to the record and try to find one's way to the heart of the man."

Secondly, a public quote by Prof. Ted Cowan, Emeritus Professor of Scottish History at the University of Glasgow, Scotland (a well-known historian and a man with a refreshing approach), sums up the author's opinion on history:

"If things are not controversial in history, then they are not worth talking about."

NOTES.

Citations of Sources Under 'Notes' at the End of Each Chapter

+ The author wrote multiple research papers from his in-depth investigations into historical, genealogical, and DNA research associated with events, places, or people linked to each chapter of this book and recorded those links, sources, and quotes.

+ As a lifetime passionate researcher and historian, he did not wish most readers lost in reams of citations listing every source of material under 'Notes' at the end of each chapter.

+ One would expect such lists from an Academic work, dissertation, or thesis and professional historians.

+ However, the author's research materials, from which he drew evidence to form his narrative in each chapter, can be made available by author-approved requests for those interested.

Historical Monetary Values Today

The *UK Office for National Statistics Composite Index*. Throughout this book, the author has used this index for all historical monetary sums, their 'approximate' value today, and their conversion rates to other currencies. Tables are based on the UK's historic inflation rate over any given two periods in time.

The author hopes you enjoy reading this book and discovering the history and events surrounding so many selected members of the Hamilton family and their ancestors. He takes you on a journey of nearly one and a half millennia back in time.

Reviewing the ensuing family trees should help put each chapter's upcoming characters, timelines, and stories into perspective. They are always handy to come back to and check where someone you read about in the book fits in.

Alexander Vereker Hamilton
A portrait by Basia Kaczmarowska Hamilton 1992.

He was a direct descendant of Sir Walter Fitz-Gilbert de Hameldone, 1st Laird of Cadzow, through his eldest grandson, David de Hameldone. The latter headed this Alexander Hamilton's Westport & Elrick lineage.

Hamilton Arms of Westport and Elrick

Alexander Hamilton, a Founding Father of America
Portrait by John Trumbull 1806.

He was a direct descendant of Sir Walter Fitz-Gilbert de Hameldone, 1st Laird of Cadzow, through his younger grandson, Walter de Hameldone. The latter, through his son, David Hamilton of Cambuskeith, headed the Founding Fathers Hamilton lineage.

Hamilton Arms of Grange

The Hamilton Genealogical Trees

Commence with Vikings, the direct male bloodline forefathers of the Hamilton clan.

Bernard "The Dane" Coat or Arms

Bernard "The Dane"
c. A.D. 880 c. A.D. 955
m. Sprota de Bourgogne
A Viking jarl (Earl) of Norway
After A. D. 909, he became Seigneur de Pont-au-demer de Harcourt, and de Rouen in today's Normandy, France.
He had 13-children.

Torf le Riche de Harcourt, et de Tourville et Seigneur de Pont-au-demer
c. 914 c. 973
m. Ertemberge de Briquebec

Touroude (Thorold) Seigneur de Pont-au-demer
c. 949 c. 997
m. Eva Duvelina
Of Beaumont town, Normandy

Anchetil de Harcourt
c. 1005 d. unknown
m. Eve de Boessey-le-Chapel
Today's Harcourt's stem from Anchetil, and Eve

Roger de Sauveur
Mathilde de Pont-au-emer
Godfrey Beaulac
Galeran de Meulan
Renaud de Meulan
Torf de Pont-au-demer

William de Eu.
Havlive de Rouen
Muriella de Normandy
Judith de Montanolier
Roger II de Sauveur
Raoul de Bayeaux

Turchetil de Tourville Seigneur de Harcourt, et de Tourville
c. 970 d. unknown
m. Adeline de Montfort
Ancestor of present, Earl Harcourt, via Bernard

Walter de Tourville

William de Tourville

Lessiline de Tourville
m. Earl of Eu.

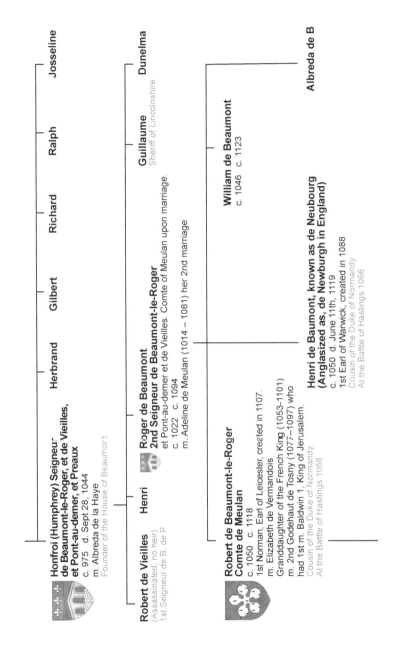

Josseline

Ralph

Richard

Gilbert

Herbrand

Honfroi (Humphrey) Seigneur de Beaumont-le-Roger, et de Vieilles, et Pont-au-demer, et Preaux
c. 975 d. Sept 28, 1044
m. Albreda de la Haye
Founder of the House of Beaumort.

Dunelma

Guillaume Sheriff of Lincolnshire

Roger de Beaumont 2nd Seigneur de Beaumont-le-Roger et Pont-au-demer et de Vieilles. Comte of Meulan upon marriage.
c. 1022 c. 1094
m. Adeline de Meulan (1014 – 1081) her 2nd marriage

Henri

Robert de Vieilles
(Assassinated, no heir)
1st Seigneur de B. de P

Albreda de B

William de Beaumont
c. 1046 c. 1123

Henri de Baumont, known as de Neubourg (Anglasized as, de Newburgh in England)
c. 1050 d. June 11th, 1119
1st Earl of Warwick, created in 1088
Cousin of the Duke of Normandy
At the Battle of Hastings 1066

Robert de Beaumont-le-Roger Comte de Meulan
c. 1050 c. 1118
1st Norman, Earl of Leicester, creted in 1107.
m. Elizabeth de Vermandois
Granddaughter of the French King (1053-1101)
m. 2nd Godehaut de Tosny (1077–1097) who
had 1st m. Baldwin 1, King of Jerusalem.
Cousin of the Duke of Normandy
At the Battle of Hastings 1066

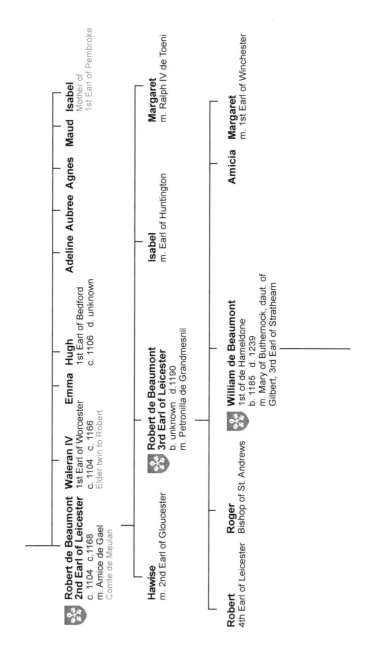

Addunt Robur Stirpi
They add the strength of stock

The Hamilton's of Westport & Elrick Family Tree

William de Hameldone
(Born in Leicestershire, and Christened, William de Beaumont as shown on the previous page. William became known from the town of Hameldone, Buckinghamshire where he lived as a young man onwards)
b. 1185 in England   d. 1239 in Somme, France
m. Mary of Buthernock dau. of Gilbert, 3rd Earl of Strathearn
The family name is sometimes spelled de Hameldun, de Hamildoun, and the modern Hamilton.

Sir Gilbert Fitz - William de Hameldone
b. 1225 d. 1293. Baldernock, East Dunbartonshire, Scotland
m. Mabel Isabella Randolph
The 1st Hamilton believed to own Scottish lands.

Sir Walter Fitz-Gilbert de Hameldone
b. 1274 c. 1346 1st Laird of Cadzow (pronounced, Kadyu)
m. Euphemia Lesley; m. Mary de Gordon
Father of David, 2nd Laird & Sir John Fitz-Walter at the time of Robert the Bruce & William Wallace.
With, 5 half brothers. Murray's.

Sir David Fitz-Walter de Hameldone (By Mary de Gordon)
b. 1310 d. 1376 2nd Laird and Baron of Cadzow
m. Lady Margaret dau. of William, Earl of Ross; 2nd m. Margaret Leslie
Father of David (the ancestor of the Hamilton's of Westport & Elrick and today's Alexander Hamilton), John, Walter (ancestor of the Hamilton's of Cambuskeith, and the Founding Father of America), and Alan.

Sir David de Hamilton (By Lady Margaret)
b. 1333   d. 1392   3rd Laird and Baron of Cadzow
m. Jonetta (Janet) de Keith of Galston
Born and died in Cadzow, Lanarkshire, Scotland
David was the first to adopt the family name to be spelled, Hamilton in 1378.
Father of Sir John, 4th Laird & Baron, George, William, Andrew, a fifth son John and one unknown child.

Sir John Hamilton
b. 1370   d. 1402 4th Laird and Baron of Cadzow, of Lanarkshire, Scotland
m. Jacoba (Janet) Douglas of Dalkeith (He died in the battle of Homildon)
Father of James, 5th Laird, & Baron, Katherine, David, Walter, Andrew, Mary, Margery, and Alexander
(de Hamilton, 1st of Silvertonhill as below)
Half brother of Sir John Stewart, 1st Seigneur d'Aubigny, Sir William Stewart of Castlemilk

Sir James Hamilton
m. Janet Livingstone
b. 1396   d. 1441 5th Laird and Baron of Cadzow
Born and died in Cadzow, Lanarkshire, Scotland.
Father of James, 6th Laird & Baron Cadzow, and the 1st Lord Hamilton, Alexander, Gavin, Mary, Elizabeth, John.

Alexander de Hamilton, of Cadzow, later 1st of Silvertonhill and
1st of Westport.
b. 1416   d. 1455
m. unrecorded
Father of James and William, Sir Robert and 7 by other women

James of Silvertonhill
c.1445   c. 1513 +
2nd of Silvertonhill

William Hamilton de Bellsyde
b. 1437   d. 1487
m. unrecorded

Lord James Hamilton, 1st Lord Hamilton
b. 1416   d. 1479 6th Laird and Baron Cadzow
Born and died in Hamilton, Lanarkshire, Scotland
m. Lady Eupheme Graham, d. of Earl of Strathearn
widow of the 5th Earl of Douglas
m. **Princess Mary Stewart, Countess of Arran (widow)**,
dau. of King James II of Scotland
Father of Lord James, Elizabeth, Robert, John and Patrick.

Lord James Hamilton, 1st Earl of Arran
b. 1475   d. 1529   7th Laird and Baron Cadzow
Of Kinneil, Scotland
m. Elizabeth Home
m Janet Bethune (Beaton)

James Hamilton, 2nd Earl of Arran 1st Duc de Châtellerault (Regent Scotland 1548 - 1542)
b. 1515 d. 1575
Heir to the Scottish and English thrones 1542
m. Lady Margaret Douglas, dau. of Earl of Morton
Father of: James, 3rd Earl; John, 1st Marquess Hamilton and
8 other children including, Claude, 1st Lord Paisley
whose eldest son, James became the 1st Earl of Abercorn.

John of Westport
b. 1485 d. 1537

Thomas of Westport
Died young brother succeeds

James Hamilton of Westport
b. 1531 d. 1578
m. unrecorded

James Hamilton of Westport
b. 1573 d. 1625
m. Janet Drummond

David Hamilton of Elrick
b. 1553 est. d. 1619
m. Marion Home

John Hamilton of Westport
b. 1593 d. unknown
m. unknown

Rev John Hamilton, Minister of Carmichael
b. 1618 d. 1674
m. Helen Ferguson

Sir James Hamilton of Westport
b. 1618 d. 1663
m. Anna dau. of Sir. Patrick Hamilton
Father of Grizel (12 children). Anna Hamilton.

Rev. John Hamilton Minister of Blackfriars Parish
b. 1670 d. 1741
m. Margaret Ballantine
Father of Margaret, Helen, Grizel, John, William, Agnes.

James Walter of Westport

Rev. John Hamilton, Minister of St Mungo's, Glasgow
b. 1713 d. 1780
m. Mary Campbell, 1 child, died
m. Mary Bogle, dau. of John Bogle, Hamilton Farm
Father of John of Northpark, Lord Provost of Glasgow. George. Patrick born in Jamaica
1757 d. 1788 William, John, George, Janet, Mary, Sarah.

George Hamilton of Glasgow
b. 1760 d. 1796
m. Agnes Bogle, m. 2nd Margaret Bogle
Father of John George Hamilton

John Hamilton of Northpark
b. 1734 d. 1829 by Mary Bogle
m. Helen Bogle
Father of Archibald, George, Mary, Helen, John plus 1

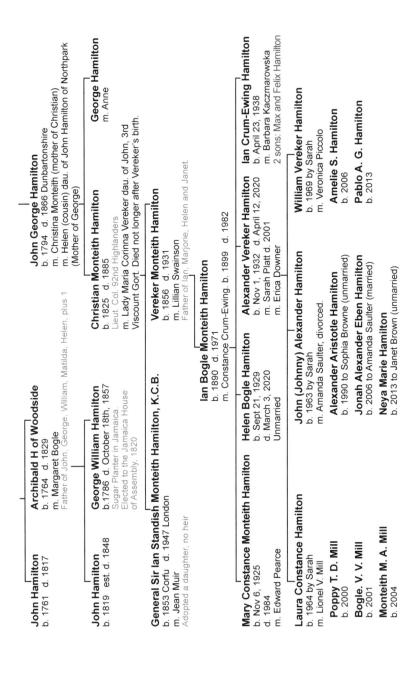

John Hamilton
b. 1761 d. 1817

Archibald H of Woodside
b. 1764 d. 1829
m. Margaret Bogle
Father of John, George, William, Matilda, Helen, plus 1

John George Hamilton
b. 1794 d. 1866 Dunbartonshire
m. Christina Monteith (mother of Christian)
m. Helen (cousin) dau. of John Hamilton of Northpark
(Mother of George)

John Hamilton
b. 1819 est. d. 1848

George William Hamilton
b.1786 d. October 18th, 1857
Sugar Planter in Jamaica
Elected to the Jamaica House
of Assembly, 1820

Christian Monteith Hamilton
b. 1825 d. 1885
Lieut. Col. 92nd Highlanders
m. Lady Maria Corinna Vereker dau. of John, 3rd
Viscount Gort. Died not longer after Vereker's birth.

George Hamilton
m. Anne

General Sir Ian Standish Monteith Hamilton, K.C.B.
b. 1853 Corfu d. 1947 London
m. Jean Muir
Adopted a daughter, no heir

Vereker Monteith Hamilton
b. 1856 d. 1931
m. Lillian Swainson
Father of Ian, Marjorie, Helen and Janet.

Ian Bogle Monteith Hamilton
b. 1890 d. 1971
m. Constance Crum-Ewing. b. 1899 d. 1982

Mary Constance Monteith Hamilton
b. Nov 6, 1925
d. 1984
m. Edward Pearce

Helen Bogle Hamilton
b. Sept 21, 1929
d. March 3, 2020
Unmarried

Alexander Vereker Hamilton
b. Nov 1, 1932 d. April 12, 2020
m. Sarah Platt d. 2001
m. Erica Downer

Ian Crum-Ewing Hamilton
b. April 23, 1938
m. Barbara Kaczmarowska
2 sons: Max and Felix Hamilton

Laura Constance Hamilton
b. 1964 by Sarah
m. Lionel V. Mill

John (Johnny) Alexander Hamilton
b. 1963 by Sarah
m. Amanda Saulter, divorced.

William Vereker Hamilton
b. 1969 by Sarah
m. Veronica Piccolo

Poppy T. D. Mill
b. 2000

Alexander Aristotle Hamilton
b. 1990 to Sophia Browne (unmarried)

Amelie S. Hamilton
b. 2006

Bogle. V. V. Mill
b. 2001

Jonah Alexander Eben Hamilton
b. 2006 to Amanda Saulter (married)

Pablo A. G. Hamilton
b. 2013

Monteith M. A. Mill
b. 2004

Neya Marie Hamilton
b. 2013 to Janet Brown (unmarried)

Hamilton, Ewing (Crum-Ewing) Family Tree connections

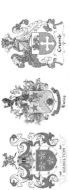

John George Hamilton
b. 1794   d. 1866

Alexander Crum of Thornliebank
b. 1757   d. 1808
m. Jane, dau. of Walter Ewing Maclae

James Ewing of Glasgow
b. 1784   d. 1853
m. Jane Crawford. No children

Christian Monteith Hamilton
b. 1825   d. 1885
m. Lady Maria Vereker dau. 3rd Viscount Gort

Humphrey Crum (From 1853 Crum-Ewing)
b. 1802   d.1887
m. Helen Dick dau. of Rev John Dick
Heir to James Ewing of Glasgow, his Uncle

Alexander Crum-Ewing
b. 1826   d. Dec 30,1912
m. Jane O'Grady dau. Admiral O'Grady

Vereker Monteith Hamilton
b. 1856   d.1931
m. Lillian Swainson

Helen Dick Crum-Ewing
b. 1862   d. 1903

Humphrey Crum-Ewing
b. 1866   d. 1946

Alexander Crum-Ewing
b. 1896   c. Nov 1914

General Sir. Ian Hamilton
b. 1853   d. 1947
m. Jean Muir

Ian Bogle Monteith Hamilton
b. 1890   d. 1971

Married

Constance Crum-Ewing
b. 1899   d. 1982

Alexander Vereker Hamilton
b. Nov 1, 1932   d. April 12, 2020
m. Sarah Platt, d. 2001
m. Erica Downer

Ian Crum-Ewing Hamilton
b. April 23, 1938
m. Barbara Kaczmarowska
2 sons: Max and Felix Hamilton

William Vereker Hamilton
b. 1969 by Sarah

Mary Constance Monteith Hamilton
b. Nov 6, 1925
d. 1984
m. Edward Pearce

Helen Bogle Hamilton
b. Sept 21, 1929
d. March 3, 2020
Unmarried

Laura Constance Hamilton
b. 1964 by Sarah

John (Johnny) Alexander Hamilton
b. 1963 by Sarah

The Hamilton's of Cambuskeith & of Grange

The tree that splits the Two Alexander Hamiltons which fell from the same tree

Sir David Fitz-Walter de Hameldone, 2nd Baron of Cadzow
b. 1310 d.1376
m. Margaret Ross

Walter Hamilton
b. by 1339 d. 1402

David Hamilton 1st of Cambuskeith
b. after 1352 d. by 1436

James Hamilton 2nd of Cambuskeith
b. 1425 d. unknown

John Hamilton 3rd of Cambuskeith
b. 1450 d. 1489

Alexander Hamilton 4th of Cambuskeith
b. 1475 d. 1513
Died at the Battle of Flodden with King James IV

Sir. John Hamilton 5th of Cambuskeith
b. 1493 d. 1543

William Hamilton 6th of Cambuskeith
b. by 1468 d. by 1571

Sir David Hamilton, 3rd Baron
b. 1333 d. 1392

**This Hamilton line leads directly
To today's, Alexander Hamilton.**
15th great-grandson of Sir David Fitz-Walter

John Hamilton of Cambuskeith 7th
b. by 1504   d. 1547

John Hamilton 1st of Grange
b. 1527   d. unknown

David Hamilton 1st of Ladieton, then The Grange
b. by 1537   d.1616
m. Not recorded

Alexander Hamilton 2nd of Grange
b. 1566   d. 1601
m. Agnes Crawford

Sir John Hamilton 3rd of Grange
b. after 1583   d. 1662
m. Margaret Crawford

John Hamilton 4th of Grange
b. 1600   d. 1674
m. Elizabeth Crawford

John Hamilton 5th of Grange
b. 1640   d. 1695
m. Rebecca Cunningham

Alexander Hamilton 6th of Grange
b. 1690   d. 1763
m. Elizabeth Pollock dau. of Sir. Robert Pollock Bt.
Father of 8 children

James A. Hamilton
b. 1718 The Grange, Scotland   d. 1799 Nevis.
Partner. Rachel Levien, née Faucette (not married to James)

Alexander Hamilton
b. 1757, Nevis   d. 1804 in a duel, New Jersey, USA
m. Elizabeth Schuyler
A Founding Father of America and 14th great-grandson of Sir David Fitz-Walter de Hameldone

James Hamilton Junior
b. 1752 Nevis   d. 1786, USA

Chapter 1

VIKING AND NORMAN ANCESTORS
TO THE 11ᵀᴴ CENTURY

You can't go back and change the beginning, but you can start where you are and change the end. C. S. Lewis

However, in this book, we can look back in time and review some of the "modern-day" Alexander Hamilton's ancestors, their stories, and their lives. By doing so, we can begin to understand the legacy and spirit he and America's Founding Fathers carried in their DNA. We can place into perspective both Alexanders' life journeys and how they faced many unexpected events in them. We can also look to Alec's continually changing story, which he'd been carving out for himself in his family's future folklore before he sadly passed away in the spring of 2020, changing the end of his life's tale himself.

As our two Alexander Hamiltons shared the same historical ancestor, they also shared scores of early ancestors, whose genes they both carried into their lives. In some way, the genes will have contributed to shaping the men they were to become. The Hamiltons are a fascinating ancient and noble family, and we have much to learn by reading their tales and history in this book.

Only in choosing C.S. Lewis's quote for this book did the author's research show that he was, in fact, of Hamilton blood, something His Grace, the Duke of Hamilton, may not have known. The author C.S. Lewis is known worldwide today primarily for his *Chronicles of Narnia* fantasy book series. But Lewis wrote over thirty books, held academic positions at Oxford and Cambridge Universities, and was a lay theologian. In January 1899, his mother was born a Hamilton in Downpatrick, County Down, Northern Ireland.

C.S. Lewis's great-grandfather, Hugh Hamilton, was an Irish Bishop, mathematician, scientist, and professor at Trinity College Dublin. For Irish and Canadian Hamilton readers' interest, one of Hugh's brothers was George Hamilton, who became baron of Ireland's Court of Exchequer. Another brother, Charles, whose son was also named George Hamilton, became an incredibly wealthy Canadian lumber merchant and politician. In the early seventeenth century, this bishop's great-great-grandfather, another Hugh Hamilton, had immigrated to County Down from the Hamiltons of Scotland. The last factoid about C. S. Lewis is that he also wrote some of his books under a pen name using his mother's maiden name—Clive Hamilton.

Reliability of Dates Before The Tenth Century

It's important to understand that many dates before the eleventh century are debatable unless evidenced by multiple sources. This is especially true of the ninth century or earlier. Due to few reliable records in this period of history, the author has chosen dates irrefutable by evidence or from the greater weight of genealogist and historical opinion, or where DNA exists.

One often finds varying dates given by various supposedly reliable historical or genealogical experts. Yet, the author had the advantage of recent DNA evidence that many earlier historical works did not. A major Hamilton DNA project has been underway for at least a decade at a central US university, overseen by a Hamilton.

2020 Viking DNA Project Results

Let us look at the Viking ancestry relevant to many Hamiltons by first sharing this Viking DNA project from 2020. In September of that year, a team of international scientists published the world's most extensive DNA sequencing of 442 Viking skeletons from sites scattered across Europe, Greenland, and Scotland. Of the skeletons, 300 were men's, but women, children, and even babies were found in Viking cemeteries. After a six-year investigation, the study of the remains revealed that the 442 Vikings were not just of Scandinavian heritage but had come "from Greenland, Ukraine, The United Kingdom, Scandinavia, Poland, and Russia," as we know them today.

It is valuable to spend a moment looking at what this means, as understanding the origins and spread of Viking genes and culture impacts everything about the Hamiltons' influence through their English, Scottish, and American genes. We will talk about two of these ninth-century Vikings and see their descendants, in one case, capture the throne of England. The other leads us straight to the male bloodline of all Hamilton descendants worldwide today. The genes of these two Vikings impact the British gene pool too. Ninth and tenth-century cultural heritage and political dynamics were changed dramatically by the Viking Age of raiding Europe and the British Isles from AD 800.

Of Viking influence, the DNA project reports that it's "still evident today in place names, surnames, and modern genetics." Professor Eske Willerslev, a Fellow of St John's College, University of Cambridge, England, and director of The Lundbeck Foundation GeoGenetics Centre, University of Copenhagen, sequenced the skeletons. Scientists collaboratively carried out the Viking DNA study from the University of Cambridge, the University of Copenhagen, the University Bristol, and the Moesgaard Museum in Denmark. Academics represented specializations in GeoGenetics, evolutionary genomics, and archaeology—a highly distinguished group of specialist scientists. DNA studies uncover myths and facts only hypothesized in earlier centuries.

Professor Søren Sindbæk, an archaeologist from Moesgaard Museum in Denmark, said that "two Orkney skeletons buried with Viking swords in Viking-style graves are genetically similar to present-day Irish and Scottish people and could be the earliest Pictish genomes ever studied." The Orkneys are an archipelago of Scottish Islands ten miles off the tip of northwest Scotland and Caithness, and north of Scapa flow. The closest mainland to their east is Norway. The DNA studies showed Viking people with varying hair colors and found significant southern European, Asian, and Pict DNA present in their remains.

This study corroborates what historians have known for a long-time—that Vikings, at least after the first 200-years of raiding, often realized that the land they appropriated was better than their land back in Iceland, Norway, or Denmark. Some settled and stayed on in the British Isles. Over the centuries, many Norse people's families or village groups settled in Caithness, Sutherland, and Galloway in Scotland in the mid-ninth century, just ahead of Bernard "The Dane," born in AD 880, whom we'll hear about shortly.

Clarifying the Type of People Vikings Were

Although some historians suggest that many Vikings were just farmers and settlers, there is a mountain of evidence that most Viking raids were appallingly ferocious and deadly. The Norse peoples were from sea-faring nations filled with fearless fighters, and they were seasoned warriors in the art of lethal hand-to-hand combat. Let's not forget that the early Norse lands were made up of many minor kingdoms frequently at war with each other, and violence was a daily way of life. Attacks were mainly on coastal village people and monasteries close to the coast of countries they invaded.

As pagans, they attacked monasteries and destroyed Christian places of worship that earned the pagan warriors prestige at home. The gold, silver, jewelry, and precious gems procured from monasteries were often achieved by torturing monks to identify hidden stashes of gold and coin (many monks' written records claim). Generally, raids enabled warriors to acquire cloth, iron goods, and weapons. Larger Viking warships could also take on board cattle and sheep for breeding stock, and all raiders would have wanted to reprovision with foodstuff for their journey back home. As acknowledged by historical records in England, Wales, Ireland, and Scotland, some of the most popular items to steal were people to keep as slaves. These records were most often written in Latin by the few that could read and write, usually monks.

A Viking Who Discovered North America

Historical documents, sagas and archaeological evidence confirm two things. Seven years of archaeological research from 1960 evidenced an ancient Norse settlement in Newfoundland. An international team joined the discoverer Helge Ingstad and his wife, Anne, unearthed eight sets of building foundations, carbon-dated to around 1000 AD.

Early expeditions of Vikings from Greenland and Norway across the Atlantic are well documented and accepted by most historians as fact. They state that Greenland-born Viking Leif Eriksson was the first European to land in North America around 1000 AD in today's Canadian province of Newfoundland. He had converted to Christianity in Norway, from where he sailed across to North America. Leif and his crew stayed some years, it seems, and returned to Greenland when the native Indian's became hostile. Leif's discovery was 500-years before Columbus's people landed on North American shores, but the Vikings didn't establish any settlement that lasted.

Christopher Columbus (Cristobal Colon) never set foot on North American land. His Conquistadors found the American continent and established the first European settlement and community to be erected that *survived* there. We can surmise that the indigenous native Indians of America would have been quite happy not being discovered by any European.

Columbus's people were the first Europeans to explore a wide area of the Americas and discover many Caribbean islands, making four separate voyages to the New World. The Americas is a term that covers Latin America, the Caribbean, today's USA, and Canada, and not any particular country. On his third voyage, Columbus discovered the Latin American continent, landing in current-day Venezuela. Columbus set foot on Venezuela soil on August 1, 1498 and spent two weeks exploring the Río Orinoco delta and river and trading with the natives. He then sailed to the Spanish Caribbean colony, the island of Hispaniola he'd already discovered, and settled the island on his fourth and final voyage; Columbus explored the coast of Central America for several months, including several land incursions looking for a passage west.

The Vikings Conquer West Francia and Settle
(Today's Normandy Region of France)

Viking (jarls) or Earls, Rollo & Bernard, Who Founded Normandy

One of the many Viking invasions of West Francia occurred in AD 909. However, this one was different—this raid, led by the Viking *jarl* (Earl) Rollo, with *Jarl* Bernard "The Dane" and others supporting him, saw them settle lands and stay in the "modern-day" Normandy region of northwest France.

To his men, Gange-Hrólfr (Hrólfr) Ragnvaldsson was known as "Rollo." There is a question mark about this being the same Rollo as the earl who conquered Normandy, and as we'll read later, some historians say that they are not the same person. Rollo was born in AD 846, and we will evidence that his birthplace was a village in the Norwegian region of More Og Romsdal and not in Denmark, as a few historiographers have claimed.

It was resoundingly evidenced by the author as the same location in Norway, as the birthplace of earl Bernard, a topic for centuries at the center of endless debate. However, recent DNA evidence exists, which was not available to earlier historians, and it is combined with a little known witness's typographical description of the town's setting by a contemporary Catholic chronicler monk who visited there. Rollo is believed to have been born in c. AD 860 and likely, therefore, was around seventy-two years of age when he died in modern-day Normandy.

Rollo conquered and ruled this "French" region from AD 909 and died in AD 932, aged eighty-six (an unusually long life for the period), and is buried at Rouen Cathedral in Normandy, France, where Earl Bernard is also buried. In a recent report, DNA from his remains in Rouen show Y-DNA Haplogroup I1, I1-P109, and the other I1-Z140*04, both found amongst the people of the Norwegian village of Fausk. They also evidence Norway as Rollo's birthplace, as several highly respected historians have. The website claims that Rollo's parents were the western Norwegian Earl of Móer, Rognvaldr Eysteinsson, born c. AD 830, and Ragnhild (Hildir) Hrolfsdottir, born c. AD 822. This site tracks his paternal grandfather, a Norwegian earl, Eystein Ivarsson, "The Noisy," of the Uplanders, and his maternal grandparents, the Norwegian earl Ivar Halfansson, born c. AD 797, and Princess Tora of Trondheim, in Norway, born c. AD 802. Several Norwegian and Icelandic historians concur.

Historians believe that Rollo had four brothers and four half-brothers, two of whom were also earls. He is considered to have first married Poppa, understood to have been the half-sister of Earl Bernard "The Dane" (as history wrongly labeled his birth country). There is also an unlikely claim that Rollo married another Poppa, the daughter of West Francia Count Bernard Berenger. This is highly unlikely as Rollo did raid the West Francia lands in AD 885 and did not return to raid, conquer, and stay until AD 990. Most sources agree he married *his* Poppa in AD 886. She could have been the booty of that earlier raid but is much more likely to be Bernard's half-sister, born in Norway in the same village. Rollo and Poppa had five children together, including his heir, William "Longsword" of Normandy, who succeeded as the region's ruler. One of Rollo's two daughters by Poppa married William, 1st Duke of Aquitaine, and after he died at age forty-eight, she married Count William "The Younger" de Auvergne. After her second husband's death, she married a regional King of Norway, Ragnald Swenosson of Haithabu.

After Poppa died, Rollo, having conquered the lands of what would become known as Normandy in AD 909 and stayed there, was granted his conquered lands to keep. With that treaty came his agreement to convert to Christianity, and he then married Princess Gisla, the daughter of the West Francia king, Charles II "The Simple." He and Gisla had one daughter, Grisaille of Normandy,

Together with what is believed to be his cousin and fellow earl, Bernard "The Dane," Earl Rollo led numerous raids from Norway to the coastal regions of France, England, Scotland, and Ireland. These men entered a battle with reckless abandon for fighting and with little fear.

They'd set out in AD 908 on a yearlong combination of sea-voyages up the east coast of England, around Scotland, down past Ireland, and the west coast of England, raiding and looting. After numerous raids on English, Scottish, and Irish coastal villages, Rollo, Bernard, and their men raided France via the Seine River in Paris. They pushed inland into what we know today as the Normandy region of France. Rollo himself had overrun Paris, France, much earlier in AD 885 but was defeated by King Ode of West Francia. The area eventually took its name from these Viking warriors who settled and stayed after this AD 909 raid.

The Latin word *Normanni* for Normans (or *Normannorum* for Normandy) describes the old Norse word for "North men," hence these Vikings became known as the Normanni, or Norman, people, and the lands they captured as Normandy. They controlled the "Normandy" region of France until the mid-thirteenth century. Viking DNA was then bred out through hundreds of years of marriage into French families.

Defeated by the West Francia army at the Battle of Chartres in AD 911, the Frankish King Charles "the Simple," in a wise strategic move, signed the Treaty of Saint-Clair-Sur-Epte with the Viking leader, Rollo. Under the treaty terms, Charles gave Rouen and the present-day upper Normandy area to Rollo, around 11,500 square miles (29,900 square kilometers). The Vikings had turned from raiders to settlers and a "pay to keep the peace" policy, it seems. King Charles also gave Rollo 310 kilograms of gold (683.43lbs) and 19.5 tons of silver .[1] This bullion in "modern-day" money is around US$36.4 million (£28 million), an excellent sweetener to the deal.

In exchange, Rollo pledged vassalage to Charles, married Charles's daughter Gisla, and agreed to be baptized in the Roman Catholic Church, as Earl Bernard and most of their men did. Rollo vowed that he and all his men would guard the Seine's estuaries against further Viking attacks, and he and his fellow earls kept their word. This began some 247-plus years of Viking

---

1 From *The Viking Age* by Christine & Tom Bjørnstad.

marriages and inter-breeding with the French nobility and peoples. Norse dialects were slowly erased over time, leaving "Normans" speaking only the old-French language by 1066.

The First Duke of Normandy Was Not Rollo

Contrary to popular myth, often stated and repeated in modern histories, blogs, books, and movies, Rollo was not created the 1st Duke of Normandy by the Frankish Kings. There is no record of Rollo being granted a noble title at the Treaty of Saint-Clair-Sur-Epte, or after that. He was early on known as the "Leader of the Norse peoples of Rouen." Once settled on his lands in Rouen, it is highly likely that his people using his Norwegian title, jarl, or Count, referred to him now as the Count of (from) Rouen.

A hundred years later, in his twelfth-century work, The Landnámabók, an Icelandic historian also referred to Rollo as the Count of Rouen. There is evidence that Rollo's son William I, William "Longsword," and his son Richard I (born in Fécamp, AD 923) were both known as "Count of Rouen" and "leader of the Norse people of Rouen" too. No mention of any dukedom. Neither does this title of "count" appear in any West Francia Royal state documents. Another likely explanation for why people thought him a count comes shortly.

By A.D.966, Richard I (Count) of Normandy was known to have "experimented" with the self-styled title of Marquis of Normandy, which he sometimes used. His son, Richard II (Count), sometimes used the ungranted title as marquis - and was later created the 1st Duke of Normandy by the Frankish king, the circumstances of the grant we'll read of shortly. However, no such designation of marquis was granted to either of them by the Frankish kings. It seems to be a case of later Norman chroniclers re-writing history. At the time, West Francia was a fragmented state whose power base was not so much with the king but with powerful regional lords like Rollo.

Many historians believe that the 1st Duke of Normandy was Rollo's grandson, Richard I, who, when aged nine, succeeded his father William Longsword, assassinated in AD 942. Later Norman chroniclers seeking to enhance Rollo's lineage appear to have woven the dukedom into their story, which did not exist. There is no formal record of Richard I, his father, William, or his grandfather, Rollo, ever being granted the title of a duke, nor is there any reference to Normandy as a duchy. Richard, I, was referred to by a West Francia chronicler of the time, Richer of Reims, as *dux Pyratorum*, which translates from the Latin as Duc (Duke) of Pirates—head of the Vikings. In other words, did this offensive slight become misconstrued or deliberately clouded over by later Norman chroniclers who referred to him as the "Duke" of Normandy?

The 1st Duke of Normandy (Normannorum)

The first time a respected institution writes about the title "Duke of Normandy" is in 1006, when the Abbey of Fécamp records a "favor granted" to it by "Richard II, of Normandy, Duc" (b. AD 963–d. 1026). The abbot believed that the then-pope, Benedict VIII, bestowed the title on Richard II. The following recorded evidence differs somewhat and is likely more accurate, as only the king granted Frank/French titles of nobility.

It was only in the reign of Robert II "the Pious," king of West Francia, who reigned from AD 996 to 1031, that the title "Duke" appears for the first time with Normandy's Richard II, "The Good," of Rouen (the *great*-grandson of Rollo). Despite claims by some that Rollo's son William and grandson Richard I were dukes of Normandy, we can say with fair accuracy that they were not and were never granted that title.

The duke's title appears regularly in officially recorded state papers only from AD 1004 onward, when Rollo's great-grandson ruled Normandy. The West Francia Kingdom's chancery State documents refer to Richard II as *dux Normannorum*, Duke of Normandy, and his land as the Duchy of Normandy. Not one of his ancestors was referred to as a duke in any West Francia state paper or royal record or communication in any previous reign. At AD 1004, the crown had grown strong and seized the duchy, and Normandy lost its autonomy. All Duchy rulers were required to wholly submit to King Robert II's power, but Richard II of Normandy could retain all his lands and wealth.

Further solid evidence that Richard II was the 1st Duke of Normandy comes from referring to him as the *Duc Normannorum*, Duke of Normandy, by the eleventh-century chronicler William of Poitiers (c. 1020–1090). He used the title of "Count of Rouen" (to Vikings, a *Jarl*) when referring to Rollo and his son William Longswood and grandson, Richard I. To Normandy's people, Rollo and his successors were counts (Scandinavian *jarls*) ruling their land.

If anyone knew the definitive truth of this, it would be the chronicler William of Poitiers. He was a Norman monk and personal chaplain and Confessor to William the Conqueror, Duke of Normandy. If Duke William (who became King William I of England) believed the dukedom had first been granted to his great-great-great-grandfather Rollo in c. AD 911 and his heirs, William would have ensured that

his chronicler, Poitiers referred to Rollo and his heirs as dukes; however, he didn't. The monk, William of Poitiers, traveled with the Norman invasion fleet to England in 1066 with Duke William. He chronicled all details of its conquest in his *"Gesta Guillelmi II ducis Normannorum et Regis Anglorum"* (*The Deeds of William, Duke of the Normans, and King of the English*). He mentions no Duke of Normandy until Richard II.

William of Poitiers was no weak monk; he had been a soldier before taking Holy Orders. He was born in Les Preaux, near Pont-Audemar, in today's France in AD 1020, just two years before Roger de Beaumont was born in the same town. Roger de Beaumont would later inherit the title of Seigneur, or Lord, of Pont-Audemar. He was a relative, close friend, and advisor to William, Duke of Normandy, and acted as regent of his dukedom when too old to participate in the invasion of England, which his two sons did instead. They would all have known the influential William of Poitiers.

Even Richard II, when he first inherited Normandy, had not been given the title of duke. It seems to have been a title he felt entitled to as the master of the nation's powerful upper-northwest. Upon inheriting the vast lands of Normandy, he self-styled himself Duke of Normandy, as he wished to grant the title of "Count" to one or two key members of his family and raise himself, it seems, to the self-appointed rank of duke. However, this was unrecognized by the Frank/French State. It also appears that to gain submission from this all-powerful descendent of Rollo, the king formally recognized his self-given title as if it had always been there. By this action, Richard II of Normandy was quietly in his king's debt and unlikely to challenge him as king.

Not having been granted the title of "King of France" by anyone, King Philip II was king of one of several kingdoms in the area known as today's nation of France. He had taken the entire country by subduing everyone else with claims to the title of the whole region we know today as France. It is no coincidence that royal documents from AD 1190 onward began to refer to King Philip II, not as King of the Franks (*Rex Francorum*) but King of France (*Rex Franciae*). He was the first monarch to style himself "King of France," born in 1165 and reigned as king from 1180 until he died in 1223.

This was an age of Gothic cathedrals and splendor, where the king's royal court had grown influential and royal authority had greatly strengthened. From the beginning of Philip's reign, French nobility first appeared in this, the Middle Ages. Having raised himself above all other regional kings in France, it was not an issue to recognize Richard II of Normandy's equal self-aggrandizement and formerly make him Duke of Normandy. It bought the new duke's support and homage too.

Hence, from at least 1203, King Philip of the Capetian Dynasty demanded recognition and vassalage from all regional lords and district rulers of "his" nation. He now had the power to enforce it and cleverly removed any last obstacles without war. Richard II, currently as ruler of Normandy, and his heirs were enrolled in France's noble ranks (*la nobility*), and he was issued Letters Patent, formally recognizing his status. These Letters Patent were registered with the court of the region, in Rouen, in 1204. The royal court of the king recorded them in the records of the *Chambre des Comptes*. So, let's put it to bed once and for all and confirm that Rollo "The Viking" was never ennobled by the West Francia kings, nor were his son nor grandson—and there are no Letters Patent issued to anyone as Duke of Normandy before Richard II of Normandy.

Where Were Our Two Viking Jarls Born

FIRST, ROLLO

Commissioned by Rollo's grandson, Richard I, Count of Rouen (AD 943 – 96) as a dynastic history, the
monk and chronicler Dudo of Saint-Quentin, originally from Vermandois, wrote his *Historia Normannorum* (*History of Normandy*) nearly seventy-plus years after Rollo's death.

Dudo claimed that Rollo and Bernard were born in Denmark. He may have simply followed the common understanding of earlier times that all Vikings came from the north. These Norse people commonly became known as Danes by many, regardless of where they were from in today's Scandinavia.

Consequently, all subsequent Historians refer to them as from Denmark.

In 2011, DNA testing was done in what was always believed to be Rollo's grandson and great-grandson's graves. But it was discovered that the skeletons far predated Rollo's life and were, therefore, not Rollo's descendants, Richard I and II. Bernard's family interred Bernard's remains in Rouen Cathedral in France. Recent DNA testing of those remains points to the weight of evidence that he was born in the small village in Norway called Fauske, as his DNA sequences align with people from this village and nowhere else. It is not an unreasonable conclusion to consider that Rollo came from the same town or region in Norway as Bernard traveled and fought under his fellow *jarl*, Rollo, known to be his cousin. Historical records and the recent DNA project on the 442 Vikings show that brothers, family, and village units were the most common Viking raiding parties' makeup. Let me explain that I have not leaped to this conclusion, and some descendants' weblinks talk of Maer, Nord-Trondelag, Norway.

Rollo was more of a roving pirate known and recorded in some records to have broken away from King Harald I of Norway. This again points to a Norwegian, not Danish, birth. However, Goffredo Malaterra, an eleventh-century Benedictine monk who the family did not commit to reflect their views, referred to Rollo confidently as Norway. He wrote that "Rollo sailed boldly from Norway with his fleet to the Christian coast." Likewise, the twelfth-century English monk and chronicler, William of Malmesbury, stated that Rollo was "born of noble lineage among the Norwegian." Both these monks were known for accurate recording of history and individuals' stories.

Later still, in his *Chronique des ducs de Normandie*, a twelfth-century monk, Benoît de Sainte-More, named a village called Fasge of Fax in Denmark as the birthplace of Rollo, 200 years after his death. He may have misinterpreted the Norwegian town's name and instead found a similar Danish name. There is no concrete evidence whatsoever to sustain the Danish claim. Still, recent research has identified that the same Norwegian town of "Fauske" exactly matches the village's mountain scenery described in detail by Benoît as Rollo's birthplace. It is nothing like the scenic topography of Fasge or Faxe in Denmark. This puts Bernard's DNA evidence and the recent DNA project of 442 Viking remains as family sticking together in Viking raids as logical. Critically, the monk Benoît's topographic evidence and the monks Goffredo Malaterra and

William of Malmesbury chronicle indicate that Bernard and Rollo came from the same Norwegian village. This collective evidence makes the town of Fauske, in Norwegian, the birthplace of both Rollo and Bernard.

SECOND, BERNARD

The Viking font of the de Beaumont and Hamilton bloodlines stretched from Bernard's birth, 1,142 years ago, through to today. In this and the next chapter, we'll look at descendants of his and some of their exciting stories. As a reminder, a glance back at any time to the family trees at the beginning of this book will be helpful to follow these stories as they unfold.

There is no concrete evidence, but later, Normans chronicled wild myths suggest that Bernard was born in France of Bruno to the Duke of the Angria Saxons and Haisla, Princess of the Holstein Saxons. Another legend is that he was born of royal Saxon blood in Denmark of Emperor Charlemagne's descent. He would have already been baptized a Christian. Suppose he was of royal birth in France or Denmark. Why on earth would he be chronicled in numerous sources as a Viking pagan earl sailing from Norway with Rollo and spending a decade as a raiding and looting pirate in England, Scotland, Ireland, and France? Rollo was also recorded as being known to have broken away from King Harald I of Norway. Chronicles of the time and the later embellished Norman myths yet do not refer to him as Bernard, Prince of Denmark or France or Saxony. He is listed, all be it mistakenly, like Bernard "The Dane," an earl. Holstein's Saxon hereditary town between AD 800–AD 100 bordered the Danish territories and Schleswig. in Bernard's time, the lines between Danish and Saxon were relatively fluid, it would seem, but Norway was distinctly separate. For many centuries, the king of Denmark was both a Danish Duke of Schleswig and a Saxon German Duke of Holstein. Schleswig was either integrated into Denmark or was a Danish province, and Holstein was Saxon German and once a sovereign state long ago. For several centuries, both were ruled by the kings of Denmark. In 1863, Prussia and Otto von Bismarck, for the German Kaiser, declared war on Denmark and won, and both Schleswig and Holstein became part of Prussia and now part of Germany.

Bernard is the Font of all Hamilton Bloodline Descendants Today

Bernard is, therefore, the first direct male bloodline ancestor of all Hamiltons, including both of this book's Alexander Hamiltons and the current dukes of Hamilton and Abercorn and the earls of Arran. DNA evidence matching America's Founding Father's living descendants today, who took part in the USA DNA study, had DNA of the Norwegian-born Viking Earl Bernard. They could not have DNA from that Viking born in AD 880 if Alexander Hamilton, Founding Father, were not a direct bloodline male descendant of Earl Bernard.

This Hamilton Founding Father of America's current living descendants were found to have Bernard's DNA marker I1-Z140*04. This evidence is thanks to Wim Penninx and Mark Pallette's research and analysis by William Hartley, a genetic genealogist. Hartley wrote his published paper in September 2011. The Pennsylvania University Hamilton DNA project also corroborates the same Founding Fathers relative's living DNA as traceable to the younger son of David Fitz-Walter de Hameldone (born 1310), the direct bloodline ancestor of the Founding Father. Walter's elder brother (Named after his father), David, is the natural male bloodline ancestor of the modern-day Alexander Hamilton's Westport & Elrick Hamilton tree.

We can rightly call all Hamiltons direct ancestors as Bernard "The Norwegian." That is a sound and proven assumption. Alec would have been interested in seeing the evidence, and the author calls him *Du er Norsk* (you are Norse) and of Norwegian Viking descent. The living ancestors of America's Founding Fathers should be delighted to see this too.

The Benefits of Converting to Christianity and Settling in Normandy

When honoring their pledge to Rollo to join him and convert to Christianity, Bernard and his men did so publicly at Rouen Cathedral in AD 912, the year following their claiming lands as their own in the Frankish/French countryside.

The second ruler of Normandy, William Longa-Spatha, Rollo's son and successor, charged Bernard with putting down an uprising by a Norman lord from the west named Raouf. As far as we can tell, the rebellion took place in the early AD 930s when Raouf besieged the city of Rouen, Bernard's seat of power, and failed. Some five years later, Bernard put down a revolt in Normandy's Bessin and Cotentin regions. These attacks came from new Viking raiders seeking to create communities independent of Normandy's early Viking rulers, stealing land from them as they had stolen them in AD 909 themselves.

After William's premature death by assassination, Bernard became a co-regent, a ruler in the name of Richard, the third ruler of Normandy in his minority, in December AD 942. He sat on a regency council with another trusted Norman of the late king's court, one Anslech de Bricqebec, and two more nobles, Osmond de Conteville and Raoul de Tarascan. In AD 945, Bernard appealed to fellow Norman Viking Harald Bluetooth and his men to defend Normandy's duchy. They had been attacked by the Frankish (Carolinian French) King Louis and Hugh the Great, Duke of the Franks. Louis attempted to retake Normandy's lands granted to Rollo and his Vikings thirty years earlier by the Franks' then-king and banish the Vikings. Bernard defeated the attempt and died a few years later, sometime before AD 960.

Bernard's sixth great-grandson was William de Hameldone (the first of Bernard's de Beaumont line known as de Hameldone, not de Beaumont). His twenty-fifth great-grandson was Alexander Hamilton, Founding Father of America, and his twenty-sixth great-grandson was the "modern-day" Alex Hamilton from a branch of the clan that lived longer lives.

Monks and Heretics

Christian Europe in the Middle Ages saw heretical pagan Viking raids on monasteries as prime targets, like the raids of Rollo and Bernard. Monks, priests, and their worship centers were, to the pagans, an unacceptable force to be crushed. Their hidden wealth within and their crops and livestock could be taken, making such raids doubly advantageous.

Throughout the Middle Ages, all learning was centered in monasteries. Catholic missionary activity sprang from them, and the nation's progress saw most of its knowledge and innovation emerge from these places. Not only were they centers of theology where monks dedicated their lives to the service of God and the learning of theological texts, but they were the center of advances in medicine, law, philosophy, astronomy, and mathematics.

English, Irish, and Scottish monks were evolving in all these sciences based on translations into Latin of early Greek texts taken in part from Arabic philosophers, mathematicians, and early medical thinkers. Giant leaps in knowledge had been occurring in the Islamic world. With the advent of the Holy Land Crusades, much-advanced knowledge was being brought back to the British Isles by knights, princes, and monks who accompanied the campaigns. Their new learning assisted them in developing significant advances in their own countries.

The Two Normandy Founding-Vikings' Burial Sites

Rouen Cathedral in Normandy houses the remains of both Bernard and fellow earl Rollo, the founder of Normandy, France, as we know it today. Rollo's wife, Poppa, and their son, William Longsword, the self-styled count of Normandy who ruled after his father, are also interred.

The cathedral also houses the bodies of King Richard the Lionheart of England; Empress Matilda, daughter of Henry I of England, who married the Holy Roman Emperor Henry V; and Geoffrey of Anjou, France. Empress Matilda became a claimant of the English throne but was not crowned after the people revolted against her, though her son succeeded as Henry II of England. He married Eleanor of Aquitaine, and their first-born male was Henry the Younger. John Plantagenet of Lancaster, Duke of Bedford, who oversaw Joan of Arc's trial and burning at the cross as a heretic in France, was buried in the cathedral at Rouen too. Sadly, his tomb was destroyed in the sixteenth century by Calvinists, but a plaque marking his life was placed there.

The Viking Bernard's Early (Hamilton Line) Descendants

The de Beaumont's to the First Hamilton Descendant

In his lifetime, Bernard (The Norwegian, we should say) went from being a Viking pirate, murdering, raiding, and looting his way to wealth, to settling conquered foreign lands. The income achieved through the granted lands made Bernard a very wealthy landed Lord, but his descendants created the Houses of Hamilton, de Beaumont, Harcourt, and others in France and the United Kingdom. Eventually, his descendants spread across England, Scotland, Ireland, France, America, Canada, Australia, New Zealand, etc.

This book's family tree and male bloodline descending from Bernard "The Dane" shows an illustrious line of men, titles, and marriages unfolding and bridging two millennia. That unbroken male bloodline takes us through the first of Bernard's descendants to use de Hameldone (Hamilton) and emerges in the 1700s and 1900s as our two Alexander Hamiltons. It is interesting to read about several of these twelfth to twenty-first-century characters whose DNA influenced the Hamilton pool's genes. Bernard's wife, Sprota, must have spent much of her life pregnant, as she bore him thirteen children.

As we've read already, Bernard is the first reliably traceable ancestor of the first Hamilton, our two Alexanders, and the "modern-day" Hamilton nobility of dukes and earls.

The de Beaumonts

Remember that Bernard was known to have married Sprota de Bourgogne, daughter of Herbert, the 1st de Vermandois, great-great-grandson of Emperor Charlamagne. The following 136 years, from Bernard's son Torf, born in AD 914 in Rouen, to Bernard's great-great-great-grandson Robert de Beaumont-le-Roger, saw Robert with his twin brother, Henri, join William, Duke of Normandy in invading England in 1066. Some five generations passed while marrying into French nobility saw the wild, pagan Viking warriors turn into Norman French nobility. After helping to conquer England for William, the de Beaumont twins stayed and settled there—a moment of déjà vu, repeating their ancestor Bernard the Earl's conquering of the lands of Normandy with and for Rollo, and staying.

The full names of Bernard's descendants, titles, marriages, and key dates can be found in the family trees earlier in the book. The author has selected interesting, historically linked descendants of Bernard in the ninth to twelfth centuries to talk more about in this book.

Bernard's Son

Torf le Riche (of) de Harcourt, et de Tourville, Seigneur de Pont-au-demer (c. 914 c. 97), one of thirteen children of Bernard, married to Ertemberge de Briquebec.

Bernard's Grandson

Touroude (Thorold); Lord (or) Seigneur de Pont-au-demer (c. 949–c. 997), born in Pont-Audemer, Eure (France). Touroude, the son of Torf, married Eva (Avelina) Duvelina and had six children, although some sources say he married Senfrie de Crépon. Tragically, Touroude was assassinated, as were several guardians of the young Robert of Normandy, while still in his minority.

Touroude was perceived as influential at the courts of three Normandy rulers, culminating with Robert I. Worthy of mention. Touroude's nephew, Anchetil de Harcourt, was the first to be known as from the town of (de) Harcourt in Normandy. Anchetil, Bernard's great-grandson, is the founder of the noble house of Harcourt, both in France where later a dukedom was raised, and in England, where eventually an earldom was raised. Bernard first acquired Harcourt's township, although it was not his principal place of residence, and neither he, his son, or grandson were spoken of or *known* as from there, Anchetil was.

The author's research suggests that Touroude's son Honfroi inherited the titles of Seigneur *de Pont-au-demer* and, over time, was granted six titles in all. These titles included de Vielles, de Preaux, and the first holder of *"Le Grand Honneur,"* de Beaumont-le-Roger. It was one of the most important groups of land domains in eastern Normandy and was the font of the de Beaumont name.

Honfroi de Beaumont-le-Roger

Honfroi (Honfroy, or Humphrey) was the Seigneur de Beaumont-le-Roger, (and of) et de Vieilles, (c. 975–c. 1044.) He married Alberée de la Haye Aubrie. His eldest son, Robert, was assassinated young, and the next eldest son, Roger, inherited from his father.

Roger de Beaumont, c. 1022–c. 1094

Another man worth writing about is Honfroi's son, who succeeded as Seigneur de Beaumont-le-Roger, de Pont-au-demer, et de Vielles. He was made Comte (Count) of Meulan upon marriage to Adeline de Meulan. It was her second marriage, and her first husband had no male heirs. Roger became a large landowner and powerful lord on the back of the wealth created from these lands.

As we read earlier, he was a trusted courtier and friend of the current Duke of Normandy's late father, Robert I, but was too old to campaign with his son, Duke William. Roger played a critical role in managing the dukedom in the absence of its ruler as governor of the duchy in his absence, with the power to make all decisions in the duchy's best interests. Duke William also willed that should he die trying to take England's throne, Roger is appointed guardian and regent of his heir and the Duchy of Normandy until William's son, Rufus, came of age.

Roger's younger brother, Guillaume (William), became sheriff of Lincolnshire. While his twin sons, Robert, and Henry, joined the invading force in England, Roger remained in Normandy and dutifully served as governor and regent. After William conquered England and was crowned king, Roger was awarded extensive lands in Leicestershire, Dorset, and Gloucestershire. He is named in the *Domesday Book* of 1086. Despite Roger never taking residence in England, these lands were split between his sons after his death. Roger de Beaumont died a year before his sovereign, William I, who died in 1087. Roger's name is listed as a tenant in chief of England's lands in that great *Domesday Book*.

Robert de Beaumont-le-Roger, later, 1st Norman Earl of Leicester.

Robert was the first Hamilton ancestor to live in England, consisting of those carrying his DNA born in the British Isles. *c. 1050–c. 1118.*

At the Battle of Hastings, Robert de Beaumont-le-Roger and twin-brother Henri fought with their cousin, William the Conqueror, Duke of Normandy. For this book, he may be the most critical descendant of Bernard "the" Dane, as it is this Robert, *the first* de Beaumont and Norman lord to rule lands in England, that all Hamiltons descend from too.

Robert had first married the granddaughter of the French king and gained her wealthy dowery. After her sad death, he married the equally wealthy widow of Baldwin, 1st King of Jerusalem, raising his power base tremendously. Robert helped his cousin become King of England, and his wife was the daughter of a king. Baldwin had led the first Holy Land Crusade, so what a coup for Robert's father to have arranged both these dynastic royal marriages through the trust and power he wielded with William, the Duke of Normandy's court.

Robert had nine children between his two wives, including his twin sons, Robert (the 2nd Earl) and Waleran. William the Conqueror gifted Robert in 1066 and beyond with a total of ninety-one manors, mainly in the Midlands. All estates had been confiscated from their Saxon English landowners. Each manor is listed in his name in the great *Domesday Book* of 1086. He also inherited titles through his mother's family when she died: Comte of Meulan, in Normandy; Viscount Ivry; and Lord Norton—English titles held by family members after the Battle of Hastings. With such a mass of landholding and manors and the doweries from two wealthy wives, Robert became one of the richest men in the new Norman England.

King William II of England followed his father's reign. On August 2, 1100, he died after being shot with an arrow in a hunting accident, at which Robert and Henri de Beaumont were present. Both Robert and Henri immediately pledged their allegiance to the king's younger brother, Henry, who became King Henry I of England. Henry in 1107 granted Robert the title of 1st Norman Earl of Leicester and Leicester Castle, and Henri, the 1st Norman Earl of Warwick. Their younger brother, Hugh, was created the 1st Norman Earl of Bedford.

The twins were given even more lands and manors by the new king to increase their income. Why William the Conqueror himself did not lavish such titles on his companions and cousins after the Battle of Hastings is surprising. He may not have won the battle without them. Maybe he feared them becoming too powerful; we will likely never know.

The title of Earl of Leicester has been created and become extant (extinct) seven times from Robert de Beaumont, the first to hold the title. Whenever a male bloodline ceased, it became in the monarchs gift to be granted the title and lands to another. The title and income-bearing lands were typically confiscated for the crown until a monarch resurrected it. His queen's favorite, Robert Dudley, was the third person to be created the 1st Earl of Leicester under Queen Elizabeth I in 1564—one such case of resurrecting an extant title. Robert de Beaumont was the very first Earl of Leicester, and his son, grandson, and great-grandson were all named Robert and became earl. But after the fourth earl, there was no male issue. The title became extant and ended the de Beaumont Earls of Leicester. The current Earl of Leicester is the eighth earl in its seventh creation, granted by Queen Victoria. We don't know why it is not known in sequence how many have held the title once extant and resurrected. The current holder logically would be the 33rd Earl of Leicester.

When Robert de Beaumont, 1st Earl of Leicester, died c. 1118 (at about sixty-eight years of age), he was the last surviving Norman noble in England who had fought at the Battle of Hastings. Their sovereign created all the de Beaumonts and earls of Leicester, Warwick, Worcester, and Bedford from his father, Roger.

Throughout history, most victors of invasions take land and wealth away from the conquered and redistribute them as favors to their people who supported them in their wars. Nothing has changed from before or since, whether in Roman or Greek Empires; Byzantine, Ottoman, or other European Empires; Asian, Russian, and Chinese Empires; communist revolutionary "Empires"; or even Hitler's Third Reich. All conquered other nations and redistributed land and wealth to their supporters.

Three Invasion Fleets Set Sail For England

Claimants to the English throne give understanding to the background of the Battle of Hastings. It all started with the January 4, 1066 death of the childless King Edward of England, known in history as Edward the Confessor. The dying king announced that Harold Godwinson, Earl of Wessex, married to his sister, was his successor to the English crown. Harold was duly and solemnly crowned and anointed King Harold I of England two days later, on January 6. Halley's Comet, which as early as 467 BC was recorded as occurring around every seventy-five years across the earth's skies, appeared in April of 1066. In his Anglo-Saxon chronicle, a Benedictine monk Eilmer recorded its appearance at Malmesbury Abbey as a bad omen for England.

A succession struggles to unseat the newly appointed King Harold of England unfolded among various claimants who did not accept Harold, Earl of Wessex, as king of England. The primary cause was that he was not of King Edward the Confessor's blood, whereas the three prime claimants were. Among these was the late King Edward of England's younger brother, Earl Tostig, who thought he should have been chosen instead. A cousin of King Edward was the Norwegian King Harold III, and he laid claim to England's Crown too. In addition, the late king's cousin once removed, William, Duke of Normandy, claimed the English crown as his by right of blood and the defense of the realm. William, Duke of Normandy, had sent troops to defend King Edward against an earlier invasion by Danes. Without William's support, it is felt that England would have fallen, and a Danish king by right of conquest would already be sitting on the English throne. William thought it quite extraordinary that he wasn't chosen to succeed the English king, but a non-blood relative was.

Prince Eadgar Aetheling was another claimant as to the rightful heir of the male bloodline. He was the grandson of the earlier English Saxon king, Edmund II, "Ironside." Eadgar was the great nephew of the late King Edward and the only next-generation direct heir to the Saxon royal line. An Anglo-Saxon prince, Eadgar was born in Hungary, c. 1051, and was the only surviving male of the royal dynasty. Eadgar Aetheling is known to have died in c. 1126, aged seventy-five. Above all others, he appears to have had the most substantial claim to the English crown because of his direct bloodline. He was only fourteen at the time of the Confessor's death. His father was in exile in Hungary when Eadgar's grandfather, Edmund, King of England, was defeated by the Danish earl, Cnut. Edmund remained King of Wessex, and Cnut took the rest of England around six weeks later. When Edmund died, the Dane was crowned King Cnut of England.

The *Witenagemot* (the shorter-term, the Witan, was usually used) was a ruling class of Saxon advisors to their kings. *Witenagemot* means "meeting of wise men." This council, chosen by the previous king, advised him to bypass Eadgar and appoint Harold, asking for the safety of his kingdom.

Before he died, Edward the Confessor seemed to have realized that the teenage rightful heir would never hold the throne in such troubled times and spared him from it. Why the Confessor did not next choose his father's blood cousin (Harold III of Norway) or cousin-once-removed (William, Duke of Normandy), we'll never know, but on his death bed, the stability of his realm must have been paramount to him. However, we can also assume that he wanted a Saxon on England's throne, not a Norman or Norwegian.

In July of 1066, King Harold of England heard from spies in Normandy that Duke William was building a fleet, and in August, that soldiers were gathering at the port of the fleet. He moved his army from York to England's south coast in preparation for a probable invasion by Duke William. Not knowing exactly where William would land, Harold placed lookouts in every port along the south coast to quickly get intelligence about the landing and immediately move his army into position.

The Norman Invasion Fleet Is The First To Set Sail For England

Hearing of Harold's coronation, William Duke of Normandy began plans in early 1066 to build a fleet of ships to invade England and seek to claim the throne of England. His advisors had chosen the seaport of Dives-sur-Mer to make what is believed to have been 700 ships and supporting materials needed. King Harold's spies alerting him to these plans formed an army and took them across the sea to the Isle of Wight. From this unexpected location in the English channel, he could push out to attack the invasion fleet before it got to English shores.

In the meantime, running out of sufficient food and supplies after seven months on the Isle of Wight, King Harold, by September 8, decided to sail his army back to England, and he returned to London.

Due to unfavorable winds and channel currents, Duke William's fleet remained in port for almost seven months. On September 12, 1066, William's fleet sailed from Normandy. Several ships sank in storms forcing the fleet to take shelter further along the French coast at Saint-Valery-sur-Somme and wait for a favorable breeze. He only had a couple of weeks to wait before he set sail again for England and his destiny.

The King of Norway Launches The Second Surprise Invasion Fleet

King Harald III of Norway also claimed the English crown. Together with the younger brother of England's King Harold, Earl Tostig, they chose that same day, September 8, as Harold of England was leaving the Isle of White, to set sail from Norway and invade England in the north.

This Norwegian army landed in the mouth of the River Tyne in the north of England, soon spotted by Harold of England's spies. It is believed that the two men made a pact, understood by all their soldiers, that if they crushed Harold of England and his troops, Harald of Norway would take the English crown, but if Harald III died in battle and Tostig survived, Tostig would take the crown.

The first battle invading Norwegian King Harald III with Prince Tostig of England occurred at Fulford on September 20. The local English lords mustered a small defense force to fight the invaders but were roundly beaten. On the 25th, the English King Harold's main army arrived from the south coast, a grueling forced march over ten days, and it defeated both claimants' armies at the Battle of Stamford Bridge in East Riding Yorkshire in the North of England. Furthermore, both England's Prince Tostig and Norway's Harald III died in the battle. Leaving Yorkshire almost immediately, King Harold was anxious to return for the expected Norman invasion and felt obliged to take his exhausted army into another ten-day forced march back to the English south coast. His worse fears were now being realized.

A Fifth-Generation Viking Becomes King of England

What happened next changed the entire course of British history and influenced the future nation of North America. Two Hamilton ancestor brothers were with William, Duke of Normandy's invading army, which sailed to England in September 1066 (The Duke, a direct descendant of the Viking Earl, Rollo). One brother, Robert de Beaumonts, a great-grandson, was the first to use de (of) Hameldone (Hamilton).

As the entire Hamilton history was shaped by the Norman invasion of England and the Battle of Hastings in 1066, we need to look at this nation-changing event. It is vital to observe how the Hamilton clan came to be in the first place. To talk of the first Hamilton, we must discover how the de Beaumonts of Viking ancestry settled in England. Without them, there would have been no Alexander Hamilton, Founding Father of America, or the British dukes of Hamilton and Abercorn, or the earls of Arran, or indeed any living person named Hamilton today.

The Norman Invasion Fleet's Second Attempt Succeeds

Many 13th and 14th century chroniclers repeating earlier monks, typically a hundred years after the event, noted that the invasion fleet of William, Duke of Normandy, set sail for England on September 27, in 1066 from the French coast, arriving on Thursday 28 and landing at Pevensey, on England's West Sussex coast. The dates of September 27 and 28 and the landing spot are now by weight of evidence to the contrary, as we'll read shortly. Let's look at several pieces of evidence that enable us to know the correct dates.

The Landing Date Needs Clarifying

The date that William's fleet landed in England, the local Northern English Worcester Chronicle, the Peterborough Chronicle, and the Anglo-Saxo Chronicle all aligned with the Bayeux Tapestry. The Norman fleet had set sail from Saint-Valery-sur-Somme, France, on Thursday, September 28, 1066, and arrived offshore from the English port of Hastings, in West Sussex on the southeast coast of England around 9 am the following day. They came ashore on a rising tide around noon that same day, it being *Michaelmas, Friday*, September 29, 1066. The Christian festival of Michaelmas celebrates the Feast of the Archangels.

The Canon of Bayeux Cathedral in France wrote that as the Duke of Normandy got out of his boat, onto the shore, he lost his footing and stumbled. Still, he rose with earth in his hands to proclaim, "I have England with my two hands," to a rousing cheer from the soldiery and averting what otherwise may have been seen by his troops as a bad omen.

Our second evidence corroborates the day of landing in England and why we know it was a Friday. A scene from the Bayeux Tapestry depicts a feast served to the Duke on the evening of the landing on English soil. The image is shown at the end of this chapter. The principal characters in it are Roger de Beaumont, a favorite of William, Duke of Normandy, and the Duke's half-brother Bishop Odo. Traditionally still to this day, devout Catholics (As the Normans were) only eat fish on a Friday. It is a whole fish on a serving platter in front of the Bishop displayed boldly in the tapestry, symbolizing the day of the week.

The Norman army landed, with, and the weight of evidence suggests up to 700 ships and up to 10,000 men. The fleet anchored in the large tidal inlet known as Crowhurst, a little to the west, northwest of old Hastings town. Crowhurst sits on the opposite side of the basin to Bexhill, some miles east of Pevensey. The Normans landed on the right of the inlet around Crouchers Farm, moved inland directly East, and established a camp to the north, northwest of Hastings, by Wilting Farm. Sea inlets and marsh wetlands surrounded this area at the time, and William could draw in his entire fleet of relatively small ships and moor them safely there.

Various historical sources agree that William's army landed unchallenged. Many military historians have said he would have been forced straight into battle with the Saxon castle, which sat by the shore, had he first landed at Pevensey.

The next day, Saturday 30, with his army rested from the sea voyage, fed and watered, William moved to secure his position. He sent a force down the coast to take the fortified castle at Pevensey, simultaneously ordering the hasty erection of a wooden defensive fortress on a nearby hill. The Hill with the fort on top when complete was said to be around 131 feet or 40 meters in height above the area's flatlands.

King Harold Races to Repel The Normans

The scout's King Harold had deployed along the south coast of England saw William's invasion force by the Saturday while William was creating defenses and taking Pevensey Castle. The scouts immediately dispatched a message to Stanford Bridge in Yorkshire, where Harold was with his army. Harold had, for his time, a state-of-the-art communication system in place. The report would have arrived by messenger pigeon, the primary source of speedy message delivery in the Middle Ages. To go from Hastings to Yorkshire would have taken a minimum of 2-3 days by horse, with at least seven changes of steed, assuming you had them all lined up in the right place! Messenger pigeons can successfully return to their home base up to 400 to 500 miles away and were used extensively, birds averaging sixty miles an hour; a pigeon could deliver a message from Hastings to Stanford Bridge in four hours.

Harold of England gave thanks for the victory over Harold III of Norway at York Cathedral. He waited another five days before his army set off south to engage William, presumably to enable his men to recover from the grueling Battle of Stamford Bridge, lick their wounds, and take care of the injured. Harold likely sent messenger pigeons to various towns to muster men to join him on his planned march south to meet William. He forced his army to march south swiftly, gathering fresh additional forces as they went. They stopped at a church in Waltham on their journey south to pray for an upcoming win against the Normans. He and his men marched 219 miles as the crow flew from Stanford Bridge.

Harold's army reached London in a six-day forced march on October 6, 1066.

After resting up overnight on Watling Street, they went through London and straight down the London road towards Hastings. It took them another seven days, as Saxon armies are known to have marched on average twenty-seven miles a day, and they did make camp on October 13, 1066, at the battle scene.

Battle Horses of the Period

It is essential to confirm that most knights' horses in the Norman army of the 11th and the 12th century were not fine thoroughbreds of dressage competition physique. Heavier horses were bred, trained, and drilled in a military warfare environment. These horses were not the vast Shire horses of today, which descended from the war-horses of the 1500s.

They were bred to carry a knight in full armor into battle, which meant not just the knight in chain mail but also plated armor over his body and helmet. A typical weight range such a war-horse had to carry on their back could be anywhere between 230lbs - 270lbs (104.33 - 122.74 kg). As a distinctive heavy horse breed in this period, records show they, on average, weighed around 1,200lbs (545 kg); we can appreciate why these mounted knights were referred to as the 'heavy horse.' Under notes, there is additional weight information for those interested.

In the 11th century, a commander would primarily send his 'heavy horse' at full gallop in a straight-on charge at enemy infantry lines. The reason becomes evident why the army with a large contingent of a heavy horse almost invariably won the day. They were the equivalent of today's military Tanks. When a wall of, say, 500 heavy horses with armored knights in the saddle weighing a combined total of at least three-quarters of a ton each (1,430lbs; 815kg), bearing down at full gallop hit a stationary row of foot soldiers, they just plowed through, crushing everything in their path. This often saw the enemy soldiers break from battle and retreat in disorder. The attacking forces, fast-moving foot soldiers, and archers could push your win home quite speedily.

Harold The Tactician

The chronicler Wace writes that King Harold had a wide trench dug across his foot soldiers' positions in his work. It was deep enough to place wooden stakes into the base of these pits, impale a Norman heavy cavalry attack and trap them. He built long stretches of logs on the other side of the trench and Harold's traditional line of Saxon shield foot soldiers. King Harold had made a barricade from trunks of trees cut down and weaved almost like wattle as a defensive wall against the heavy horse and enemy infantry assault.

Harold was more prepared and tactically minded than most historians give him credit. He chose his manor grounds, which he knew well, and the best defensive position, showing shrewd defense tactics. The Bayeux Tapestry depicts this trench in one panel and shows multiple Norman mounted Knights stumbling with their horses into this long ditch, being killed by stakes or spears thrown at them by Harold's troops.

Most battles in this period lasted one to two hours. The army with a more significant tactical advantage, such as a massive heavy horse charge, slammed into the line of enemy foot soldiers. Surviving ranks nerve broke, and they ran en-masse, and the battle was soon over. That the Battle of Hastings lasted 7-hours is a testament to some degree to Harold being a clever military tactician, something few have accorded him the credit. Harold chose, contrary to many earlier historians claiming the land by the Abbey was the Battle scene (where zero artifacts have been found), Crowhurst manor lands.

Harold owned this land and knew the ground well. Recent archeological digs are beginning to yield evidence of this ground being where the battle took place. Encased in parts with heavy woodland and by the barriers that Harold created (the trench and log wall), Harold could narrow the battlefield to best suit him and position his army on higher ground, which would force the Norman army to fight uphill somewhat. It was a clever strategy for someone who knew he might have an equal force of men; however, he knew he had few horses versus William's large contingent of heavy horses. He also had few men with bows, whereas he knew William had a large contingent of not just bowmen but men wielding the latest, more accurate, and deadly crossbow.

William's only rival in his path to grab the throne of England was its current occupier, King Harold, as the other two main claimants had been killed in battle by Harold in the previous month. William had been sending out scouts daily in different directions from his camp near Hasting's to ensure that any army of King Harold's could be found in time to ready William's men for battle.

The Battle of Hastings - Saturday, October 14, 1066

It appears from chronicles of the battle that both sides underreported their numbers and inflated the other numerical size, so when action was over, the victorious could claim it against all odds, and the losers that they were overwhelmed. Middle Ages' Spin Doctors.

William's scouts did find Harold's camp. They reported it to William, who sent emissaries to Harold's headquarters on Friday, October 13 (another example of such a day being unlucky for some, in the English psyche), demanding Harold relinquish England's throne in his favor. When rejected, William then offered it up to arbitration by the pope, which Harold also dismissed. We can be sure Harold knew only too well that the pope had already chosen sides and had backed William—or why would William's army be carrying the pontiff's golden staff? Pope Alexander had given William the Holy Roman Gold Cross of St. Peter to take into battle to inspire his troops with the knowledge that they fought with God and the pope on their side. The honor of carrying it into battle went to Count Eustace of Boulogne, and he rode to the cavalry's left flank on a heavily armored horse.

William proposed a final avoidance of the entire battle, and likely the deaths of thousands, offering to let God's will decide the crown of England as he and Harold entered single combat. I am not sure if he intended to enter single action personally or choose champions to represent them, as was not uncommon. In either case, Harold rejected the offer.

Harold's battle plan saw the men from London guarding the king himself, and the Kent soldiers granted the right to man the front ranks and create the famous Viking-Saxon wall of shields in defense. With a moderate-to-brisk march of rested, well-fed men at an average of twenty minutes a mile, as often recorded in those days, William most likely set off around 5:30 am from his fort just northwest of Hastings on Saturday, October 14, 1066, to confront Harold's army in the field. William rode a black stallion, a gift from Alfonso, King of Asturias, one of the then-many kingdoms in "modern-day" Spain. The Spanish Crown Princes today are crowned Prince of Asturias.

The Normans arrived opposite Harold's battle camp at around 8:00 am. As William's troops appeared out of the woods, Harold's troops were still mustering and deploying into position. The violent, pitched battle about to ensue would be bloody, and neither ruler would give quarter. The few mounted knights on Harold's side would have dismounted and fought on foot, as was the traditional way of Viking and English battle tactics. All foot soldiers carried long shields and were famous, as were Vikings, for creating an impenetrable wall with them. They likely had axes with shorter shafts and foot soldiers, who would step through from behind the wall with long spears to thrust into the enemy. The Norman foot soldiers likely had similar weapons and tactics.

William had arranged his army with his men on foot to the fore and his extensive archers behind them. His heavy cavalry of 600 horses was placed behind the archers, ready to be directed in battle. William's forces had an array of new war weapons, which Harold's did not. William's 600 horses with mounted Norman knights were in tough defensive armor, primarily chain mail. They would all be men of quality, landed men with significant income, or their lord's squires, as ordinary men could not afford the quality of armor they wore.

They would have had long, heavy chain mail coats, metal helmets, and lethal, well-forged long swords. William's knights carried long lances, too, as one thinks of later medieval jousts. They had sharp, pointed tips for impaling the enemy before engaging with swords and axes wielded from on high. Split into squadrons, William's large company of archers had the new lethal and more accurate crossbow. They also had old-fashioned balusters, throwing large stones into enemy lines with deadly or debilitating force to foot soldiers.

The Battle Begins

A short time before 9:00 am, William raised the Papal Flag and the Golden Staff of the Pontiff (as if Harold needed any further evidence of how hollow William's offer to avoid battle and allow the pope to decide the outcome of his kingdom was). The two armies started to shout and trade insults, building bravery, morale, a sense of anger, and a desire to win. English monks began to sing a sacred hymn, and the Normans responded with a Latin *Te Deum*. At 9:00 am, the bells of the local village church pealed the hour (they rang the matins five times a day, when workers in the fields stopped momentarily to pray, just as Muslims in today's world are called to prayer five times a day). William gave the signal for his Breton forces to move forward. The battle had begun.

William signaled his army to move forward at a walk-in three columns.

His Breton foot soldiers were on his left flank, and Flemish and French mercenaries on his right, with the 600 war-horses coming up behind them. A release of a thousand arrows falling from the sky at once was a terrifyingly destructive action, and two or three flights of arrows let loose while William's foot and mounted troops moved forward. Each landed amid the Saxon army to devastating effect. Many noted that the sky turned dark with arrows crashing from the sky, hitting most Saxons in the head, face, or shoulders, as often occurred in such incidents. Fierce hand-to-hand combat followed on three fronts, with several pushes by the Norman foot soldiers, but somehow, the Saxon wall of shields held or regrouped amid the carnage and death. Amidst the screams of the injured, the blood-soaked grass underfoot on a sloping hillside made footing difficult.

On the first push forward as they neared Harold's shield wall, the Breton foot soldiers on William's left flank met an avalanche of spears, axes, rocks, and the odd arrow loosed by Harold's soldiers behind the wall of shields. The Breton foot soldiers of the Norman army momentarily wavered and started to break, with some retreating and crashing into the main Norman cavalry coming up from behind. The Norman cavalry pushed them forward to re-engage with Harold's forces. Stories of a deliberately planned retreat by the Norman Bretons to draw the enemy in and pounce on them from the side with the Norman cavalry appear baseless, and likely a later Norman desire to cover up the panic of the Bretons.

Some of Harold's English foot soldiers, led by their lords on foot, gave chase to the panicked and retreating Bretons but, by most accounts, were soon driven back. Twice during the morning, one of Harold's few archers, who must have been a good bowman, shot William, the Duke of Normandy's horse from underneath him, the black beauty that had been a gift from Asturias. Much of the Norman army suddenly hesitated, stunned to see William crash to the ground and thinking he was slain. But he staggered to his feet, removed his helmet, and shouted out to let his men know he was alive and encourage them to attack.

Both leaders agreed to a truce and break of battle to remove the field's injured and to drink water. King Harold's English shield wall was still very much in place, bolstered by his well-disciplined and seasoned, war-ready troops. Fighting began again with repeated showers of arrows loosed by the

Normans, Flemish, and French archers. Duke William's infantry and cavalry plowed into the Saxons as the light was fading. Recalling how quickly the Saxon right flank had broken ranks to chase the running Bretons earlier, this time William instructed his left flank to break and run to the rear, as if in full flight and retreat, as in reality they had done in the first battle of the day.

As William anticipated, Harold's right-wing of a now much-depleted force rushed forward to chase the "retreating" Normans with their Saxon lords shouting them on. The ruse worked, and as the Saxons passed the main body of Norman's foot and mounted troops on their left, William gave his cavalry command to swoop in behind the Saxons and his foot soldiers to about-face and attack the Saxons. Harold's troops were caught in a pincer movement and slaughtered.

After Harold received a head wound from an arrow, he was hastily treated and fought on for some time. Three or four of William's mounted knights had gotten up high into Caldbec Hill behind the Saxons in this bloody battle, and they tore downhill to attack from behind as the Normans' main forces were battering those forces from the front. The Knights broke through from the rear to the corner, attacked King Harold, and hacked him to death. Whether William was one of them is not recorded as some have suggested. Even then, Harold's lords did not give up but continued the battle around their king's dead body to defend it, and one by one, they were struck down by the Norman knights and killed. The remainder of Harold's army fled the field, and as darkness fell, they ran into the nearby woods to regroup, care for their wounded, and rest from the day's exhausting defeat.

After some skirmishing, survivors headed for London with their leaders. William surveyed the now eerily calm battlefield, covered with thousands of dead and dying and men moaning in pain and calling for help. Crows and other birds would soon be flocking to peck at the flesh of the corpses and those on death's door. Every man had given his all for their country. Nearby villagers would soon be looting the bodies of fallen knights for what they could get, in between being chased away by compatriots who'd survived.

William asked for Harold's body to be brought to him and decided to carry it to London to demonstrate that King Harold was dead. Harold's main banner was the golden dragon on an appropriately blood-red background, the Wessex Wyvern. The flag was dispatched as a gift to Pope Alexander in

Rome with the knights accompanying the Gold Cross of the Pontiff, returning it to His Holiness. It remains at the Vatican today.

A Matter of Scholarly Debate – an Eye to Detail

At this battle stage, the Normans had begun to seriously inflect carnage on the Saxon right flank, exposed in the open, when Harold caught an arrow in his head and probably not his eye. There was no arrow in King Harold's eye on the original Bayeux Tapestry of the Battle of Hastings. Popular belief has always claimed that King Harold died from an arrow that pierced his eye on entering his head. Every British schoolchild learned that.

The Archdeacon of the Diocese of Lincoln.
In his work, the *Historia Anglorum*, Henry of Huntington wrote that Harold died from an arrow to the eye. Henry and other chroniclers were writing in the next century multiple decades after events.

Guy, Bishop of Amiens, France.
Later Chaplain to Queen Matilda, William the Conquerors wife traveled with her to England for the Crowing of William as King of England, and Matilda as Queen. Guy wrote the earliest record of the Battle of Hastings amongst other things in this work, *Carmen de Hastingae Proelio* ("Song of the Battle of Hastings;" a poem). He states that Harold died from an arrow striking him in the eye.

The chronicler Wace,
Wace was the Canon of Bayeux Cathedral in France and wrote the *Roman de Rou* from secondhand accounts, direct from next-generation decedents of those who fought in the battle. The stories passed down *appear* to be very detailed and aligned. Wace comes across as relating stories in a balanced, fair, and honest way.

Wace wrote that Harold's right eye was put out by an arrow that struck him from *"above the eye."* Suggesting, not in it, but hitting his skull with sufficient force, it seems to have popped his eye out of its socket. Semantics, maybe, but he continues,

"And now the Normans had pressed on so far, that at last, they reached the standard" (the Saxon battle Flag which stood by the armies King). "There Harold had remained, defending himself to the utmost, but he was sorely wounded in his eye by the arrow and suffered grievous pain from the blow. An armed man came in the multitude of battle, struck him in the ventaille of his helmet, and beat him to the ground. As he sought to recover himself, a knight beat him down again, striking him on the thick of the thigh, down to the bone."

Yet, he survived this first attack. The ventaille (ventilation) slit was often built into the metal helmet from the forehead down for breathing and a slit across for a good line of sight. Most accounts agree that when four Norman knights broke through from the rear of the Saxon army's remnants, they charged directly for Harold, now without shield, and they cut him down then and there and killed him.

William of Malmesbury

In his *Gesta Regum Anglorum, the Anglo-Norman monk said* that "Receiving a fatal arrow from a distance, he died. One of the Norman soldiers with a sword then cut off his leg as he lay." This is interesting as we appear to have varying chroniclers agreeing that Harold was both hit by an arrow in the head or eye and attacked by Norman mounted knights and cut down.

The Bayeux Tapestry Death Scene of King Harold

Of thirty-two key panels, the 31st depicted an entire battle scene of Norman and Saxon soldiery and mounted knights, and the famous scene, of King Harold being killed. A full panel image and a close-up clipped copy of the image area at the end of this chapter. Across the top right section of this 31st tapestry panel are the Latin words:

Harold: Rex: Interfectus: Est (The translation reads, Harold: King: Killed: It is). King Harold is killed.

Yet, take a close look at those embroidered words as they stretch across this scene, above two standing Saxon knights and a mounted Norman. Depending on which chronicler you read, Harold is the knight on foot, center-left of the image in full armor, shield, helmet, and lance. This man appears with an arrow striking his head or eye. Other chroniclers describe Harold's death from being set upon by mounted Norman knights and cut down. The Saxon knight on the right of the clipped image is depicted falling to the ground in body armor and helmet but without a shield and is struck by a sword across his thigh or leg.

The Probable Answer to Which is Harold

Nick Austin is a historian and author of *Secrets of the Norman Invasion*, first published by Ogmium Press in October 2011. From exhaustive research and analysis of every known source and document on the Battle of Hastings, Austin suggests that the Bayeux Tapestry *depicts Harold twice* in one scene. This is in much the same way that a static cartoon strip would show more than one image of the same person in a different scene side by side.

In wrapping up his manuscript, the author has only recently read Austin's book on the Norman invasion. The author supports Nick Austin's hypothesis that the knight on the left of this clipped image is King Harold, depicted when struck by an arrow in the head or eye. The author also supports Austin's belief that the image on the right of a knight falling and being attacked by a mounted Norman knight is King Harold, showing his death.

The Normans Had Not Won England Yet

On hearing of Harold's defeat and death, the Witan met. This was the council of Saxon chiefs who'd not gone south, had survived and returned to London as Saxon lords or earls, or who had elevated themselves into their dead father's shoes. They elected Eadgar Aetheling, by now aged just fifteen (Edward the Confessor's rightful blood heir), to be King of England. The young earls Eadwin, Morkere, and Waltheof readied themselves for a most certain head-on collision with William, who they knew would soon be heading to London, the capital.

News soon reached them that William, Duke of Normandy, was making his way to London via Kent with his victorious army, including 600 mounted knights. As that was how many mounted knights William had had before the

Battle of Hastings, I doubt that number was heading to London; however, it was a large, mounted force—something the Saxons had not dealt with before Hastings. They must have been deeply fearful of the defense of London, a battle that was looming. On October 21, after days of resting his men, reprovisioning, and taking care of the injured, William took submission from the south's Saxons at Dover. Eight days later, the Saxons of Canterbury had submitted too.

Before the Saxon nobility could hastily crown young Saxon Prince Eadgar King of England, as they now planned, the Norman army, with William at its head, arrived late morning at Southwark on London's outskirts. William again offered the Saxons a chance to concede to him and avoid other battles and bloodshed. But Eadgar, the intended new Saxon English king, and his earls refused, and the action commenced on the road from Southwark to London. Numerous times William's cavalry threw themselves at the Saxon shield wall, which held. The wall did not sustain heavy losses, but many Norman knights and horses were lost each time, mainly from slingshots and arrows, with more significant archers now deployed to defend Saxon ranks.

By accounts of the day, the London road ran red with blood like a stream of red, running water. Yet William resorted to trying to break the dangerous deadlock by setting fire to all the Southwark homes. As dusk was falling, he knew he had to take London now or never. A final assault on Eadgar's shield wall lost William more men. Shamed and under cover of darkness, he signaled a retreat. William's retreat saw the end of fighting that day and was Eadgar's hour of glory, which led him to sense he could defeat the Norman invader and opportunist on the morrow.

The following day, William renewed his attack on the Saxon forces. Eventually, his men's superior fighting ability, with so many mounted knights, won the day, and he moved on to London, where the city submitted to him without a fight. Most of the Saxon leaders were dead, and the only surviving male relative of Edward the Confessor is thought to have been Eadgar, whom William captured. Eadgar submitted to William as the new and rightful king of England. William now set about taking control of the English government and did so with ruthless efficiency.

The Aftermath

On Christmas Day, 1066, William was crowned King William I of England and the first Norman king of the realm. The ceremony was conducted at Westminster Abbey in London, a Benedictine Catholic abbey. It was the third major royal event for the Abbey within twelve months: the burial of King Edward the Confessor, the crowning of King Harold, and now the crowning of William as King of England. It was coincidently one of the few times in English history that there were three kings in one year. Though the Saxon Witan as the rightful heir to Edward the Confessor, Eadgar Aetheling served William I and his son, Rufus, who became William II of England. A town sprang up around the site of the Battle of Hastings and was called Battle. William had a great abbey built on the field to commemorate the dead. It was named Battle Abbey and still stands in use today.

Not long after, William set about turning a temporary wooden defensive fort built in London on the bank of the River Thames into a stone castle. Right after Christmas, the Tower of London would commence what, 954-years later, stands firm and is one of the most potent symbols of Norman English monarchy and power. William also built great defensive castles across England to defend his crown, starting with Norwich, Wallingford, Chepstow, and Exeter.

King Harold's mother, Gytha, petitioned William for her son's body, which he unchivalrously rejected. In February 1067, Gytha led a rebellion against the Normans at Exeter, but her forces were defeated. When William returned to Normandy for nine months in March, he made his half-brother, Bishop Ode, who had been made the English Earl of Kent, his regent in his absence. Further uprisings against the Normans in 1068 in the north of England and an actual rebellion led by Harold's brother, the Saxon Earl Morcar, at Peterborough in the north. These also ended in their defeat. It was the last serious uprising of the Saxons, but William was to face two further invasions. His reign was not entirely settled until 1102.

French became the king's court language and gradually blended with the Anglo-Saxon tongue to modern English. French with the Normans became the language of most royal courts in Europe over the following centuries and was commonly taught to all princes and nobility. William was illiterate, like most nobles of his time. In this era, scribes, monks employed by kings and nobles, wrote letters and records. William didn't speak a word of English when he ascended the throne of England, and despite his advisors' efforts to teach him English, he never mastered it.

William, the 1st proved an influential king of England, and among his notable achievements was the *Domesday Book*, which we'll talk about shortly, the first great census of the lands, manors, and people of England as William would describe the victory in Latin, *Voluntatem Dei*—God's will. For the ordinary God-fearing man, this summed it up.

The newly crowned William I, King of England, was challenged continuously for some years. In 1069, just three years after William took the throne, King Sweyn of Demark led an invasion of England.

King William, Duke of Normandy, died September 9, in 1087, and Rufus, choosing to take William's sovereign name, was proclaimed King William II on his succession to the English throne. In 1098 and again in 1102, King Magnus of Norway invaded England, claiming its throne, but William's descendants and their fellow Normans triumphed over them all.

The Domesday Book

It is worth taking a moment to tie the story so far to this book, which was embarked upon and created in England, but whose approach formed many new nations' ways of assessing people for taxes. The lands of Roger de Beaumont and his son, Robert, the future Norman 1st Earl of Leicester, were listed in this extraordinary book. Domesday is the old Middle English spelling of the word doomsday—the day of reckoning. This established the font of Hamilton lands that followed. As this was to be a "Great Survey" of England's entire nation, it would be the final authority on all matters for which it was created. It became known as a "great reckoning" of who owned the land and its production value that the king could tax. It was the precursor to every other country's land and property valuation for government taxes.

This book was the most detailed record of landowning and values ever created, and another wouldn't occur for 787 years. It greatly impacted everyone's lives, including the conquered and the newly landed Norman families whose English holdings were assessed for taxes due to the crown. It was a very unpopular move with the Saxons.

NOTES:

Viking DNA.
DNA projects were coordinated by St. John's College, the University of Cambridge in England, the Lundbeck Foundation GeoGenetics Centre, the University of Copenhagen, the University of Bristol, and the Moesgaard Museum in Denmark. Professors, assistants, and associate professors represented specializations in GeoGenetics, evolutionary genomics, and archaeology—a highly distinguished group of specialist scientists associated with FamilyTreeDNA.

Sources of Rollo's Place of Birth Are Important to Share
William of Malmesbury, in his chronicle *De Gestis* said, "Then Rollo, born of noble lineage among the *Norwegians*, though obsolete from its extreme antiquity, was banished, by the king's command, from his own country, and brought over with him multitudes" to Frankish, Normandy.

Goffredo Malaterra was an 11th century Norman Benedictine Monk. He wrote his *De Rebus Gestis Rogerii Calabriae et Siciliae Comitis et Roberti Guiscardi Ducis fratris eius* (The history of the Normans in Italy). He noted that "Rollo sailed boldly from *Norway* with his fleet to the Christian coast."

Benoît de Sainte-More, a twelfth-century monk and chronicler, got it wrong in his *Chronique des ducs de Normandie* c. 1175. He misinterpreted a Danish town's similar but different spelling to the proven by contemporary chronicles, topography, and more recent DNA as the Norwegian birthplace of Rollo being "Fauske." The Norwegian town of "Fauske" matches the village's landscape and mountain topography described in detail by Benoît as Rollo's birthplace. It is nothing like the scenic topography of Fasge or Faxe in Denmark.

Confirmation of The Nobles at The Battle of Hastings
Three sources aligned on fifteen Norman nobles who fought with Duke William at the Battle of Hastings. The sources are The English Benedictine Monk, Orderic Vitalis's *Historia Ecclesiastica* (*The Ecclesiastical History*). William of Poitiers, a former military Knight, contemporary chronicler, cleric,

and chaplain to William, Duke of Normandy, was present at the battle and confirmed the principal nobles in his "*Gesta Guillelmi II ducis Normannorum et Regis Anglorum*" was published in 1073. Thirdly, there is the Bayeux Tapestry.

The Bayeux Tapestry Itself

It is, in fact, needlepoint but has been known as a tapestry from time immemorial. The work is vast and 224.3 ft × 1.6 ft wide (68.38 meters long and 0.5 meters wide) and depicts the events leading up to and including the Battle of Hastings in 1066.

A Weighty Subject in the Battle of Hastings

An 11th-century knight on a heavy horse typically wore around 50lb (23 kilos) in armor, a shorter sword than for ground fighting, and maybe a dagger, a mace, or lance. Now add a man's weight, which could be around 180lb (81.65 kilos) for a solid young warrior or 220lb (99.7 kg) for an older heavier knight. Hence these horses were bred to carry anywhere between 230lb's - 270lbs (104.33 - 122.74 kg) on their back. A typical heavy horse breed at this time would have weighed around 1,200lbs - 1,300lbs (545 - 590 kg).

The Duke of Normandy, Today

Interestingly, the British Crown Dependencies of the Channel Islands are the Bailiwicks of Guernsey and Jersey (Separately, they include the Isle of Man off the west coast of England). Both Dependencies have broad powers of self-government and legislative assemblies, and a Lieutenant Governor for each Bailiwick is appointed as the Queen's representative. The Bailiwick of Guernsey comprises the islands of Guernsey, Alderney, Sark, and Hern, Brecqhou, Jethou, and Lihou. The Bailiwick of Jersey also includes the uninhabited islets of Minquiers and Écréhous.

A Bailiwick is an area of land under the jurisdiction of a bailiff. The term survives in the Channel Islands. All of these Islands lay some 10-30 miles off the coast of France in the English Channel are the last remaining part of Normandy's former duchy to remain under the rule of the British monarch today. They were inherited from William the Conqueror, Duke of Normandy, King William I of England.

Despite the English claims to the Duchy of Normandy, formerly relinquished in 1259 at the Treaty of Paris, they remain British Crown dependencies. France abolished the aristocracy and ducal titles included in 1790. However, in a very British quirk of custom, the Channel Islands officially recognize the British Sovereign today and raise the loyal toast to 'The Duke of Normandy.'

Bernard "The Dane" a Viking Earl (NCA) *The sketch from 'The Little Duke' by Charlotte Mary Yonge* published 1854 (CE) The author evidenced that Bernard was born in 'Norway' a Pagan warrior who invaded France in 909 A.D. with "Rollo" later the 1ˢᵗ ruler of Normandy and is the earliest proven male bloodline ancestor of all the Hamiltons (CE).

The Bayeux Tapestry (CE)., depicting Roger de Beaumont, with beard (an ancestor of all Hamilton's today). His cousin, William the Conqueror, Duke of Normandy seated to his left, and his half-brother Bishop Odo, blesses a feast after landing near Hastings, England, on Michaelmas Friday, 1066 (CE).

A larger stretch of the same segment of the Bayeux Tapestry depicting the Battle of Hastings and the final scenes leading to King Harold I death (CE).

The Bayeux Tapestry depicting the death of King Harold of England. The Latin inscription is stretched above these two standing Saxon knights: *Harold: Rex: Interfectus: Est* (**King Harold is killed**). The latest research suggests that King Harold is depicted twice in this panel, once as the Saxon knight standing on the left when struck by an arrow, and on the right, falling and attacked by a mounted knight who killed him (CE).

Chapter 2

The 12th – 13th Century Hamiltons

Robert de Beaumont, 2nd Earl of Leicester

Robert was born in c.1104 and died in June 1168. He and his twin brother, Waleran, were just fourteen when they became wards of the court in the royal household of King Henry I (grandson of William the Conqueror). The latter had succeeded to the crown when William II died without issue. The twins were raised at court as favorites of King Henry. No doubt, the king utilized the income from their lands for himself after paying the costs of their household support.

The de Beaumont twins had inherited all their father's titles, lands, and wealth. Robert inherited his father's English titles, and Waleran inherited his father's Norman French titles. Robert, as 2nd Earl, married Amice de Gael, and they had four children. Their son, *also* named Robert, became the 3rd Earl of Leicester. The second earl's three daughters married well—Hawise to the 2nd Earl of Gloucester, Isabel to the Earl of Huntington, and Margaret to Tonei (Tosny), de Conches of Normandy—Ralph (Raoul) IV. Ralph's father had been granted lands in England after its conquest in Flamstead and Hertfordshire, and he was the Lord of Flamstead and Clifford.

During 'The Anarchy' civil war (1135-1154) England and Normandy, in 1139, by now under King Stephen's reign (Henry I's son), which lasted almost a decade, Robert, the second earl, had supported the king, as did his twin brother. He would have known King Henry I's friend and later his nemesis, Thomas Becket, the Archbishop of Canterbury, murdered in his Cathedral in King Henry's name on December 29, 1170 after Robert's death. Robert became justiciar (prime minister) of England (1155–1168) and lord high steward under King Henry II, the first king of the House of Plantagenet.

Robert de Beaumont, 3rd Earl of Leicester

When his father died c. 1168, this Robert inherited the earldom and married Petronilla de Grandmesnil. From his children came yet another Robert, who would become the fourth earl. A son, Roger, became a bishop, one daughter, Margaret, married the future 1st Earl of Winchester and William de Beaumont. Their other daughter, Amicia, married Simon de Montfort, who, after his brother-in-law, the fourth earl, died without living issue, became the fifth earl. His heirs carried the de Montfort name.

This same Robert, the third earl, joined a revolt against King Henry II of England in April 1173, an uprising in both Normandy and then England. In response to the king seeking to sequester lands from other family members for his young son, Prince John, the king's other three sons objected and fled to the French court of Louis VII, where Robert de Beaumont joined them. In a coordinated attack with their ally, the Scottish king, Robert, they invaded Normandy, and the three princes invaded the north of England. With a force of Flemish mercenaries, Robert later joined the princes' invasion of England, landing in Suffolk in late September, most likely.

Robert sought to join up with the 1st Earl of Norfolk, where later the Battle of Fornham in Suffolk took place on October 17, 1173, known as the "Great Revolt." Robert de Beaumont led his forces, which were split half on land and half trying to ford the River Lark when the king's cavalry and an army commanded by Robert de Lucy attacked at this crucial weak moment.

With most of his 3,000 mercenaries driven into nearby swampland, Robert lost the battle, and most of his men were killed by local peasants loyal to the king. The king imprisoned Robert and his wife, Petronilla, who had donned the armor. The king also stripped Robert of all his titles and lands. In January 1177, the king released Robert and Petronilla, restoring Robert's Earldom and lands, but *not* his four castles. Two had been destroyed, and two were forfeit to the king, including Leicester Castle, the de Beaumont family seat. He remained though out of favor at court.

In 1185, Petronilla gave birth to their third of five children, christened William de Beaumont, at Leicester Castle. The key to the 'Hamilton' name is this third son of the 3rd Earl of Leicester, the font of all named Hamilton today, as we'll read about shortly.

When England's King Richard I inherited the throne, Robert came back into favor at court, and on September 3, 1189 at King Richard I's coronation, Robert carried the king's Sword of State during the ceremony. He later joined his king on the Third Crusade to the Holy Land and Palestine in 1190. He died at Dyrrachium, later known as Durazzo and the "modern-day" Durrës, during his journey in Albania. Its port was one of the largest on the Adriatic Sea and was often used as a staging post for Crusade armies to or from the Holy Lands. Some historians suggest he died on the way home from the Crusades. However, as he died in the same year, he'd set off to join the campaign, he may well have been killed on the way there, as Crusaders were usually some years on Crusade.

William de Hameldone, the First Named 'Hamilton'

He was born William de Beaumont in Leicestershire in 1185, the third of five children and the third son of the 3rd Earl of Leicester. Interestingly, by the time of his birth, his father, the Earl of Leicester's 'seat,' Leicester Castle, had been forfeit to the Crown. Hence, the assumption made by some that William, born a de Beaumont, was born in Leicester Castle is *highly* improbable. William married Mary of Buthernock, the daughter of the 3rd Earl of Strathearn, in 1215 and died in c. 1293 most likely at the Battle of Amiénois, the "modern-day" town of Amiens, in the Somme district, the capital of France's Picardy region. The town had been incorporated as a French rather than a Norman royal domain in the year of William's birth.

William's elder brother, Robert, became the fourth earl, but the title became extant of the de Beaumont line with his death without male issue. Robert split his property and wealth between his two sisters. The earldom was designated for William's eldest sister, Amicia de Beaumont's husband, Simon IV de Montfort. This Simon was to become one of the great military commanders of the Middle Ages, who took part in the Fourth Crusade to the Holy Lands. We do not yet know why Robert didn't leave the earldom to one of his two brothers, Roger, the Bishop of St. Andrew's, or William.

King John Plantagenet of England (Who lost the Dukedom of Normandy lands after nearly 200-years in the hands of the de Beaumont family) inherited the throne in AD 1199 from his brother, King Richard the Lionheart. He almost immediately confiscated the Leicester lands and revenues for himself and refused to issue Letters Patent to the designated fifth earl, Simon de

Montfort IV. After his death, Simon IV's son was granted Letters Patent and, as Simon de Montfort V, became the 6th Earl of Leicester.

At a time of major religious battles with the Crusades (1095–1291), William lived in the period when the Knights Templar sought to defend the Holy Land route for Christians from Europe to Jerusalem. The Fourth Crusade took place in 1202 (when William was seventeen), and others followed in 1204, 1228, and later.

William de Hameldone's Birth-Place

The Patronymica Britannic, states that, *William de Hameldon, a younger son of Robert de Beaumont, third Earl of Leicester in the year 1215, went into Scotland, where he was well received by,* (King) *Alexander II. From him* (William de Hambledon) *sprung all the noble and other Scottish lines of Hamiltons.* William would have been aged 30 at the time.

Many historians put weight behind William being born in Leicestershire in the original village of Hamilton. Some say that this village was initially called Hameldun, which sits between Scraptoft and Barkby-Thorpe just outside of the city of Leicester. This name is from the old English word for Hamlet "Hamel," and the old English word for hill, "Dun." Hamlet-on-the-hill. It's said therefore he was known as from or of (de) Hameldun in Leicestershire. Let us read about the case for his birthplace.

It is critical to spend some time on this topic as it is the foundation of the Hamilton name, mired in past controversy as to which town the name hails from and why. Settling this debate is valuable, as everything that follows stems from that truth.

Not linking any such claim but purely as land records, *Historic England* lists a *deserted* village in Leicestershire (now open agricultural fields) named Hamilton since medieval times Hameldun. The village is located between Scraptoft and Barkby-Thorpe on the northeast side of the city of Leicester.

This location's records include archeological imprints of a 'moated site and a fishpond contained within the village earthworks.' The area of earthworks today shows an agricultural village measuring approximately 330m x 300m, which is 22.24 acres. According to Historic England, 'the village name of Hamilton was first recorded in c.1125' (60-years before William was born – the first to use the name) 'when it contained 374 acres of land. By 1377 there were only four taxpayers,' and desertion took place sometime after that. This suggests that as archeological imprints cover 22.24 acres, the rest was purely agricultural land yielding crops most likely.

The records show that 'the hollow ways evidence of a well-defined internal street system' and 'a series of house platforms are evident, at least ten of which lies in the northern part of the site. A platform on the south-western side of the site is believed to be the site of a chapel.' 'On the northern side of the close is a rectangular moated area measuring 55m x 45 m' overall (26,701 square feet), and within this would have sat a Manor House, likely built as a defensive property for a local squire or even Lord. See notes at chapters end.

Evidence of The Town He Was Known as From

For William to have been born here is highly unlikely and stretches reality a tad too far. His father, the Earl of Leicester, had been deprived of Leicester Castle for falling foul of the King by the time of William's birth. However, he is unlikely to have stooped so low in fortune that he would be living in a comparatively small rural agricultural village. While the author has no fully-evidenced location of William's birth (as no one to date seems to have), most historians agree it was in Leicestershire - somewhere.

Growing up, William would always have been known by his father's lineage, William de (of) Beaumont. His father *never* changed the name of where he was known from in Normandy; he didn't suddenly become Robert de Hamilton, 3rd Earl of Leicester of that village he *would have lived* in for many years, if William was to be known as from there. He was always Robert de Beaumont. As we have read, the name de Beaumont springs from the name of the Normandy town where Honri (Humphrey). From Honri to William's father some 141 years by the time William was born, every generation was known by their name as heralding from de Beaumont - keeping their Norman ancestry and pride in place.

Finally, William de Hameldone's names spelling does not appear in any records spelt Hamilton, nor do his son's, grandson's, or great-grandson's names. It was not until his great-great-grandson, born in c. 1333 registered as David de 'Hameldone' that *he* changed the spelling in 1378 after becoming the 3rd Baron Cadzow to the simplified 'Hamilton.' The castle and town of Cadzow were known as Hamilton *after* that. David changed the spelling to

Hamilton 93-years after William de Beaumont, later known as from de (of) 'Hameldone' was born.

The Town of Hambleton (Hameldone), Buckinghamshire

Over the centuries this has been variously recorded as Hambleden, Hambleton, Hammelton and Hameldone. The evidence of William being known as a young independent man living in the village of Hameldone in Buckinghamshire close to the river Thames, from 1205, as we will read, is substantial. The evidence that his great-great-grandson changed the name to Hamilton is clear, too, as the de Beaumont line has never wavered from using that name until William. The author is satisfied with all evidence that the de Beaumont name remained unchanged from c. 995 and Honri until 1205. From 1205 until 1378, all sons were known as de Hameldone and only from 1378 as Hamiltons.

Buckinghamshire Counties historical records confirm that a young adult by the name of William de Beaumont, *named* as the third son of the Earl of Leicester, made the town of Hameldone, Buckinghamshire his home. He became known to be from that town but not born there. This Buckinghamshire town's records of this being the source of what became a family name and was later simplified to "Hamilton" are to the author the most solid evidence he has found.

Multiple 'Hamilton' Name Variations

The Spelling of the Hamilton name has variously appeared over earlier centuries.

Hameldone, Hameldon, Hambledone, Hambledon, Hameldun, Hambleton, and Hamiltoun are variations in 12th, and 13th-century records for the same family morphed to the spelled, Hamilton.

Multiple Claims to the Origin of the Founding Town

There are Hambledon (variation spellings) in Parishes in at least six English counties. Rutland, Lancaster (Shire), Buckingham (Shire), York (Shire), Leicester (Shire), and Northumberland. The author is sure that there will have been a Hamilton connection to each town or village named at some time or other over the last 1,142-years. There is a *far* greater weight of evidence for this than for any other place, including 'Hamilton' in Leicestershire or Northumberland, as proposed by particular historians. A similar coat of arms is not the same.

Additional Evidence of the Correct de Hameldone/Hamilton Town

It is the first man to cease using the family name of de Beaumont, William, whom we have focused on where he and his immediate heirs were known to have come from, that resulted in his and they are known as de (of) Hameldone.

At a time of major religious battles with the Crusades (1095–1291), William lived in the period when the Knights Templar sought to defend the Holy Land route for Christians from Europe to Jerusalem. The Fourth Crusade took place in 1202 (when William was seventeen), and others followed in 1204, 1228, and later.

William most likely died in the Battle of Amiénois, the "modern-day" town of Amiens, in the Somme district, the capital of France's Picardy region. The town had been incorporated as a French rather than a Norman royal domain in the year of William's birth.

The Patronymica Britannic, states that, *William de Hameldon, a younger son of Robert de Beaumont, third Earl of Leicester in the year 1215, went into Scotland, where he was well received by,* (King) *Alexander II. From him* (William de Hambledon) *sprung all the noble and other Scottish lines of Hamiltons.* William would have been aged 20 at the time.

Gilbert fitz-William de Hameldone, Son of William Hameldone

Gilbert was born in 1225 d. 1293. The genealogical record of the Hambleton family, in the "Patronymica Britannica," states that, *From Hambleton, the seat of Sir Gilbert de Hambledon, the founder of the Scotch Ducal family of Hamilton, in the 13ᵗʰ century;* and goes on to say that *Hambledon, a manor in Buckinghamshire* from where they hailed.

Gilbert relocated to Baldernock, East Dunbartonshire in Scotland, which is about 9-miles north of Glasgow, and 15 miles east from where Alec Hamilton was born, at Strathleven House in West Dumbartonshire, in the heart of Clan Hamilton territory in the middle ages. Gilbert's son Walter stayed in Hameldone in Buckinghamshire becoming Lord of the Manor.

Gilbert fitz-William *de Hameldone* (as spelt on official records) was stated as born in Hambleton (Hameldone) in Buckinghamshire, in 1225, the eldest son of William de Hambeldone; adding further conclusive weight to the fact that his father had moved there as a young man – hence from 1205 when William de Hameldone the son of the Earl of Leicester is recorded there from 1205 onward, he became known as William from, or de (of) Hameldone (Hambleton). William would have been aged 40 when Gilbert was born.

Fitz is pronounced "fits," was a patronymic indicator used in Anglo-Norman England to distinguish individuals lineage by identifying their immediate predecessors. Fitz (usually spelt fitz) means "son of", it would precede the father's forename. Hence, Gilbert 'son-of-William de (of) Hameldone.

When Gilbert fitz-William de Hameldone died, the lands of Kinneil were transferred to his son Walter.

The Magna Carta—the World's First Charter of Liberties

The Magna was Carta signed by King John Plantagenet on June 15, 1215 and is now an 807-year-old charter of civil liberties established in England during William de Hameldone's lifetime. It was to affect both Britain's and its colonies' basic rule of law, and indeed, the United States of America's constitution and initial civil liberty laws. This charter of freedoms only came about as a large body of rebel English barons forced King John by a coup d'état to give his assent to it and sign it or be deposed for his dictatorship-style rule.

The Magna Carta constituted a fundamental guarantee of rights and privileges. Under this charter's terms, the nobles were granted the right to trial by jury and given protection, in theory, from the king's arbitrary acts. Sir William de Hameldone (a de Beaumont by birth, remember) was in the thick of these times of change, and his complete absence from all records of those opposing the king confirms that he supported the king, like many landed nobles. In 1215, William was thirty years of age and had just married when the Magna Carta came into force. "How amazing were the times and the changes in which William lived;" modern-day Alexander Hamilton reflected in his discussion with the author. No Hamilton or de Beaumont signed or was witness to any charter or document against the king – and remained loyal to the crown. See Notes.

Sir Walter Fitz-Gilbert de Hameldone, the 1st Laird of Cadzow

Walter was the son of Sir Gilbert Fitz-William and grandson of William de Hameldone (who had died many years before his grandson was born). Walter was born in 1274 and died in 1346.

From Walter, most historians say, sprang the multiple cadet branches of Hamiltons. When talking about the fountain of Hamilton ancestry, it is odd that many quote this de Hameldone, Sir Walter, or his father, Gilbert, but fail to mention his grandfather, William de Hameldone, the actual Hamilton name's fountain.

Walter's story is crucially entwined with the times of Robert the Bruce and William Wallace. William Wallace was born just four years before Sir Walter, who lived through an extraordinary period of Scottish history. It is essential to spend a while looking at the events occurring currently, as there were some earth-shattering changes to Scottish history during Sir Walter's lifetime. In Scotland in 1291, Walter was present at Berwick Castle to sign documents by which Scotland's nobility and gentry vowed allegiance to King Edward I of England. His father, Sir Gilbert, was the first de Hameldone to be born in Scotland rather than England

Sir Walter & The Early Struggle for Scotland's Throne

King Edward I of England was known to the Scottish patriot William Wallace and the Scots people as "Longshanks" because he was unusually tall for this century, at 6' 2". A 2017 University of Oxford study of the average height of a man in the British Isles in the thirteenth to fourteenth centuries suggests that in Longshanks' time, it was about 5' 8" for men aged twenty-one to forty-nine. Hence, King Edward stood a good six inches taller than most, creating an imposing stature that enhanced his regal bearing.

In documents, Sir Walter was listed as giving loyalty to the English Crown as "Walter fitz Gilbert de Hameldone, formerly with lands in Renfrewshire," Scotland. He also appears in Paisley's monastery charter around 1294, when he would have been aged twenty. First, there was John de Comyn III; then Robert de Bruce, the VIII de Bruce, Earl of Carrick, Lord of Annandale; and finally, John de Balliol III (one of his sons, was later to be crowned King John I of Scotland in 1292). Balliol College at the University of Oxford is named after him, his having donated funds during his life and his will established and built Balliol College. John de Balliol IIIs daughter, Mary, married John de Comyn II, and son was John "the Red" de Comyn (father of the "Black Comyn).

A further claimant to the throne was John, Lord of Badenoch, in Inverness shire, Scotland, and John Balliol's nephew. What an intricate web had been weaved.

John de Comyn's father had been Ambassador to France for King Alexander I of Scotland and was himself was a direct descendant of King Donald I of Scotland. Stretching down from his Norman ancestors, John descended from several Comyn's who Earls of Northumberland in England were. His claim was as good as John Balliol III and Robert the Bruce. John's ancestor, another John de Comyn was born c. 991 (died c.1021), and his son, Robert (c.1022 – d.1069) was all too briefly the first Comyn Earl of Northumberland, granted by William the Conqueror in 1069. This raising to nobility suggests he came to England with William, Duke of Normandy in September 1066 and played a critical part in the conquering of England

Loyal or not

While both Balliol and Comyn were staunch defenders of Scotland's autonomy, as was William Wallace, born of a noble family. He never wavered, and always stood for Scotland, whereas the Bruce had wavered from Scottish to English Crown allegiance and back more than once. Many Scottish nobles did not trust Robert the Bruce (who later in 1306 became King Robert I of Scotland for thirteen years).

At this time of a significant turning point in Scottish history, the Hamiltons had sided with the English king the Scottish kingship claimants. The Hamilton fortunes ebbed and flowed with the king's patronage, so it is worth spending time on this matter, as it had a significant effect on Hamilton fortunes.

It is believed that in secret negotiations, Comyn eventually agreed to recognize the Bruce to be King of Scotland. In exchange, he demanded significant tracts of Bruce's lands and income, and that the Bruce commit to rising against the English with him. The Bruce, believing that John Comyn had broken their secret pact, asked to confer with Comyn at the Franciscan Church of Greyfriars in Dumfries, Scotland.

They are said to have entered the church alone on February 10, 1306, just the two men. The Bruce is understood to have accused Comyn of betraying him by telling the English king of their secret pact. A fight ensued, and Comyn was stabbed to death. Whatever happened between them in the church, and whether the Bruce murdered Comyn in cold blood or acted in self-defense, will likely never be known. However, most sources accept that the Bruce killed John Comyn and fled initially to caves in the hills. Then he moved on to Dumfries Castle, which was held by the English, attacked it, and took their surrender.

Murder, Excommunication, and the Crowned King of Scotland

The Catholic faith was the predominant religion of Scotland then, and to kill in a church was grounds for ex-communication. Not only that, but the Bruce killed Comyn under a flag of truce against all standards of chivalry among knights and lords in the Middle Ages. A man's honor was his life's code.

The Bruce arrived in Glasgow six weeks after Comyn's murder, where he met the Scottish Catholic bishops with Bishop Robert Wishart, Bishop of Glasgow. The Church of Greyfriars sat within Bishop Wishart's diocese. Extraordinary for his triple crime (murder in a church, at the altar, under a flag of truce), the bishop, sympathetic to the Bruce and his claim to Scotland's throne, forgave him. Instead of the Bruce being excommunicated by the Catholic Church, Bishop Wishart crowned him Robert, King of Scotland, on March 25, 1306, in Scone, with additional Scottish bishops present.

The bishop was of French-Norman descent yet was a significant supporter of Sir William Wallace and Bruce's claim to Scotland's throne. He saw the Scottish church's freedom entwined with ensuring Scotland was free from the English. He took the considerable risk of backing the man he believed was the best bet to protect Scotland as its king. If he was wrong and another won the throne from the Bruce, he would be dispatched to the next world, and the church might not be so safe. In time, the bishop was to pay dearly for crowning and supporting the Bruce as King of Scotland, as we will see.

Scotland almost immediately teetered on the brink of civil war with the Bruce's crowning and multiple claimants to the throne revolting against him. By that same summer of 1306, an English army marched into Scotland and, on June 19, challenged the Scottish army in the Battle of Methven, during this long period of Scotland's wars for independence. Both sides appeared evenly matched in numbers of men at around 4,500 each. The English defeated the Bruce. Fleeing the battlefield with his remaining troops, he was ambushed by members of the MacDougal and Macnab clans led by John MacDougal, a relative of the murdered Sir John Comyn. The Bruce had nearly been killed himself when MacDougal's men grabbed his cloak to pull him from his horse, but he managed to release the brooch holding it around his neck. Cloak and brooch (the latter now a MacDougal Clan treasure) were ripped away, and he was able to flee into the hills and hide in a cave.

Despite his advancing age and his enemies' surprise, Bishop Wishart personally led Scottish troops later that same year, 1306, besieging Cupar Castle in Fife, which was held by the English. A holy warrior monk for sure. However, the English gave battle to the enemy, beat them, and captured Wishart, and he was carried away in chains.

The Catholic bishops of England asked the pope to remove Bishop Wishart from his Scottish office, but the pope declined. However, Wishart was brought south and imprisoned in a dungeon in England, possibly in Wisbech Castle on the Isle of Ely. King Edward "Longshanks" was said to be delighted by Wishart's capture and saw this man, a Norman by decent, as a traitor to his kind. He only saved Wishart's life because he was a man of Holy Orders appointed by the pope. Wishart was kept in squalid conditions and chains for eight years, going blind in the process. It was only after the Scottish King Robert beat the English army at the Battle of Bannockburn that Wishart was released in a prisoner exchange. He lived out his last few years in Glasgow, dying in 1316.

After the Battle of Methven in 1306, the Bruce spent the next few years on the run, fighting skirmishes and terrorist-style raids. He was harassing King Edward of England's troops in Scotland while slowly but surely winning over more and more clans to back him. History suggests the strategy worked well for him.

The Bruce began to attack and destroy many English castles in the Scottish Lowlands, but Stirling Castle and Bothwell Castle were still in English hands. The former was considered the most critical crossroads to control the Scottish Highlands at the time, as it was the gateway to them. His goal was to weaken the English in Scotland before raising a big enough army to take on Comyn's followers and allies and wipe out their competition to his crown. Then he'd deny the English all supply lines and safe havens to gain supremacy over other claimants to the Scottish throne.

The 14th and 15th Century Hamiltons

In 1307, the English King Edward I, Longshanks, also known as the "Hammer of the Scots," died unexpectedly, having developed dysentery after setting off north from southern England on another campaign against the Bruce. He had encamped the day before on the Burgh Sands just south of the Scottish border on the English side, but when his servants awoke him to eat on the morning of July 7, the king died in their arms.

Many historians said his son, whom many believe due to his very close relationships with young men, was gay or bi-sexual. Prince Edward ascended to the throne as Edward II, King of England, without solid support from his barons.

Sir Walter Hamilton remained loyal to the English, supporting the new king's son, Edward II. Before June 1314, Sir Walter de Hameldone was appointed constable of Bothwell Castle in South Lanarkshire, Scotland, by Edward II. The English king charged Sir Walter with its security quite some time before the Battle of Bannockburn. The king's note to Walter de Hameldone read:

"The King commands Walter Fitz Gilbert de Hameldone, constable of his castle of Bothwell, to see that it is safely and securely kept and delivered to no other person whatsoever, without the King's letters patent under the Great Seal of England directed to himself."

Bruce's brother, Edward Bruce (later appointed High King of Ireland in 1315), was besieging Bothwell Castle and close to taking it. Thinking it would bring peace and save the unnecessary loss of hundreds of lives of both sides, Edward Bruce agreed on a truce sought by Sir Walter Hamilton, holding the castle for the English. Surprisingly Edward Bruce approved a pact that if an English relief force didn't arrive within a year, Sir Walter would surrender the castle to the Bruce without a fight. But if an English army did come in time, Edward Bruce would end his siege and leave the castle to the English.

The Bruce was livid at his brother's act, as he felt he'd missed the chance to crush the English, but as a matter of a knight's honor, he agreed to uphold the pact. How clever of Walter Hamilton to have pulled such a deal off. It's mind-boggling that the Bruce happily broke his code of chivalry to murder a rival at the altar of a church under a flag of truce. However, he wasn't willing to be seen to force his brother to break the arrangement he had made to Scotland's potential significant disadvantage.

The Battle of Bannockburn – Changed Scotland's Future

The English met the Scottish challenge, and military preparations to defeat the Scots were made once and for all. However, it took much of the year to raise an army of 20,000-foot soldiers and 2,000 men and horses, as the English barons were not enthusiastic about supporting their king. Edward II had initially wanted 30,000 men and 3,000 heavy horse to crush the Scots. As it was, the Bruce only had around 7,000 men and 500 "light" horse. In any traditional battle of the times, this would almost certainly have seen the Scottish army annihilated, or great swathes of his army turning and running from the field of battle under attack from a company of "heavy" horse.

However, it was now or never. If only his brother had not lifted the siege of Bothwell Castle and enabled Sir Walter de Hameldone to survive that siege, weighed heavy on the Bruce's mind. The Scottish light horse might be good at quick maneuvers and skirmishes on the battlefield, but the Bruce knew he could not attack thick infantry lines with great success.

The Scottish troops were primarily made up of peasants and farmers trained up, and every man from the age of sixteen was required to come forward and serve their Lord and their country. This was the battle the Bruce had sought to avoid: a frontal, formation, standard field battle, as he knew the English outnumbered him greatly and had a large contingent of "heavy horse." Typically, the side with a large troop of a heavy horse broke the back of opposing infantry by crashing through them, which swayed most medieval battles in favor of such mounted troops.

The Bruce had been learned lessons from earlier Scots battles featuring a stationary group of pikemen. Called "schiltrons," such formations lay at the heart of Bruce's battle strategy. A schiltron was a "great oval" (or sometimes a circle used at the Battle of Bannockburn, or a square). It was a battle formation with anything from eighty to as many as 2,000 men tightly knit, carrying massive twelve-foot-long pikes (spears), facing out. Their structure bristled like a giant lethal hedgehog. Weighing-in typically at 22.5 lbs. or ten kilos, it was unlikely that a weak or elderly soldier would be able to hold such a weapon for hours at a time during battle, even if he rested an end on the ground between enemy charges. Enemy archer arrow attacks usually broke pikemen's ranks, as they needed two hands to hold the heavy, long pikes.

Pikemen could not defend themselves with shields simultaneously, so they had to drop their pikes to pick up their shields. Such an action momentarily rendered pikemen defenseless if an enemy's light horse charged in at the right moment behind an avalanche of arrows falling out of the sky. If their ranks broke, leaving gaps to penetrate and scatter the schiltron, the whole company of soldiers would be routed. The three schiltrons were considered such a vital element of Bruce's strategy that on the first day of the battle, he commanded one full-circle schiltron himself. He had his brother, Edward Bruce, command one, and the third was commanded by Thomas Randolph, Earl of Moray, a trusted nephew of the Bruce.

The Bruce had drilled his pikemen in a new technique that took the English by complete surprise. As the schiltron blocked and destroyed the first wave of English heavy horse sent against it, the Bruce instructed his men to remain in their wholly defensive, bristling hedgehog shape while moving to where he needed them on the battlefield. Being on the move enabled them to avoid any sudden attack by arrows. Holding formation, they could move away rapidly between a torrent of arrows being loosed and their arrival as drilled by the Bruce. They would simultaneously avoid the deadly falling missiles, hold formation, and defend against heavy horse attacks. It is believed that this mobile schiltron was a never-before-seen tactic in Scotland, and this innovation worked brilliantly in favor of the outnumbered Scottish troops.

Let the Battle Begin

The Battle of Bannockburn took place on June 23 and 24, in 1314, just outside the Scottish town of Stirling, in Scotland. Two Hamiltons played critical roles in the battle and its aftermath, and titles, and lands were gained, so we must understand this battle as Hamilton's wealth was propelled from here.

As King Edward moved his English archers on his right flank into position to attempt to destroy the Scottish schiltrons, the Bruce, as a double safety measure, broke his fast, light horse troops off to his left side to attack. He was able to scatter and rout the English archer formations just as they were forming. Because they were usually behind infantry lines, safe from attack, the archers were not armed with anything but their bows. The bulk of Bruce's light horse cavalry destroyed or rendered useless the enemy's archers, leaving his schiltrons free to take on the English heavy-horse attacks, which quickly came as soon as King Edward II's commanders saw what was happening.

The first English cavalry charge of the day was led by the Earl of Gloucester and the Earl of Hereford. They encountered Robert the Bruce and Henry de Bohun and faced off in single combat. Bohun lowered his long lance and charged the Bruce, and Bruce, armed only with an ax, maneuvered his horse in a slight sidestep to miss the lance. It was witnessed that he then stood up in his stirrups and with one mighty, well-timed swing of his ax, split de Bohun's head in two. Bohun was the grandson of the 2nd Earl of Hereford. Meanwhile, the schiltrons' deadly walls caught a remainder of English knights.

A second cavalry attack was launched by King Edward, led by Sir Robert de Clifford and Sir Walter de Hameldone's distant cousin, Henry de Beaumont. It was defeated by the Scottish forces and schiltrons, with hundreds of knights killed or captured. Henry de Beaumont escaped with some English knights and men and fled to the protection of Sir Walter de Hameldone at Bothwell Castle.

Obligingly or tragically, the English heavy horse and the mounted knights thundered wave after wave into what they expected by then to be weakened schiltrons. Yet the English heavy horse plowed into a concrete, unmoving wall of twelve-foot spikes. The first one or two waves of heavy horse realized too late that the schiltron formations were not breaking, and the waves of knights and horses behind the front rows could not see anything ahead of them but other horses. Row after row of heavy horse plundered headfirst into the schiltrons' deadly walls of giant, iron-tipped spikes. It was utter mayhem as horses were impaled and men fell or were pulled from their horses and killed.

John IV, the son of John III "the Red" Comyn, died fighting on the English side on the second day, June 24. He was one of the heavy horse cavalrymen who charged against the Scottish schiltrons. He had sided with the English fighting against the Bruce, who had murdered his father.

Once a knight in heavy chain mail and armor fell or was pulled from his horse, he would find it very hard to stand up under such weight and became an easy target for ground troops to stab daggers into his neck or between armor plates. Hence, many English nobles died or were captured in these attacks at the Battle of Bannockburn on these two June days. Ten English knights, lords, barons, and earls died, and another eleven were caught at battle's close, to be swapped for Scottish prisoners.

With the unique tactic of the moving schiltron, the Bruce had routed a far greater, better-trained and equipped English force with mainly peasant highlanders. Edward II fled the battlefield and escaped for England in a ship waiting at the coast. Edward's senior commanders, who had stood back at the rear of the battle with the king, were stunned by their defeat as they sought to get Edward to safety. Defeated knights and junior commanders were left on the field to muster survivors and find escape routes and their own way back to England.

The victors claimed Scottish casualties and deaths to be only two knights and 400-foot soldiers. Yet seven-hundred English knights and men at arms were reported killed, and 500 English barons (including thirty-four earls, barons, and knights) and men at arms were reported captured, together with some 4,000-foot soldiers. Scottish victor spin-politics of the day at play.

When Switching Allegiance Pays Off

Sir Walter de Hamilton had remained loyal to the English King Edward II. Before June 1314, Sir was appointed constable of Bothwell Castle in South Lanarkshire, Scotland, by Edward II and charged the English king with its security before Bannockburn's Battle. The Castle was very close to the battlefield. The English king's note to Sir Walter read:

"The King commands Walter Fitz Gilbert de Hameldone, constable of his castle of Bothwell, to see that it is safely and securely kept and delivered to no other person whatsoever, without the King's letters patent under the Great Seal of England directed to himself."

After the battle, many leading English nobles who survived sought shelter and protection from Sir Walter, who took them into the Castle. The Bruce sent his brother Edward with a Scots army to besiege Bothwell Castle, and this time, with the English military crushed, he was in a strong position and gave Sir Walter the chance to yield the castle to Scotland. With the English army defeated and its remnants running for home, Sir Walter realized he could not withstand the siege. Thus, he decided to surrender the castle, himself, and the English nobles he was sheltering. Bruce asked Sir Walter if as a Scotsman he would pledge his allegiance to Scotland and its king and forsake the English king. Sir Walter pledged his loyalty, and in return, King Robert granted Sir Walter de Hamilton the lands of Cadzow in Scotland, along with Cadzow Castle, situated on the bank of the River Clyde, creating him the 1st Baron of Cadzow.

Cadzow (pronounced Kadyu), which is in South Lanarkshire, Scotland became Hamilton's town. Eight years later, in 1322, Sir Walter received a Scottish knighthood as Sir Walter de Hameldone. The previous year he had been made a justice of Lanark by King Robert. He was granted lands the following year yet again in Kinneil, Larbert, Auldcathy, and Kirkcowan, some of which were ironically but not surprisingly formerly owned by the Comyn family. Changing sides was a lucrative business where loyalty to kings was involved, yet it could result in losing everything, including your head, if you played the wrong cards.

After the same battle as we'll read shortly, another de Hameldone was propelled into wealth with lands granted by Robert the Bruce for this knight's part in the campaign won.

Defeating the English opened the north of England to Scottish raids and later a Scottish invasion of Ireland. Under a treaty signed between Scotland and England, England acknowledged the complete independence and creation of Scotland's kingdom. Edward II recognized Robert "the Bruce," his heirs, and successors as kings and rightful rulers of Scotland. Edward's father, Longshanks, must have been turning in his grave.

After Bruce dominated the English at the Battle of Bannockburn, he paraded his power to support the English king over the next few years. He did help the English time and again, and in return was offered support from Edward II when he needed it and was granted vast land and titles of nobility in England. The Bruce finally swore allegiance to the English king and paid homage to him while being allowed to rule Scotland in a power-sharing deal that worked for them both and the Hamiltons.

When Sir Walter fought for the English king at the Battle of Bannockburn in 1314, so did Henry de Beaumont. They were both Normans of the same de Beaumont family bloodline. Henry de Beaumont was made Earl of Buchan in 1333, in right of his wife, whose father was the earl without a male heir. The de Beaumonts were widely rewarded long term for their continued support of England's Norman Crown, with quite a lot of earldoms sprinkled around over the following 250-years of England's conquests.

By the time of Bruce's death, Sir Walter Fitz-Gilbert, de Hameldone, was one of his seven royal knights of bodyguard. In 1329, Sir Walter gave the funeral oration at the Scottish king's burial in Dunfermline Abbey. In 1333, Sir Walter was still fighting battles in Scotland for Bruce's successor, his son, King David II, but we hear little else of Sir Walter until his death, believed to be in 1346

Sir David Fitz-Walter de Hameldone and the Founding Father of America

Sir Walter's son David became the 2nd Laird and Baron of Cadzow, and his third son, another Walter de Hameldone, is the prime ancestor of the Cambuskeith line of the Hamiltons (and of the Sanquhar line). The Cambuskeith line is that of Alexander Hamilton, one of the Founding Fathers of America. Sir David was captured at the Battle of Neville's Cross, west of Durham in England, on October 17, 1346, an English victory over the Scots. Sir David's grandson, James, was the first to change the name from de Hameldone to Hamilton.

Sir David Hamilton, 3rd Baron of Cadzow

Sir David Fitz-Walter's son was born and died in Cadzow, like his father. Born c. 1333, he died on May 14, 1392. He had married Jonetta Keith of Galston and had six children. Sir David de Hameldone appears across our path in 1361 when endowing Glasgow Cathedral with a chaplaincy. In reward for giving King David II continued support, the English king gave his approval in 1368 to give back Hamilton's lands of Cadzow. Hamilton is next recorded taking part in the Parliament of Scotland in 1371 and again in 1373. In the latter Parliament, the Earl of Garrick, John Stewart, and his heirs were named to Scotland's throne and kingship.

Sir David is the first of the family recorded to formerly pronounce Hamilton as a surname in a writ of 1375, which stated, "David de Hamilton, son, and heir of David Fitz-Walter Hameldone." By 1378, he had styled himself David de Hamilton, and by 1381 as David Hamilton, Lord of Cadzow. So here was the final version of the name from de Hameldone, which William de Beaumont had chosen from his home in Hameldone, Buckinghamshire. For his clan's name, Sir David is as significant to the Hamilton Clan globally as his great-great-grandfather William de Hameldone.

Sir John Hamilton, the 4th Baron, Alec Hamilton's Silvertonhill Ancestor

Sir John died of wounds after the Battle of Hamildon Hill in Northumberland at just age thirty-two. He is known to have sired ten children, of which five were illegitimate, and he found himself imprisoned along with his son James, the 5th Baron, in a diplomatic spat between England's King Henry V and the Scottish Crown. The Silvertonhill Hamiltons descended to Westport and Elrick Hamilton, right through to the modern-day Alec, his siblings, and their male descendants.

Sir James Hamilton, 5th Baron Cadzow, the Modern-Day Alexander Hamilton's Bloodline

James was born in Scotland c.1390 in Cadzow and died in West Lothian in May 1441. He was perceived to be the fourth baron's son and the great-great grandson of Sir Walter Fitz-Gilbert de Hameldone. James married Janet Livingston sometime before 1422, when he received a charter of the lands of Schawis (forest land south of Hermitage Castle in Roxburgh, Scotland) from his father-in-law, Sir Alexander Livingston of Callendar. James and Janet had seven children; two were illegitimate and not of Janet, yet they were raised all together as one family. One son, another James, who was to become the 1st Lord Hamilton of an English title, married Princess Mary Stewart, as we will read shortly, the King of Scotland's daughter. His younger brother, Alexander Hamilton, was the first of Silvertonhill, the ancestor of the Hamiltons of Silvertonhill, which later became the Westport and Elrick line of modern-day Alec Hamilton in Jamaica.

James Hamilton, 6th Baron Cadzow, 1st Lord Hamilton and Royal Marriage

James was born c. 1415 at Cadzow Castle in Lanarkshire, Scotland, and died on November 6, 1479. In 1426, he appears in a charter granting him lands of Dalserf. Like his father, he was, at some time before 1440, knighted. In

1450, he traveled to Rome and was granted permission from the Vatican authorities to convert the new Burgh of Hamilton Parish Church into a collegiate establishment, and he made endowments to fund a provost and six canons, which the Holy See granted. His paternal grandmother was born a Douglas of James Douglas, Lord Dalkeith.

Some historians claim that he married three times, the first to Janet Calderwood, although there's no evidence of a marriage record or issue. He either married secondly, or first, Lady Euphemia Graham, daughter of the Earl Palatine of Strathearn and Caithness. (She was the very young, widowed wife of Archibald Douglas, 5th Earl of Douglas.) They had six children together. James and Euphemia had one daughter, Elizabeth, who married the 1st Duke of Montrose, and the sixth laird was to have four additional illegitimate children by three other women.

The author diverts momentarily to share with you that Lady Euphemia had one daughter who married Sir John Lyon, 1st Master of Glamis Castle, from her first marriage. Sir John was an ancestor of HM Queen Elizabeth, the Queen Mother of Great Britain, HM's family name being Bowes-Lyon. Sir John had a son later created the Earl of Monteith.

James Hamilton's first known father-in-law's family, the Earls of Strathearn, hail from a southern Perthshire region in Scotland. The Earls of Strathearn sprang from three hundred years earlier, in 1115, where the title is first mentioned in official documents. Lord Malise, Earl of Caithness, was granted a second earldom as the 1st Earl of Strathearn since he had fought with King David of Scotland at the Battle of the Standard in 1138. Interestingly, the earldom became extant when forfeiting to King Edward Balliol. The Earl of Strathearn is a title oft resurrected as a royal title from the 1300s onward.

The current Earl of Strathearn is HRH Prince William of Wales when in Wales and Scotland, Duke of Cambridge when in England, and Baron Carrickfergus when in Ireland. Prince William is the second in line to the British Crown. The present British queen, Elizabeth II, granted the title to her grandson upon his marriage to Catherine Elizabeth Middleton, now HRH the Duchess of Strathearn when in Scotland.

This James, now the 1st Lord Hamilton, had substantially increased his lands, wealth, and status but then offended the king by siding with the 9th Earl Douglas against the king in a nasty argument. The king laid waste to both

Douglas and Hamilton lands in Clydesdale in 1455 to teach them a quick lesson of his power. A truce was reached later that year, and in the following one, James was back in England arranging the release of the English king's prisoner, his brother-in-law, the Lord Malise Graham, Earl of Strathearn. For obtaining his release, Lord Malise granted Hamilton his lands of Elliestoun in Linlithgowshire, Scotland.

As a reward for James Hamilton's about-turn support of the Scottish king, the king gave back the sixth laird's manor, lands, and castle and granted him more land as an additional advantage. He also made Hamilton Sheriff of Lanark and granted him certain forfeited Douglas lands—confirmed by Royal Charter in October of that year. He was given by the king the lands of Drumsergard, Cessford, Finnart, and Kinneil. He was also made Baillie (then a type of provost or secular head of an ecclesiastical body and magistrate) with powers of appointment of the Priory of Lesmahagow. All these appointments and lands brought increased revenues to Hamilton. In the same year of 1445, a second Royal Charter was issued, naming James' estates, lands, and the castle and town of Cadzow, Hamilton, as they are named today. By letters patent that same year, James Hamilton, the 6th Laird, was also created a Lord of Parliament of Scotland and the 1st Lord Hamilton. The title of Baron Cadzow faded away with the town and castle's name change. And in the orchard of these lands is where the lavish Hamilton Palace was later built.

His Marriage to the Scottish King's Daughter

James Hamilton the 6th Baron's first wife, Lady Euphemia, sadly died in c. 1434. James then made a highly advantageous marriage to HRH Princess Mary Stewart, widowed Countess of Arran, daughter of the King of Scotland. Princess Mary's late husband was Thomas Boyd, Earl of Arran.

Princess Mary, the Lady Hamilton, and James had three children with royal Scottish Stewart blood that was to flow down to the current Dukes of Hamilton, Abercorn, and the Earl of Arran.

1. Elizabeth Hamilton married Matthew Stewart, 2nd Earl of Lennox. Her descendants included James I, King of England and VI of Scotland, who succeeded Queen Elizabeth I of England to the English throne. He united England and Scotland as one realm,

which remains united today.

2. James Hamilton.

3. Robert Hamilton, Seigneur d'Aubigny (1476–1543).

All Hamilton descendants from this union claim a distant link through the Stewarts' blood to the royal family of England and many royal houses in Europe.

James Hamilton also sired three illegitimate children—a son, Patrick, whose son was burnt at the stake for heresy at St. Andrews in 1528 during Catholic James V's reign and, after that, declared a Protestant martyr. He was the most famous Protestant put to death under James V, who would not tolerate heresy. The monarch across the border at the time was England's King Henry VIII, who just five years later broke from the Church of Rome and made England Protestant.

James Hamilton also sired an illegitimate daughter, who married the 11th Chief of Clan MacFarlane, and another son, John of Broomhill, whose birth in 1512 was later legitimized. He is the font of the Broomhill Hamiltons.

The 16th and 17th Century Hamiltons

James, Lord Hamilton, Later the 1st Earl of Arran

Born c. 1475 possibly two years later, he died c. 1529, with royal Scottish blood. He was, through his mother, the grandson of King James II of Scotland and first cousin of King James IV of Scotland. James, the 2nd Lord Hamilton, succeeded to the Hamilton Barony and lands in 1479 when he was just four years old when his father, the first earl, died. In 1490 when Hamilton was fourteen, James IV made him Sheriff of Lanark, a position his father had held, and a Privy Counselor to the Scottish Crown. Such titles came with annual income, though young James would not have been expected to adjudicate court cases at such an age.

His first marriage:

In c. 1490, James aged only 15 or 17 at the time, married Elizabeth Hay (née Home), daughter of the 2nd Lord Home. Some fourteen years later, when it came to light that Elizabeth's first husband, Thomas Hay, had not died as presumed but was very much still alive overseas, James Hamilton petitioned for a divorce. Elizabeth bore no children in their marriage, whereas James had sired several illegitimate children by other women. In 1510, the divorce award was repeated, suggesting that he was still living with Elizabeth twenty years later and had not moved to end the marriage. James was obliged to petition afresh, having, one presumes, always hoped for an heir, though he still loved his wife. Eventually, he gave up and had the marriage allowed in 1506, even hoping to sire a much-needed heir.

James Hamilton negotiated Scottish King James IV's marriage to Margaret Tudor of England (King Henry VIII's sister) and was present at the wedding on August 8, 1503. On the same day, James IV elevated Lord Hamilton to become the 1st Earl of Arran (his widowed grandmother's title). It is stated in the formal grant of arms, "for his nearness of blood and his service successfully negotiating the marriage." The following year he was appointed a lieutenant-general and commanded a naval expedition to put down an uprising in the Western Isles of Scotland. He was later sent as an Ambassador to the Court of King Louis XII of France.

The Single Worst Crushing Blow to Scotland's Nobility and Throne

The Battle of Flodden Field also saw the largest number of troops assembled between Scotland and England ever before this date. On August 22, 1513, King James IV of Scotland crossed the border into England across the River Tweed, bombarding and taking submission from four English castles with an estimated 40,000 troops. He stopped just outside the village of Branxton in Northumberland and made camp on Flodden Edge. This hill rises to over 500-feet, and King James intended to attack King Henry VIII's army of some 26,000 troops in retaliation for his earlier attack on France, James' alliance partner.

The Battle of Flodden Field near Branxton Moor in Scotland on September 9, 1513. The Earl of Surrey, aged seventy, led King Henry VIII of England's 26,000 soldiers into battle with Henry's queen, Catherine of Aragon, not just watching from the rear but also as Henry's regent while in France, commander of the field of battle. She was a highly popular queen in the English people's eyes, and she worked hard rallying the troops before the action, which the militarily experienced Earl of Surrey commanded. It is estimated that up to 4,000 English troops were killed.

Still, an estimated 10,000 Scots were lost in an overwhelming defeat by the English, which saw not only a large portion of Scotland's nobility slaughtered, including King James IV himself.

Lord Dacre discovered the Scottish king's body noted by a chronicler, John Stow, as on "Pipard's Hill." While it is not named today, it is believed to be the small hill overlooking Branxton Church., known as Branxton Ridge. His surcoat, drenched in blood over his body which both had multiple lacerations. Scotland had lost its King buried amongst the thick of the fallen in battle.

King James' natural son out of wedlock, Alexander Stewart, Archbishop of St. Andrews and Lord Chancellor of Scotland, died in conflict with his father. Four other bishops and abbots were killed at Flodden Field; they had taken up the sword to defend their realm and sovereign.

Ten Scottish earls died at Flodden, including a grandson of King James I of Scotland. Nine sons of earls and lords who would have inherited titles died at this engagement with their fathers as well. In total, an estimated 218 Scottish nobles from earls to lords, lairds, clan chiefs, and knights died this day—fathers, sons, brothers, nephews, uncles, and cousins. This confrontation devastated the whole Scottish nobility, leaving many small children as heirs. Heirs to titles of nobility or widows appeared before councils after such wars; hence, an accurate list of deaths can be attributed even in these Tudor times. This one combat truly devastated an entire generation of Scottish nobility, from king to knights. Some forty-six English lords and nobility were knighted after the English victory, and the Earl of Surrey was made Duke of Norfolk by Henry VIII.

James IV of Scotland was the last monarch of the British Isles to die in battle. Nobles and commoners alike had seen him as a good king. His son, Prince James, was crowned James V of Scotland three weeks later, at not yet two years old, which created an unsettling time for Scotland. Power plays were made by several close to the throne to be Regent of Scotland and control its income and policies.

James, 1st Earl of Arran's Children by his 2nd Marriage, to Janet Bethune

+ Lady Helen Hamilton, who married the 4th Earl of Argyll, Archibald Campbell, from where Hamilton and royal Stewart blood, no matter how thin, flows through the current Duke of Argyll's veins.
+ James Hamilton became the 2nd Earl of Arran, later a French Duke and a Regent of Scotland and heir to the Scottish crown.
+ Lady Janet Hamilton married the 5th Earl of Glencairn.
+ Another son, Gavin, died before 1549 and may have been stillborn.

Hamilton had a further five, "illegitimate" issue, three by one unnamed woman:

+ James Hamilton of Finnart.
+ Elizabeth Hamilton married Thomas of Kirkton Weir (born c. 1570).
+ John Hamilton became Archbishop of St. Andrews, Treasurer of Scotland.

Two of his illegitimate children were by his known mistress, The Hon. Beatrix Drummond, daughter of John Drummond, 1st Lord Drummond:

+ Margaret Hamilton married the 2nd Lord Avondale, the 1st Lord Ochiltree.
+ Sir John Hamilton of Samuelsson married Janet Home, only legitimate daughter and heiress of the 3rd Lord Home and Lady Agnes, née Stewart.

James Hamilton, Duke of Châtellerault, 2nd Earl of Arran, the 8th Laird

He was to become the Regent, Governor, Protector of his sovereigns child, and Heir Presumptive to the Crown of Scotland.

James was born c. 1516, he died on January 22, 1575. In 1529, at just thirteen, he became the 8th Laird and 2nd Earl of Arran on his father's death. Born in Hamilton, Lanarkshire, Scotland, his paternal grandmother was HRH Princess Mary Stewart and his great-grandfather King James II of Scotland. In 1532, James married Margaret Douglas, ten years his elder. She was the daughter of James Douglas, 3rd Earl of Morton, and his wife, Catherine (Née Stewart, who was a natural but out-of-wedlock daughter of King James IV of Scotland). It was a very fruitful marriage. They had nine children, five of whom were boys.

+ James (c. 1537–c. 1609) became the 3rd Earl of Arran.
+ Gavin, who died young.
+ John (c. 1540–c. 1604) became the 1st Marquess of Hamilton (and in a later generation the title was raised to the Dukedom of Hamilton).
+ David died young in 1611.
+ Claude (c. 1546–c. 1621) became 1st Lord Hamilton of Paisley, later Lord Abercorn, and Baron Hamilton. His son became the 1st Earl of Abercorn, raised in later generations to Marquess, and then a Dukedom.
+ Barbara married James Lord Fleming in 1553.
+ Jean married the 3rd Earl of Eglinton in 1555.
+ Anne married the 5th Earl of Huntly.
+ Margaret married Sir Alexander Pethein.

Through his grandparents, the 2nd Earl of Arran was a Hamilton of Hamilton, related to the Douglas clan, the Lords of Dalkeith, and Lords of Livingston. He was blood-related to the Dukes of Guelders. One set of great-grandparents were King James I of Scotland and Queen Joan (née Lady Beaufort), and he was related to the Dutch Duke of Gelderland and the Royal House of Cleves.

Cleves was then an independent Holy Roman Empire Vassal State and a Rhineland Duchy of the "modern-day" Germany. The Duke of Cleves was a hereditary Prince of the Holy Roman Empire, and it was Prince John II, Duke of Cleves, whose daughter, Anne (Anna von Kleve), became the fourth wife of King Henry VIII of England in July 1540 in this James Hamiltons lifetime.

In 1544 when James the 2nd Earl of Arran's wife, Margaret, seemed to be suffering mental illness, he divorced her. Their son James, the 3rd Earl of Arran, tragically went insane aged just twenty-five. After a long and extraordinarily successful and loyal career to the Crown of Scotland, their son Claude Hamilton eventually, in old age, suffered mental collapse too, it is believed. Mental illness appears inherited from their mother.

A Hamilton as Heir Presumptive to the Throne of Scotland

John Stewart, Duke of Albany, grandson of King James II of Scotland, had spent most his life, on and off, as the Heir Presumptive to Scotland's throne, as numerous monarchs came to the throne as infants. During the minority of King James V (he inherited the Scottish throne aged only seven months), Albany acted as regent on more than one occasion between 1514 and 1524. After the Dowager Queen, Margaret remarried to the Earl of Angus, who was opposed to Albany's duke being so close to the young king, Albany left for France, where he died in July 1536. King James V was by now aged twenty-four and had ruled since his minority ended. James V's son James VI was to take the thrones of both Scotland and England.

While born and raised a Catholic, as an adult, John Stewart had Calvinist, reformatory leanings towards Protestantism and held a tolerant view of all religions. He was Elizabeth I's closest male blood relative, and her council was deeply concerned with avoiding a Catholic sovereign again on the English throne after Elizabeth's elder sister, Queen Mary. They courted James VI of Scotland as Elizabeth was dying, though she had refused to name James VI or anyone else as her heir. Lord Cecil, her Chancellor of State, had been holding secret correspondence with James VI. The moment Elizabeth died, he extended England's throne to James on behalf of the vacant monarch's Council of State, which James accepted as James I of England and James VI of Scotland.

Several royal children of the Stewarts proved to be short-lived. In 1536, on the Duke of Albany's death, since the king had no legitimate living children at his death, King James V of Scotland, according to the rules of cognatic primogeniture, formerly declared and appointed James Hamilton, 2nd Earl of Arran and his first cousin, closest living male blood relative, and Heir Presumptive, to the throne of Scotland. In case of the king's death, Hamilton was to be regent of Scotland to any legitimate child of the king until they reached their majority.

The king's army had suffered a massive defeat by the English on November 24, 1542, at Solway Moss near the River Esk, on the English side of Scotland's border. By December 6, the king had taken ill, whether by nervous collapse or fever, or potentially both. Either way, he was by now lying seriously ill back at Falkland Palace when his council realized he was dying. At this time, on December 8, 1542, his only legitimate child was born, the future Mary, Queen of Scots.

The king proclaimed that James Hamilton, 2nd Earl of Arran, was also the child's governor and protector of her life and realm. He further declared that if Princess Mary did not survive before producing an heir, James Hamilton, his cousin, would become King of Scotland. Within six days of Princess Mary's birth, the king died. His body was moved to Holyrood Abbey in Edinburgh, where it was buried with his first wife, Queen Madeleine, and his two sons who had died before him: James, Duke of Rothesay (born May 1540, died April 1541), and Arthur, Duke of Albany, born April 12, 1541 and died eight days later. It's possible both died of some sort of fever. How tragic for the king and his wife, Mary of Guise, of France. Their children's deaths left the door open to chaos and power struggles for control of the Scottish throne.

James V of Scotland had nine known illegitimate children, three of whom he sired before reaching twenty. Four of his illegitimate sons were granted dispensation to take Holy Orders and enter the Church's service. He fathered children with the 3rd Earl of Lennox's daughter and with the wife of the 5th Earl of Argyll. With his favorite mistress, Margaret Erskine, he sired the illegitimate son, James Stewart, whom he had created 1st Earl of Mora. James Stewart was appointed Prior of St. Andrews and became an advisor to his young, "legitimate" half-sister, Mary, Queen of Scots. This is the illegitimate son who later usurped his sister's rights, placing her baby boy on Scotland's throne, which enabled him to rule Scotland through the baby prince. Power and wealth drove this bastard son to deprive his half-sister of her rightful crown.

The Hamilton Who Might Have Become
King of Scotland and England

Mary's son, James, went on to become the most likely heir to Queen Elizabeth I of England, and at Elizabeth's death, on March 24, 1603, he succeeded her as James I of England and James VI of Scotland. Had Princess Mary died without producing an heir, or her child died before her, James Hamilton, 2nd Earl of Arran, would rightfully have become King. James would have become James VI of Scotland and James I of England, subject to Mary's treacherous illegitimate brother, the Earl of Moray. The Earl of Moray would not have been able to raise his traitorous head so quickly against a healthy male bloodline relative. However, it was not meant to be, but if Mary died without a child, a Hamilton would likely be the English Monarch today.

Though Elizabeth's council sought to avoid another Catholic on the English throne, they couldn't prevent her closest blood relative from becoming King of England and Scotland. James may have won over the fearful council to rule tolerant of all faiths, as did James VI, and he allowed England to remain primarily a Protestant state.

But before all of this, when Queen Mary was still a baby, there was a challenge to the Earl of Arran's Regency of Scotland. After the earl's appointment, the king died just six-days later. The knives, politics, and clan rivalries emerged immediately. Matthew Stewart, 4th Earl of Lennox, challenged James Hamilton's claim to be in succession to the throne and suggested he was not of legitimate birth, which would ban him from being heir to the baby Queen Mary. Lennox claimed that James' father's divorce from Elizabeth Home and marriage to Janet Bethune were invalid. This was unfounded, as his divorce from his first wife was legal. On this basis, Lennox raised his flag against James Hamilton and demanded that the 2nd Earl of Arran be removed from his role as Regent, Governor, and Protector of Scotland.

Initially, James Hamilton was outwardly Protestant leaning. This might have won over Lord Cecil and the English State Council as strongly as Mary, Queen of Scot's son did, proving a religiously tolerant heir to the English crown. Neither was likely to force Catholicism upon a nation of Protestants and think they'd survive. In 1543, a year after King James V's death, Hamilton was involved in negotiating a possible marriage of the Catholic infant, Mary, Queen of Scots, to the infant Prince of Wales, the future Protestant King

Edward VI of England. Henry VIII of England stated in his memoirs that he doubted James Hamilton's allegiance to the English in negotiating his son's marriage.

During the negotiations for that marriage, the pro-English party in Scotland believed that James Hamilton left Edinburgh to meet the Catholic Cardinal Beaton. James Hamilton and the cardinal did indeed clandestinely meet. Hamilton converted entirely to the Catholic faith to show homage to Scotland and its king and joined the pro-French cause. This proved the Scottish nobility English sympathizers and Henry VIII right. Hamilton now secretly supported the Catholic Queen Mary's marriage to Catholic Prince Francis, France's dauphin.

In 1548, the Queen of Scots lived in the Scottish court and married the dauphin by a proxy exchange. For successfully negotiating the marriage, the French king created Hamilton the 1st Duke of Châtellerault of France and a Knight of the French Order of St. Michael. The dauphin, Francis, would later rule France as King Francis II from 1559, and Mary, who had been wed to him as Dauphine the year before in 1558, became Queen Consort of France and Queen of Scots. During much of this time, James Hamilton, 2nd Earl Arran and now Catholic, remained the accepted heir to Mary, Queen of Scots. He was governor of her education and her regent, managing the country on her behalf until she came of age. He was very loyal to his duty and the princess's protection and as devoted to her as he had been to her father, James V, who trusted him.

A French Queens Promise –So Easily Broken

Pressured to give up the regency but not his right as Heir Presumptive, Hamilton seems to have continued as regent despite the 4th Earl of Lennox's challenge. It wasn't until twelve years later, in 1554, that he was put under intense pressure to surrender the Regency of Scotland to the French Mary of Guise, Queen Mary's mother-in-law, the dowager Queen of Scotland. In return, he was appointed her lieutenant in Scotland, and we can assume had riches bestowed on him too, to ease his pain in surrendering to a powerful Catholic queen. He built in one non-negotiable condition—that he would submit the regency to the queen if she gave her word that he would remain the heir to Mary, Queen of Scots, if she died without children. The dowager queen gave her word.

Little did he know that the Scottish succession had been secretly promised to the Dauphin Francis by his mother. She intended that all future French kings would rule over an aligned France, Scotland, and England. This would create a Catholic realm of Western Europe, and His Holiness had given his blessing to the plan. Mary of Guise became Queen Consort of Scotland upon her marriage to King James V of Scotland in 1538, a year after her first husband, the Duke of Longueville, had died. Now she was regent of her twelve-year-old daughter.

Trusting the dowager queen, Hamilton naively continued to support Mary of Guise and fought Protestant armies for the crown. However, he changed sides again in 1559, taking up arms with the Protestant lords against the Regent, Mary of Guise. To be utterly fair to this Hamilton, who had kept his word to his late king resolutely, I suspect he'd discovered that Mary of Guise had no intention of allowing him to succeed to the Scottish throne. Consequently, the French king stripped him of his French dukedom, lands, and income due, and it was never reinstated to him or his heirs.

The closer you were to the extraordinary solar power of an autocratic monarch's sun, the closer you were to being burnt by it. One could rise to fame and fortune and collapse into the misery of its ashes and have everything taken from you if, at any time later, you upset the hand that had raised you up. Many a risen star in King Henry VIII's court and his daughter Elizabeth I's court in England learned that lesson; some gave their heads to their monarch's displeasure.

The Hamilton Who Nearly Became Queen Elizabeth I, Husband

After Mary of Guise's death, Hamilton, the 2nd Earl of Arran persuaded the Scottish Parliament to present his son James, the future 3rd Earl of Arran, to Queen Elizabeth I of England as a worthy husband and bring the Scottish crown with him. Unfortunately, and interestingly, Elizabeth of England rejected him as a suiter.

After Mary, Queen of Scots, married Lord Darnley in 1565, James Hamilton went overseas. Four years late, upon returning to Scotland, after his Queen had been illegally deposed, he was imprisoned by the regent of her son, the Earl of Moray. Hamilton, undoubtedly under threat of being assassinated, agreed to formally recognize Mary's infant son, James, as King of Scotland and was released from prison. As the infant Prince James usurped his mother's crown through his regent and half-uncle deposing his mother, he became king of two nations on March 24, 1603, after the death of Queen Elizabeth I. Under James' reign, England and Scotland were joined together, but not as a Catholic triumph with France, as his grandmother Mary of Guise had hoped. England remained a Protestant nation under James, and the Hamilton Clan's opportunity to become kings of Scotland and England passed away.

NOTES:

Putting Broader Sixteenth Century World Events Into Perspective

Europeans were discovering the East. By 1517, Portuguese traders had discovered Indonesia, and in 1521, its spice islands. Charles V was elected Holy Roman Emperor in 1526. For the first time, the printing press appeared in Sweden, and Christians across Europe were beginning to theorize and challenge Catholicism. The Augustinian Friar and Professor of Theology, Martin Luther, published his ninety-five theses to herald in his branch of the Christian religion. From 1518 to 1523, Erasmus' humanist works were appearing across Europe and influencing people's thinking. Henry VIII, King of England, was aged twenty-seven at this time, and two of his six wives, Boleyn, and Parr, later influenced him to consider Erasmus's works.

In 1542, the Portuguese introduced musket guns to the Japanese, and Ivan the Terrible, the future Tsar Ivan IV of Russia, was twelve years old. The 12th Ming Dynasty's Jiajing, Emperor of China, experienced the most significant earthquake ever seen in Shaanxi's region in 1556, killing 800,000 people. The Portuguese Francis Xavier, the Jesuit Missionary, landed in Goa, India.

In January 1547, Henry VIII, King of England, died, and his Protestant son, Edward, ruled for just over six years from age nine to his death at just under sixteen years of age. He named his Protestant first cousin once removed, Lady Jane Grey, as his successor. Jane ruled just a hundred days before King Henry VIII's eldest and Catholic daughter overthrew him. Mary was crowned Queen Mary I of England and died after only five years. Her half-sister, Elizabeth, was crowned the Protestant Queen Elizabeth I in 1558.

In just eleven years, England had seen five crowned monarchs: Henry VIII, Edward VI, Jane I, Mary I, and Elizabeth I.

Origin of the de Comyn Name

Robert being known as de (of) Comyn, suggests that he originally came from Comines, then in the County of Flanders aside France. He arrived with William, Duke of Normandy's invasion fleet to England in 1066. He was sent to the north by the now, King William I, of England as his newly ennobled Earl of Northumberland in 1068; after playing a significant role in England's conquering.

The Saxon Uprising in the North of England

King William's subsequent brutal suppression and scorched earth policy of the north England is listed by contemporary chroniclers. William's scale of destruction and the level of looting and violence by the Normans was massive. The north of England at the time was considered to be modern-day Yorkshire, Durham and Northumberland, Lancashire, Westmoreland, and the southern parts of Cumberland. The king's reprisal for the Saxon killing of Comyn as overlord of the north was widespread famine. The king moved swiftly to subdue the Saxon population long-term by replacing all Saxon authority figures with Norman Nobles. Norman Barons being generally the ultimate power in over half the county's or shires in England; they're appointing Norman Sheriff's, Lords of Fiefdoms, and even Church Bishops.

The Hamilton DNA Project (Source) USA

This DNA shows that after John Hamilton, the 4th Liard of Cadzow, the two main trunks of Hamilton descendants' from his two eldest sons have had two distinct Hamilton DNA components for over 680-years. The Dukes of Hamilton and Abercorn, and Earl's of Arran, carry a Haplogroup I1a2a1a1 (I-L338), while the other branch has the Haplogroup were I1a3a (IL1237).

The Author Doubts Sir Walter fitz-Gilbert de Hameldone Was Poor

Walter was the grandson of William de Hameldone, whose father, was the wealthy 3rd Earl of Leicester. Some eminent historians say that Sit Gilbert was a poor man, just a clerk, whose son Walter was a poor nobody given into service with the church. Others dismiss these claims as a different Gilbert and Walter, not the men later at the Battle of Bannockburn.

It may be a simple misunderstanding of the Latin meaning of words used by monks at the time, who recorded both Gilbert and, in time, Walter, signing official Abbey documents.

In a charter of December 12, 1272, to the monks of Paisley – there appears as a witness a certain "Gilbert de Hameldus clericus." The Latin, Clericus can be interpreted as a scribe, Priest, Cleric, Monk, or Scholar amongst other uses and likely depicts a man of standing in the case of Gilbert. Yet the first group of witnesses is labeled Militibus, literally meaning Knights. The author believes that this is where confusion has entered for some past historians. Gilbert fitz-William de Hameldon held a Lordship over a manor and lands - with sufficient income to own a fine war-horse and equip himself in knight's armor and weapons and be known to the Royal Court.

Many have said that Walter was simply a scribe, yet at the time, all scholarly writers from a Parish to the King's Court were monks and Priests, which no one is suggesting Gilbert was.

Who Was the 'Great Lieutenant of England, Slain at Bannockburn?

There appears no definitive record that the author can find or has missed; however, he believes that the *Great Lieutenant of England* could be none other than the young Gilbert de Clare, 8th Earl of Gloucester, 7th Earl of Hertford. He was a 1st cousin to King Edward II, his mother the daughter of England's King Edward I, and at the same time, a second cousin to Robert the Bruce. The rationale for this, in the absence of any evidence to the contrary, is severalfold.

Gloucester was one of four earls with Edward in the English army, which included Welsh and Scottish Lords loyal to the English king. The other Earls were the English Earl of Hereford, the Wels Earl of Pembroke, and the Scottish Earl of Angus. It is interesting to note that among the many knights fighting under the English banner was the Scottish Sir John Comyn (son of the John Comyn murdered by Robert the Bruce, fighting with the English king). Also present was Sir Henry de Beaumont (A Norman-French favorite of the King) married to the murdered John Comyn's niece.

Sources amongst others were from the Stirnet Genealogy, The Scots Peerage, and Burkes Extinct Peerages. The Bruce, Robert Bruce's Rivals; The Comyn's; The Scottish Civil War: The Bruce's and Balliol's and the War for Control of Scotland. The Wars of Scotland, Robert the Bruce. A Life Chronicled, Vita Edwardi secundi, Bannockburn. The Scottish War and the British Isles, Patronymic Britannica. The genealogical record of the Hambleton family and descendants of James Hambleton.

Sir Walter Fitz-Gilbert de Hameldone, 1st Laird of Cadzow (1274–1346), grandson of the first known Hamilton. From him come our book's Alexander Hamilton, the Dukes of Hamilton and Abercorn, and the Earls of Arran (CE).

James, Hamilton, b. 1515 d. 1575, the 8th Laird and Baron Cadzow, 2nd Earl of Arran, and the Duke of Châtellerault of France. Regent, Governor, Protector of Scotland and Heir Presumptive to the throne as the king's first cousin and closest blood relative, should Princess Mary die without issue (CE).

Map of the Battle of Bannockburn won by King Robert de Bruce, which resulted in Scotland's independence from England. Map by John Fawkes (NCA).

English Knights hitting a Scottish schiltron wall of deadly pikes in the Battle of Bannockburn, June 23 and 24, 1314. Scotland and England's battle (NCA).

81

Chapter 3

CLAUDE HAMILTON AND MARY, QUEEN OF SCOTS

Here is one of the most intriguing Hamiltons from antiquity, a true warrior: Hamilton, whom our modern Alec Hamilton was proud to call an ancestor. Alec said that from a young boy, this was his Hamilton hero; the man was the stuff of legend. We'll read of his resilience, power plays, and his ability to be a cunning tactician. These traits, combined with loyalty and duty to the Crown, are a thread we'll see through Hamiltons over the centuries to the Founding Father of America and the modern-day Alexander Hamilton.

Claude was the younger son of the 2nd Earl of Arran (who was, for a time, the 1st Duke of Châtellerault of France). His elder brother, James, became the third earl, and another brother, John, was later created the 1st Marquess of Hamilton, his heirs becoming the first Dukes of Hamilton. Claude's son became the 1st Earl of Abercorn, and Claude was a cousin twice removed of James Hamilton of Westport, a direct ancestor of the "modern-day" Alexander Hamilton. Claude was a man who came within a cat's whisker of being made a Scottish Duke himself, as we will read.

As 1st Lord Paisley, later Lord Abercorn, and later still made a baron, Claude Hamilton was born in 1546 and died in early 1621. Claude was the great-grandson of Princess Mary Stewart and the great-great-grandson of King James II of Scotland. He had royal blood, as do all the Dukes of Hamilton and Abercorn, and the Earls of Arran, and proved one of the most loyal Scotsmen in history.

Living to the age of seventy-five was quite a feat in those days when the average life expectancy of a man of noble birth was aged forty-nine, and that of an ordinary working citizen was aged forty. In 1553, aged just seven, Claude was granted the lands and income of the Abbey of Paisley by a Papal Bull dated December 5 of that year. At the same time, he was appointed nominal Protector of the Abbey by Pope Julius III. He received an annuity of profits, a grant won through his father's efforts for the young man's future independence, as Claude would not inherit the earldom, being a younger son.

John Knox, a Scottish religious minister, and theologian founded the Presbyterian Church of Scotland in the 1500s. His second wife was Margaret Stewart of a staunchly Protestant family, related to the royal family and the Hamiltons. One of her brothers was James Stewart, Earn of Arran. In self-exile in Switzerland, Knox met the reformist, John Calvin. On his return to Scotland before Mary, Queen of Scots returned from exile to retake the Scottish throne, Knox had converted many of the nobles and much of the country to the reformed faith. He took to the pulpit and strongly opposed a Catholic being on the throne of Scotland. Heading support amongst Scottish nobility for the new Presbyterian faith was Mary, Queen of Scot's stepbrother, the king's illegitimate child, given the name James, and his family name, Stewart. The king made James Stewart, 1st Earl of Moray.

Claude Hamilton grew up to be a fine young man of honor. He remained loyal when Mary, Queen of Scots was dislodged from her throne by her illegitimate stepbrother, who sought to rule Scotland on behalf of her son, a 'wee' baby. He could look forward to 14-years as king in all but name and the power and wealth he could amass before baby King James was free to rule in his name. The Earl of Moray was assassinated within three years, but his successors as regents had no interest in placing Mary back on her throne.

Mary imprisoned would not surrender but did not have the power to reign or fight back. By May 1568, with the aid of George Douglas, brother of Sir William Douglas, the castle's owner, and with an escort of fifty horse under his command, Claude Hamilton, age just twenty-two, led Mary, Queen of Scots' escape from Loch Leven Castle. She had been imprisoned there by Moray to rule without interference. Claude escorted his queen to safety in "his" town of Hamilton and Hamilton Palace. Her freedom enabled her to encourage her supporters to take up arms against her stepbrother, James Stewart, 1st Earl of Moray.

When later imprisoned again by her stepbrother, Queen Mary was forced (in writing this time) to abdicate the Scottish throne in favor of her son, James. The regent, Moray, arrested and imprisoned a lawful reigning queen, a member of the same House of Stewart. He was an illegitimate son of King James V, unable to inherit and rule legitimately. The infant King James VI, in effect, deposed his mother from the throne. So bitter was the battle for the throne that Moray sought to control and deny Queen Mary access to her ten-month-old son, whom she never saw again. One can imagine her grief and distress at such betrayal, and she did not have most of her Scottish lords' backing to drive her stepbrother off.

Mary's Final Battle to Save Her Throne

When free, Mary raised an army to win back her throne, believing that it was an act of treason to force God's anointed sovereign to surrender under threat of death. She made it clear that she had not relinquished her throne by choice but was moved to do so by threats to her and her baby's life. Now she was free; all were under no illusion, least of all her stepbrother, that she intended to win back her throne. One of her champions, Claude Hamilton, was her man.

The Battle of Langside

The battle is a story worth telling, as it was to change Scotland's and Claude Hamilton's fortunes forever. Queen Mary met her step-brother Moray's smaller forces at the famous Battle of Langside on May 13, 1568. It was an extraordinary event that the sister gave battle to her stepbrother (an illegitimate child of their shared father), seeking to keep her infant son and not her on Scotland's throne. Such is the lure of power and wealth that deposing a rightful queen was a stepbrother's goal, so that in effect, he could rule as de-facto king for fourteen-plus years until the baby monarch's majority, assuming he planned to allow the child to live. Such a regency would bring him great power and personal wealth.

Archibald Campbell, 5th Earl of Argyll, led Queen Mary's forces, supported by General Claude Hamilton, who commanded the vanguard (the front) of her army. The Earls of Cassilis, Rothes, and Eglinton, the Lords Sommerville, Yester, Livingston, Herries, Fleming, Boyd, and Ross, and Sir James Hamilton and others rallied their men to their queen's cause. She mustered 6,000 troops in all to the regent's 4,000 and had the numerical advantage.

A fantastic painting of the Battle of Langside, some twenty-four feet wide and over seven feet tall, was painted onto the wall of Alec Hamilton's library at his estate in Melrose, Scotland, and is reproduced in this book. It shows Claude Hamilton on the painting's left side on a white charger while conversing with Mary, Queen of Scots. The image's to the right are understood to be the Earl of Argyll, Mary's overall battle commander and herself. Mary had intended to avoid battle at this stage, if possible. She determined with her commanders to make their way to Dumbarton Castle, outside of Glasgow, take stock of her situation, and build her forces to an even more significant number.

Mary prearranged to receive reinforcements at this castle upon arrival and planned through greater strength to take opposing fortifications and enemy Scottish troops first. Her goal was to weaken Moray's ability to win battle when she gave it, and probably scare support away from him as well. If she required shelter from opposing forces, she intended to bypass Moray and his troops and march to another castle on the route before swinging in a complete circle around Glasgow itself. They planned a route through Langside and Paisley and on to Dumbarton (coincidently close to the late-built Strathleven House in Dumbarton, where the modern Alec Hamilton was born). But her scouts seemed to do an abysmal job and were unaware of Moray's troops across the river.

Moray's scouts had been following Mary's army's progress from a distance on the river's opposite bank for some days. Moray had his main army drawn up on the moor across the river close to Langside village. This town was several miles south of Glasgow at the time but is today well within the city's more significant metropolis. The regent's commander then ordered his hack-butters (heavy-musket-wielding musketeers) to mount behind each of his horsemen and sent them some miles upstream, out of Mary's army's sight. They crossed the river onto the same side as Mary's troops some miles to the south. Moray's commander had his men march into Langside village, where he correctly perceived Mary's army would have to pass. He placed his hack-butters among the cottages and the town's hedges in guerilla tactic style. Hedges bordered each side of the village's narrow lanes through its length. He felt that he could not take on greater forces with a familiar face-to-face battle, drawn up in lines in the field, and had to rely on the element of surprise and rapid-fire.

Meanwhile, Moray, the regent himself, led the usurper army's vanguard across a nearby upstream bridge unseen, his men under the Earl of Morton's command. Moray sent a 200 strong mounted detachment ahead of his force under the command of Sir William Kirkcaldy of Grange with each horseman carrying a hack-butter (musketeer) as pillion. He then split his main force to either side of the village and thoroughfare where Mary's troops would unwittingly march. No sooner was this complete than the queen's vanguard, commanded by General Claude Hamilton, Lord Paisley with and Sir James Hamilton began its advance through the town, unaware of the trap set.

A Surprise Attack Commenced Battle

Mary, Queen of Scots stood some distance to the rear of her army as Claude Hamilton, and James Hamilton led their troops unsuspecting through the village. As the surprise attack unleashed, Claude's troops through Langside. The barrage of gunfire, which his troops sustained time and again in the narrow country lanes from all sides, must have been devastating. The deadly hack-butter fire at close range resulted in much loss of life. Still, somehow, driven by survival and their determination to protect their queen, most of Claude's vanguard amazingly managed to reach the top of the hill on the other side of the village. Imagine their shock before they could recover their breath, only to find Moray's main army lined up in the battle formation of pikemen charging at them.

There followed a terrible combat led by men wielding their long pikes, which were the leading lethal weapon of the day. One can only imagine the horrific melee that ensued: the noise, battle cries, the clashing of steel, men screaming in agony, confusion, and fear that left so many dead and dying, the lane and hills covered in bodies.

The local laird fighting for the regent was said to have acted with great courage and rallied Moray's troops along the line when it seemed near breaking at one stage. The battle was at its height, and when the laird's right flank seemed to falter and was at risk of giving way to Hamilton and Queen Mary's superior number of troops, he sent in his main force of Highlanders, the MacFarlane's, to steady the flank and a final charge. Leading his mounted troops at a gallop into his enemy, he punctured Claude Hamilton's line and Mary's troops were routed, Hamilton's ranks broke, and a full flight from battle occurred with the queen's troops in disarray. The retreating army fled the field on what is today appropriately known as Battlefield Road having lost around 300 men killed. The Regent, Earl Morey having defeated Mary, which was seen as her total defeat, and now to rule Scotland for many years until Mary's son, James VI as he was to become, ordered his men not to pursue the Catholic army's remnants. He now had to rule those same people and didn't need to make any greater enemy of himself. The battle of Langside had lasted less than one hour.

The queen and her forces were routed and fled the field. Not only was the Battle of Langside lost, but the queen also lost the bigger prize: to win back her throne from her traitorous stepbrother.

Queen Mary's commander, the Duke of Argyle, lost the battle despite having 50 percent more troops than the Earl of Moray. His generals were defeated by clever, guerilla-type tactics and the failure of their scouts to spot any enemy nearby, and they were outperformed by enemy field leaders. Mary fled the field to the south, escorted and protected by Claude Hamilton himself and twenty trusted mounted knights, who took her to the English border. Getting his to safety was now Claude's only focus when he realized they had lost the battle.

They spent the night at Dundrennan Abbey. The abbey, near Kirkcudbright, was a Cistercian Catholic monastery in the Romanesque architectural style, established in 1142 by Fergus of Galloway, King David I of Scotland (1124–53). Monks from the sister Rievaulx Abbey (which is in the North Yorkshire Moors) helped found the abbey. It still stands today but in ruins, as does Rievaulx Abbey.

Farewell to His Sovereign

Mary crossed the Solway Firth waters into England by a fishing boat on May 16, 1568, disguised as an ordinary woman in simple village clothes. The same day, she arrived Cumberland in the north of England and stayed overnight at Workington Hall. Originally established as a fortified tower house, Workington Hall was built around 1404. From here, as one anointed sovereign to another, Mary wrote to Queen Elizabeth I, seeking her support and temporary shelter.

Early in the morning, two days later, she declared herself as Mary, Queen of Scots to English officials. They were in some befuddlement as to what to do with the foreign queen suddenly appearing in their jurisdiction. It was May 18, 1568, when Claude Hamilton escorted his Queen to Carlisle Castle after resting at Cockermouth on their journey. Claude bade his queen farewell, not realizing that he'd never see her again. She gave him a lock of her hair as a memento of her until they met again.

That night at Carlisle Castle, she was treated as an honored guest and a royal cousin to the English queen. Queen Mary was just twenty-five years old. She expected her royal cousin, Queen Elizabeth, to host and protect her until she could regain her throne, and she hoped her English troops would help her win back her country.

Elizabeth allowed Mary to feel like a guest, but she was cautious, ordering a secret inquiry as to whether Mary was guilty of her husband Darnley's murder, as was believed in England. Mary, who could not realize that she would be a captive for nineteen years, was moved to other castles and eventually to Fotheringay Castle in Northamptonshire. By this time, Mary realized that she was being pushed further and further from any chance of rescue and held a prisoner, as slowly her "jailors" curbed her freedoms. She learned that her sealed letters and communications to Scotland were being read.

Claude Hamilton Declared a Traitor

Because of his crucial part in the Battle of Langside for Mary, Queen of Scots, Claude Hamilton was declared a traitor by Moray, Regent of Scotland. In 1568, Claude was found guilty by Moray's appointed judges and was sentenced to forfeit the Abbey of Paisley, its lands, and its considerable income. Mary's supporters in Scotland continued the civil war with Moray and his supporters for some five years. Claude was believed to have been involved in the murder of Mary's stepbrother Moray, the Regent; James Stewart, 1st Earl of Moray in 1570; and in the following year, a Protestant regent, Matthew Stewart, 4th Earl of Lennox. Warrants were issued for Claude's arrest, and little is heard of him for the next few years. However, in 1573 he is seen to have recovered his estates of Paisley, according to Scottish government records. The proof and hard evidence to convict him could not have been there, and the Crown likely pardoned him.

On February 8, 1587, Mary, to whom Claude Hamilton had given his all and risked his own life and lands for, was executed at Fotheringay Castle, nineteen years into her captivity in England, aged just forty-four. She was a tragic pawn in power politics and was a "God-anointed" sovereign, put to death while in her cousin and fellow queen's captivity. Mary's son James was compliant in legitimizing his former regent. Having usurped his mother's throne for him, he was robust and secure enough not to fear that his former step-uncle would challenge his throne. In 1579, six years later, the regent's privy-council again issued warrants to arrest both Claude Hamilton and his brother John to punish them for new misdeeds. New evidence may have come to light. They fled to England before they could be found and arrested, where Queen Elizabeth used them as pawns in the diplomatic game that followed, effectively holding them captive.

Reconciliatory Merry-Go-Round

Five years later, in 1584, King James VI of Scotland reached a private agreement with Claude Hamilton. By now, the king was an adult (and the future James I of England and VI of Scotland), and he issued a writ that allowed Claude Hamilton to return to Scotland in 1584. However, the custodian appointed to watch over Claude those last five years, the Earl of Huntley, ignored his release and forced him to go abroad in exile in France. Claude may not have been aware of the writ of discharge from the Scottish king. A few months later, Claude was welcomed back to Scotland with Huntley's fall from power and was admitted to the Scottish king's privy council in 1585. In 1587, Claude Hamilton was created a baron and 1st Lord Paisley by King James, and his past deeds fighting against the king seem to have been forgiven.

Claude Hamilton sought to reconcile Protestant King James VI of Scotland with his Catholic, usurped mother, "Queen" Mary, still in English care. On Mary's instructions, he was secretly negotiating with the King of Spain, Philipp II, who hoped to restore both the Roman Catholic faith and Scotland's throne. Even the uncovering of Catholic attempts against the English Queen Elizabeth's life did not stop Claude Hamilton. There was the Catholic Babington plot, and later the defeat of the Spanish Armada, which sought to overthrow Queen Elizabeth, restore Mary, Queen of Scots, to Scotland's throne, and rule England jointly with the Spanish King. Claude was Mary, Queen of Scots' man through and through, and while history shows him as having chosen the wrong side, he stayed loyal to his queen until her death.

In 1589, two years after his queen was executed, some of Claude's correspondence was seized by the Scottish authorities, and it suggested that he may have been involved in more plots against Moray, the former regent, and of more direct involvement in past treasonable crimes. The evidence could not have been conclusive, as Claude was only imprisoned for a short time during the investigation and then released. After that, he seems to have disappeared from public life and must have decided, with his queen dead, it was time to remove himself from any further intrigue or risk and retire. Later, Claude was created Lord Abercorn by the king. This branch of the Hamilton family also prospered (one brother's heirs becoming the Dukes of Hamilton eventually, as mentioned earlier). Claude's eldest son and heirs, who successively became Lord Abercorn, were advanced to the Earldom of Abercorn in 1606 and later still to a Dukedom of Abercorn in 1868.

Claude's Twilight Years

In 1597, Claude was visited by King James VI (Mary, Queen of Scot's son) at his Hamilton estate in Scotland and recognized for his compliance, the visit suggests. After that, he seems to have quietly slipped into history. Sadly, by 1590 he is known to have become insane during his concluding years, but the legacy he left is one held in great pride by modern-day Alec Hamilton's line, as the painting of the Battle of Langside on the wall of Alec's library attests.

NOTES:

Dodds, G.L (1996). Battles in Britain 1066-1746. Arms & Armor, London.

Sir William Kirkcaldy of Grange – and the Hamilton connections

A brilliant soldier of a staunch protestant Scottish family who, in 1557, was the Protestant Lord Provost of the Royal Burgh and City of Edinburgh. Civil war broke out in Scotland, and Mary's army prepared for battle at Carberry Hill on June 15, 1567. However, no conflict emerged as most of Mary's army deserted during negotiations between the Regent and Mary and Lord Bothwell.

The Queen and Lord Bothwell were forced to surrender. Bothwell was driven into exile in Denmark, where he was imprisoned, went insane, and died in 1578 a broken man. Meanwhile, on June 17, the Queen was imprisoned in Loch Leven Castle on an island in the Loch, following her surrender and taken there by Sir William Kirkcaldy. The Queen was forced abdicated on July 24, 1567, and on May 2, 1568, after 11-months of imprisonment and with help from the powerful Douglas family Claude Hamilton, she escaped and raised an army. Within two weeks, they would all be at the Battle of Langside.

Kirkcaldy began to sympathize with her cause and must have been struck by a God-anointed Queen. Yet, at the Battle of Langside some two weeks after her escape, Kirkcaldy led the vanguard of the Regent Moray's protestant army, routing Mary, Queen of Scot's army, and vanquishing Claude Hamilton for a second time. This battle sealed Mary's fate, her fleeing to England aided and protected by Claude Hamilton, and her eventual execution.

Then an extraordinary thing happened. Sir William Kirkcaldy changed sides and held Edinburgh Castle for the exiled Mary, Queen of Scot's against the. Regent Moray. No doubt he was then helped by Claude Hamilton, and he managed to rebut all attempts by Moray to take the castle for 5-years. Sadly, for Kirkcaldy, his luck ran out, and he was eventually forced to surrender the castle to Moray and was promptly hanged for treason.

The Kirkcaldy's and Hamiltons of Grange

As Kirkcaldy came from Grange, in Ayrshire, and no doubt he knew the Hamilton's of Grange well, the Hamilton founding fathers ancestor 200-years earlier. A complete research paper on Sir William Kirkcaldy is available with the author.

A Lock of Mary, Queen of Scots' Hair

A link of pride for Alec Hamilton to his ancestor, Claude Hamilton, was having possession of a gold and crystal glass locket in which there's a braid of Mary, Queen of Scots' hair. The queen gave the locket of hair to Claude Hamilton in May 1568 after the Battle of Langside. Generation after generation of Hamiltons passed down the locket and the story to Alec. Sadly, there was no dukedom for Claude as promised him before the battle *if* the queen won. Claude and his queen were not to meet again after she entered England. He never wavered in his support for his queen throughout her internment in England and lived with anguish that he could not rescue her again. No doubt, Claude grieved heavily when his queen was executed.

The Most Extensive Collection of Mary, Queen of Scots Memorabilia

His Grace, the current and 16th Duke of Hamilton, is known to have one of, if not the most extensive collections of personal items and memorabilia of Mary, Queen of Scots. These are on display at his family seat's public galleries at Lennoxlove House during an annual season when the house is open. The author would encourage everyone to take an opportunity in the future to visit Lennoxlove House and view its incredible collections.

Mary, Queen of Scots, painted around the period of the Battle of Langside, 1568, when Claude Hamilton, 1st Lord Paisley and Abercorn, commanded the vanguard of her army. The painting is on public display at the Palace of Holyrood house, Scotland, from the Royal Collection Trust (CE).

A locket of Mary, Queen of Scots' hair given by her to Claude Hamilton after the Battle of Langside as a keepsake; now held by Alec's Hamilton Trust (WOP).

The Battle of Langside (May 13, 1568). A painting around 24' wide on Alec's library wall, Scotland. Mary, Queen of Scots, mounted on the grey, on the right with the 5th Duke of Argyll. Lord Hamilton on the grey horse on the left with the Hamilton standard. (PBA)

Mary, Queen of Scots at the Battle of Langside, May 13, 1568, a painting by Giovanni Fattori. Lord Douglas lays dying and receives last rights, as Claude Hamilton, on the grey seeing the battle lost, prepared to escort his queen to safety with eleven knights (NCA).

Claude Hamilton, 1ˢᵗ Lord Paisley, and Mary Queen of Scots champion (NCA).

Queen Mary is embarking on the Solway Firth to England after her defeat at the Battle of Langside. Claude Hamilton is standing with one foot on shore and one in the water. Engraving by John Smith, after Henry Melville, painted. c. 1830 (CE).

Chapter 4

ALEXANDER HAMILTON, A FOUNDING FATHER OF AMERICA

The First of This Book's Two Apples

Here we will read a summary of Alexander Hamilton's life, contributions, and achievements from the many resources researched and studied. They lay the foundation for this Alexander Hamilton, an apple who fell in 1757 (more anon) from the same Hamilton tree of 1185 as did Alec Hamilton, our second apple, who fell in 1932 from the same family tree. One was born of Scottish blood in the West Indies (Nevis) and made his career in the Western world (America); the other was born in Scotland in the more modern Western world and made his career in the West Indies (Jamaica).

In the way of an opening summary, this Alexander's story began when he was born out of wedlock on January 11, 1757—the bloodline son of James Hamilton, a Scottish trader of noble ancestry. His birth was in Charlestown, on the island of Nevis, the capital of the then-British Leeward Islands of the West Indies. These islands are now known as St. Kitts & Nevis. His birth year was registered in government records in Nevis as 1755. However, Hamilton always claimed it was 1757, and several historians believe it may have been a Nevis error, not a Hamilton error. As Hamilton was adamant, for whatever reason, that he was born in 1757, the author will stick with that date of birth.

From the recent Hamilton Surname DNA Project, Alexander Hamilton is confirmed as descended through his father, James Hamilton, from a younger son of John Hamilton, 4th Baron Cadzow (b. 1370 d. 1402). Therefore, he carries original Hamilton blood through William de Hameldone (1185) and his bloodline ancestors to AD 880. More anon.

Alexander Hamilton's Scottish Heritage

Alexander's great grandfather, another Alexander Hamilton, the Laird Hamilton of Grange in Ayrshire, Scotland, traces his lineage back through the Cambuskeith line of Hamiltons.

Alexander Hamilton's Father

James Hamilton was the fourth son of the Laird of Grange of Scotland and was born there in 1718 (he died on the Isle of Nevis, British West Indies, in 1799). We'll evidence shortly his Hamilton bloodline questioned by some in the last decade. As the fourth son of eleven children, he was not expected to inherit any wealth, and typical of the day for a young gentleman, would have been expected to go into the army, navy, the clergy, or make his way in the business world. At this time, many left Scotland for the New World of the Americas, and the West Indies, in the hope that they would make their fortunes. James was raised in Kerelaw Castle, which the family inherited or purchased in 1685 when his father acquired it. The grandfather, formerly of Cambuskeith, changed the castle and grounds' name to Grange, after the family home in Kilmarnock.

James Hamilton was educated well for the times but failed to get a degree at Glasgow University. While he made various attempts to make his way in different business or investment schemes in Scotland, he seems not to have succeeded at anything he touched.

His elder brother, John, had inherited the lairdship on their father's passing and, with business partners, was trading with the West Indies from Scotland, so the lure for the younger brother likely stems from there. John paid for his younger brother to undergo an apprenticeship with a local business friend, who with John and others had launched a textile manufacturing business producing linen-wear. As was common in those days, an apprentice received board and lodging, clothing, and training, but no wages as such. He was expected to work hard in return for the training he received and be free after his apprenticeship to leave and start his own business.

In the summer of 1725, some sixteen years before James Hamilton arrived in Nevis, tensions were running high on the island, home to approximately 1,500 white settlers and 6,000 African slaves. This number was to rise significantly, as we'll see later. There was a momentous drought at the time, which resulted in a shortage of water across the island. This drought badly impacted food availability and caused a crash in sugar crop prices and income, with reports of "much livestock and many slaves" dying. The authorities' actions resulted in a planned slave rebellion, which was brutally put down by the Leeward Islands' governor, based in nearby Antigua, before the uprising occurred. His retribution resulted in ten slave conspirators being jailed, and he burned two to death. These underlying earlier tensions simmered just below the surface much of the time during James Hamilton's days.

As with many younger sons of the Scottish, Irish, Welsh, and English gentry in these times, James dreamt of the chance to make money, as many were, by acquiring a sugar plantation in the West Indies. Hence in 1741, when he completed his four-year apprenticeship, he set sail for St. Kitts.

The Dumbartonshire countryside outside of Glasgow has many grand estates and houses built on the wealth of prosperous sugar planters like the Ewings, who were the modern Alec Hamilton's maternal ancestors. Alec was born in one such house and estate, Strathleven, one of Scotland's first Palladium-designed homes acquired by James Ewing on the back of his tobacco and sugar wealth in the mid-1800s.

James Hamilton, as the grandson of a Scottish laird with lands and a castle, had a certain society cache upon arrival in St. Kitts. He started trading in sugar and plantation supplies. Historical records suggest that James was no more successful in St. Kitts than in Scotland, and he got into debt. He was bailed out by his brother John and friends back home in Scotland, and they kept their support discreet to such a degree that James was not fully aware of those underwriting him. He then faltered severely and went into debt again, and when his brother didn't bail him out a second time, he lost his trading business and was forced to take menial, low-paying jobs, such as a clerk or watchman, to survive.

Alexander Hamilton's Mother

Born Rachel Faucette on the island of Nevis in 1729, she died in St. Croix aged thirty-nine on February 19, 1768. She was the daughter of a man who was at first a relatively successful French-Huguenot sugar planter and doctor. Dr. John Faucett of Nevis married an English-born wife, Mary, née Upington. They kept seven slaves. Rachel was of half-Scottish and half-French Huguenot descent. She and her sister Anne survived the ravages of Caribbean island diseases, which were so prevalent at the time and ranged from malaria, dengue fever, and dysentery to yellow fever, all of which took many lives annually. She was one of seven children, and three of her siblings died in an epidemic: her sisters Frances and Elizabeth and her brother, Peter.

By 1737, the Faucette plantation's fortunes declined due to crop failures in a period of drought and wide-scale loss of vegetation by plant diseases on the island. The Faucettes, with a mass exodus of others, left the island and moved to St. Croix. With the strain of financial losses, and having to clothe and feed seven children, her parents saw their marriage falling apart, and in 1740 a separation was agreed upon. Mary renounced all rights to her husband's inheritance in return for a small annual stipend. After the couple separated, Mary moved back to St. Kitts and took Rachel with her. Rachel may well have first met Alexander Hamilton at this time, as Europeans were relatively small in numbers on the island. However, no written evidence of her having done so was unearthed in researching this book.

Rachel's father died in 1745, leaving her everything. As his fortunes seem to have recovered somewhat, Rachel, as a teenager, was suddenly relatively well off and a desirable match in the marriage market. Rachel's mother, Mary, may also have moved them to St. Croix because Rachel's sister Anne and her husband, James Lytton, had moved there and prospered, it seems.

Rachel Faucette Marries her Danish Prize

It is here on St. Croix that Rachel met a Dane, Johann Michael Lavien (c. 1717–February 28, 1771). St. Croix was then a Danish colony known as the Danish Virgin Islands. Johann was by all accounts good-looking and had a swagger of apparent success and wealth about him. Some historians have claimed he was of German origin, although Hamilton believed him Danish.

Some have gone as far as to suggest that Lavien was born a German Jew and sought to hide his religion on the small Danish church island of St. Croix. This hypothesis is based on the spelling of Lavien being 'claimed' as one commonly used by those of the Jewish faith in Germany at the time, in a *fictionalized* biographic of the future Founding Father of America, published in 1902 by a *novelist* suggesting Lavien was Jewish. Since there is absolutely no factual evidence of any kind, no records, or first-hand accounts, we must dismiss such suggestions as what they were - fiction, until written evidence from records or DNA proves otherwise. The fact that Rachel Lavien (Hamilton), a decade later, was lucky enough to have a Jewish neighbor volunteer to tutor for her sons in Nevis has no connection. At the time, no school would accept the boys due to their illegitimate birth.

Lavien attended the Danish church. He had his son, Peter, Christened there, which would not have been possible in the relatively tiny community of "Danish" people in St. Croix at the time had he been of German or Jewish origin. The lack of a paper trail as a Dane would have stood out to the authorities. Therefore, the author will assume him to be Danish, as Hamilton himself believed. The leaders in St. Croix must have seen sufficient evidence that he was Danish, or he would not be listed as such. Had there been any evidence of his origin being German and Jewish, it would be apparent in St. Croix archived government records.

Rachel's mother was attracted to Lavien's apparent success and wealth and pushed Rachel into accepting his offer of marriage. Lavien had already invested his savings into a small sugar plantation, known later as Estate Ruby, and by 1744 had established a reputation as a sugar planter. He and Rachel married in 1745 when Rachel was just sixteen years of age, and with some of Rachel's inheritance, Lavien boosted investment in his modest sugar plantation. In 1746, the year following their marriage, they had a son, Peter.

In 1748, Lavien bought a half share in another small sugar plantation, which slowly ate away at Rachel's inheritance, at a time when his businesses were beginning to flounder. Rachel appearing across his bow three years earlier must have seemed like a heaven-sent source of wealth, which by law across the whole Western world at the time meant that what a wife brought to the marriage became her husband's to command. However, he nearly demolished the entire cash windfall with poor management of his investments. Lavien could not afford enough slaves to compete with sufficient production against the more significant established plantation outputs or make enough profits. He is believed to have had sixteen slaves, including five children. Lavien landed in debt when trying to make money from a third venture, a fifty percent share in a cotton plantation he had bought. He landed up squandering *all* of Rachel's capital, it seems, leaving them in total debt within two years by 1750.

Rachel's Divorce From Lavien

Their marriage may have become violent with all the strain when Rachel had had enough, and she refused to live with her husband. She moved in with her mother and filed for divorce. However, her husband made a counter-suit against Rachel, stating adultery by his wife and that she had refused to live with him. At the time, a wife was simply "chattel," as was a cart, chair, slave, or pot, so her refusal to live with her husband, no matter his behavior, was punishable by St. Croix's Danish law, and Rachel was imprisoned. She was incarcerated in the military fort in Christiansted, St. Croix, for several months in a cell just 10 X 13, with a tiny window high above. There would have been horrendous conditions, surrounded by wayward slaves, drunks, thieves, pirates, and murderers, with appalling sanitation and little food.

Any husband had sole rights to custody of his child, regardless of the divorce case outcome. Rachel felt the need to escape her husband and what she saw as prejudice and injustice, as she was not a Dane, before the divorce hearing concluded, which could drag on and did for many years. With her husband willing to put her into prison, she determined she would neither be forced to live with her husband and could not take being sent back to prison.

Within a week of leaving jail, in 1750—a week she spent with her mother, who was living with a senior Danish military man herself—Rachel determined to abandon her husband and child, fearful of what court decisions were yet to be made. Together with her mother, she sailed for St. Kitts, then under British colonial rule, and out of the grips of her husband before he could have her put back in jail for not coming home to him once released. This time, life and men would be on her terms, she decided, though now in a perilous financial position. By doing so, she lost any claim to a financial settlement.

The Laviens - Life After Rachel

In 1753, three years after Rachel abandoned him and their son in St. Croix, Lavien sold his last remaining plantation to pay off his debts. He retained his sixteen slaves and rented them out to work on other planters' properties to give him a small income. It was not until 1759, nine years after Rachel had fled to St. Kitts (then Nevis), that the St. Croix courts finally granted Lavien a divorce, which we'll return to shortly. Rachel was glad that she had not waited in St. Croix for the divorce settlement. She would, she feared, either have been forced to move back in with her hated husband or may have been imprisoned again for those nine years.

By 1761 Lavien had moved to Frederiksted, where, on the other side of the island of St. Croix, he made some income speculating, eventually unsuccessfully, in real estate. By 1768 he is listed as a "hospital janitor" in Frederiksted and poor. He remarried and had two sons and a daughter with his new wife, but sadly it is recorded that the children all died in early childhood. One month before Rachel's death in Nevis, his second wife died in 1768. Lavien himself died in St. Croix on February 28, 1771.

Alexander Hamilton Meets and "Marries" Rachel Lavien, née Faucette

In 1748, two years before Rachel arrived in St. Kitts and met James Hamilton, James is listed as a clerk in St. Kitts government records. Having failed in business, he was accepting basic wage jobs to survive. Sometime after arriving free in St. Kitts, most likely in 1751, Rachel met and fell in love with James. They both had suffered losses in family, finances, and social standing. Both were reeling from lives wrecked by others, which formed a keen understanding of each other's sufferings—they were kindred spirits in need of love and security. Unlikely to be on the A list of invitations to the island's British society events and dinners, they were forced to mix with the European commoner society. It was noted as a difficult time for James, having come from a noble family of lairds and castles.

James and Rachel entered a "common law" marriage arrangement. They were unable to formerly marry, as she was still married to her husband—the divorce decision was yet to be determined by the courts in St. Croix. After becoming a couple, James and Rachel decided to move to Nevis and make a fresh start. He called her "Mrs. Hamilton" for appearance's sake. By 1753, when she was twenty-four, she gave birth to an illegitimate son, James (Junior). Four years later, she gave birth to little Alexander Hamilton—the child destined to help shape a nation.

Doubts of Alexander Hamilton's Bloodline - Dismissed

Ron Chernow's book, *Alexander Hamilton* first published in 2004, says that some people have expressed doubt whether the Founding Father is biologically a Hamilton. A Hamilton Surname DNA project wrote at the time of his excellent biography of the Founding Father that, "As Chernow has pointed out, there have been suggestions that his father (Hamilton's) was a Stevens, in which case he would not be a Hamilton."

Since then, seventeen years have passed by, and the DNA from some

Stevens' lines have been analyzed. None of those results matched, but they were yet to test the West Indies branch of the family. However, this project's more recent DNA developments show that Alexander's descendants carried DNA matching Bernard "the Dane," born in AD 880 in Norway, the earliest proven Hamilton ancestor by the author of this book. This confirms that the Founding Father was of the legitimate bloodline of James Hamilton. He carried the male bloodline DNA of Bernard, as all the Hamilton Founding Fathers' descendants who were tested did.

The founding father's descendants could not have DNA traceable back through de Beaumonts to that Viking earl born in AD 880 unless their ancestor Alexander Hamilton carried that same Hamilton DNA. Bernard "the Dane's" Viking warrior DNA went through all the de Beaumont, de Hameldone, and Hamilton descendants. It is reliable to say that the Hamilton Founding Father of America is of the well-established Hamilton bloodline, which puts an end to speculation.

The Church Denied the Hamilton Brothers An Education

With James Sr.'s meager income as a clerk, and a so-called "wife" and two sons, these proved tough years financially for the family. Due to James and Rachel's "illicit" partnership, no church would grant their illegitimate boys a baptism or give them an education. At the time, all schools on the island were run by religious organizations. With a relatively small white population in a highly religious British environment, not attending church was the same as being seen as lepers by society.

The boys received their early education through private tutoring by an elderly Jewish lady who empathized with the family, and Alexander supplemented his education with thirty-plus books from the Jewish family's book collection. The future Founding Father is understood to have learned many Hebrew passages and certainly had a lifetime acceptance of Jewish peoples from his childhood gratitude to the woman who opened his eyes to learning. He was to embrace all races and religions throughout his life.

It was not until 1759 that the St. Croix courts finally granted Lavien a divorce on the grounds of adultery (now proven). Rachel had been living with Alexander Hamilton for at least eight years by this time and had two children by him, and Lavien filed for desertion, as she had left St. Croix. He was granted the freedom to remarry, but as the guilty party, Rachel was banned from remarrying and couldn't apply to the courts to have her sons by Hamilton legitimized.

In 1764, unknown to Alexander Hamilton or his mother, the Hamilton boys' half-brother, Peter Lavien, moved to South Carolina in the American colonies. Peter rose high in the shipping merchant trade, owning and eventually running a merchant house of his own. In 1769, a year after Rachel had died, Peter returned momentarily to St. Croix to take the procession of his inheritance from his mother Rachel's estate, bound there for his claim. There is no evidence that Peter had to deal with the Hamiltons during his brief return before going back to South Carolina, despite the small community.

Interestingly, during the American War of Independence, when Peter Lavien's half-brother, Alexander, was a young revolutionary, Peter turned to smuggling in South Carolina, making an illicit fortune. In 1777, he moved to Savannah, Georgia. Peter died in 1781 when Alexander was twenty-four years old, a half-brother the Founding Father never met.

Their Father Moved Them to St. Croix and Then Abandoned Them

In 1765, James Hamilton moved his little family to St. Croix, where he felt he'd have better opportunities to make money again in the sugar trade. Despite her hated ex-husband being there, Rachel was now formerly divorced from Lavien, and he had no hold on her. Her relatives were there too, so she must have felt it okay.

When he relocated them to St. Croix, the sugar trade (white gold as it was being called) was at a new peak, and James felt this was his chance to make a success finally. At this time, 92 percent of this Danish colony's population were slaves—some 22,000 enslaved Africans lived on St. Croix at the time, and just 1,913 European-descent occupants appeared in its census.

No one is sure why James Hamilton left his family, but it is only speculated that he couldn't face them as a complete failure again and felt unable to care for his "wife" and children. In 1756, James, when little Alexander was just eight years old (and James Junior, twelve), suddenly abandoned Rachel and the children, never to return.

Some historians say he did so to avoid Rachel being cited for bigamy when her Danish husband came after her through lawyers and sought a final divorce.

However, they had been divorced six years already by then, and she had been banned from remarrying. If James and Rachel never married, bigamy could not be a charge levied against her. In any case, James left St. Croix forever. His family never saw nor heard from him again, as far as is known.

Various sources suggest that he wandered from one job to another and from one island to another, ending up in a refuge for the poor on the tiny island of Bequia in the Caribbean. Alexander and his brother, James Junior, now had no father to guide or protect them. Being abandoned by him must have been hugely traumatic, let alone the economic loss for them and their mother. They had left behind Nevis and their friends there, despite being illegitimate outcasts, which they would remain.

Rachel moved into small lodgings with her two boys, which she rented above a shop on a busy high street in Christiansted. According to various sources, she now owned five female slaves, and she augmented her livelihood by renting them out as house servants while retaining two house slaves for her home. She took over the running of the trading store, and some sources suggest that she bought the shop, but where the money came from is not proposed.

Over time, two of her female slaves had children, and when old enough, one each was assigned to Alexander and his brother as houseboy servants to help care for them. Rachel by then "owned" nine slaves.

An Orphan's Life Ahead

By early to mid-February 1768, both Rachel and her son Alexander, the future Founding Father of America, were struck down with yellow fever, which rapidly took Rachel's life on February 19, 1768. Alexander was eleven years old and had been in St. Croix for three years, surviving with his mother and brother on their own. Alexander recovered, and he and James were noted as having attended their mother's funeral, though the Church refused her burial in sacred ground. Therefore, she was buried in the gardens of a friend, Mr. Tuite, at Grange Plantation in St. Croix.

No sooner had Rachel been buried than the children were flooded with bills of debt. St. Croix being a small island, her ex-husband heard quickly of Rachel's death and immediately petitioned the courts to claim all her wealth, goods, and chattels, and if she owned the shop, its sale value and contents.

Her chattels included her nine slaves, and he claimed "all" her goods as his son Peter's by right of law, being their legitimate child. He sought to have Rachel's will, which left everything to her two illegitimate sons, ruled null and void.

Lavien used the 1759 divorce agreement as evidence to the Islands Danish court of probate and inheritance claims. It must have been at least a year in court, and Rachel's probate and court settlement languished. During that year of court probate, Alexander and his brother (while not technically owning any slave) held those nine slaves. Ajax, Alexander's houseboy, continued his duties caring for Alexander, which some historians seem to forget.

The courts favored Peter Lavien as the rightful owner of all Rachel's property. Any faint hopes the boys, or their employers had of them inheriting any of her funds were squashed. They received nothing.

If there is record of Alexander and James Jr. being denied Rachel's home and using her slaves until the court case ended, it does not appear to be evidenced anywhere. Presumably, the five slaves rented out by their mother for some income continued to be rented out by an intelligent, business-minded Alexander, as none of his mother's "chattels" could change hands until the court case announced its findings. There was nowhere for those slaves to run on a small island, so they stayed put in Rachel's home with the boys or were rented out and carried on with their duties, it can reasonably be assumed.

Before she died, Rachel named her St. Croix-based nephew, Peter Lytton, now thirty-two, her sister, Anne, and her brother-in-law, James Lytton, to hold "wardship" over her sons. Peter had an African mistress and an illegitimate child by her, and when he is said to have committed suicide a year later, his last will and testament left everything to his mistress and their child. Less than a month later, Peter's father, James Lytton, died, and his last will left nothing for his abandoned, orphaned nephews, Alexander and James Hamilton.

The brothers had been hit by an avalanche of calamities in a short space of time. Aged sixteen and fourteen respectively, by 1769 they were alone, penniless, and without family. Soon, the bequests left them by their mother and stuck in probate would have denied them too. No money, no longer a roof over their heads, no furniture, no slaves or pots and pans—all chattels went to their mother's son from her first marriage. They indeed became utterly penniless and homeless. Their father had turned their lives upside down in a harsh, unforgiving world, yet two men came to their rescue.

New Homes and Employment for Alexander and James Junior

James was taken in as a carpenter's apprentice by a family friend and given training in a trade, along with food and lodging. Within seventeen years, he was taken seriously ill from tropical fever, which took his life in 1786, fourteen years after Alexander had left to make his future in America. They are not known to have met again after Alexander moved to America.

Alexander, the fourteen-year-old boy, the homeless orphan, was taken in by a prosperous local merchant and friend of his mother, Thomas Stevens. Stevens saw Alexander's sharp mind and capability even at such a young age. He gave him food and lodging and recommended him to his friend, Mr. Nicholas Cruger, who employed him as a clerk handling record-keeping and tasks for his employer at his company, the St. Croix trading firm, Beekman and Cruger.

On behalf of his employer, Hamilton would, in time, write to ship captains and traders seeking slaves for clients. Beekman and Cruger imported anything for what was primarily a plantation economy revolving around sugar, including goods, fabrics, machinery, and especially slaves from Africa.

Alexander handled record-keeping, balancing orders -v- received goods and slaves, the price paid the ship's captain, the housing, feeding, and preparing the captives for the slave markets. He would often be left in charge of inspecting the slaves and, in time, helping put a sale price on them. Evidence by way of a surviving letter written in Hamilton's hand in 1772 is often quoted in several sources and books. In it, he reached out to a known supplier when aged fifteen. Parts of the letter read, "two or three poor boys" for plantation work, and Alexander asked that they be "bound in the most reasonable manner you can."

Alexander was quite proficient in French, which he likely learned from his mother. This must have helped when dealing with French ship captains. In later years, he was an aide-de-camp to General Washington as Washington worked alongside French troops and closely with the French Admiral Marquis de Lafayette.

Alexander Hamilton's Early Involvement in Slavery

There is no evidence from the time that Alexander struggled as a young man against the slave trade he was involved in or felt it wrong. By the age of fifteen, he worked for the import trading firm in St. Croix, which specialized in slave imports and sales. However, he was later to be clear, as he stated on many occasions as a politician in America, that he had an abhorrence of slavery.

As a child and teenager surrounded by the trade, which was simply a way of life across his world at the time, he may have had no thoughts about or felt the great weight of slavery's horrors nor whether it was right or wrong. He was raised by a father and mother who owned slaves, and he had his slave houseboy, Ajax, whom he had anticipated 'owing' after his mother's last will in probate. There is no evidence that he would not have accepted this bequest in his mother's choice of the slave boy, Ajax, had her Danish husband not been awarded those "chattels" for his son. The author was unable to establish what happened to Ajax and his fellow house slaves after the courts awarded them the property of Peter Lavien. No doubt the senior Lavien sold them for his son's profit.

This appears to suggest that their dispersal and the fate of his houseboy since childhood meant little to him. He happily earned a living out of the misery of slavery as a clerk. He grew up with a house full of slaves, and his education was sponsored by a group of businessmen from St. Croix, whose wealth primarily came from the slave trade. We'll see going forward that he was supported in his education by academics who held slaves. He cherished his friendship with General George Washington and rose through the ranks of government in the new, free nation under President Washington. The fact is that the president and most of the Founding Fathers all owned slaves, and Alexander married into a family that happily kept slaves. All of this seems highly contradictory to his political statements abhorring the trade.

Slavery enveloped Alexander's world in various periods of his life. When he joined Mr. Nicholas Cruger and his company, he soon found himself trading commodities, including slaves. During his work, he regularly recorded and assisted in slave auctions with his employer (his employers brought in 200 to 300 slaves at a time on ships). Cruger saw early on that this young man had a sharp business brain, was quick at mathematics, was thorough and accurate in his record-keeping, and maintained first-rate expense accounts and profit ledgers.

When Alexander was still only fifteen, Cruger found him an excellent communicator, whether dealing with sea captains, their agents, or local authorities.

Whenever Cruger traveled off the island, he left Alexander in sole charge, numerous sources suggest. This meant that any slave ships docking would have seen their captains dealing with young Alexander Hamilton to sell their slave cargo on the docks, make payment to the ship's owners, and receive compensation from planters and others buying slaves.

One of Hamilton's grandsons interpreted some journal entries in America as slave purchases for Alexander. However, most historians do not accept it, as the same purchase he made, he sold to his sister-in-law, for whom it would seem he was purchasing the slaves. Buying slaves for members of his in-law family didn't seem to trouble him at all. Some had written that Hamilton had no deep abhorrence of slavery and accepted that it was the norm in his time. Was it only when it became politically expedient to say so that he appeared to find it abhorrent?

There is no evidence that Hamilton owned slaves at any time, early in life or later, but he was nevertheless complicit in the slave trade, working for employers trading in people from Africa. However, one thing is clear: he became an avid abolitionist later in life. Watching the suffering of fellow human beings set aside merely because they were African must have influenced him over time. Hamilton's eventual actions showed that he saw Africans no matter what he accepted around him before, not as persons of color or "inferior beings" nor "property," as so many Europeans saw them in that era, but as human equals. At the same time, working in the slave business, he learned much about trading, buying, selling, and managing a company, as well as accounting and bargaining—all skills that would stand him in good stead for his later career as America's first head of the treasury.

Alexander's Opportunity of a Life in America

Alexander's luck changed as a group of St. Croix businessmen (likely board members and friends of Nicholas Cruger, of the trading firm Beekman and Cruger) proposed acting as his benefactor and underwrote Hamilton going to New York to pursue his education. New York at the time, as with all North America, was under British rule. He arrived by ship in Boston in 1772 and traveled overland to New York, lodging with his benefactor's family member, Hercules Mulligan, a merchant with trading connections to St. Croix. Alexander likely did not realize that he'd never see his elder brother again. With Mulligan's help, the arrangement expected Hamilton to sell cargo in his spare time when not at his studies, and his labor was bartered to pay back the cost of his education to his benefactors.

When he was preparing for college entry, he attended a local preparatory school for over one year to close his learning gaps. There he met William Livingston, a leading intellectual and revolutionary, with whom he lodged. In 1773, Alexander won a place at King's College in New York City, now Columbia University, and graduated a year later. Because they saw great potential in their young protégé, he was sponsored by merchants, including Mr. Cruger, to further his education to an even higher level.

Alexander was just sixteen when he went off to New York City's King's College. Many of the trustees of the college were slaveholders, as were all those putting up his education costs upfront. His education in America was 100 percent achieved on slave-trade profits, as he would have well known.

He published some papers anonymously to answer British Royalist propaganda and became very active politically for the revolution to come. He is known all the same to have saved his college president, a loyalist to the British Crown, from being attacked by an angry revolutionary mob by talking the mob into calm and reason. Such were the man's sensitivities to right and wrong despite, or maybe because of, being aligned to American independence. He believed in the right of all men to be free to choose their government.

He had to temporarily abandon his studies when British forces occupying New York City closed the college down as a hotbed of rebellion. By 1782, when the revolution was won against the British, and after some challenging self-study, Alexander passed his bar exam in law and received a license to practice in the Supreme Court of New York. "What a self-driven result for one who, as a young boy of fourteen, was orphaned, abandoned, and penniless in the West Indian island of Nevis; it's the American dream, I suppose, isn't it?" Alec Hamilton said to the author when discussing his namesake together.

Hamilton Compromised on Slavery

Even later, Hamilton compromised when voting in the new Constitutional Convention in 1787 to form the Union of all States (the prelude after it collapsed, to the American Civil War, which followed in 1861). He supported a clause that counted each *enslaved African as three-fifths of a person* when determining each state's population. "How bizarre is such a thing today," Alec Hamilton said during interviews when the author touched on the topic. In 1787, Alexander Hamilton believed that such a compromise, insisted upon by the Southern states, was needed to pull the new nation together after the British had been forced out. He stated to the Convention floor debate: "Without this indulgence, no union could have possibly been formed."

The American Revolutionary War (War of Independence) 1775–1783

Hamilton supported arming and enabling slaves to fight in the Revolutionary War to oust the British, which promised them freedom afterward. Parts of Hamilton's letter to Congressional colleagues lent full support and encouraged Congress to support the concept too. They read: "I have not the least doubt, that the negroes will make very excellent soldiers, with proper management," and "their natural faculties are probably as good as ours." He didn't sound too convinced, but he did feel that no human, regardless of race or color, should be enslaved.

His lobbying, however, failed to win support. He appears to have been a pragmatist who, while against another human's enslavement, accepted that this was the way of life surrounding him, and that he would have to influence change over time. After colonist troops engaged the British in 1775, the first engagement of the revolution, King's College students, including Hamilton, joined the volunteer New York Militia company. He took charge of drilling them and led a successful raid on British shore batteries while under fire from a British naval ship, capturing cannon and turning his militia into an artillery company.

During his teenage years in St. Croix, we can recall that slave revolts were often simmering, and all non-disabled European men were formed into a militia by the local Danish authorities. Hamilton was raised in an environment of protectionist militia and would have learned to shoot early on. He built a new artillery company with sixty men in 1776, and they elected him their captain.

George Washington - Hamilton's Career Enabler

As the American Revolution raged, Alexander Hamilton was invited to become aide-de-camp to Washington's generals. He diplomatically declined the offer, as he was holding out for a front-line fighting commission. Not long afterward, he felt unable to decline General Washington's invitation to become his personal aide-de-camp in 1777 with the rank of lieutenant colonel in the newly formed Continental Army.

Hamilton took part in many battles and skirmishes, the first of which was the Battle of White Plains led by George Washington, which was lost. Then in the Battle of Princeton, still in 1777, Washington led American troops and forced a British retreat to a nearby building. Hamilton took the initiative on his own to bring up three cannons, and after firing at the facility, his troops rushed the front door and broke it down. The British defending the hall surrendered. While Hamilton was stationed in New Jersey over the winter of 1779, he met and married his life partner, but more anon.

In 1781, the American Revolution looked close to being won, and after continually asking for and being denied a field battle commission, Hamilton offered his resignation. Washington refused to accept it and, relenting, gave him command of four infantry companies, both regular and provisional. In the assault on Yorktown, which was to prove the final major battle of the War of Independence, Hamilton was now given command of three battalions, which, together with French forces, were under the leadership of his companion and ally, the Admiral, the Marquis de Lafayette. Armed with bayonets and axes, some 400 of their combined infantries stormed two stronghold redoubts of British fortifications on the hill. (A redoubt is a fort-like system usually consisting of an enclosed defensive emplacement, typically relying on earthworks to protect soldiers and cannon and invariably on a hilltop defensive placement.)

Hamilton and his battalions fought bravely while attacking Redoubt 10, and he led his troops in a bayonet charge while the French, fighting equally as fearlessly, attacked the other redoubt, number 9. Hamilton and Lafayette took both redoubts, and within two days, General Lord Cornwallis was forced to surrender the British Army at Yorktown, effectively ending the war. Lord Cornwallis, Commander of the British Army in America, was too shocked and proud to attend the ceremony of handing over his sword, so he had one of his generals do it on his behalf. That surrender was in the presence of Alexander Hamilton. The loss of the continent of North America (other than what was to become Canada) caused King George III great distress, for which the king roundly blamed Cornwallis.

Two Hamiltons on opposite sides of the Revolution

The "modern-day" George, Lord Hamilton put a question to the author in his interview with him in 2020, while the author sat at his desk in his study in North Carolina and Baron Hamilton was in a room at the British House of Lords in London. Lord Hamilton's question was: Did the author know why Hamilton, the capital of Bermuda, was given that name, and was there a Hamilton family link?

The author did not know the answer to His Lordship's question, so he researched the topic. This led to the discovery of the Anglo-Irishman Henry Hamilton (born c. 1734 in Dublin, died September 1796, aged sixty-two, Antigua, West Indies). Henry's father was a member of the Irish Parliament. His elder brother, Sackville Hamilton, served as undersecretary to the Lord Lieutenant of Ireland and as a privy counselor to the British king. Sackville had married Arabella Berkeley, and their son, Henry Berkeley, married the daughter of the 2nd Lord Longford. A sister married the Duke of Wellington, "Old Ironsides" himself.

Henry Hamilton was a British Army officer and a senior diplomatic official of the British Empire, fighting for his king during the American War of Independence and based in the British Northern Territories, the "modern-day" Canada.

Henry was a direct male bloodline descendant of Claude Hamilton, 1st Lord Paisley. Claude's father was the first cousin to James Hamilton of Silvertonhill Hill, ancestor to modern-day Alec Hamilton. Claude Hamilton's great-great-great-grandfather was Sir David Hamilton, the 3rd Baron Cadzow, whose brother Walter's son, David Hamilton, became the 1st Hamilton of Cambuskeith. As we established earlier, the Cambuskeith direct male bloodline descendants became the Hamiltons of Grange, leading directly to the Hamilton Founding Father. (See the family trees in this book). The Hamilton founding father, Henry Hamilton, Claude Hamilton, and the modern-day Alec Hamilton are all connected.

During America's French and Indian wars, Henry started his military career as a captain in the British Army's 15th Regiment of Foot. He was at the 1758 attack on Louisburg and the Battle of Quebec, Canada. As Canadian Hamiltons may know or be interested in, Henry rose to become a brigade major with the support of Guy Carleton, then the British Lieutenant Governor of Canada.

In 1775, after seventeen years in the Americas, Henry Hamilton sold his commission in the British Army to launch a diplomatic career in the region. In the same year, the British authorities appointed him Lieutenant Governor of Quebec and Superintendent of Indian Affairs. In the province of Quebec, he was posted to Fort Detroit, a posting he held for some four years. At this time, the province of British-governed Quebec stretched from the Atlantic Ocean of eastern Canada, known as British North America, down to Fort Detroit, which is today in the City of Detroit, Michigan in the Great Lakes region. The fort was situated north of the Rouge River. The American Revolutionary War was underway when, in 1778, Alexander Hamilton was appointed a captain of the artillery at age twenty-one.

Henry had very few regular troops, and to avoid conflict, cultivated good relations with the French Canadians and local Indigenous tribes on both sides of the "modern-day" border between Canada and America. He successfully built mutual trust with them, although not all the Indian tribes supported the British.

After Henry had received instructions from the British Army command to encourage and arm Indian tribes, they became supportive of the British. Henry's charge was to promote the attack and harassment of American settlements by friendly-to-Britain Indian tribes across revolutionary held territories. British raids occurred as far afield as in Kentucky, Pennsylvania, and Virginia. Henry Hamilton realized that to carry out such orders inevitably meant civilian casualties. To limit civilians being killed, Henry sent British and French-Canadian officers with the Indian war parties. It was an attempt to prevent such casualties, which sadly failed most of the time.

'Hair-Buyer Hamilton'

Tragically, in western Pennsylvania and Kentucky, hundreds of American settlers—men, women, and children—were slaughtered and brutally scalped by Henry Hamilton's Indian war parties. The British and Canadian officers could not stop the Indians, who once entering battle fell back on warrior pride to take scalps. Henry Hamilton was horrified; this was the last thing he wanted to happen. Thereafter, the American colonists and authorities nicknamed Henry "Hair-Buyer Hamilton," a name which somewhat unfairly stuck, and he noted that he was "sickened by the name and the scalping of people"

With continued raids from Henry's Quebec Militia and native Indian tribes across and into American patriot country, the American colonist Lieutenant Colonel George Rogers Clark took a stand. He demanded reprisals be made against the British. Clark called for his Virginia Militia to be permitted to attack the British forts of Kaskaskia, Cahokia, and Vincennes. He hoped that by taking these posts and eventually capturing Fort Detroit to better protect American settlers in Kentucky against Indian raids.

After Clark's rapid and daring campaign took the British by surprise, and he captured the British outposts of Kaskaskia, Cahokia, and Vincennes, Henry Hamilton called for a pre-emptive counterattack with 500 British regular troops, French Militia, and loyal Indian tribes. He planned to march to Fort Detroit (Michigan) and retake Vincennes and the fort that had been constructed there. Clark himself, with his American troops, had designed to move to capture Fort Sackville in Indiana. On his march to Fort Detroit, Henry Hamilton enlisted friendly Indian tribes to join and support him and the British and, with their help, hold Fort Sackville after that. He captured Fort Detroit on December 18, 1778, and he is said to have had the French townspeople take a new oath of allegiance to the British Crown.

Hamilton went on to Fort Sackville and stayed to hold it against an impending attack from the American colonists. His actions led to a daring counterattack by Clark, whose combined forces of American Militia and French volunteers who'd escaped Fort Detroit did, on February 25, 1779, take Fort Sackville quite quickly. As the Americans lay siege to the fort, it was clear to Henry Hamilton inside that he could no longer hold the post.

Henry Hamilton Surrenders

On the morning of February 25, Henry did not raise the British flag over the fort because he wanted to be spared the humiliation of taking it down in front of his enemies. He surrendered the fort and garrison to Clark and the American colonists. Clark would have sent a message about such a high-profile capture to General George Washington, and, likely, Alexander

Hamilton would have learned that a fellow clan member was his enemy. In a book on this lesser-known Hamilton of the American Revolutionary War, there is an image of him surrendering his sword and Fort Sackville to the American militia commander.

As the British Lieutenant Governor of Quebec, Superintendent of Indian Affairs, *and* the infamous "Hair-Buyer Hamilton," Henry Hamilton was quite a high-profile prisoner. Because he had allowed deadly Indian raids on their colonial settlers, the Virginians regarded him as a war criminal. Henry was not afforded the same treatment as a more conventional senior officer of war or an aristocratic gentleman. He was lucky, all the same, not to have been executed by the colonists. Many suspected that the possibility of using him for prisoner exchanges stopped his being executed. Henry Hamilton was sent to Williamsburg, Virginia, where, ironically, he was jailed and placed in irons by none other than Governor Thomas Jefferson, another future Founding Father of the United States of America.

In March 1781, having been kept in irons for nearly two years, Henry Hamilton was released in a prisoner exchange and deported to England. In that same year, Alexander Hamilton was by now an aide-de-camp to General Washington, as we've already heard. The surrender of Great Britain to George Washington happened in the same period that Henry was released from prison and on his way to England.

Henry Hamilton returned to Canada from London in 1782, again becoming Lieutenant-Governor of Quebec, although with earlier chunks of that territory, such as Indiana and the Michigan lake districts, under American colonist rule. In 1782, fighting in the American War of Independence ceased entirely. In September 1783, a formal treaty was signed, leading to the creation of the independent nation of the United States of America from the former British American colonies.

Now Baron Hamilton is about to have the answer to the question he put to the author. From 1785 -1794, Henry Hamilton served as Governor of Bermuda, and a British Royal Charter company managed the island until 1684 when it became a British Crown Colony. Its original capital was St. George's, founded in 1612, which had a reputation in later years of being too close to malaria-infested swampland. The government had set aside 145 acres (59 ha) for new future capital and a seat of power before Hamilton arrived. He oversaw the establishment of that town in 1790 and 1793 by an act of the British Parliament approved by the House of Lords. Today's Baron Hamilton now sits. The colony's new capital was officially approved and named Hamilton, after Henry Hamilton, then-governor who had done so much to help the cities establishment.

In 1794, Henry Hamilton was posted to Dominica, another island in the Caribbean, as governor. While still Governor of Dominica, he died on the island of Antigua while visiting it in 1796.

One Hamilton, Henry, fought for the British during the American Revolution and was jailed and kept in irons by another of America's future Founding Fathers, while the other Hamilton, Alexander, became a future Founding Father.

Hamilton Place Names

There are many places named for Hamiltons worldwide—Henry Hamilton was not the only Hamilton to have a city named after him. There is one in New Zealand and two in Canada. There are also twenty-two in the United States, the majority most likely named after the nation's Founding Father.

As one example, George Hamilton (1788–1836), a merchant son of a Scottish immigrant to Canada, was a soldier fighting with Canada's British colonists in the North America War of 1812–1815. George Hamilton was a captain in the Niagara Light Dragoons and fought in the Detroit Fort capture, which laid out a township in 1815 after the War with the United States—named Hamilton.

Alexander Hamilton Takes a Wife

While Hamilton was stationed in New Jersey over 1779 during the Revolutionary War, he met Elizabeth Schuyler, a daughter of General Philip Schuyler and Catherine, née Van Rensselaer. Just a year after meeting, Hamilton and Elizabeth were married on December 14, 1780, at the Schuyler family estate in Albany, New York, as the Revolutionary War raged around them.

Elizabeth, nicknamed Eliza, was born in August 1757, and she lived to be ninety-seven. Being of a wealthy Dutch family who first settled in British New York in the 1600s, she grew up around slavery, and her father owned many slaves. She later became a friend of George Washington's wife, as much as her husband was close friend of Washington.

Elizabeth and Alexander Hamilton had eight children, although there is often confusion because two of their sons were named Philip. That's because the younger Philip was named after his elder brother who had died in a duel, as we will read.

After her husband's untimely death, Eliza founded an orphanage and went on to help widows with small children.

After the American War of Independence

After the war and resigning his commission as a major general, Alexander Hamilton sought to enter and influence politics in the new nation. It needed to form a foundation by which it could govern itself going forward. In 1782, he was appointed to the new Congress of the Confederation as a New York City representative. So began his path in politics and in the government of the first presidency and beyond. Even though he may not have been recognized for all his contributions during his lifetime as he should have been.

Hamilton had been an avid proponent of the future United States Constitution. He believed in a federal government, a central administration, and federally controlled taxes, versus Thomas Jefferson's belief in stronger independent state governments. Hamilton is credited with founding the nation's financial system. As President George Washington's first Secretary of Treasury, he was the president's primary forger of monetary policy and established the first national federal bank. He was a leading negotiator with trade links to the new nation's former masters, the British Government, and he drafted tariffs, tax, and customs systems. What an extraordinary individual this man was. He was known to be dedicated and have a strong work ethic, focused feverishly on every project and writing prolifically.

The "Federalist" hands-off-each-state approach to government was considered weak by Hamilton, who led a movement calling for a Constitutional Convention and a more centralized government. He wrote over half the papers proposed to Congress, which today form reference to constitutional interpretation. As a member of President Washington's cabinet, Alexander was one of Washington's most trusted men. However, Hamilton's constant disagreements with Thomas Jefferson and John Adams caused Washington much anxiety.

America's First Government Sex Scandal

Alexander Hamilton has the dubious distinction of being the new nation's first senior government figure to be caught in a major sex scandal. His extra-marital affair started in 1791 and became a public scandal eight years later, in 1799. It had all the hallmarks of a modern-day political sex scandal with a key government minister. A husband-and-wife team blackmailed him, and he paid hush money. Allegations were made against him for corruption, and the only way he could prove these were lies, was to come clean on the extra-marital affair, so he did as he was seen as straight as an arrow with the finances of the nation.

This scandal wrecked Hamilton's chances of becoming the future president of the nation, potentially its second president behind his career mentor, general, and now president, George Washington. In 1791, a Mrs. Maria Reynolds had approached Alexander Hamilton at his family home in the country, in Philadelphia. A fine-looking blonde, twenty-three-year-old woman, she sought his help, as her husband had abandoned her and her child, and she was destitute. She expressed that she needed help to get her back to New York and to stay above complete destitution and feed her child. Later that same evening, Hamilton took a thirty-dollar check (called a note-bill) to her boarding house. Maria invited him upstairs, and their sexual relationship began.

It is surprising, considering Hamilton's exemplary military and government career and loyal behavior, that he should have become involved in an affair and put himself in the position of being blackmailed. He soon realized that Maria was in cahoots with her husband and that he'd been set up, as it wasn't long before Maria wrote him a letter, on December 15, advising that her husband had become aware of the affair. Duly, the following day he received a letter from Maria's husband, James Reynolds, who proposed to Hamilton that if he paid him $1,000 (about $28,800 today, or £20,000), he would leave town with his daughter forever, and Hamilton could carry on his affair with Maria. He was demanding $1,000 not to publicize the affair.

Hamilton paid the money in two parts assured that he'd never hear from his blackmailers again. However, in time, his blackmailers wanted more money, and Hamilton paid, but by February 1792, he said enough was enough and ended the affair. The total he'd paid to keep his affair silent came to around $1,300 in all. Until now, the affair was totally unknown to the American people.

James Reynolds, the conspiratorial husband, and an associate, Jacob Clingman, were later arrested on counterfeiting and other charges about claiming
dead war veterans' back pay. Clingman was released on bail, and in November
1792, seeking to get his friend out of jail, he decided to break the news of
Hamilton's affair. Clingman told the then US Senator from Virginia (and
future fifth president of the USA), James Monroe, that Reynolds had evidence
to incriminate Hamilton, Treasury Secretary of the nation, in wrongful and
corrupt financial dealings.

In company with Congressman Abraham Venable and Frederick Muhlen-
berg, First Speaker of the House, Senator James Monroe confronted Hamilton with the charges and letters from Hamilton that Maria Reynolds had
given Monroe. To the surprise of Monroe and the two others, Hamilton
shared more than they expected. At that moment, Hamilton chose honesty
and integrity to the nation and his president over his career, knowing that
what he was about to tell Monroe would clear his name of wrongdoing in
any financial dealings. However, to do so, he'd need to come clean about his
extra-marital affair and shred any chance of one-day becoming president.
Hamilton evidenced his innocence in illicit dealings but shared the truth
about his extra-marital affair, which had led to bribery and blackmail, evidenced by Reynold's letter and his payments from his bank account. The
three men left satisfied that Hamilton was innocent of all wrongdoing other
than adultery and gave Hamilton their word to keep the matter confidential.

The Future President Broke His Word

James Monroe claims he gave some of the information to a Congressional
Clerk to transcribe and claimed that the clerk informed Thomas Jefferson,
Hamilton's long-time adversary. Whether this is true, or Monroe told Thomas
Jefferson to cause trouble directly, Jefferson set off a whisper-mongering campaign in Washington. After a while, Hamilton quietly stood down from the
cabinet, withdrew from other government posts and committees, and decided
to take up his law practice again. Hamilton was succeeded as Secretary of
the Treasury by Oliver Wolcott Jnr. on January 31, 1795. Yet this scandal
was still not public knowledge, nor did his wife yet know of it.

Hamilton had cleared his name of any government or financial wrongdoing and retained his reputation as an honest man, although exposing his

adulterous affair ruined his chances at the prize of the presidency. He had spectacularly shot himself in the foot.

In 1797, after he told his wife of the matter, he wrote a pamphlet of his affair for release to the American people. Hamilton evidenced in this newssheet that his payments to James Reynolds were not linked to treasury misappropriation of funds but to his being blackmailed. His reputation in the eyes of everyday Americans was maintained as an honest man. His wife, Elizabeth, moved out of their home. They separated for around a year; however, she eventually forgave him and moved back to share their lives.

Supporting Haiti's Revolution Against France

Meanwhile, in August 1791, six years earlier than Hamilton was too out himself to the American people over his sex scandal, together with his fellow Federalists in Washington, placed his support behind a full-blown slave revolution on the Caribbean island of Haiti. What had originated as a slave revolt against what was now the French Republic became a significant clash for France, and the British Navy lent support to the Haitian's. It is somewhat ironic that the revolution in France (instigated in 1789 and concluded in 1799), which had deposed and executed their king for a government of the people, should fight to keep slaves in bondage in Haiti.

Later, Hamilton called for the mobilization of American troops against the French Republic over what he saw as a dishonorable long-drawn-out game of negotiations by the French Republic and a waste of time. He became active in helping to bring legislation that would see the end of slavery in America at the same time.

Hamilton's suggestions to the Haitian revolutionaries helped the Haitian constitution when Haiti became the first independent black nation in the Western world in January 1804. Hamilton urged closer economic and diplomatic ties with Haiti but tragically was to die in July that same year.

Hamilton's Growing Advocacy to End Slavery

From the 1780s, Alexander opposed pro-slavery southern interests, which he saw as defeating the values of the revolution. He believed firmly that every human being should be free, regardless of color, race, or religion. He now clearly was anti-slavery, and his childhood and past experiences no doubt spurred him to accept that slavery could not be correct—this no one can deny Hamilton.

Hamilton proactively promoted the abolition of the international slave trade in New York City, and shortly after his death, the city passed a law to end slavery. After that, a decades-long process of emancipation ensued, which finally saw the ending of slavery in the state on July 4, 1827, fifty-one years after independence. It took another 140 years to see the segregation of people of color outlawed, mainly those descended from African slaves, and full voting rights for all in the USA only came in the mid-1960s.

Hamilton Named Commander-in-Chief

On December 14, 1799, Hamilton was named Senior Officer of the United States Army, taking over the role from George Washington back in the position of Commander-in-Chief of the army again. Hamilton was, however, the Commander-in-Chief for just 6-months – cut short by his unexpected death.

The Deadly Duel

The French Republic had accused the new nation of America of not paying loans back, which the previous Kingdom of France had given to support it gain freedom from Great Britain. Now France threatened war. Hamilton became commanding general of the newly reconstituted US Army, which he modernized and readied for battle. Hamilton's army never saw combat, and Hamilton was outraged by Adams' diplomacy in the conflict with France. He opposed Adams' re-election, and much of his rhetoric and accusations against his opponents helped cause the Federalist party's defeat in 1800. This led to Aaron Burr and Thomas Jefferson seemingly being tied in the race for the presidency in 1801. Hamilton helped defeat Burr, whom he found unprincipled, and he said so publicly and loudly. Like in the game of Roulette, Hamilton had placed his chips on the board and made his bet, mother nature had called, *Plus de paris, s'il vous plait* (no more bet's), and everyone waited for the Roulette wheel to stop.

Vice President Burr ran for Governor of New York State in 1804, and Hamilton again actively worked against him and said publicly for all to hear that Burr was unworthy. Taking offense, Burr challenged Hamilton to a duel.

On July 11, 1804, early on a Wednesday morning, Hamilton was rowed across the Hudson River from New York City (very different from the "modern-day" massive city, of course), accompanied by his physician and dear friend, Nathan Pendleton. Nathan would be Hamilton's "second" in the duel. Imagine the scene, with likely an early morning mist silently wafting across the river and clinging to the grassy banks and woodland. The duel was to take place in a clearing on the Weehawken side of the river, and Alexander's destiny awaited him.

On the eve of the duel, he had written to his wife, making it clear that he intended to waste his shot and shoot high to serve his honor by taking part in the duel and give satisfaction to Burr. Therefore, neither was to die, as he certainly had no intention of leaving his loving wife and family over the illegal practice of dueling, which he did not believe in either.

An eerie sense of foreboding may have gripped Hamilton and others as their boat silently slipped across the Hudson with no sound but the oars clipping the water. July in New York typically sees temperatures in the upper eighties Fahrenheit (early 30c) with high humidity; hence, an early morning duel would have worked best in that climate.

Much debate ensues to this day as to whether Alexander shot first and deliberately high or was hit first by Burr, and his shot went high as he fell. Either way, he was mortally wounded, as Burr had certainly aimed to kill. It's said that Alexander Hamilton died in great pain at a friend's house, where he'd been carried after the fatal shot. The discharge lodged a steel ball in his abdomen, fractured a rib, and likely damaged significant organs, such as his kidneys.

Alexander Hamilton, a Founding Father of America, Dead

On July 12, 1804, Alexander died tragically at age forty-seven. In a twist of fate, the duel was close to the same spot on the Weehawken bank of the Hudson River where the life of Hamilton's eldest son, Philip, had ended three years earlier. As a wife and mother, Elizabeth had to live with such losses. Burr ran away from New York immediately and laid low for quite some time. He was never brought to justice for dueling in breach of the law, even when he returned to New York. Some have often queried why there is one rule for the people and another for the rulers. He should have faced justice, his opponents maintained.

After Hamilton's death, Elizabeth commenced the preservation of his legacy. Organizing Alexander's letters, papers, and writings with her son, John Church Hamilton, she finally published them as a biography. It was the first of many to be written about her extraordinary husband. With help from the Scottish Government Archive department, the modern-day Alexander Hamilton's wife, Erica Hamilton, started documenting these last three years or so, all the essential documents, memorabilia, and historical family records in Alec's possession to preserve them for future generations and give access to historians.

Despite his infidelity, Elizabeth was so devoted to her husband's memory that she wore a locket around her neck containing a sonnet that Alexander had written for her during the early days of their courtship. The early 1800s were a difficult time for Elizabeth, as her mother had died, one of her sisters and one brother had died, she'd lost a son in a duel, and then lost her husband in the same way. A few months later, her father died. The grief that Elizabeth Hamilton had to bear was overwhelming, losing five immediate family members in quick succession, two to duels.

The Grange in America is the only home Alexander Hamilton ever owned. It was built on Hamilton's thirty-two-acre country estate, called Hamilton Heights, in upper Manhattan. In 1802 when the house was complete, Hamilton named it "The Grange" after the ancestral family estate in Scotland. Great things were achieved by many of Alexander's eight children.

Hamilton's Children Left Behind

Alexander and Elizabeth had eight children, six of whom were boys. Full research summaries are available to Alec's family or those interested. The author shares brief highlights of only these children, born between 1782–1802.

Philip (1782–1801) attended Columbia College like his father, and as did at least three of his brothers. Tragically in 1801, he challenged George Eacker to a duel over a slight to his father by a Burr supporter. While dueling by this time was illegal in nearby New Jersey, it was quietly accepted in New York. This saw Philip mortally wounded, just as his father would be three years later. Philip died invincible in his mind, I am sure, at only nineteen years of age—proud, strong, a young man of honor, with his whole life ahead of him.

What a tragedy and devastation for his parents.

Angelica (1784–1857) and Eliza (1799–1859). Angelica suffered a complete mental breakdown after her brother's death. She died at aged seventy-two, and her sister Eliza died two years later.

Britain's General Wellington, and the Hamilton Son

Alexander Junior (1786–1875), who joined his elder brother Philip at his first boarding school in Trenton and studied at Columbia before leaving without graduating. He is a child not to be passed over quickly is their third child.

Alexander Junior went on to learn and practice law before sailing to Spain at the beginning of 1811, where he joined British General Wellington's forces, fighting against Napoleon's armies in Portugal. At this time, Wellington was a viscount, as stated in the *London Gazette* on August 26 (not yet a duke): "The King has been pleased to grant the Dignities of Baron and Viscount of the United Kingdoms of Great Britain and Ireland unto the Right Honorable Sir Arthur Wellesley, Knight of the Most Honorable Order of the Bath, and Lieutenant-General of His Majesty's Forces." Wellington continued to take on the French in Portugal, Spain, and France for some five years.

At least nineteen battles, skirmishes, and sieges were waged by Wellington when Alexander Hamilton Junior was part of Wellington's Peninsular Wars. I am sure that the younger Hamilton must have taken part in many, of which six saw Wellington defeated, and four neither army won. These wars saw Wellington and his troops winning nine significant battles all the same. After nearly two years Alexander Junior is believed to have spent with Wellington's army in Portugal, he returned to America and received a commission as a captain in the newly formed United States Army, joining an infantry regiment.

Fresh with his own combat experience in Europe fighting for the English, at the end of 1812, he now took part in fighting against the English on American soil. It strikes many as somewhat ironic that the son of a Founding Father of the United States of America, who fought against the English in the American Revolution, fought for the English in the European Peninsular Wars.

After the War of 1812, Alexander Junior returned to law, became a government attorney for part of Florida, received the military rank of colonel, and was elected to the House of Representatives for Florida. Fate would enable him to take on his father's old enemy, Aaron Burr, when he became the attorney prosecuting divorce proceedings against Burr by Aaron's wife, which closed after some two years due to Burr's death.

James Alexander (1788–1878), served during the 1812 War as brigade major of the New York Militia. He later served President Andrew Jackson as Secretary of State of the United States, a cabinet-level post like his father had held, and he served as US Attorney for the Southern District of New York.

John Church (1792–1882), took part in the 1812 War as a young lieutenant and aide-de-camp to Major General William Harrison, just as his father had been to George Washington. Harrison was another future president of the United States. Two of John's sons fought in the American Civil War that was to follow—one as a general, one as a lieutenant colonel—and a third son fought in the Mexican War and reached a captain's rank. A fourth son fought in two Indian wars in the mid-West and attained the rank of colonel in the militia. Later, he wrote a seven-volume biography of his father, Alexander Hamilton, and published, after her death, a biography of his mother, Elizabeth.

William Stephen Hamilton (1797–1850), attended West Point Military Academy and, before graduation, resigned and served in two Indian wars. He reached the rank of colonel in the Illinois Militia, dying most likely in the cholera outbreak in Sacramento, California in October 1850.

Philip Hamilton (1802–1884) was the final son of Alexander and Elizabeth Hamilton. Known as Little Phil, he was named after his older brother and was carried in his mother's womb when Philip, the elder, was killed in the duel. Without a college education, he went into the law and raised himself to assistant US Attorney under his brother James, the US Attorney. By the end of the Civil War, he had become a judge advocate of the Naval Retiring Board. As his father had become a staunch abolitionist, he is believed to have sheltered at least one slave until they could escape to Canada, and likely dozens more.

Judge Philip Hamilton married a lady named Rebecca McLane, daughter of Senator Louis McLane. The senator had served as Secretary of the Treasury as Philip's father had, and Secretary of State for President Andrew Jackson.

Alexander Hamilton's Grandson, and General George Custer

Louis M. Hamilton (b. July 2nd, 1844–d. November 27th, 1868) was Philip and Rebecca Hamilton's son, and Alexander Hamilton, the Founding Father's grandson, though Alexander died before Louis was born. Louis's brother, Allan, was a professor of psychiatry at Cornel Medical College and founded the New York Psychiatry Society. He wrote the biography of his grandfather, *The Intimate Life of Alexander Hamilton*, in 1910.

At just eighteen years of age, with some family arm twisting of contacts, Louis was commissioned as a second-lieutenant of infantry and took part in five major Civil War battles by May 1864. These battles included the famous Battle of Gettysburg, by which time he'd been made a first lieutenant. By July 1866, Louis had become the youngest captain in the regular American army when he joined the famous 7th Cavalry under General George Custer. Custer was to become renowned, dying in the Indian massacre of Little Bighorn in the battle scorched in American history annals as "Custer's Last Stand" in 1876. This was twelve years after Louis' last fight.

On November 27, Captain Louis Hamilton was assigned officer of the day by General Custer, riding on his left. They approached the Cheyenne Indian camp on the Washita River in Roger Mills County, Oklahoma, and the ensuing battle became known as the Battle of Washita. Captain Hamilton was placed by Custer to command the initial cavalry charge into Chief Kettle's village by the riverbank. As he led his troop off, he was heard to shout to his men before they broke into a gallop and charged into the village: "Keep cool, fire low, and not too rapidly." He was almost immediately struck and killed by a bullet through the heart. A postmortem after the battle, which Custer won, confirmed that Louis would have died instantly, and he was buried at their nearby camp. Later his body was reburied in Poughkeepsie, NY, where his parents had raised him.

Most of America's Founding Fathers' Collective Support of Slavery

Fourteen of the twenty-one key Founding Fathers of America held slaves: Thomas Jefferson, Benjamin Franklin, George Washington, John Hancock,

James Madison, Patrick Henry, Charles Carroll, Samuel Chase, Button Gwinnett, John Jay, Richard Lee, Charles Pinkney, Benjamin Rush, and Edward Rutledge. *Alexander Hamilton, John Adams, Samuel Adams, Oliver Ellsworth, Robert Paine, and Roger Sherman did not keep slaves.*

The Proclamation emancipating 4.9 million enslaved Africans came into being by the end of December 1865. The Thirteenth Amendment was ratified by Congress twelve months later, some three years after first being announced by President Lincoln. He never got to see the mass freedom of slaves as in April 1865; he was assassinated.

The earlier Emancipation Proclamation during the Civil War only applied to Confederate states in 1863 and did not apply to the 500,000 enslaved Africans in Lincoln's own Union states, which came later.

Washington Dies the Same Year as Hamilton

In the same year, 1799 that George Washington handed over his post as Commander-in-Chief of the army to Alexander Hamilton, he had become an advocate in support of Hamilton to end slavery and called to free all enslaved persons, it was the year the French monarchy fell. Yet, he'd been a slave owner from the age of eleven when his father died, and he inherited ten slaves. Later he purchased eight more slaves and when he married, his wife brought with her 84 slaves, which became Washington's property. His slaves were whipped and another form of punishment for wrongdoing, separated from their families for a period of time.

In Office, Washington pursued laws to track down and punish escaped slaves many historians have written. At his death that same year as Hamilton, but on December 14, 1799, Washington owned 123 slaves at his property, Mount Vernon. While he declared in his last Will & Testament that upon his death, his slaves were to be freed but were Martha's to decide during her lifetime. She did free one slave, William Lees who had become a revolutionary war hero but had no intent on freeing the remainder, she was committed to slavery as her right. It was about a year later when 'his slaves' became restless and a fire at Mount Vernon and rumors of a plot to poison her occurred from these people, that she freed George Washington's slaves in January, 1801.

However, she still personally owned 153 slaves she had inherited post her marriage and when she died on May 22, 1802 some 16-months after her husband. There seemed absolutely no suggestion for her to free her slaves. All 153 of her slaves were left in her Last Will & Testament to be distributed to her two Custis children she brought to her marriage with George, as a widow from her first, and she also bequeathed at least one slave to a grandson. Neither of Martha Washington's Custis children freed those slaves.

Jefferson's – "Ship Freed Slaves Back to Africa" Proposal

Thomas Jefferson, another Founding Father of America, advocated removing all freed slaves in the south and north to sparsely populated western US territories, or proposed shipping them back to Africa.

Some have said that the new nation's economy would collapse altogether if the freed slaves, now with the right to earn a living, did not form the backbone of the workforce of paid laborers, but as free men, they chose what work they did and where they lived. Shipping them back to Africa or creating a "ghetto state," as we may term it today, would not help them let go of the shackles of slavery to build equality and success for all, and it would not allow the new nation to grow. Leading lights were clear that the new government needed everyone, regardless of their color or race, to pull together.

Thomas Jefferson, who wanted to get rid of all these freed African slaves, became the third president of the United States, from 1801–1809. Alexander Hamilton pressed for emancipation without any such provisions and denounced slavery as morally wrong. Hamilton would have made a great president and moved forward the cause of true freedom for African Americans.

A typical sugar plantation mill across the West Indies in the 1700s during America's Founding Father, Alexander Hamilton's, days living in Nevis (NCA).

An antique map of Nevis. Alexander Hamilton, Founding Father of America, birthplace. Captain Horatio Nelson was stationed here in the 1780s (NCA).

The Storming of Redoubt No.10 by Alexander Hamilton on October 14, 1781, painted by Eugene Lami, 1840. General Washington's decisive battle that soon saw the end of the Revolution with the British leaving America (CE).

General George Washington, Commander-in-Chief, and aide-de-camp, now Major-General Alexander Hamilton, the American War of Independence. (CE).

A mural at the George Rogers Clark Memorial National Historical Park (CE). British Lieutenant Governor Henry Hamilton surrenders the British held Fort Sackville at Vincennes, Indiana on February 25, 1779, to Lieutenant Colonel George Rogers Clark of the Virginia militia. The American Revolutionary War.

British Lieutenant Governor Henry Hamilton of the Province of Quebec, covering Michigan lake district and Indiana, also. c. 1734–September 29, 1796 (CE).

Alexander Hamilton as Secretary of the US Treasury under President George Washington (CE).

Alexander's wife, Elizabeth
Hamilton, née Schuyler, by
Robert Earl, c. 1787, Museum of
the City of New York. (CE).

Phillip Hamilton, Alexander and
Elizabeth's dashingly handsome
eldest son, who died in a duel
aged nineteen, defending his
father's honor (CE).

Chapter 5

GENERAL SIR IAN STANDISH
MONTEITH HAMILTON

British honors granted by his Sovereign: Knight Grand Cross of the Order
of the Bath (GCB); Knight Grand Cross of the Order of the St. Michael and
St George (GCMG); Distinguished Service Order Territorial Decoration
(DSO, TD), and Lieutenant of the Tower of London. Honors bestowed
by foreign Monarchs: Order of Red Eagle (Prussia), Order of the Crown
(Prussia), Order of the Sacred Treasure (Japan), Order of Merit (Spain),
and he was made Rector of the University of Edinburgh by that institution.

This man lived through the reigns of Great Britain's Queen Victoria, King
Edward VII, and King George V.

Ian was one of the family's more fascinating members, especially as he had
a massive influence on Alec. His great-nephew saw him as a family hero who
took part in or first-hand witnessed many of the most significant battles
and wars that straddle the boundary of two centuries of the British Empire.
He experienced the Empire's height and decline, an Empire that rules other
nations no more. He fought in the Second Anglo-Afghan War of 1878 in
India and Afghanistan, the First Boer War from 1881 in South Africa, and
the Mahdist War in Sudan.

Ian also served in the Northwest Frontier War of India in the 1890s, the
Second Boer War, witnessed Japanese maneuvers ahead of the Russo-Japanese
War in 1904, and took part in the First World War from July 1914. The
'Great War,' as it was called, ended on the 11th hour of the 11th day of
the 11th month of 1918. In its wake, 17.6 million people had died, and
multiple European empires had been swept away while revolution broke
out in several nations.

Ian Standish Monteith Hamilton, his nephew, Alec's father, and Alec's brother were all called Ian, so to distinguish the three of them, Sir Ian was known as Big Ian. The future Sir Ian is someone who stands out in this branch of the Hamilton tree, and it is a little amusing that his nickname was Big Ian, as in reality he was a relatively small man in height.

His Early Life and Family

Big Ian's military career formed the bulk of his life, so let us first read about his early years. Ian Standish Monteith Hamilton was born in Corfu in the Mediterranean Ionian islands on January 16, 1853, and he died in England aged ninety-four on October 12, 1947. HRH Prince Philippos of Greece and Denmark, later to marry the future queen of England and become HRH Prince Philip, Duke of Edinburgh, was also born in Corfu.

Big Ian's father (Alec's great-grandfather) was Lieut. Colonel Christian Monteith Hamilton (1825–1885), commanding officer of the 92nd Highlanders regiment, which in 1861 was granted the right to ad the Gordon to its name. By 1881 the 92nd Gordon Highlanders Regiment of Foot, amalgamated with the 75th Regiment of Foot to form the Gordon Highlanders.

Sir Ian's mother, the Honorable Corinna Vereker, was the 3rd Viscount Gort's daughter, and her grandfather was John Prendergast Vereker (July 1, 1790–October 20, 1865), an Irish peer and politician. Viscount Gort was a Member of Parliament for Limerick in Ireland and later mayor of that city, eventually taking his seat in the House of Lords. Alec Hamilton was christened with a forename, Vereker, in honor of his great-grandmother's family.

Tragically, Sir Ian's mother (Alec's great-grandmother) died on July 20 after giving birth to his younger brother, Vereker, on February 14, 1856, in Corfu, where her husband was stationed. Ian was just three years old. On the same day his mother died, her sister, Julia, died in Dublin in Ireland. Ian's father, Colonel Hamilton's mother, died after his birth also, quite a tragic history of children growing up having never known their mother.

Ian Hamilton's early education was at Cheam School in Surrey, the most expensive private school in England, and soon became a feeder school for boys going on to Eton. HRH Prince Charles attended Cheam some ninety 94-years after Ian Hamilton had enrolled there.

Ian went from Cheam to Wellington College, Berkshire (named after the Duke of Wellington), before attending the Royal Military College, Sandhurst, in 1870 to complete his army officer training. He was then sent by his father to stay in Dresden, Germany, with General von Dammers, a Hanoverian military man who had fought against Prussia. Dammers had commanded the Hanoverian Army in the Austro-Prussian War; a battle lost to the Prussians. After this decisive battle, the reign of King George V of Hanover ceased, and with the entire Hanoverian royal court in September 1866, they had then been exiled out of the kingdom. Until the king's death, Dammers remained aide-de-camp to the exiled and crest-fallen King George of Hanover in the Kingdom of Saxony's key city of Dresden, where they had been given asylum. To Ian's father, this was the best possible man to educate his son in all things military.

Interestingly, General von Dammers' father was of Danish descent and had fought at the Battle of Waterloo on June 18, 1815, in the 3rd Hanoverian Brigade under a British Colonel H. Halkett. The 3rd Hanoverian Brigade was attached to a British division supporting the Duke of Wellington's far-right and were kept in reserve for much of the day. When Wellington knew the time was right, he sent this fresh Brigade into battle against the exhausted French troops as he saw that the defeat of Napoleon was close.

At the age of seventeen in 1870, Ian spent six months with General Dammers in Dresden. Hamilton traveled to Germany with an armed escort, as the region was in the early days of the July 1870 – January 1871 Franco-Prussian War which, lasted just over six months. Prussia leading the North German Confederation, sought to crush the French Empire/Republican state, having destroyed today's German states of Hanover and others.

In one of his stories, Big Ian, when visiting Scotland in retirement, mentioned to Alec that he had to be escorted to Dresden and General Dammers via Hamburg and Berlin to avoid active battlefields en-route. The Franco-Prussian War was in full swing during those two years. During his time in Dresden, Ian was taught by one of the best military men of his age about military tactics, surveying, drawing, army organization, provisioning, keeping supply lines open, and even astronomy. He was also tutored heavily in German at Dammer's request.

Ian left Germany fluent in the language and apparently with a high-Deutsch accent, a sort of German version of speaking the Queen's English is how it can best be described. This German fluency was to stand him in great stead later as a general in the British Army, visiting the Kaiser before the First World War, and indeed useful during it. Sir Ian must have shared these stories on his last visit to Scotland about a year before he died in 1947; Alec would have been about age fourteen. As Alec said to me, such stories stay in your mind.

The exiled King George of Hanover's father was Ernst Augustus, King of Hanover, the British Duke of Cumberland. This king was himself the son of the British King George III (uncle to Queen Victoria of England), who carried the title of King of Hanover. The Kings of Hanover also inherited the Hanoverian title of Duke of Brunswick-Lüneburg, and the Electorate and Kingdom of Saxony lands were part of the German Empire under Germany's Kaiser or Emperor. After World War Two, Saxony fell under East German Communist rule and was abolished as a State in 1952 until German unification in 1990.

Some seven years after leaving Dammers and returning to England, in 1887, Ian married Jean Muir, a prosperous Glasgow businessman's daughter. Seemingly unable to have children of their own, they later adopted two. Their adopted son was to tragically die in action in North Africa in 1941 in World War Two, as so many did, and just weeks later, Jean, Lady Hamilton, Ian's wife, passed away. It was a massive double blow to lose his son and wife simultaneously when he was eighty-eight in the twilight years, his lifetime military career behind him.

The celebrated author, biographer, military, and Churchill historian, Celia Lee, published her biography of the wife of General Sir Ian Hamilton, entitled: *Jean, Lady Hamilton, 1861–1941: Diaries of a Soldier's Wife*. It is an excellent read and assists in understanding more fully the life of Sir Ian, which the author broadly summarizes in this book.

Sir Ian was fluent in English, German, French, and Hindi. Alec said that he rarely saw him but remembered him as a fascinating man to a young boy, who was efficient at everything he turned his hand to. He was clearly used to commanding and being in charge, was charming, kind, generous, and a jolly good shot. Ian retained a confident soldierly and courtly bearing and often shared stories of his life's adventures. The head of a tiger Sir Ian shot in India, which he had stuffed, sat in the entry hall of Alec's house in Scotland (and a photograph of it is in this book, along with a photo of the hunt camp).

At the time, tigers were esteemed trophies of bravery. Tiger hunts in the days of the Raj were the continuity of sport practiced by the Indian nobility for centuries, with the British immersing themselves in it after taking over the ruling of India. Game shooting in India at the time was a way of keeping a soldier's keen eye and ability to shoot accurately under fear and stress. In this era, there was an unlimited abundance of such wild animals, or so it seemed. We must remember that the 1800s were a hundred years before wildlife conservation became a realization essential to wild animal survival. The same applied to elephants, as no one ever foresaw their numbers dwindling. How quickly man has nearly driven them both close to extinction in less than 150 years.

His Early Military Career

When young Hamilton attended the Royal Military College, Sandhurst, in 1870, it was the first-year men entered Sandhurst officers' training by regulated academic examination rather than purchasing or buying an officer's commission. When he graduated in 1871, he received a commission as an infantry officer with the Suffolk Regiment. Not long afterward, he asked for and was granted a transfer to The Gordon Highlanders and assigned to the 2nd Battalion.

As they were serving on Imperial Garrison duty in India once he joined the regiment, it was clear that's where he would be sent to join the battalion. Once he arrived, Hamilton threw himself with enthusiasm into what was the Second Anglo-Afghan War. During the Afghan War, he nearly lost his sight from a shell exploding close to him and was twice mentioned in dispatches and awarded the Afghan War Medal with two clasps.

While serving in Afghanistan, Sir Ian met his long-term mentor, General Sir Frederick Roberts, who commanded the British Army in India's Northwest Frontier. Over the next thirty years, Roberts became Britain's most famous soldier of the age and never lost the opportunity to support Hamilton in his rise up the ladder.

At the time of his retirement, Sir Ian lived through World War Two, and 'goodness, what an extraordinary military career and life,' as his great-nephew, Alec, remarked.

Ian Hamilton, and General Charles Gordon

Before Ian had embarked for Bombay some years earlier, Gordon was about to leave for Cairo to lead British support of the Egyptian Army under its khedive (ruler)—where he would become Britain's hero of the Sudan.

Gordon read in the 1871 *Army Gazette* of a young officer named Ian Hamilton, who like Gordon had been born in Corfu. The *Gazette* listed Ian as being transferred with the Gordon Highlanders and about to depart for India. Gordon wrote to Hamilton to invite him to meet him in Gravesend, on the east coast of England, where he was due to leave for Cairo. Having heard of the reputation of the famous "Chinese Gordon," who had contained and managed the situation with the Emperor of China and subdued China's Army when stationed there, he genuinely saw Gordon as a hero. Ian gladly accepted and made his way at once to Gravesend.

Gordon, the son of an artillery officer, had fought in the Crimea war, was promoted to captain in 1859, and volunteered to join the British forces fighting the Chinese. In 1860, Gordon took part in Peking's occupation and personally directed the burning of the Chinese Emperor's summer palace. His engineers strengthened the European trading center of Shanghai's bulwarks to defend it during the Taiping Rebellion. He then became commander of a 3,500-man Chinese peasant force to defend Peking. When he returned to England in 1865, the press had already been dubbed him "Chinese Gordon," which is how his nickname came about.

Gordon and Hamilton had amicable meetings in Gravesend in England, which sits on the River Thames and is a secondary port down from Tilbury going out from there into the North Sea. Gordon wished Ian well as they parted after a few days and told him that if he could ever do anything for him, he was to let him know. Eleven years later, Ian Hamilton was part of the relief force on its way to Khartoum to rescue Major-General Gordon.

The First Boer War

MAJUBA HILL

Ian Hamilton was present at the decisive final battle of the First Boer War, the Battle of Majuba Hill, on February 27, 1881, which the Boers won. Historically, it was one of the British Army's most humiliating defeats.

When a mere subaltern during the height of the battle on a mountain top flat plateau, Ian Hamilton ran up to his commanding officer and asked, "Forgive my presumption, sir, but will you let the Gordon Highlanders charge with the bayonet?" With icy calm and approving reply, the general was heard to say, "No presumption, young gentleman. We'll let them charge us; then we'll give them a volley and charge." This is the battle in which Ian was shot through the wrist, severely damaging it and later taken prisoner.

When apprehended, he refused to give up his officer's sword, which had been given to him by his father. Just as the Boer officer was losing patience with him, General Joubert, commander-in-chief of the Boers, who had heard the exchange, walked up to him and permitted him to retain his sword on trust that as a gentleman he would not use it against them while a prisoner.

The injury to his hand was quite severe and badly damaged the use of his fingers He always referred to the paralyzed fingers of that shot hand as "my glorious deformity from Majuba." Once released by the Boers, Ian was shipped home to Scotland to recover, aided by his brother Vereker, who came out to escort him home, as we'll read in his brother's account in the next chapter. He was welcomed as a hero, was presented to HM Queen Victoria, and awarded the Afghanistan War Medal and mentioned in dispatches twice. Sir Ian is a man who served Queen and Country under Prime Minister Gladstone early in his military career and ended that career under King George V and Prime Minister Asquith. He lived under the reigns of five British monarchs and was an active soldier in three of them.

General Gordon and the Siege of Khartoum, in the Sudan

A year later, in 1882, and now recovered from his shattered wrist, Ian was promoted to the rank of captain and joined the British Army in Egypt in the Nile Expedition of 1884— the expedition to relieve the siege of Khartoum and General Gordon by the Sudanese leader Muhammad Ahmad "the Mahdi" in the Egyptian-colonially administered Sudan.

But though the expedition was to see repeated action on its way along the Nile, they arrived just two days too late. Khartoum had fallen and General Gordon, his brave Egyptian army soldiers, and thousands of civilians were dead. After a brief gun battle with the Mahdist defenders and having satisfied himself that both Gordon and the entire garrison were dead or lost and that he could not take on the army of the victorious Mahdi's full force, Lord Beresford, leading the relief advance with Captain Ian Hamilton in tow, ordered a tactical retreat downriver. Soon afterward, the Mahdi himself abandoned Khartoum and later created a new capital city of Sudan, at Omdurman.

The Gods Aligned

A fantastic coincidence occurred, a moment linking Ian Hamilton and his fallen hero, whom Hamilton did not forget all his life. With only two days to reach Khartoum, Ian had written home to his brother, Vereker, with his news that they were now close to rescuing the garrison and Gordon. Ian handed his letter to the postmaster in the town where they had stopped on the Nile to take on final provisions for their journey's final leg. The postmaster stamped his letter received at 6:00 a.m. on January 26—the day and hour that Khartoum's hero, General Gordon, was murdered, Ian arriving with the relief army two days too late in Khartoum. "God works in mysterious ways, as the saying goes." Ian Hamilton, in his retirement years, told Alec. "To arrive just two days too late to help save Gordon was personally devastating."

The Aftermath of Losing General Gordon at Khartoum

The British press blamed Gordon's death squarely on Prime Minister Gladstone, charged with deliberate and excessive slowness in sending relief to Khartoum, hampering Gordon by refusing earlier troop requests, and thereby losing pride of Empire. Gladstone was also soundly rebuked by Queen Victoria in a telegram, which became known to the public. His government fell shortly afterward. Isn't that karma at work?

Gladstone had always viewed the Egyptians as ruling with rough colonial behavior over the Sudanese. He had an open distaste for them, treating them as inferior people, it has been said, and once declared in the British House of Commons, "Yes, those people are struggling to be free, and they are rightly struggling to be free." Gordon acted towards Gladstone with superior-officer arrogance, and Gladstone felt this insubordinate manner, as he described it. A mere general had publicly challenged the prime minister and ultimately paid for it with his life.

The Nile Expedition of 1884–1885 Closes

For outstanding service and bravery shown throughout the campaign, Captain Ian Hamilton was promoted to the rank of brevet major and mentioned in dispatches. He was awarded the campaign medal with two clasps and the Khedive of Egypt's Star. Brevet is a title previously used in both the British and American armies. It denoted a commissioned officer given a higher rank as a reward for conspicuous gallantry or meritorious conduct in the field, without granting the authority, precedence, or pay of a full officer of that rank. All the same, it was a steppingstone on the ladder of command to that rank.

In 1896, an expedition led by Lord Kitchener was sent to avenge Gordon's death, and Kitchener's troops defeated the bulk of the Mahdi's Army in September 1898 at the Battle of Omdurman. Two days after hostilities ceased, and in front of the palace's ruins where he had died, a memorial service was held for Gordon. Ian Hamilton was present.

Many years later, in 1913, by which time Hamilton had been promoted to a general himself, he wrote a rather long poem in tribute of his hero, General Gordon. Its style is reminiscent of Rudyard Kipling, his friend, whose work may well have influenced him. Let me just share the opening of it to give you a sense of Ian's admiration for Gordon:

> 'Where the Blue Nile into the White Nile slips,
> Where the long betrothed at last link hands,
> The ghosts of the dead men move their lips,
> And the sound of the wind o'er the desert sands,
> Bears the whispered name—Charles Gordon.'

General Sir Ian Hamilton's nephew, Ian Bogle Monteith Hamilton (Alec's father), wrote a book on Sir Ian published in 1966. In it, he stated that "Gordon was not the best choice to effect an inglorious retreat from Sudan. His daring and resource, no less than his sudden and inconsistent impulses, were incompatible with administration and diplomacy, and the government was soon at loggerheads with their envoy."

Back in India and His Future Wife

In early 1886, before he went to Burma, Brevet Major Ian Hamilton had arrived in Bengal, India, from the Nile expedition. On his return from Burma, he was posted back to India and stationed in Calcutta. On December 5, 1886, he was dancing the cotillion (four couples in a square) at the Viceregal Lodge Ball in Calcutta with the beautiful Miss Jean Muir, and he fell in love. Ian and Jean married in 1887, and marrying a career soldier, she would live a relatively lonely life for much of their marriage with his long-postings overseas.

As one can see from a painting reproduced at the end of this chapter, she was an absolute beauty and was a wonderful society hostess. After the king knighted Ian Hamilton, his wife became Jean, Lady Hamilton. You can read more about her in the fantastic biography by Celia Lee, 'Jean, Lady Hamilton, 1861–1941: Diaries of a Soldier's Wife.'

Rudyard Kipling and the Hamiltons

Joseph Rudyard Kipling was born in British India in December 1865 and died in London, England, in January 1936. Kipling's works of fiction include the globally famous *Jungle Book* in 1894 (still today, new versions of the book in cartoon and movie form are being produced), *The Man Who Would Be King* in 1888, the poem "Gunga Din" in 1890, *Kim* in 1901, and many, many others. Henry James, a famous American author and critic in the late 1800s, described Kipling, thus: "Kipling strikes me personally as the most complete man of genius, as distinct from fine intelligence, that I have ever known." James was considered by many to be among the most celebrated English language writers in America.

In a letter from India to his younger brother, Vereker, Ian Hamilton said he'd seen a good deal of a young fellow named Rudyard Kipling, who had a pretty talent for writing and was anxious to publish something in England. He said he had suggested that Kipling send one of his works to Vereker and asked him to show it to Lang & Sharp, publisher friends. In due course, Vereker received a story from Kipling with simple instructions that he show it to the publishers he knew for their feedback and then to editors of two magazines Kipling hoped might print excerpts from them.

One of the publisher friends was Andrew Lang, whom Vereker had known since they were at school together at Loretto's, where they met first in a fencing class. After receiving Kipling's short story from Vereker, Lang wrote back deploring it. Years later, after Kipling had become famous, no doubt he somewhat regretted his remarks. Another publisher rejected the work with even worse remarks

He returned the results of his efforts to Kipling, sharing his circle of friends' admiration for the work and apologizing for the magazine and newspaper publishers' rejections. A few years went by, and nothing more was heard of Kipling's works until one day, in 1890, Vereker was surprised to see in a blaze of national publicity in Great Britain and roundly praised by many critics, a volume of short stories by Rudyard Kipling. They included the dismissed short-story, now renamed and published unaltered as "The Mark of The Beast" in the *London Pioneer Mail* and *The New York Journal*. It was the bestseller of the year, with the public eager to soak up anything Empire. It was satire; with spellbinding stories and humorous poems, it introduced the British people to the fascination of the Orient and India.

As European empires receded, Kipling was recognized as an incomparable, if controversial, interpreter of how the British Empire was lived and experienced. There is a photo in this book of Rudyard Kipling around the time he was good friends of the future Major-General Sir Ian Hamilton.

Burma (Modern-Day Myanmar)

The year after the Nile expedition, Ian Hamilton was posted to Burma and promoted to full major. By this short campaign's end, he was promoted again, this time to brevet lieutenant-colonel, and awarded the campaign medal with a clasp. Little is written about this brief expedition to Burma.

Hamiltons India Military Appointments and the Afridi Uprising

In 1890, Ian was shipped back to Bengal in India, where he was to spend eight years and served with distinction. The Indian Army was the collective term for the three British Raj Presidencies or their Indian regions' military battalions: the Bengal Army, the Madras Army, and the Bombay Army. Within a year of arriving in Bengal, in 1891, Hamilton had been promoted to full colonel and, in that same year, received the DSO, the Distinguished Service Order.

Vereker Hamilton, an artist (Alec's grandfather), arrived in India and spent quite some time in Kashmir and up in the British hill station, Shimla. This is where the Raj government, senior officers, and British India colonial "high society" withdrew during the heat of the Indian summer on the plains. What magical stories I am sure both brothers shared of their travels when they met.

In 1893, appointed as military secretary (attaché) to Sir George White, Commander-in-Chief British Forces India, Ian took part in the Chitral Expedition. Chitral was a princely state that had an alliance with British India, in what is today Pakistan. In 1895 he was appointed as the Deputy Quartermaster General, India, for the army, a massive command for a country made up of nearly 1.27 million square miles. Its population was recorded in the British Indian Government's 1893 census as 287 million.

Ian would have been responsible for supporting and overseeing the strategic distribution of the army's supplies and provisions to all parts of British India, broken down into the Bengal, Madras, and Bombay presidencies or regions. The checks and balances system required every army battalion and regiment's quartermaster, no matter how remote their station, to go through their presidency quartermaster. He would filter up to the India HQ quartermaster's office. Every quartermaster was typically commissioned after serving as a warrant officer. That army rank came from senior non-commissioned officers, such as a company or regimental sergeant major. With what was known as quartermaster commissions, these men tended to hold the rank of captain or major. British India Command HQ had Colonel Ian Hamilton of the Gordon Highlanders, as he then was, as its Deputy Quartermaster General, India.

in 1895, Hamilton led the Chitral Relief Force, for which he earned his GCB (Knight Grand Cross, The Most Honorable Order of the Bath), the campaign medal with clasp, and mentions in dispatches. Two years later, he commanded the Third Brigade in the Tirah campaign, was again mentioned in communications, and was awarded the campaign medal with clasps. Yet little is reported about this short period in his career.

In 1897, his last two years in India, he commanded the 3rd Brigade of the British Army in the Tirah Campaign, with nearly 3,500 men. This was the Indian frontier war of 1897–1898 in the "modern-day" Pakistan mountains and centered around the famous Khyber Pass, home to the Afridi tribe. For an annual stipend, the Afridis safeguarded the Khyber Pass for the British. Trained and outfitted by the British Army, they had done an excellent job for nearly two decades.

Unexpectedly, the Afridi tribe revolted in 1897, and they attacked several British forts in the Peshawar region. Fearing the loss of the strategic Khyber Pass, and other mountain tribes joining against them, a British expeditionary force with British and loyal Indian regiments was pulled together to put the uprising down and secure the Khyber Pass, which was a priority. During the first battle, Ian's right arm was injured in an artillery shell explosion, but the revolt was successfully put down, and the Afridi regiment disbanded.

South Africa and the Second Boer War

Ian arrived in South Africa in 1899 as a colonel. After leading his men in playing a critical part in numerous battles, such as Elandslaagte, the Relief of Ladysmith, Wagon Hill, and Diamond Hill, he was promoted to major-general. His commander, Lord Roberts, became a lifelong friend. Roberts wrote a note to Ian to say, "I am delighted at your repeated successes." For the balance of the Second Boer War, Ian played a vital role commanding a rapid movement column in the Western Transvaal, fighting several essential actions.

As a seasoned officer from the First Boer War, he was assigned to the KwaZulu Natal Regions Field Force as acting adjutant general. The Boers had superiority of numbers and had settled large swathes of South Africa before the British. During this bloody guerilla-tactic war, Ian commanded the infantry in two significant battles and was frequently mentioned in dispatches. The future British Prime Minister Winston Churchill took part in the Second Boer War campaign too. He was attached to the Commander British Armed Forces, Lieutenant General Sir George White, where Ian and Winston Churchill first met, got to know each other, and became lifelong friends.

Winston Churchill, Soldier and War Correspondent

Winston Churchill was a young cavalry officer with the 21st Lancers while simultaneously granted permission to be a war correspondent for the then national newspaper of the UK, *The Morning Post*. He arrived in South Africa as the war commenced with his valet and personal supplies of eighteen bottles of scotch whiskey in a specially made liquor cabinet. Having been dispatched with alacrity to serve his country and earn himself a reputation as a journalist at the front and in the face of danger, he landed in Cape Town.

Not long after that, on November 15, 1899, Churchill was captured during a Boer ambush of an armored train. On December 12, he shimmied up and over the prison fencing and tore away into the night. It was a massive embarrassment for the Boers, who launched a manhunt. This was just the tonic the British troops needed, as they were in the slump of losing several battles in succession at this time. It was a likely 300-mile journey through enemy territory, and Churchill traveled and foraged for food by night, hid and slept in the day—a genuinely remarkable escape and journey of survival.

It was pure luck of the gods that Churchill was taken in, exhausted and hungry, by an "Englishman" managing a coal mine. After hiding him in the mine shaft for some time, John Howard, the benevolent countryman who had risked his life in Boer country hiding Churchill, smuggled him out to safety after dark when he deemed it was the securest moment to do so. They hurried through the night to reach a rail track stopping post, where Howard, under cover of darkness, smuggled Churchill unseen into a freight train wagon, which carried him to freedom and into Portuguese-held East Africa.

Thanks to John Howard, the escape was an extraordinary feat of Churchill's. His dispatches written and sent to London in the immediate aftermath of his arrival in Portuguese East Africa made him a hero in England. They buoyed the spirits of the nation and the British troops serving in Africa. Churchill was soon back in South Africa, and he covered Ian Hamilton's campaign from Bloemfontein to Johannesburg and Pretoria.

Ian Hamilton liberated the very same prison camp Churchill had earlier escaped from, the Pretoria Prison. Churchill rode into the city and saw 180 British prisoners released. Churchill and Hamilton's lifetime bond of friendship and trust was only made stronger from that moment.

Ian Hamilton's March, a Book by Winston Churchill

Winston Churchill wrote a book from his dispatches for *The Morning Post*, titled *Ian Hamilton's March*, which was a great success and made Hamilton a national British hero too.

The British public eagerly awaited every dispatch, story, and drawing Churchill made. The entire nation was hanging on his every word. When Churchill returned to England that summer, he was received with tremendous excitement. Churchill immediately used his fame to contest a seat as a member of the British Parliament. His hero status helped him win the seat.

The Boers Attacked the British Cape Colony

In one conflict, the Siege of Ladysmith at which Ian Hamilton fought, a Boer attack and blockade of the city saw the British under the command of General White. The Boers had crossed over the border into the British Cape Colony to regain their land taken by the British. The Boers had originally bought the land to form their independent republic from the Zulu king in 1847, fifty-three years earlier, but within three years it had been invaded by

Great Britain. White made his stand at Ladysmith, his point of operation to hold the Natal region.

Numerous battles ensued from October 1899 onwards as the Boers sought to take back the Natal region. After sustaining heavy losses, White retreated with his surviving troops into the town of Ladysmith itself. The Boers then surrounded it and placed it under siege. The siege lasted just over four months in early 1900.

General Sir Reders Buller (who knew Ian Hamilton in Sudan) made three attempts to break the siege, having brought up his army for the relief of Ladysmith. He lost each of these first three battles, and interestingly, war correspondent Winston Churchill was present at the relief of Ladysmith with Hamilton. In his fourth attempt, General Buller succeeded in battle.

It used to be said in South Africa that the Boers were good shots because when they were youngsters, their fathers used to supply them with one cartridge and send them out on the veldt (the plains) to get food for the larder. They got a good licking if they came back empty-handed. I assume if a lion got them, another son was available!

Mohandas Gandhi, the future "Mahatma" of Indian independence fame, was part of the British Army's Indian stretcher-bearing corps, and he took part in Ladysmith's relief to help the wounded. One can reflect on the probability that they passed each other on numerous occasions.

As acting adjutant general, Ian Hamilton was attached to the British Natal Field Force and commanded the infantry at the Relief of Ladysmith, where he fought well. Following this battle, he was promoted to major general and created a Knight Commander of The Order of the Bath (KCB) before returning to the United Kingdom in early 1901. Ian was now Major General Sir Ian Hamilton, KCB. In his article "Ian Hamilton's March," Winston Churchill told of Ian's campaign from Bloemfontein to Pretoria (London, 1900, reprinted in the second half of the Boer War).

Hamilton traveled 400 miles from Bloemfontein to Pretoria, fighting ten significant battles against Boer forces on that journey (including the struggle of Rooiwal) and fourteen minor conflicts. His superiors twice recommended Hamilton for the Victoria Cross. It was considered that the first was withheld, as it was inappropriate because he was too young. He was not awarded the second because of his then seniority of rank, it's believed.

Hamilton, appointed Military Secretary of the War Office in May 1901, was by November appointed back to South Africa as chief of staff to the commander-in-chief, Lord Kitchener. Given the local rank of lieutenant general, Hamilton landed back in South Africa in November 1901. In April 1902, he took command of the military columns operating in the Western Transvaal. When the Boer hostilities ended in June 1902, Hamilton returned to England, accompanying Lord Kitchener. In July, their ship arrived in Southampton, where they received an enthusiastic hero's welcome, with thousands of people lining the streets to watch their procession through the city of London.

In a dispatch dated June 23, 1902, Lord Kitchener wrote the following about Ian's work in South Africa:

> "At much personal inconvenience, Lord Roberts lent me his Military Secretary, Ian Hamilton, as my Chief of Staff. His high soldierly qualities are already well known, and his reputation does not require to be established now. I am much indebted to him for his strong and constant support to me as Chief of Staff, also for the marked skill and self-reliance he showed later when directing operations in the Western Transvaal."

British Casualties

At the outset of this conflict, British troops numbered over 12,500 men in South Africa. From the beginning to the end of this conflict, some 448,000 British officers and men served in the war. As is usual in most wars, figures vary of deaths and casualties; official records show that over 700 officers and nearly 7,600 men were killed in action or died of their wounds. Some 400-plus officers and over 13,000 men died of disease, typhoid fever being one of the biggest killers. Nearly two-thirds of all British troops who died in this war died of disease.

German and Japanese Military Maneuvers

In September 1902, Hamilton accompanied Lord Roberts, Commander-in-Chief, and St John Broderick, Secretary of State for War, on a visit to Germany to attend the German army maneuvers as a guest of Emperor

Wilhelm. Ian was to meet the Emperor on more than one occasion going forward, and his fluency in the German language must have helped enormously. The Kaiser created Sir Ian a Knight 1st class of the Order of the Crown of Prussia, greatly impressed by his military understanding.

British Military Command HQ appointed Sir Ian Quartermaster-General to British Armed Forces in 1903 and 1904 after he returned to a War Office post. In 1905 Ian became the military attaché to the British Indian Army visiting the Japanese in Manchuria, where he attended the Japanese Army's Manchurian maneuvers before war broke out between Japan and Russia in September that year. Afterward, he published a *Staff Officer's Scrapbook* on his experiences and observations during the conflict.

The Emperor of Japan had received multiple reports from almost every Japanese general in attendance at the maneuvers of how thoughtful Sir Ian's questions were, and how he openly shared his wisdom on tactics. It was rare that the Japanese Emperor granted a private audience to anyone. Yet General Sir Ian Hamilton was invited to one at the express wish of the Divine Emperor Meiji. In gratitude for the wisdom Sir Ian had readily imparted with honesty and openness to the Japanese military elite, the Emperor of Japan awarded him the Order of the Sacred Treasure, 1st class (then the highest rank of eight forms of the award) with an Imperial Order Star chest decoration. Today, the 1st grade is referred to as the Grand Cordon Gold Star. The emperor's chamberlain would have read out his honor with words: "By the grace of Heaven, Emperor of Japan, seated on the throne occupied by the same dynasty from time immemorial, we confer the Order of the Sacred Treasure, 1st class upon General Sir Ian Hamilton."

England and Senior Military Appointments

Succeeding Lieutenant General Sir Evelyn Wood, who had served during the Indian mutiny between 1909 and 1910, Hamilton returned to England and served as General Officer Commanding Southern Command. His next appointment until 1910 was as adjutant-general to the forces. Following this appointment, he became Inspector-General of Overseas Forces in 1911. Within just two years, in 1913, he was, in addition to this role, General Officer Commander-in-Chief, Mediterranean Command. The major generals in charge, respectively, of Egypt, Malta, and Gibraltar all reported into him, as did the British military commanders in Cyprus and the Anglo-Egyptian Sudan. What a massive pair of jobs this was, but he proved to be a top-class military man, with an extraordinary ability to lead, motivate, and get things done, combined with a flair for strategic planning and logistics.

Sir Ian's Visits to the Last Emperor of Germany, and Last Tsar of Russia

Alec's great-uncle hastily made trips to Germany and Russia upon the death of King Edward VII in May 1910, and traveled with Field Marshall, Earl Roberts, Commander-in-Chief of British Forces, as his General-in-Waiting. Lord Roberts was a slight of stature man like Ian, born in India, and attended Eton and Sandhurst. This was four years before World War One was to decimate Europe and wipe half the European monarchies off the face of the map forever. As Sir Ian spoke fluent French, German, and Hindi, he was well suited to this diplomatic journey. A common language used in almost all Royal Courts was French, and both the German Emperor and Russian Tsar were also fluent in French. At the time, virtually all royal households in Europe were connected by marriage or family ties, something Queen Victoria of England was good at creating. Many of the wives chosen to marry senior royals in other countries, especially future kings and emperors, were German princesses with common ties.

Ian Hamilton and Lord Roberts set off immediately to meet the Kaiser of Germany, en route to Russia, to likewise notify the tsar first-hand of the news he carried with him. Sir Ian wrote down his memories of his meetings with these two mighty sovereigns, and his impressions of them: that they were both complete autocrats answerable only to God. He shared a little of their personalities and circumstances with his great-nephew, Alec, who recalled him sharing such stories when a teenager.

Ian Hamilton's Memories of the Last German Kaiser, or Emperor

In the summer of 1910, Sir Ian, at the time Adjutant General of The British Army and Military general-in-waiting to Lord Roberts and envoys of the newly raised King George V, arrived in Berlin to deliver the message they'd later deliver to the last tsar—that King Edward VII had died, and his son, their cousin George, was now monarch.

Kaiser Friedrich Wilhelm Viktor Albert, of the house of Hohenzollern, chose to reign under the name Emperor Wilhelm II. He was born in 1859 and reigned as the Emperor of Germany and King of Prussia from 1888 to November 9, 1918. This was a crucial stage in history.

Kaiser Wilhelm's mother was the eldest daughter of Britain's Queen Victoria. The Kaiserin's son's traumatic breech birth, his left arm wrapped around his neck, and the doctor's use of forceps resulted in the permanent paralysis of Wilhelm's left arm. He underwent many treatments over several years, from relatively useless to quite aggressive ones, in an attempt to bring the arm back to everyday use. Sadly, they all failed.

Wilhelm was left with a withered arm about six inches shorter than his right one as he grew into manhood. Many have commented (as did Sir Ian) that the Kaiser hid this disability quite well by placing his hand on his sword hilt. Sometimes he put his hand in a specially raised jacket pocket on the left side, or he held a pair of gloves. These moves with his withered arm were designed to draw one's attention away from his infirmity, Sir Ian believed. He rarely used his left arm in public. He had a very structured, almost harsh, education and upbringing to prepare him for his future role leading the German Empire. Twenty-seven separate German kingdoms, principalities, grand duchies and duchies, free Hanseatic cities, and an imperial territory, all came under the umbrella of his Empire. Wilhelm himself was King of Prussia and Emperor of Germany. Prussia was the largest of the states that made up unified Germany and covered some two-thirds of it.

In addition to German, Kaiser Wilhelm was fluent in English (it's said without a trace of a German accent), French, Russian, and Dutch. Most royals, as in England, Russia, Germany, and most European royal houses, were educated to speak French, not only seen as a good education, but with most Houses interconnected by marriage, it served as a common form of communication for the dynasties that collectively ruled the continent.

Sir Ian found that Kaiser Wilhelm had a quick, sometimes brilliant mind and was evolved enough to adopt modern scientific discoveries and technology. Sir Ian and many who knew him well, however, felt he was somewhat superficial, that he never seemed to relax, and he was quick to jump to conclusions. Sir Ian saw him as a little unsure of himself, despite his autocratic monarchial role, which he balanced by being somewhat arrogant. He could be brutal, and force was his first solution to every domestic or international problem, militarily or in conversation. It was who he was.

Sir Ian believed him to have had a very quick temper, and he was warned that the Kaiser could become quite hysterical if he was not happy at how things were being done, and he frequently had bouts of depression. Pre-warned, pre-armed. He often infuriated public opinion with his outbursts. He was almost paranoid, some say, in getting his way and in dominating his will on others, both domestic and international. This led to the general German population often being concerned at his ability to govern, and it caused great concern amongst the other ruling heads of state across Europe. They were anxious at the Kaiser's aggressive approach to everything.

Sir Ian recalled to Alec that the Kaiser looked delighted when he used flawless fluent German, making the Emperor more comfortable. The Kaiser's aide-de-camp mentioned after Sir Ian's first meeting that the Kaiser had felt touched that Sir Ian chose to speak to him in German. He also appreciated his cousin, King George V, sending such an eloquent messenger of both the sad and happy news. This more comfortable form of discussion without interpreters enabled them to discuss things more openly, as the rapport built between them was very genuine, Sir Ian felt.

The Last Tsar of All the Russia's

As a military emissary of his king traveling from Berlin to Moscow, Sir Ian was sent to deliver the same message to the tsar he had given the Kaiser. To inform them that King Edward VII had died, and their cousin George, was now monarch. Sir Ian's journey would have taken four days, passing out of Germany, across the Congress of Poland, and through Lithuania and Belarus. After passing today's Russian border, the train would have traveled through the beautiful region of Smolenskoye Poozerye, with its wilderness of low fir tree forests, lakes, and wetlands. A warmer time of year in Russia with typical 46f (7.8c) – 65f (18.3c) and the tail end of snows falling before the summer.

Tsar Nicholas II, or Nikolai Alexandrovich, Emperor and Tsar of all Russia, King of Congress Poland, and Grand Duke of Finland, was born on May 18, 1868, and reigned from November 1, 1894–March 15, 1917, with his abdication. During his reign, the Russian Empire stretched across Europe and Asia. The empire stretched from the Arctic Ocean in the north to the

Black Sea in the south; it traversed the Baltic Sea west to Alaska east. Some 80 percent of the population of Russia were peasants, and Tsar Nicholas was a total autocrat of patriarchal German descent. His bloodline descended from the House of Holstein-Gottorp-Romanov. This royal house ruled Russia from 1792, technically to the fall of the Romanov Dynasty, with the Tsar and his family's execution in 1918 wiping out the nation's imperial rule.

Sir Ian arrived speedily in the Russian capital, taking the train across more than a thousand miles of open countryside, hastening to share his news with the tsar. Family connections were again crucial here as the tsar's mother, the Dowager Empress Maria of Russia (born Maria of Hesse-Darmstadt, Denmark), was the sister of Princess Alexandra of Hesse-Darmstadt. Alexandra had married King Edward VII of Great Britain. The tsar's maternal uncles were Denmark, and Greece's kings, King George V of England, Kaiser Wilhelm II of Germany, and the King of Norway were all cousins. Both Nicholas and Wilhelm were also descended from King-Emperor Frederick of Prussia and great-grandsons of Tsar Paul I of Russia.

In this book, her Highness Princess Olga Romanov says that she loved reading of Alec Hamilton's great-uncle, General Sir Ian Hamilton, meeting her great-uncle Tsar Nicolas II, of Russia. She now has the opportunity of reading Sir Ian's comments on the last reigning member of her imperial family dynasty.

Ian Hamilton's Memories of the Last Tsar of Russia

Once in Moscow, Sir Ian became aware of the vastness of the Russian court and its incredible opulence compared to Germany's or England's. The fabulous palaces, the men's elegant attire at court, and the ladies' stunning court dresses and jewelry—everywhere he turned was a scene of extraordinary wealth and grandeur. Yet, he caught glimpses of the poverty in the streets as he was whisked from one imperial event to another as the tsar's guest.

Sir Ian attended the Russian Orthodox Christian Mass of Remembrance held by the tsar for his relative, King Edward VII, at St. Basil's Cathedral in Moscow. He had said that the tsar had him seated with the Imperial Romanoff family as personal envoy and representative of Great Britain's king. Sir Ian had said to his interpreter sat next to him that the Russian Orthodox chants sounded more like Scottish monks than Russians with their Gregorian chanting and incense. The *grand duke*, who acted as interpreter for him during any spoken parts of the service, explained that *the man singing was a Scotsman* chanting old Gaelic monastic chants. It was the Tsar's request in honor of the late British king. Sir Ian said he would share such a touching moment with his king and was himself greatly moved by the thoughtfulness of the tsar to do such a thing.

Ian found His Majesty extremely diplomatic, of a calm, warm personality, and kind in his attention to him, and his genuine sadness at the loss of his relative. He also recalled how gentlemanly the tsar was and what a thoughtful host he was throughout his meetings and confidential conversations.

In Sir Ian's experience, all members of the Imperial family he met were exceedingly polite, well educated, spoke several languages, and were engaging, gracious, and impressive as individuals. The Tsar's utter fluency in English made it easy for them to hold conversations together without interpreters.

The Tsar was educated in his native tongue, Russian, which he used with court officials and ordinary people. He was tutored fluently in French, German, and English from childhood also. Sir Ian himself had told Alec that the Tsar spoke English as clipped and plummy as any English Oxford Don. With a cheeky smile a member of the Romanov family, told Sir Ian in a quiet voice that the Tsar spoke Russian with a slight foreign accent, as he generally spoke English with his wife and family.

Languages of the Russian and European Courts

Romanov royalty by the 19th century was, apart from Russian, educated since childhood to be fluent in French, English, and often German. Russian and French were *de riguer*; most were raised by British governesses, so English was a given. Whereas French was *the* common language across a multitude of European royalty through which they could communicate.

Up until the last Tsar's grandfather, Alexander II, Russian Society preferred and used French as the language of Society. The perfection and fluency in French distinguished the *nobility and inner circle of Society* against all others. Alexander II was fluent in six languages, including Latin and Polish.

The last Tsar's father, Alexander II, forced Russia's mother tongue to be the only language spoken at court anywhere in his presence. Even as a young man and Tsarevitch, he answered Courtiers and Russian nobility who talked to him in French, in Russian.

The world of inter-connected royal families of Europe proved valuable for Russia. Most princesses from Germany were of the Protestant faith, more easily converted to the Russian Orthodox church - and were a significant source of wives for Russian royalty. It was much more complicated to gain a European Catholic princess's father's consent to convert. They generally forbade conversion. Consequently, the German family connections were myriad, as many tsars and grand dukes married German princesses from one or other of Germany's twenty-two royal courts over the centuries. Great Britain and other non-Catholic countries in Europe found a plentiful supply of princesses from German royal houses too. When royal houses of Europe met or fell out with each other, it was invariably as family.

World War One

By the outbreak of World War One with the declaration of hostilities announced on August 5, 1914, between Great Britain and Germany, General Sir Ian Hamilton was appointed Commander-in-Chief, Home Army, based in Whitehall in London. At the same time, he was appointed to the primarily territorial army role as Commander Central-Force. Both appointments placed him in military command of repelling any seaborne German invasion of the east coast of England, where it was expected in the early part of the war. Getting to know Hamilton through researching his career and reading his own words, the author suspects he was honored to accept such appointments but would be champing at the bit to have a field command where the action was, in Europe. He didn't have to wait too long.

Austro-Hungary declared war on Serbia in 1914 after its crown prince and his morganatic[2] wife were assassinated in Serbia's capital by Serbian nationalists. Soon the war would engulf all of Europe. Before describing the breakout of action, it helps to understand the two major treaties, or agreements of mutual aid in time of war, that were in place among the three major countries. "The Triple Entente" of 1904 was signed by the Russian Empire, The British Empire, and the French Third Republic—it did not guarantee that the parties would come to the defense of a member, but they

---

2 Of unequal rank. In a morganatic marriage, titles do not pass to a spouse or the children.

would offer support. The French also had an entente with Japan, signed in 1907, to stave off hostility to its Indo-China possessions, and a robust mutual defense treaty with Serbia existed with Russia.

The other major treaty was the "Triple Alliance" signed between Austria-Hungary, Germany, and Italy. It was a full treaty of mutual defense in time of war. Now we can understand that the Kaiser was required by a pact with the Austro-Hungarian Empire to declare war on Serbia the moment the Austro-Hungarian Emperor did. Italy was drawn in to defend both of its allies. The Kaiser's military leadership may have jumped at the chance with enthusiasm, but that's beside the point. By its treaty with Serbia, Russia was obliged to declare war on Austro-Hungary and Germany in return. Russia's allies, Great Britain and France, made it a joint declaration of the war supporting Russia.

Suddenly, the whole of Europe was at war, but it did not end there. It became a World War, as the then-British Empire meant that Canada, Australia, New Zealand, South Africa, Rhodesia, and India were by default at war with the Triple Alliance. Belgium and Portugal joined in, and Romania, Montenegro, and Poland were pulled in. Finally, the United States of America joined in 1917, three years into the war. Without question, America's entry into the action aided it to finish a year later, as Alec said when we touched base on Sir Ian's life. The war culminated in a massive loss of life and the downfall of most of Europe's monarchies. By war's end, nearly 20 million military personnel and civilians had died, and 20 million were wounded or disabled for life.

The Gallipoli Campaign, Turkey, World War One

Lord Kitchener, who had been deeply impressed by Ian Hamilton in Sudan, asked Sir Ian to lead British land forces, known as the Mediterranean Expeditionary Force. As First Sea Lord of the Admiralty and close friend of Sir Ian, Winston Churchill planned for a naval attack on the Dardanelles. The assault of the combined allied naval forces was the first to knock out all severe threats to Sir Ian's land forces. This was to clear the path for him to land his troops and capture the Dardanelles coastline. Secondly, it was to ensure that the navy could drive through the straits of the Dardanelles to Turkey's capital, Constantinople (the "modern-day" Istanbul). Constantinople, being the seat of Ottoman Empire power, was the home to their palace and naval base, near this harbor. The action was intended to force Turkey's capitulation in the war, releasing ships and troops to the Western Front in Europe. In the harbor at the time were ten German warships that had evaded British Royal Naval pursuit and been granted passage through the Dardanelles by the Turks.

The Gallipoli Campaign was to prove the defining moment of, and many say the tragic and unfair end to, Ian Hamilton's career.

The Naval Battle Begins

On November 2, 1914, a Royal Naval squadron bombarded the Turkish forts at the entrance to the Dardanelles. Yet the British government did not declare war on Turkey until four days later. Eleven days after the bombardment of the Turkish forts, with ample time to repair and restock, a British submarine sank an obsolete Ottoman ship. Another month passed by, giving Turkey and their German allies plenty of time to complete reinforcements and rebuild their forts and guns. It would be another six days before February 19, 1915, when the British would launch their first naval bombardments against the Turkish shore batteries.

It seems extraordinary in hindsight that it would be another thirteen days before a final naval attack at night on the Turkish gun and fort placements occurred. The British Navy assumed they had now significantly weakened the Turkish forces and knocked their guns out.

On March 12, Major General Sir Ian Hamilton, who had already arrived on station, was officially appointed General Officer Commanding the Mediterranean Expeditionary Force by the Secretary of State for War, Lord Kitchener. Hamilton's troops were coming from across the whole British Empire, from Great Britain (with English, Scottish, Welsh, and Northern Irish regiments), and from India, Canada, Australia, New Zealand, and French colonial allies. Roughly, as varying accounts differ slightly, Sir Ian started the campaign with 489,000 troops of the British Empire and its Allies, of which 345,000 were from the British Commonwealth, including those from the United Kingdom, Indian, Irish and Canadian Newfoundlanders, 50,000 Australians, and 15,000 New Zealanders. There were also 79,000 French Allied troops. There were some 315,500 Turkish and German troops holding the high ground and an advantage everywhere. They had well-entrenched large-gun installations on land overlooking the relatively narrow Dardanelle Straights waterway.

The Allied Navy began with a sweep for mines in the Dardanelles Straits with some success at night on March 13. From March 15–16, the main Allied Naval Force commenced its bombardment to knock out the Turkish guns, forts, and positions, but naval command was shocked that the Turkish gun batteries bombarded the Allied fleet, causing severe damage. Under such heavy fire, Turkish forces were obliged to abandon some of their fortifications temporarily. However, the majority were still fully operational, and to the navy's total surprise, managed to inflict devastating firepower and damage on the approaching Allied ships coming up the Dardanelles channel, whose advance they halted.

The admiral of the British fleet suffered a nervous breakdown as his fleet sustained substantial unexpected damage, losses, and vessels being put out of action; he resigned on March 16 and was replaced.

Undamaged Allied ships forged ahead farther up the straits on March 18. An attack from additional Turkish battery gunfire on land and previously undetected mines floating in the channel destroyed, incapacitated, or warded off the whole fleet. The British Royal Navy and its allies lost eight battleships, with three battleships sunk by mines. An additional three battleships and a battlecruiser were badly damaged, limping away. The Turkish and German guns, and the vast number of mines laid, had done a first-rate job in destroying an entire navy fleet. There appeared to be poor reconnaissance in advance of the fleet arriving off the Dardanelles, with no advance spying on and assessing the state of the straits and shore gun batteries. It appears that they assumed the British Royal Navy would blast away whatever resistance they found. It was an utter disaster.

The Allied Navy Knocked Out

The Allied navies were, in effect, out of the picture and unable to do their job of clearing the Turkish ground forces from the peninsula. Sir Ian's troops would now go in with high risk, and the chances for taking control of and commanding the Straits' entrance and choking off Turkish and German movement were looking slim. British High Command, Kitchener, and Churchill should have issued orders to Hamilton to call off the troop landings, and their naval troop carriers ordered to weigh anchor and withdraw from a situation virtually untenable. They should not have landed or lost a single man; some military Historians have since suggested.

The plan for large-scale troop landings on the Gallipoli Peninsula was now one of excessive-high risk. Sir Ian made it clear to London and Churchill (recorded in Hamilton's private notes) that he did not have enough troops to take the Turkish land forces. His troops were exposed to their gun batteries, and a Turkish Army insufficiently damaged by the Royal Navy's bombardments would stack the odds against them.

No orders were issued to abandon a landing. Hamilton decided to follow his original orders to launch a land offensive and take the Dardanelles Straits entry; he gave orders to prepare for landing. Hamilton must have been in communication with Lord Kitchener and Churchill, and they decided to go for it. As a team—this was a fatal decision.

During these delays, with more than four weeks since the last bombardment, the Turks had plenty of time to reinforce troops, strengthen gun placement and troop hides, and be ready. These Turks, we must remember, were fighting for their country's survival and were supported by battle-seasoned World War One German military officers' tactics and ammunition. They also had a surprise weapon waiting for the Allied troops if the British did not think the Germans had supplied them.

The Land Battle Begins

On March 22, Hamilton held a conference with his commanders, and they decided to make an amphibious landing on the Gallipoli Peninsula with maximum troop numbers. Unbelievably, it was more than another five weeks before the British and Allied troops landed on April 25.

By April 28, when the two sides engaged in the first major ground battle, two British Naval submarines slipped up through the Dardanelles. The struggle of Kithira saw 4,000 Allied casualties. Some days later, a second French submarine was sunk by a mine in the Straits. Battles raged back and forth between May 8 and 18, with ANZAC[3] forces landing on various days.

---

3 Australia and New Zealand Army Corps

On the 18th, a massive attack was mounted on Hamilton's ground forces by 42,000 Turkish soldiers, which was repulsed at an enormous loss of 100,000 Allied killed and wounded casualties.

More allied ANZAC troops land on May 19 – 22, including a mounted regiment. After a brief armistice to take a breath and bury the dead, two British warships were sunk by German U-boats over two days. A Royal Navy submarine sank an Ottoman troopship in the Bosporus Strait at the entry to Constantinople, causing panic in the city. Battles continued throughout June, July, and September, with massive losses on both sides. The Germans had supplied the Turkish troops with the deadly Maxim machine gun, which could cut hundreds of men down in just a few minutes. From well-encased positions uphill, this devastating machine looked down on the British and Allied troops.

Despite suffering extensive casualties over six months, the Allied troops managed to establish two beachheads. However, with heavy losses mounting, Hamilton (with Churchill's support) petitioned Kitchener for 95,000 more soldiers to be sent immediately. Still, he barely got a quarter of that number, making the task an uphill one.

At some time in September, the decision was taken in London to order Hamilton to evacuate his troops from shore and leave the theater of war. It was now clear to all that this was a war they could not win. Hamilton was ordered to evacuate with immediate effect on October 15, but he argued that doing so could cost the lives of 60,000 men. He asked that more troops be sent to enable him to swing the war for the British and Allies, and in the meantime held to a decision not to order an evacuation until he received a reply.

Lord Kitchener's reply was quick and simple: he "sacked" Hamilton and relieved him of his command for not enacting a direct order. It took another thirteen days for General Sir Charles Monro to assume control of the Mediterranean Expeditionary Force as Hamilton headed back to England. By November 22, Field Marshall Kitchener arrived in Gallipoli to survey the scene. A week later, he recommended the evacuation of ANZAC troops just ahead of a fierce snowstorm and blizzard that lasted three days on the peninsula. Sir Ian estimated from what he witnessed of the enemy and their gun emplacements that retreat would result in a bloodbath for Allied troops. Not for the first time, the author quotes the line from William Shakespeare's play sharing how difficult it is for commanders on the ground, *Henry IV:*

"Uneasy lies the head that wears the crown."

Between December 7, 1915, and January 9, 1916, all remaining British and Allied troops were evacuated, and with their naval troop carriers and surviving escort vessels, they departed the Gallipoli Peninsula. Had Hamilton judged the risk wrong, or had the situation on the ground changed dramatically in the weeks that had passed? Either way, the evacuation went relatively successfully; of course, losses occurred, but a bloodbath did not occur.

The Aftermath - the Blame Game Unfolds

In the thirty-eight years of his military senior command, Sir Ian was known at home and across Europe and Asia as a brilliant commanding general and tactician. The elite of the German and Japanese Officer Corp revered his skills. He seems to have independently made the right call and military decisions in the field for all his career.

The Cost in Men, Lives, and Humiliation

Considered as the senior service and the world's best navy, the Royal Naval Fleet with its Allied ships was, to all intents and purpose, wiped out by the Turkish gun placement, sea mines, and tactics. It was for the Royal Navy a colossal humiliation and loss. Land forces were under General Sir Ian Hamilton's command. Regardless of where the blame lies—the navy, British High Command, the government, Kitchener, Churchill, or Hamilton, the British Allied troops lost many men.

Some 489,000 Allied Troops Started in the Gallipoli Campaign

41,150 were killed by the end of the campaign, about 8.42%, but 91.58% lived. 97,397 men were injured or wounded and unable to fight: about 19.92% 158,000 men were incapacitated by diseases, such as cholera: about 32.3% With over 60 percent of Hamilton's force incapacitated, and just over 30% of his fighting force were able to fight.

The Ottoman Empire and German Axis paid a hefty price for their victory too. An estimated 250,000 Turkish, German, and Arab troops were casualties of war. Some 57,000 were killed or died of disease, and 174,500 were wounded, injured, and or evacuated with illness, or were declared missing in action, which would add to the death toll in their defending Gallipoli.

As we've read earlier, both the German and Ottoman totalitarian empires collapsed at the end of World War One and became republics.

Whatever the reality, Sir Ian's removal from command and recall to London ended a remarkable, brave, extraordinary, and honorable military field career.

No matter how much he thought he was doing the right thing, time would prove that Sir Ian Hamilton had, under the circumstances of not getting more troops, which he and Churchill asked for, called the withdrawal scenario wrong. Had Hamilton listened to Kitchener, he could have evacuated his army and might have come out in history as the man who could have won the battle but saved his men first. He could have been sent to the European front and continued his glorious career.

On the other hand, had Kitchener listened to Hamilton and Churchill and found a way to supply the necessary extra troops, they might have overrun the Turks and hastened the end of World War One. The Allies could have made a far more significant saving of life in Europe by not fighting on a double front. Hindsight and "if" are easy conclusions for historians to draw on with all the perceived facts in their hands years later. In the safety of their armchairs, academics can debate endlessly without the slightest risk. Hindsight experts have all the time in the world to analyze a myriad of options and apply theories of what should have happened and who is to blame. However, men in command on the ground, often without a complete picture, must decide based on what they know, see, and believe about the enemy and their troops. As some historians and military men go back and forth over the decades with opposite views on this battle and its players, it is what it is.

The British Government's Gallipoli Inquiry

Firstly, one can feel a sense of great regret and distress in Sir Ian's own hand-written words. His notes are clear: he could not believe that his distinguished military career from the Second Afghan Wars to pre-Gallipoli counted for nothing, nor that his requests for more troops could be considered anything but the right strategy. Having made a career of faultless strategic decisions, you're conscious that he felt let down and used as a scapegoat, whatever any of those in government, military, or the press thought at the time, or whatever historians have made of him since. One is also aware that he did not seek to blame others but held himself accountable for every injured man, lost limb, or death.

Secondly, he comes across, from varying accounts and unbiased reviews, as an honest and humble man who based his decisions on the hand of cards God dealt him. He played that hand the best he could. He was known for his great sensitivity to his men's welfare and a sense of fair play. The author does not doubt that he was a military genius, as his earlier unblemished career testifies. He was a man who followed orders and maybe did not deserve the label given him politically at the time, nor did Churchill—that they alone caused defeat and massive loss of Allied life.

Prime Minister Asquith remarked in deflecting accountability from himself, no doubt, that General Sir Ian Hamilton had "too much feather in his brain." Charles Bean, a war correspondent covering the Gallipoli campaign, considered Sir Ian the opposite of the stuck-in-the-mud old military leadership when he said that Hamilton had "a breadth of mind which the army, in general, does not possess."

Blame, if any, for the Gallipoli campaign's disaster likely lies equally shared among them all: the prime minister, his war cabinet, Kitchener, Churchill, Hamilton, and Naval Command, their poor intelligence, seemingly total lack of knowledge of the enemies' capabilities, and Hamilton's desire to push on. All share the blame, but the horrific cost of lives lost on both sides is still hard to reconcile today.

Devastating for Sir Ian was that the inquiry would not decide or hear his defense, stating that they could not share everyone's facts and justifications at the time, as there was a war on. To divulge all the necessary data would be to risk military and naval secrets and reveal the British strength or weakness to the enemy. So, the inquiry was closed, leaving Hamilton accused as a critical person blamed, and no ability for him to defend himself publicly. He retired in a cloud of doubt, convinced his evidence would have cleared him of gross misconduct of any kind.

European Empires Fell – Like a Stack of Cards

By 1918 and the end of World War One, the Russian Empire and the German and Austria-Hungarian Empires had fallen. Their autocratic rulers, whom Ian Hamilton had visited just a few years earlier in their regal splendor, were assassinated or in exile. With them were swept away the Principality of Albania and the Kingdom of Montenegro. We must not forget that the former German Empire was made up of twenty-six states, twenty-two of which were ruled by royal dynasties. There had been four kingdoms, seven principalities, six grand-duchies, and five duchies that fell with their empires, and all their families were swept from power. By 1922 the Ottoman Empire fell, and by 1924, the Kingdom of Greece fell, lost in a coup d'état, and both monarchies were abolished. After the two great wars, the Italian, Romanian, Bulgarian, and Serbian monarchies fell and were dissolved.

General Sir Ian Hamilton's Life in Perspective

What an extraordinary, forty-seven-year military career Ian Hamilton had. From participating in the Afghan wars in 1880, through both Boer Wars in South Africa, to commanding British and Allied forces as a major general in a critical theater of World War One. He retired in 1920 from a desk job in London, five years after dismissal from his field command. He lived and breathed military. In hindsight and on fair balance, he was a highly valued British senior military asset in the British Empire, particularly in South Africa and Imperial India. He was a man with an exemplary record for his entire career, lauded by both the top German and Japanese Military command. That he faltered in a final action not entirely in his hands is a sadness beyond compare.

The author watched a rare old black and white film of General Sir Ian and listened to the now aged Hamilton family member, splendid in military uniform. He was a charming, matter of fact, courtly, distinguished man, and one felt kind-hearted with a classical military bearing. He was very slight, yet was, as Alec said, a bundle of energy even in old age—a man whose mind was sharp and analytical and who always reflected on and recognized talent when he saw it. Slight of stature he may have been, but in his career until that last action, he was a giant amongst men. Indeed, he was held in the highest esteem in his regiment, the military establishment, and overseas.

Sir Ian wrote a volume of poetry and a novel contemporarily described as risqué. In introducing his published *Gallipoli Diary*, he commented:

"There is nothing certain about war except that one side won't win"

A Highlanders Lad's Kiss From The Duchess of Gordon.

Ian Hamilton wrote a book, 'The Commander,' a story of the Gordon High-landers founding and Jane Gordon, the 4th Duchess of Gordon. The Duchess was quite a racy Lady of her time, a sponsor of Robbie Burns and intimate supporter of William Pitt. The Duchess made a bet with the Prince of Wales, the future King George IV, that she could raise more men than he for the war declared on Britain by the French Revolutionary Government in 1793. She toured the Duke's expansive lands and highlands wearing a military uniform and a black feathered highland bonnet, encouraging men to join the new regiment her husband was raising for the war against France. First called the 100th Highlanders and later the 92nd Highlanders in 1798, the regiment for which the modern-day Alec Hamilton's great-grandfather Christian Hamilton was Lieutenant. Colonel. The Duchess of Gordon gave the King's shilling to all who signed up, and each 'lad' could kiss the Duchess and take the shilling she held between her lips. The highlanders called it the "Kiss of Life," which many a happy highland lad accepted along with the silver shilling.

General Sir Ian's Later Life

He carried five titles or decorations bestowed by his king and country and the highest decoration orders from three foreign sovereigns as listed at the beginning of this chapter.

When he eventually retired from the military, Sir Ian was a leading figure in the British Legion, the ex-servicemen's organization, holding the Scottish president's position. The king appointed him Lieutenant of the Tower of London in recognition at last of his outstanding pre-Gallipoli army career. Sir Ian also served for some time as rector of the University of Edinburgh.

When he was appointed as "colonel" of his old regiment, the Gordon High-landers, this honorary appointment gave him enormous pride. He attended their reunions and major events, from parades to funerals. In retirement, he donated money to help create *The Gordon Highlanders Museum*, something he was proud of—*his* regiment. After his death, all these organizations sent representatives to attend his funeral and spoke of him with high esteem.

He was undoubtedly a man of letters and a prolific author, having written and published thirteen books all told. He liked to write poetry and was a founding member and vice-president of the Anglo-German Association in 1928, which promoted pro-German sentiment in Britain to heal World War One wounds. It seemed typical of the man to seek to heal the wounds of war with his enemy and make new bonds of understanding.

The Passing of a Legend

Major-General Sir Ian Standish Monteith Hamilton, GCB, GCMG, DSO, T.D., died aged ninety-four in 1947, two years after World War Two ended. As one chronicler wrote, "the old warrior faded away" rather than suddenly died. He passed away at his home in Hyde Park Gardens in London. His body, with full military honors, was transferred to the Kirk and Kilmadock Cemetery, where he was buried in Doune, in Stirlingshire, Scotland. His passing deeply saddened one of his greatest admirers: his fifteen-year-old nephew, Alec Hamilton.

In April 1962, a memorial plaque to General Sir Ian Hamilton and his brother, Vereker Hamilton, the artist, and grandfather of Alec, was unveiled in Glasgow Cathedral's "Blackadder Aisle." The Hamiltons have had a long connection to this cathedral and the city. Six Hamiltons have been buried there, including the Rev. John Hamilton, Moderator of the General Assembly of Scotland in 1766, and his son, John Hamilton of North Park, three times Lord Provost of Glasgow (both men are shown in this book's opening family tree pages). The memorial stone was made from a single slab of Iona marble from a quarry no longer working, situated in a small inlet on Iona's southeast in the Inner Hebrides of Scotland.

General Sir Ian Hamilton was known among his troops "as the man who never talks," since he only did when necessary and not for the sake of it, whilst being extremely popular with the troops. He was a soldier's soldier. A fellow senior officer once said of Sir Ian,

'He is a man that was recognized as knowing as much about active soldiering in his day as any man living.'

NOTES:

The author sought to write a balanced summary of Sir Ian's life and career, taking all that private data and learning he had access to into consideration. To reflect on one man's impact on his nation's history and his great-nephew, Alec, was essential to get right. The author came to deeply admire Sir Ian and his astonishingly successful and unblemished record if one leaves off the debatable end to his active field career.

The author wrote in-depth research papers on the background to General Gordon's Sudan, the emergence of the self-declared God's redeemer of Islam, and the Siege of Khartoum itself.

Articles written also cover the relief force efforts, with Ian Hamilton at the forefront and Gordon's heroic death seen in Great Britain.

A young Australian-born private whose Father of French ancestry had a plantation in Mauritius. The soldier marched past his "cousin" and General Ian Hamilton in the desert by the Egyptian pyramids and died at Gallipoli. His family claimed his father was a cousin of Sir Ian, written about more fully in reserved papers. These, as with others in the book, are available to approved individuals.

Ian Hamilton's signature.

A Tiger shot by Ian Hamilton in India,1876, which sat in the hall of Alec's home in Scotland. From a time when tigers were abundant, and not an endangered species. It was a different time, which within fifty years would change. (PBA)

General Wolseley with a 5,400-man relief force, including Ian Hamilton, January 1885. They arrived up the Nile River to Khartoum on January 28, just two days too late. They found Major-General Charles Gordon, Governor-General of the Sudan, and virtually all 10,000 civilians and soldiers slaughtered (NCA).

Lieutenant Ian Hamilton at Camp Baramulla, Kashmir, India in 1876. Alec's great-uncle. He stands holding a one-horned Markhor's skull, next to Rajvelli, his trusted shikari (meaning tracker). (WOP).

Colonel Ian S. M. Hamilton (later Major-General, Sir Ian) by John Singer Sargent, 1898. (CE)

Jean Hamilton, wife of the the-Colonel Ian Standish Monteith Hamilton By John Singer Sargent, 1896 (CE).

General Sir Ian Hamilton (The closest rider) riding aside Britain's King George V, the Kaiser, and HRH The Duke of Connaught. King Edward VII's London funeral, 1910. (WOP)

Lt. Ian Hamilton with French and Russian friends in Burg-Bei-Magdeburg Prison Camp, c. 1916. It is a small town in Jerichower, in the northeast part of Germany, which had around 24,000 people in 1916. The town is in the Saxony-Anhalt state and has had a military garrison since the 1700s (NCA).

Rudyard Kipling, British India-born poet and writer, Calcutta, India, 1892, age twenty-seven. A friend of Brevet Major Ian Hamilton, Alec's grandfather's brother (CE).

Chapter 6

MODERN-DAY ALEXANDER HAMILTON'S GRANDFATHER AND FATHER

Alec's Grandfather: Vereker Monteith Hamilton

Vereker Monteith Hamilton was born at Hafton House in Argyll, Scotland, in February 1856 (often, due to its castellated walls and tower, the property was called Hafton Castle). He was the son of Lieutenant-Colonel Christian Monteith Hamilton of the 92nd Highlanders and Lady Maria Corinna Hamilton, née Gort. Vereker was to die aged seventy-six, in 1931, in Kent.

Vereker was born and raised in the Victorian Era of Great Britain and lived through the Edwardian Era and into the House of Windsor Era of the British Monarchy. He was born into an upper-class world of landed wealth, refinement, and leisure. As with Alec's parents, his life gives us a look through an open window into that world, through their stories passed on firsthand to Alec Hamilton, along with stories from his great-uncle, his grandfather's brother.

Vereker was the paternal grandfather of Alec and brother of General Sir Ian Hamilton. In his day, he was a Scottish artist of some renown, creating both military and historical works of art, often on giant canvasses. Twelve of his most famous paintings sit in major museums and national art galleries around the world. A picture entitled "The Storming of the Kashmir Gate at Delhi, India" sits today above Alec's dining room in his Melrose, Scotland estate. The bugle a soldier is holding in the painting, sounding the attack to storm the gate, sits on the Lowood dining room serving table under the picture. Vereker painted a second original of the gate's storming, which was displayed at Wellington College (the private English boarding school), where Vereker was a pupil.

His mother, Lady Hamilton, was the 3rd Viscount Gort's daughter. It is a tragedy that the boys grew up without their mother, as she died within months of giving birth to Vereker. Ian, their eldest son, was three years old when his mother died. Sadly, losing a mother during birth was not uncommon in earlier centuries; childbirth was a dangerous moment in a woman's life.

Vereker had an otherwise idyllic childhood, living at Hafton House with his grandparents, surrounded by endless lawns, fields, and paddocks filled with wild grass and flowers and dotted with landscaped trees, woodland, and forest. They all rolled down to a Loch on the other side, from which arose the Mountain of Benmore. Fields of corn, come harvest season, were reaped in the old way, threshed with flays on the barn floor.

All of this is Scotland at its best, with the Hafton Estate covering at the time 5,740 acres. The house and estate sit on the southern shore of Holy Loch, Argyll. The man who designed the house, called the "father of architecture in Scotland," was David Hamilton (May1768–December 1843), a Glasgow-based man. He also designed Lennox Castle, The Royal Exchange, Glasgow (built on top of James Ewing's former home) and was runner up in the competition to build Great Britain's Houses of Parliament in London in 1835.

The Hafton Estate's grounds were filled with fruit and nut trees, flower gardens, and a walled kitchen garden. Typically, the estate's dairy, livestock, crops, and kitchen garden met all the kitchen's needs for seasonal vegetables, herbs, and fruit, flour, and meat. Sheep and cattle grazed on their land, so they raised lamb and beef for the house, and their chickens and ducks provided the eggs and poultry needs of the home. An abundance of woodlands provided logs for winter fires, and rivers through the estate could provide fish. Family shoots would provide seasonal gamebirds. They were almost totally self-sufficient.

With their father overseas serving with the 92nd Highlanders for years at a time, the brothers, Vereker and Ian, were raised mainly in the home of their paternal grandfather, John Hamilton, and grandmamma Maria Hamilton. An elderly aunt lived there too. This grand Victorian family home saw the boys surrounded by estate servants and tenant farmers, all set in the most delightful Scottish countryside. It's no wonder Vereker grew up appreciating nature and people and became an artist. The boy's maternal grandfather, Viscount Gort, often visited them; the Gort family lived in even grander style in their home, where the boys would stay from time to time. Their liveried servants still wore powered white wigs.

Because of their mother's death and father's absence, both sets of grandparents spoilt the boys with love and care but raised them as sound young men with a good education and exceptional manners, along with a sense of duty and accountability. They grew up with a reliance to changing circumstances and early lessons in adaptability.

Henriette was the boys' nanny, who took great care of them as babies and young children. Vereker remembered her bringing apples from the orchard, roasting them in the nursery fire for them, and endlessly telling magical nursery rhymes and stories. They may have lost their mother, but the boys were indeed not short of loving family care.

Little Vereker also recalled that as a small boy, the butler, while serving lunch one day, announced, "shepherd's pie." Poor Vereker was shocked and anxious all day, as he thought cook had minced up William, the shepherd, and made a pie with him. Late afternoon, he was relieved to find William in the pasture and learn that the pie was made from lamb meat from the lambs the shepherd tended.

Ian, Vereker's brother displayed early signs of martial genes; Vereker said Ian once attacked the family doctor when he vaccinated Vereker, who had let out an agonized scream as the rather thick injection needle plummeted into his soft little flesh. In the early 1800s, doctors still used leeches to suck the blood out of a patient to relieve the body's "humors." After having their fill, the leeches proceeded to "vomit back the blood they'd sucked," as little Vereker so delicately put it when describing the process of leeches at work.

The boys Gort grandfather would arrive on a visit to see them, always dressed immaculately in a black top hat and topcoat and flawlessly polished shoes. Vereker recalled that one of his mother's sisters, Lady Emily, had married the relatively wealthy and eccentric Mr. John Bassett. They were the fourth largest landowners in Cornwall in 1873, as revealed by the *Return of Owners of Land records*, with 16,969 acres. Land records are an excellent resource of family ownership and movement in past centuries for authors

The Bassett's lived in grand style between their estate in Cornwall and a townhouse in London. Both were fully stocked with staff, including footman still in full livery and powdered wigs as were the Gort's. At one luncheon in the dining room of the great house in Cornwall, where Vereker had gone one summer with his nanny in attendance, the French chef was serving roast hare. It was a little undercooked with blood visible. As the bewigged footman brought it to the table, young Vereker, in total innocence, shouted, "Look at that bloody hare!" His literal meaning was not realized, and assuming he was being vulgar, his aunt sent him to his room in disgrace, while he plaintively tried to explain that he wasn't swearing.

School and an Early Art Awakening

Vereker followed his elder brother at Wellington College and believed he was destined for the army too. The school was founded in 1859 by Queen Victoria in honor of the Duke of Wellington. However, to his surprise, in 1872 when he was sixteen, his father, as a lieutenant colonel, told him that he thought it a mistake for both his sons to be in the same profession (Ian was already enlisted to attend the Sandhurst Military Academy). He suggested looking at other "outdoor" pursuits. Vereker was quite taken aback at first but saw an opportunity. In the end, with his father's blessing, he decided that he should go to Ceylon as part of the then-treasured British Empire (the "modern-day" Sri Lanka), buy land, plant coffee, and make his fortune. I suspect that with the school's input, his father realized that he was more of a sensitive boy and unlikely to cope well with battle and a soldier's harsh life.

Consequently, Vereker left Wellington College at Easter in 1873 and was funded by his family, as most "gentlemen of means" and the aristocracy were at the time. He spent just over two and a half years in Europe studying languages, art, and traveling on "The Grand Tour." He experimented with his passion for drawing and art and having fun. The following year, he returned to Scotland for part of the shooting season.

With a natural talent and enthusiasm from childhood for sketching and painting, Vereker's painting career emerged more seriously as he copied images expertly in the Dresden Gallery when studying there and then from real life in Rome. He found himself painting at every opportunity, often at an artist friend's studio, where his talent was remarked upon by well-known artists.

A Ceylonese Planter's Life, and India

It was not unusual for a younger son of a typical Victorian aristocratic family to go into the Church or army, or move to the colonies, as in Vereker's case. Money could still be made in rubber, tea, coffee, and sugar in places like India, Ceylon, Malaya, or the Caribbean.

In December 1875, Vereker set sail from London. After some research with British shipping registers, the author found that Vereker could only have embarked on the P&O Steamship *Surat*, which in December was bound for the Island of Ceylon, the "modern-day" Sri Lanka. The island sits off the southeast of the Indian sub-continent, where the predominant local peoples are ethnic Tamil. The Peninsular & Oriental Steam Navigation Company was formed in 1836, and according to the ship's register, the *Surat* had been built in 1866 and weighed 2,578 tons. There is a painting of the ship at the end of the chapter.

After landing at Pointe de Galleon, Ceylon's southernmost tip, Vereker spent the night in a local hotel although he never listed it. Until the mid-seventeenth century, Galle had been the island's largest port, but Colombo, with one of the world's largest natural harbors, overtook it later that century. Vereker traveled the sixty-five miles (105 km.) the next day to Colombo (Kolamba in Sinhalese), up the island's west coast. His transport would have stopped for tiffin each afternoon, traveling by coach and horses to Colombo, the Ceylon capital, over a two-to-three-day period most likely. The railway between the two cities was not built until 1895. (See notes on tiffin at the end of the chapter.)

On Vereker's ocean passage to Ceylon, he traveled in a portside cabin and booked a starboard-side cabin when he eventually returned to England. Let me offer a quick clarification for those who may not be aware. Those passengers who could afford the extra cost would travel to India and Ceylon portside out/starboard home in these days of steamships of the 1800s and sail ships earlier in the 1700s. You can find a helpful explanation in this chapter's notes as to why this was essential for those that could afford it.

Home in the Ceylonese Hills

After some days of rest upon arrival, he traveled to a residence in an outlying district called Madulseema, some sixty miles beyond Badulla. Having rested there, he traveled on to the Haputale District's mountain range, whose mountains climb to some 6,000 feet from the south side. He was headed to the Haldumulla Estate at around 5,400 feet, an ideal elevation for a coffee plantation, best grown above 4,000 feet. He soon discovered that a path from a gap at this elevation led to Beauvais, the only estate on the opposite side to the mountain. Here he became good pals with Edie Moss, who lived there with his brother Lewis. They were coffee planters. Luckily, they all enjoyed hunting and bird shooting and spent much time together.

To learn the ropes, Vereker started at the coffee estate of an acquaintance's plantation, as assistant manager/planter; tea was by far the greatest product grown in Ceylon, however. The head manager was a Scot, like Vereker. Very few Sinhalese were employed on such estates; most were Tamils, and Vereker set about becoming fluent in Tamil to manage his workforce better. He was later in the Haputale district, some 5,000 feet up in the southern hills of Ceylon, on a plantation called Ginnegadulla, which he managed, often visiting his friends higher up Haldumulla to go snipe shooting.

He took over the plantation of a neighbor who had fallen ill and left it in his care. The only relief from the heat and humidity day and night would be the breeze flowing off neighboring hills and mountains. One evening Vereker had a huge scare, when staying in a bedroom at one end of the long, narrow plantation house. A planter friend who'd come to help him manage the plantation slept in another bedroom at the other end, fronted by a verandah that spanned the width of the home. A blood-curdling scream went up in the middle of the night from his friend, and Vereker hastened to his room with nothing more than a candle and a smile (no electric lighting in those days).

He found a giant and fearful-looking tarantula spider clinging to the room's curtains, the size of a man's hand, its hairs bristling. None of the house staff would come into the room, whereas had it been a scorpion or cobra snake, they would not have hesitated, apparently. After some period of standoff and concern, the two men eventually managed to get it down by shaking the curtain. Just as Vereker was about to stab it with his knife, he dropped the candle, and it went out.

They momentarily stumbled around in the dark with no shoes or slippers on with a tarantula spider on the loose! A panic and a feared agonizing death were avoided as, in the glimmer of moonlight now registering in their eyes, Vereker spotted the just-as-frightened tarantula scuttling around the room. He stabbed the poor creature and dispatched it. Life in the tropics in the 1800s was not for the faint-hearted. Both men slept with one eye open that night.

Vereker traveled to India late in the same year and spent some years there painting in Shimla and Kashmir. Numerous early photographs held by the family record his time there. He also spent time learning and becoming fluent in Hindi. Being fluent in English, French, Hindi, and Tamil was quite a blessing in India.

Shimla—the British Raj Government's Summer Retreat

By 1864, Shimla (pronounced Simla by the British) was the summer capital of the British government and high society for three months of the year, from mid-March to mid-June, after which the monsoon rains came for the next three months.

The excessive heat and humidity down on the plains below and in the British Raj capital of Calcutta became unbearable. For "the season," it was a five-day, 1,200-mile bumpy journey by horse, horse and carriage, elephant, sedan chair, or even a bullock cart with people's luggage and personal belongings. The train and cars up to Shimla would come after the turn of the century, as would electricity and electric fans.

Summers on the Indian plains saw temperatures often exceeding 40°C (104°F) during mid-March to mid-June before the monsoon rainy season started, whereas the average daytime temperatures simultaneously in Shimla were 21°C (70°F). It is no wonder that everyone who could head for the Shimla hill station in the summer did. The dense forests of the Himalayas 7,500 feet above sea level were, during the devastating summer heat, like being in the Scottish Highlands, with fires often needed at nighttime when temperatures dropped to 4.4°C–17°C (40°F–62 °F) in Shimla. Ian Hamilton had described summer in Shimla as "blissful."

By 1864 it was well established. With the viceroy, the entire government would come: some 5,000 imperial clerks, staff, military officers, wives, children, and a few thousand British India Society servants. One either owned a home in Shimla or rented one for the season. As the population increased, a lot more bungalows were built, and they established a bazaar. There is a broader summary in the notes section at the end of the chapter for those interested.

While Vereker Hamilton was based at Shimla for the 1889 summer season, his brother, now Brevet Lieutenant Colonel Ian Hamilton, made plans to go on an expedition into the Kashmir region. Ian would have met his friend Rudyard Kipling at Shimla, who visited most summer seasons, with the hill station township centered on a flat plain at 7,000 feet high. Rudyard Kipling once described Shimla as the "center of power as well as pleasure."

The Hamilton Brothers Go Hunting.

From Shimla, Ian and Vereker traveled with one or two friends and a small retinue of staff and bearers, including their cook and their khitmatgar (a personal servant, rather like a valet). They moved deliberately light in rough mufti clothes, with only a spare shirt and underwear and an extra pair of puttees each (strips of cloth worn wrapped around the lower legs in a spiral pattern, from ankle to knee, to provide cover from dirt and insect bites). They also wore a Puggaris, a local form of turban typically made of felt or goats' wool—round, flat headwear. Both brothers being fluent in Hindi would have helped their travels enormously.

They spent their time in daily marches towards Srinagar for the shooting and just relaxing together. Srinagar is in the Kashmir Valley and sits on the banks of the Jhelum River. The city is at an elevation of 1,600 meters (5,200 feet high). The enormous Dal and Nagin Lakes are situated there. On the last stretch of their journey, they all boarded a local boat to go upriver to the city, disheveled and untidy. They were delighted to bathe in the river and be free of dust and dirt and to have their clothes washed too. Vereker especially enjoyed being away from polite society: the stiff colors and jackets, formal dinners, and polite conversation, all of which he would trade in any day of the week for casual clothes, an easel, and brushes, and days painting in the hills on his own.

Since the seventh century, the river was the major transport route to and right through the city and was the final part of the journey. It became challenging to navigate this river many decades later, with lack of care and clearance of blockages, and boats seemingly assigned only to the big lakes like Dahl, primarily for vacation and tourism. There are currently moves afoot by the Srinagar Municipal Corporation to dredge the river and make it fully navigational for the transport of goods again

Both Vereker and Ian were thoroughly enjoying the peace, calm, and splendor of slowly gliding down the river. The boatman alerted them to a long, grandly decorated barge—propelled by a crew of forty liveried oarsmen moving their oars in unison and dressed splendidly in official government crimson uniforms. It was a splendid sight to the brothers, but both thought it somewhat ominous. Both men's foreboding was realized as the barge slowed and the oarsmen were instructed to raise oars, which they held straight up towards the sky. The barge officer asked permission to steer alongside. An Indian Army orderly delivered a message from the British Resident of Srinagar (a sort of the regional governor). He had heard somehow that they were making their way to the city, and he invited them to transfer to his stately official barge for the final passage to town and to stay as his guests at the British Residency.

They chatted amongst themselves to find an excuse, not wishing to go, as they were woefully underdressed and unprepared in wardrobe to be presented to the Resident or other guests. Vereker didn't want to spoil his relaxing holiday with his brother by such a formal society attendance either. Eventually, he agreed with Ian that they could not reject such a kind offer from a senior government official, which might offend, so they transferred to the grandly decorated barge.

In the end, their host was very kind and disarming about their dress and mentioned how sensible their clothes were for the heat and travel and how he envied them, making them entirely at ease. They saw him as most charming and hospitable, as was his wife, and when it came time to leave, they almost regretted it, as they much enjoyed their stay and the Resident's company.

Vereker's Paintings in India

Vereker's paintings of battles in India and the western frontier, such as the Tirah campaign and his famous depiction of the storming of Piewar Kotal (shown in this book), were inspired by conversations with Sir Ian's old mentor, Lord Roberts. The Battle of Piewar Kotal was at the western end of the Kurrum Valley on the border between Afghanistan and India, at which Ian Hamilton was present, a battle the British won. Vereker wasn't happy with his painting depicting the 92nd Regiment of Foot (The Gordon Highlanders) at Kandahar, and after exhibiting it at the Royal Academy, he repainted it, adding in additional figures. It was shown again at the Royal Academy under his new title, *MacPherson's Brigade at Kandahar*, the following year. Around this same time, Vereker did a painting titled *Missing Afridi*, about the tribe driven from the Khyber Pass by his brother in the military campaign.

Art School, and Marriage

Finally, in 1883 and back in England, Vereker joined London's famous Slade School of Art, tutored by a Mr. Legros. Vereker once said that Legros was too important a personality to have a mere Mr. tagged on to his name.

Vereker met a young woman he fell in love with at the Slade School of Art, where she was a prize-winning artist who had won one of the school's several scholarships. He, too, won a prize in 1886 for landscape painting, and together they made a wide circle of eclectic friends. Lillian Swainson, whom he was destined to marry, was a granddaughter of William Swainson. He was a famous ornithologist, malacologist, conchologist, entomologist, and naturalist. Nine bird species discovered by him carry his name, and he became famous for his bird illustrations and for being the first illustrator and naturalist to use lithography.

After Vereker and Lillian married, they stayed in London and took up residence in St. John's Wood. They were to have four children in time. He frequently had art works accepted by The Royal Academy and showed at Burlington House events. Burlington House was completed in the late 1600s for the first Earl of Burlington. Later it was sold to the Dukes of Devonshire and eventually sold again and then acquired by the British government in the mid-1800s. After that, it housed The Royal Academy amongst other societies. Here the greatest artists of the day displayed their works, if accepted by the academy.

Vereker had worked for many weeks on a grand Italian landscape, which he submitted to the committee to accept and hang. Moreover, he provided a rapidly drawn rough sketch of his brother that he did in thirty minutes. His brother was dressed in the Gordon Highlanders' complete tartan kit for the new role he was about to embark on as aide-de-camp to the Commander-in-Chief, British Armed forces, India. Vereker's stunning oil painting was rejected, but his quick sketch was accepted and displayed. He learned later that the entire committee of the Royal Academy had dismissed his drawing too. However, the president of the Society, a keen fan of Vereker's works, exercised his right to overrule the committee and approved its display.

Vereker exhibited at the British Royal Academy and, from 1886 onwards, at the Salon d'Art de Paris, in Glasgow. He also exhibited at the Grosvenor Gallery, London. In 1899, his Royal Academy painting was titled *Sniping the*

Rear Guard. During the First World War, Vereker, a conscientious objector, served with the British Red Cross, to Ian's great concern and embarrassment. Quite a contrast indeed for a man from a military family; his brother led armies, while he would not participate in the fighting. One can only imagine what Vereker's father thought of his decision, as neither Vereker nor Ian ever said. However, like many artists, Vereker was a sensitive man with a sensitive soul and put his energy into saving and caring for others' lives to do his bit for King and Empire.

Off to South Africa

In mid-1894, between the two Boer Wars, skirmishes constantly flared up between British troops and Boer militia in South Africa. Vereker learned by telegram that Ian was in a field hospital there after having had his wrist shattered by a bullet wound and succumbing to malaria at about the same time. Vereker was assured that the diagnosis was good, and doctors predicted he'd survive malaria. Within a month, he'd be fit enough to withstand the journey back to England, where he could convalesce fully. Vereker took the next ship out to South Africa and met people who would take him across the veldt to the railhead at Maritzburg, which sat close to the mountain range where Ian was in the hospital. Now known as Pietermaritzburg, it is in the KwaZulu Natal Province of South Africa.

During the Second Boer War in 1899, the future world-renowned Mahatma Gandhi gathered around 1,100 fellow Indians and organized the Indian Ambulance Corps to support the British troops fighting in South Africa. He himself ran ambulances and stretcher parties. Later from 1893 until 1914, Gandhi worked as an attorney in South Africa, based in Durban. It was from Pietermaritzburg that Ian would be brought down by mule-wagon from the mountain, still very weak. Ian's superior officer had ordered Ian's batman to stay by his side until he was safely delivered home in England (a batman is a soldier assigned as a personal servant to a commissioned army officer). Before the advent of motorized transport, an officer's batman was also in charge of his officer's horse. This animal was affectionately known as the "bat-horse," and it carried the packsaddle with his officer's kit during a campaign. Escorted by Vereker and his batman, they set off through the South African town of Newcastle and on to Durban. From Durban, they crossed by ship to Cape Town, and from there by another vessel to England via St. Helena and Ascension Island in the South Atlantic Ocean.

Having a whole day in Cape Town before the long ocean voyage ahead, they had planned for a fishing boat to meet them early in the morning, most likely at the Victoria and Albert Dock. They longed for a day's fishing together, and Ian, with his batman's agreement, felt that his wrist's bandaging was sound enough for the fishing not to cause further injury. Both men loved fishing, whether in a river, lake, or the sea, and fishing remained one of their favorite sports throughout their lives.

Ian's batman, who was as keen on fishing as they were, alerted them that their fishing boat had pulled into the harbor. It was about to approach the quay and load them aboard. Just as they were picking up their belongings, a liveried orderly approach and handed Ian, to his surprise, a message on "Government House" British Cape Colony-headed paper. It was an invite to both brothers to attend a luncheon with the governor that very same day.

Ian felt that as a serving officer on leave, he could not refuse the invitation of the governor and Lady Robinson, and they'd have to forgo the day's fishing; however, Vereker said an emphatic no. He felt under no such obligation as a private citizen and knew it was improbable that they'd ever meet the Robinsons again. He and his batman would still go fishing, and Ian could give their apologies—Vereker was adamant. Ian felt that it might be seen as a snub, but there it was. Vereker was on board the fishing vessel and apologized to Ian that he would not change his mind. Luckily, Ian had his ship trunks with him by now and his batman to assist him in retrieving the clothes he needed. He went to the formal luncheon on his own and made his brother's apologies.

Vereker had an excellent days fishing and said that he did what he had most looked forward to after the long voyage: relaxed, spent time with nature and the elements, and fished. He was especially pleased to catch several of the South African snoek fish. Snoek is the Dutch word for a pike fish, typically 50 cm.–140 cm. in length (1'6"—4'6").

Vereker's Moment of Karma

By August 1894, they arrived in Great Britain to complete Ian's recovery, and after a brief spell in London, the brothers headed home to Scotland for the grouse shooting season. A few days afterward, they were invited by Campbell Finlay to come to stay and shoot at his home, Toward Castle in Argyll, the former seat of the Clan Lamont. The ruins of the earlier castle sit within the grounds destroyed by the Campbells in 1646.

At dinner that first evening at the castle, having arrived in the late afternoon ready for tomorrow's first shoot, karma struck Vereker. Dinners at Toward were always formal, white-tie affairs with a huge mahogany dining table designed to seat many guests comfortably and laid with lavish amounts of sterling silver, silver candelabras, crystal glasses, and flowers no doubt. Vereker dressed a little late for dinner and missed pre-dinner drinks. He hurriedly found his way to the dining room to join the other guests, who had just sat down and were busy chatting and laughing amongst themselves. His host, looking a tad disapproving, waved him towards the one empty seat between two ladies, whom he had not had time to be introduced to yet. A rather stately lady with bold aristocratic features sat to one side of Vereker and turned to him. She said in a somewhat haughty tone of voice, "I was very sorry the other day in Cape Town, Mr. Hamilton, to hear you preferred catching snoek to making my acquaintance, but you see, we are fated to meet." It was Lady Robinson, the governor's wife from Cape Town! Vereker merely smiled and complimented Lady Robinson on her dress with a somewhat embarrassed glance, a very gentlemanly response.

Vereker's life passion was shooting, even more so than fishing. He was especially keen on grouse and snipe shooting and made frequent trips as a young man to stay with an uncle in Aberdeenshire to shoot there. His uncle, years earlier, had purchased a house and shooting estate from the Earl of Fife, owned initially by the last Skene or chief of Clan Skene. Skene is a village next to Echt in Aberdeenshire, just outside Aberdeen City, where the Scottish Highlands rise. Here Vereker remembers excellent pheasant and partridge shooting and duck flighting on the Loch. George Skene had been the last of the Clan Skene and died in 1835. Echt and Skene are usually referred to as a pair. Knowing them well, the author described Echt as a charming, beautiful village, the Old Manse a perfect example of a Georgian grand house.

A Life Well-Led

There were years when Vereker's paintings sold well both privately and to galleries and museums, and his Ceylonese plantations, which he owned as an absentee landlord by now, were doing well. At some time in later years, when coffee and tea were not doing so well, he sold his plantations in Ceylon, I believe at a loss.

He painted countless works in his life, and thirteen of his most significant pieces hang in museums and national art galleries in London, Scotland, New Zealand, and South Africa. Many more of his finest works are in private collections around the world, and one painting he painted twice hangs both in his old school, Wellington College in Berkshire, England, and one in his own home. That painting was left through Alec's father to Alec and hung in his home in Scotland.

In later years, life's odds seemed stacked against Vereker, and he and his little family took to living rurally in France to cut costs. Income was only just dribbling in from his artwork and an invested past family bequest. He leased out his more substantial house in London and rented a small pied-à-terre close by to paint in when he was able to win commissions. Sometimes when he received commissions, he'd temporarily leave the family in France, return to London, paint, sell his work of art, and return to France with funds to keep them going.

In 1925, Vereker published his autobiography. His main intent was to write down the memories of his life for the amusement of his children. Indeed, they became of much value to his grandchildren and now his great-grandchildren and great-great-grandchildren too. It was titled, *Things That Happened*. He had written his memories from his home in France in 1923 and 1924, at à L'epine Île de Noirmoutier. Later still, Vereker released his house in France and the pied-à-terre in London and purchased a home in Cowden, in Kent, where in 1931, aged seventy-six, he died before Alec was born the following year. Sadly, Alec never met his grandfather, the famous Hamilton artist. Alec said that he was delighted that the author was fulfilling, for him, the same gift his grandpa wished to leave his descendants: memories of his life and times.

Alec's Father: Ian Bogle Monteith Hamilton

The Early Years

This Ian Hamilton was born on October 1890 in Argyll, Scotland, and died aged eighty in 1971 at Cowden, in Kent, England, the home he'd inherited from his father, Vereker. He chose to be buried at Bowden New Cemetery near his Scottish estate in Melrose, Scotland, which his son Alec Hamilton inherited.

Lieutenant Ian Bogle Monteith and His World War One

While his uncle, General Sir Ian Hamilton, took command of an entire theater of war in Eastern Europe, his nephew with the 1st and 3rd (Special Reserve) Battalion, the Gordon Highlanders, is in one of its first battles in France. The younger Ian was soon to be an unexpected German prisoner for the entire war.

Ian Bogle Monteith Hamilton was commissioned as a 2nd Lieutenant in the 3rd (Special Reserve) Battalion, the Gordon Highlanders, on August 30, 1911. Before receiving his commission, Ian had been a cadet corporal in the Oxford University Contingent Training Corps and underwent his training after completing a degree at this, one of the preeminent UK universities.

Special Reserve Battalions were established in January 1908 to provide additional support to regular battalions in war. Such reservists were hitherto part-time soldiers who enlisted for a six-year term and committed to undergo six months of basic training upon recruitment and three to four weeks of training annually. Ian was the only Special Reserve officer commissioned into the Gordon Highlanders full time; the other officers required to manage and supervise the 3rd Battalion were seconded as necessary from the regular, full-time battalions.

A Family at War

On June 28, 1914, after the assassination of the Austro-Hungarian Crown Prince, Archduke Franz Ferdinand in Sarajevo and Serbia failed to meet an ultimatum by the Austro-Hungarian emperor, he declared war on Serbia on July 28, 1914. The alliances between some states saw the German Emperor come to the Austro-Hungarian Emperor's aid and the Russian Tsar to Serbia's aid. So, it rapidly escalated into an entire European conflict, as we know. Virtually every royal house in Europe was headed by family relatives. It truly was a family at war.

By August 4, all reservists, including this young Lieutenant Ian Hamilton, were mobilized, and ordered to report to the Gordon Highlanders Regimental Depot in Aberdeen, the Castlehill Barracks. A group of Special Reservists was then sent to the south coast of England port of Plymouth on August 6 to join the 1st Battalion of the Regiment, including Ian. He had been promoted to lieutenant the day before. The 1st Battalion had already landed at Boulogne-Sur-Mer on the coast of France on August 14 as part of the British Expeditionary Force (BEF). They were almost immediately thrown into the Battle of Mons against the Germans.

Alec's father, Ian had been assigned to C Company, 1st Battalion, the Gordon Highlanders Regiment, which was placed within the 8th Infantry Brigade under the command of Brigadier-General Doran. Three infantry brigades (the 7th, 8th, and 9th), four artillery brigades, engineers, and divisional mounted troops of Hussars and *cyclists* were all part of the 3rd Division of the BEF, commanded by Major-General Hubert Ion Wetherell Hamilton.

Ian faced the German Army at Mons on August 23, 1914 where the British forces were significantly outnumbered, virtually 2:1, including artillery. Remarkably, this was the first battle fought by the British Army in World War One. The BEF attempted to hold the Mons–Condé Canal line against the advancing German First Army Division and fought well. The First, had around 1,600 casualties, but inflicted a disproportionate number of German casualties, who suffered 2,500 losses. The sudden and unexpected retreat of the French Fifth Army took British command by surprise. The sudden loss of a sizeable part of the Allied Army from the theater of war exposed the British right flank. The tactical decision was made by the British supreme field commander, Sir John French, to withdraw over the next few days. While supposedly a simple withdrawal executed in good order, it took two weeks to affect the escape.

On August 26, however, at Le Cateau the Gordon Highlanders, and Royal Scots formed a defensive line to protect their Battalions' retreat. They were ultimately forced to withdraw more speedily, but this defensive line of men had become detached from the main British force. Surrounded by the German

Army, they were forced to surrender. Over 500 Gordon Highlanders, including Alec's father, by now Major Ian Hamilton, were taken as Prisoners of War (POWs) on August 27 and 28, 1914.

Major-General Hubert Ion Wetherell Hamilton was with the main force withdrawing and was pushed to the outskirts of Paris in France before counter-attacking in concert with the French. He was tragically to die on October 14, 1914, in the thick of battle, aged just fifty-three. He was killed by a single bullet to the head in a later engagement with the enemy. Mons in Belgium fell to the German Army, who held it until November 28, 1918, after four years and two months of occupation. The Canadian Army Corp. recaptured the city. Coincidently, the last shot fired in World War One was at Mons, where the British Army had their first battle in this world war.

Following a lengthy series of journeys by train from Mons, Belgium, the Allied prisoners of war (POWs), including Ian, arrived in Germany at the small town of Sennelager directly east northeast, some 226 miles or 363 kilometers as the crow flies. A prominent prisoner of war camp had been set up there by the Germans, from where they moved prisoners further into Germany. Here the officers and men were separated and sent to different camps. Ian was temporarily sent to a camp in Freidberg, near Augsburg in Baden-Württemberg in the southwest of Germany, requiring more long train journeys to the west-northwest of Munich. Allied officers were held here in the old Freidberg University building on the grounds of the Mainz Citadel.

After this temporary prison encampment, Ian was transferred one last time by a series of trains almost directly north to a POW Officers Camp in Burg-Bei-Magdeburg, where he spent the remainder of the war. The camp on the outskirts of the old town held 900 POW officers. Here they were close enough to German High Command in Berlin, just 68 miles, or 109 kilometers, away.

There are files on Lt. Ian Hamilton, the Gordon Highlanders, Lt. Colin Campbell, the Argyll, Sutherland Highlanders, and Arthur Gallie, a Glasgow Yeomanry Officer, at the National Records Office in Scotland. While Ian documented with sketches and graphic descriptions of his surroundings, the town, and his friends, he also made close friends with one of the Russian officers, who taught him Russian to some degree. Meanwhile, Lt. Colin Campbell led fellow officers in building an escape tunnel out of the camp, under the walls and the riverbanks! Nineteen Allied officers escaped, although most, like Campbell, only remained free for ten days before being picked up and reinterned in prison. Lt. Gaillie, from a wealthy Glasgow family, fought bravely as an infantry officer before being captured in 1918. Luckily for him, the war was very close to its end, so he spent less time as a prisoner.

Following the Armistice of November 11, 1918, Ian was one of a group of British officer POWs who were repatriated from Germany via Rotterdam in Holland, landing in Hull in England, which is around halfway up the east English coast. They landed on November 16 aboard the 'Screw Steamer' the SS *Stockport*. After landing in Hull, each man was interviewed by government-appointed lawyers about their time as a POW. Following their intensive debrief and medical checks, the officers were free to return to their families.

The Special Reserve Battalions were abolished immediately after the war, and Ian then resigned his commission (most likely around year-end, 1918) and returned home to Scotland. It appears that he did not maintain any significant links with the Gordon Highlanders, other than through his family connections.

He studied architecture in Paris and led a very active architectural practice of some renown in London. As an example, he designed the classical Royal Bank of Scotland offices in London. Ian was a Fellow of the Royal Institute of British Architects (RIBA). He served in World War One as an officer with the Gordon Highlander regiment and was taken prisoner in Europe and incarcerated in a German Castle quite early in the war. Alec's father had a self-portrait sketched when he was in prison, and a photograph of him was taken around the same time. Both are in this book.

Alec's Father Gets Married

Ian was to marry Constance Crum-Ewing, great-granddaughter of Humphrey Crum-Ewing, who inherited as a nephew all of James Ewing's property, including the Caymanas sugar estate in Jamaica.

Miss Crum-Ewing Marries Mr. Hamilton

Alec's father, Ian, spent the night before his wedding at Boturich Castle on Loch Lomond, the Findlay's home, close to Strathleven House. Bill Findlay's father and Alec's father were close pals, and Alec and Bill, their sons, became the very best of pals. They went to boarding school together and kept in touch until Alec's sad death on Easter 2020.

The Daily Gleaner, the principal national newspaper of Jamaica, published a feature article on January 9, 1925, picked up from the *Lennox Herald & Weekly Advertiser* of Scotland's December issue. It was a feature article on Alec's parents' wedding, held on Wednesday, December 10, 1924. As Constance's parents owned one of the largest estates in Jamaica, this was important news there too. The article read:

> The marriage of Miss Crum-Ewing, Strathleven House, at the Dumbarton Parish Church, was bedecked with chrysan-themums on Wednesday, December 10th afternoon. When she arrived, the bride had added lily of the valley and orange blossom, the two blending in the early Victorian posy she carried. The occasion was the wedding of Miss Constance Beryl Crum-Ewing, (daughter of Mr. and Mrs. Alexander Crum-Ewing, and Mr. Ian Bogle Monteith Hamilton, son of Mr. and Mrs. Vereker M. Hamilton.

There were some one hundred guests present at the wedding: ladies in stunning dresses, wrapped in sumptuous fur coats, exquisite hats, and magnificent jewelry; and the gentlemen in their top hats and tails looking very dapper. Her father gave her away, and the church had a full choral choir.

Among those present were Sir Archibald and Lady Campbell of Succoth, Sir Alexander and Lady Leith-Buchanan of Ross Priory, the Lady Helen Graham of Buchanan Castle, Sir James Guthrie, General Sir Ian and Lady Hamilton, Brigadier-General and Mrs. Hamilton of Skene, the Hon. Mrs. Godley, and Major and Mrs. R. E. Findlay of Boturich Castle (Alec's best pal Bill's parents).

Alec's Parents

Constance was a very serious-minded lady, but generosity personified; Ian was a highly amusing man, which made them an ill-matched but devoted couple. There was an event at Castle Hill in Caithness (Constance's home on Scotland's northernmost point, which Alec's sister inherited). Bill Findlay,

Alec's oldest Scottish-born friend, remembers Constance saying, "Off to bed, boys, or you will not shoot straight in the morning." Ian was just heard to quietly say right after, "Boys, who's for a game of bridge?"

Alec's parents were always such a loving couple, and their children recalled that their mother was stricter than their father. Their mother was still interested in all the farms, and their parents would go together in a pony and trap around the estate at Strathleven to visit them. There was a farm at the top of a hill, which was really for sheep but had plentiful grouse, and there was a funicular railway that went up, which she used to enjoy. Alec's parents sometimes shot grouse up there, joining with the next-door neighbor to have grouse beaters on hand.

Their father was much more social than their mother was, who was learning to shoot and had her gun, a 16 bore. Father shot with a 22 bore and shot everything, including snipe at Castle Hill in Scotland's northern reaches on the family moor. They had liked to fish on the Clyde but couldn't in those years due to carpet makers using what was called Turkey Red Dye at the weaving works, which washed out untreated into the river and the Clyde, ruining the fishing and polluting the river.

In her later years, Constance was cared for full-time by her daughter, Mary, until she died. Alec said Mary gave up her personal life to care for their mother, and while she had many young men after her, she followed up with none, as she felt her duty to their mother came first. It is into this loving parental home that Alec and his siblings were born.

The Heiress

In 1944, Constance Hamilton became heir to the Crum-Ewing's 26,000-acre Caymanas Sugar Estate in Jamaica and the Strathleven House and estate's 8,000 acres of farms in Scotland. There was capital wealth trust behind her too. Her only brother and heir to the estates, Alexander, had been killed in World War One, hence Constance became heir. Several years later, the Scottish Board of Trade issued a compulsory purchase order for Strathleven Park Estate and all 8,000 acres to build an "industrial estate." Oddly, the purchase excluded the listed palladium house and a few acres sitting smack bang in the middle of the entire estate.

Constance, not wishing to live in the middle of an industrial estate filled with factories and warehouses, forced the purchase of the historic house by the local council, along with the rest of the estate. A surprising claim against the estate emerged. The Free Church of Scotland filed a lawsuit against Constance for 80 percent of the sale price of the Strathleven Estate. They gave evidence that under a change to the deed executed by her ancestor, James Ewing, 80 percent of the sale price would go to the Church if his heirs or future generations ever chose to sell the estate.

Constance vigorously disputed the Church's claim in court based on it *not* being a voluntary sale. They had not "chosen" to sell and therefore had not breached the terms of the deed. The estate had been forcedly taken from her by the regional government. She won but bizarrely lost at the Court of Appeal at the High Court when the Church appealed. Constance, showing great fortitude and determination, appealed to the final arbitrator in the land, the British House of Lords, and won (somewhat akin to the American Supreme Court). She filed for legal expenses and received 100 percent compensation for *all* her legal costs at the expense of the Free Church of Scotland.

Strathleven's eventual sale went through in 1947, when Alec was just fifteen and away at boarding school. Alec's maternal family had once farmed crops there, their tenants bred sheep, and doves cooed in the ancient dovecote; it is still there, but now surrounded by factories and warehouses. The house, which survived a fire after the sale, was rebuilt and stands today, grade II listed.

Alec's mother was bitterly upset to have her family's property forcibly removed. She used the eventual payment to purchase the 300-plus acres Lowood House and estate on Scotland's east coast. Lowood is close to Melrose, south of Edinburgh, almost as if she couldn't get far enough away from her lost heritage. An additional 300-plus acres nearby was purchased by Mrs. Crum-Ewing and inherited by Alec's sister, Helen, along with some 6,000 acres of moorland with some homes on it in Caithness, the northern tip of Scotland.

As the eldest son, Alec would inherit through his mother the 26,000-acre Caymanas sugar estate in eastern Jamaica, and the beach house on the north coast. While she was still alive, his mother allowed Alec to manage the estate and learn the business, as we will read in a later chapter on Alec himself. He also inherited the 300 acres in Scotland, near Melrose.

Dear friends of Alec's, Johnnie, and Claire Blair, recalled how during Alec's mother's final illness, she kept a clutch of goose eggs under her bedclothes to make the best of being bedridden and focus on caring for the goslings before they hatched. Alec's eldest son, Johnny, said they called their paternal grandma Mummy Crummy. When Alec's younger brother was born, he was christened Ian Crum-Ewing Hamilton to honor his mother's maiden family name. Consequently, everyone nicknamed young Ian, Crummy.

Winston Churchill and Belted Galloway Cattle

Alec's father had once recalled the story of his great-uncle, General Sir Ian Hamilton, who was very close to Winston Churchill and purchased "Lullenden Farm" from him. It comprised seventy-seven acres in East Grinsted, in West Sussex in England, around twenty-one miles south of London. With the land came a large Tudor manor house, which Churchill had only had for two years, from 1917, after he resigned as First Sea Lord over the Dardanelles fiasco— something that connected Sir Ian and Churchill at the hip. Churchill eventually settled at "Chartwell" in Buckinghamshire.

Churchill had re-established the belted Galloway breed of cattle, which General Sir Ian took on. As his obituary noted, Sir Ian had moved his herd of Lullenden heifers and bulls up to Lowood in Melrose, Scotland, when his nephew, Alec's father, Ian, purchased the herd from him. They remain at Lowood today under Alec Hamilton's care, having been taken on by him after his father died. See notes at chapter end.

Ian and Constance's Life

In the 1930s, Alec's parents lived at a lovely country home, "Whinns" in Surrey. Alec's father commuted to London every day by train to his architect's office, sharing a compartment with, among others, T.S. Eliot, one of the twentieth-century's most celebrated British poets. Eliot was an essayist, publisher, playwright, literary, and social critic too. He had moved to England from America, the country where he was born, when he was twenty-five.

Ian and T.S. became good friends and did the *Times* newspaper crossword together every day on the train up to London, Monday to Friday. This was at the time when Eliot commuted each day to his office at the publishers Faber & Gwyer in London, where he'd become a director and remained so for the rest of his life (publishers now known as Faber & Faber). At her parents' request, T.S. Eliot became godfather to Alec's sister Helen.

Alec's friends remember his father, Ian, as a talented artist, besides being a leading architect of the day.

Alec's mother Constance was a very keen sportswoman who rode to hounds side saddle, as was expected of a lady in those days. She was a super shot and a lover of deer stalking. Many have described her as the archetypal British countrywoman. She seemed happiest in the field with country sports and was always full of energy and go. She was known to be a straightforward, no-nonsense woman with impeccable manners and someone who always knew what to say in conversation with anyone.

As he aged, Alec's father did not grow old mentally and was known as a very able communicator, particularly with the young. He was enthusiastic right to the end about many interests: design, painting, writing, sport, and wildlife—and everything that was going on around him. In retirement in 1966, he wrote and published the book *A Happy Warrior* about his illustrious uncle, General Sir Ian Hamilton's, life and times.

Ian Bogle Monteith Hamilton was known for his gentle manner and kindness, his great sense of humor, his patience, and mainly his perpetual courtesy to everyone, no matter their class or rank. These are a set of traits that the author has witnessed as having been inherited by Alec. Alec encapsulated all these traits for sure, and Ian had a dry and engaging sense of humor while being someone known for not suffering fools gladly. Such an encounter would have resulted in a polite but dismissive remark, leaving the recipient dead in the water.

Alec's father was a keen fisherman; it must run in the genes, as that sport passed down to Alec, who loved nothing better than to be out fishing, whether on his estate in Scotland fishing for salmon on the family's 1.5 mile stretch of River Tweed or wherever he might happen to be. He loved fishing in his younger days off the coast of Caymanas Estate in Jamaica too, or on its river outlets.

Constance's Love of Horse Racing and Breeding

Constance had a passion for breeding racehorses both in England and in Jamaica, a love her sons were to take on. Her most successful British horse was Peaty Sandy, who won the Welsh Grand National; he had been trained by Helen, her daughter. Peaty Sandy won the big race at Newcastle four times and was eighth in the English Grand National. Alec's younger brother, Ian, carried on his mother's passion and for many years bred racehorses at his stud farm at Newbury, Berkshire, in England.

Caymanas, Jamaica, and The New House

When Alec's mother inherited the Caymanas Estate in Jamaica, her husband designed and built the new, modern great house out of traditional local granite stone. The house is known as Caymanas House. He also designed and built the family beach house on Jamaica's north coast. The house sits on a hundred yards of yellow sandy beach with calm waters, as it sits on the inside of a reef onto which the north coast Atlantic waves crash and tumble. The beach house is known as "Kling-Kling." Ian and Constance usually visited the Caymanas estate in Jamaica once a year as absentee owners. They relied on an estate manager to run to show for them.

Alec's father's design for the present Caymanas Great House saw to it that the house sits on a stunning flat ridge of land above the Caymanas sugar plantation. In front of the house on this ridge, the lawns drop away downhill to the sugar plantation below, and in the distance can be seen Kingston and the Blue Mountains—breathtaking views day or night. The mist lays across the plains below as the sun rises over the horizon in the early morning. As dawn breaks, the wafting aroma of flower beds rises, wherein evening falls with glorious red sunsets that light up the sky and land below in a dream-like vision. The tropical sound of bird song welcomes the sunrise, and there's an evening serenade of cicadas and crickets as the sun sets.

There is a marvelous painting of the Caymanas cane fields by the famous Jamaican artist - Hamilton and the author's friend, Judy McMillan, with mutual friends who live in Montego Bay. To stand on the paths between the cane fields at Caymanas, with the blue mountain range soaring above the cane fields, is quintessential Jamaica, something Judy catches instinctively in all her work.

What an adventure it must all have seemed to Alec when, in 1954, he arrived in Jamaica to live at and manage the estate himself. Alec's father passed away in 1971, and his mother in 1982. His children were all born in Jamaica, and while he still visited Scotland for a few months each year, Caymanas and Jamaica became his home after his bachelor days sixty-seven-years before. His parents would have been proud to see how Alec managed his inheritance.

NOTES:

From Grandfather Vereker's Years of This Chapter

Tiffin: A word that emerged in British India and Ceylon in the 1880s and typically referred to having a light snack in the afternoon, instead of a traditional English afternoon tea. Eating light meals in the heat of the day was preferable, which often left one feeling hungry by mid-afternoon. The British were copying the sensible native Indian habit. Tiffin was carried in a series of small round boxes (dim-sum-looking boxes stacked one on top of the other), usually metal or wicker. Different foodstuffs were put in each layer. A curry, rice, naan bread, and maybe eggs made up a typical stack of four with a carrying handle. Tiffin, as a word, was most likely created by the British in India, as it derived from the old English word tiff, meaning to eat between meals.

P&O Ships and the Acronym, POSH

On the outward leg of the sea journey from England to India or Ceylon, the sun rose on the ship's port side in the morning in the tropics. When it was at its highest point and its hottest from noon onward and set on the ships' starboard side, you would have been glad you booked your cabin on the port side of the ship, as your room was in the shade and cooler! With no air conditioning and not even electrical fans in the earlier Raj years of the 1800s, the cabins on the starboard side became unbearably stifling. Of course, the reverse applied to the journey home to England, creating the term Port Out/ Starboard Home (POSH).

Some say the acronym is a myth, and that phrase did not exist in the modern vernacular until the 1930s. Port Out/Starboard Home was *absolutely* in use and spoken in full by most well-to-do passengers from the late 1700s onwards. However, it was *not* put into an acronym format, as far as the author can tell, until the mid-1930s. Literacy only became more widespread within the European population in the twentieth century. By 1935, newspapers were creating acronyms for everything to explain common phrases in a shorter print space. P&O's acronym, POSH, only came into regular vernacular from around 1935 - but whether spoken in full or as an acronym, it was always used to mean something exclusive and more luxurious. So, both story *and* myth are correct.

A Rudyard Kipling Poem – The Rival

The poem is seven paragraphs long and one epitomizes that Shimla Hill Station, and it's romantic trysts:

> *The young me come, the young men go,*
> *Each pink and white and neat.*
> *She's older than their mothers, but,*
> *They grovel at her feet.*
> *They walk beside her rickshaw wheels,*
> *None ever walk by mine,*
> *And that's because I'm seventeen, And she is forty-nine.*

Painting by Sir Thomas Jones, President of the Royal Hibernian Academy. The devilishly handsome Lieutenant Colonel Christian Monteith Hamilton and Lady Maria Hamilton 1855—Alec's great-grandparents. Sir Ian and Vereker Hamilton's parents (WOP).

Vereker Monteith Hamilton, Alec's grandfather and the well-known nineteenth century artist's, self-portrait . The portrait hung in Caymanas House, Jamaica (WOP).

The *Surat,* the P&O Steamship that took Vereker Hamilton to Ceylon as a coffee planter. England to Ceylon was around forty-one days' sailing (CE).

Vereker Hamilton, Alec's grandfather sketching his wife in his St. John's Wood, London artist's studio, while friends entertain, c. 1890 (WOP).

A portrait of **Alec's father, Ian Bogle Monteith Hamilton**, in his Gordon Highlander uniform when a prisoner of war in Germany during World War One. The painting hung in the drawing room of Caymanas House, Jamaica. (WOP).

Chapter 7

THE EWING AND CRUM-EWING CONNECTION

When Alec's father, Ian Hamilton, married Constance Crum-Ewing, Constance brought into the marriage vast family wealth from the Ewing's 26,000-acre sugar estate of Caymanas in Jamaica and several other plantations in the Caribbean and America.

She also inherited Strathleven Estate in Dumbartonshire, Scotland, which came to the Crums through the Ewings. James Ewing purchased the estate in 1830 after making his fortune in tobacco and sugar in the Americas and West Indies. Therefore, we ought to step back from our story to date and look at Alec's maternal ancestors, from where his inheritance sprang. Their family tree is in this book too.

James Ewing

Some 246 years ago, James Ewing was born in Glasgow, Scotland, on December 5, 1775, the younger son of Walter Ewing of Cathkin. His mother was Margaret Fisher, the daughter of the Rev. James Fisher, one of the Scottish Secession Church's founders.

To place this in perspective, this was during the lifetime of Robbie Burns and Bonny Prince Charlie, and the year when the American War of Independence erupted. It was when Alexander Hamilton, the future Founding Father, fought alongside General Washington. The tobacco and sugar trades dominated Glasgow, when only eighteen streets made up the entire city of just 40,000 souls.

James' father had sold the lands of Gilmore Hill to another West India merchant, with the surname Bogle (the Bogles later intermarried with Hamiltons). Mr. Bogle subsequently sold these lands where the buildings of Glasgow University stand today. James' parents, Walter and Margaret Ewing, were pious, and James was raised in a like manner. Margaret came from a well-known ecclesiastical family, with many family ancestors a crucial part of Scottish history. She believed she descended directly from Halcro, a Prince of Denmark.

James was known to be rather vivacious and active when at Glasgow High School. In 1786 when he was only eleven, he entered Glasgow University and was an undergraduate in arts and business. His masters marked him out for a career in commerce or law. Upon graduating from university in 1790 at fifteen, he was appointed to manage the Glasgow end of the family consignments of sugar, molasses, and rum, Because of his young age, his legal responsibilities were delegated to a friend of his father's, a magistrate and justice of the peace.

It had been expected, based on his masters' expectations of him, that James would become a lawyer and be called to the Bar (become a senior legally qualified person, known as a barrister in England, managing cases in the high court). James was admitted a "burgess" by his father's right in 1808, aged thirty-three. In the eighteenth and early nineteenth century, a burgess was the representative of a borough in the British Parliament. A sort of junior member of Parliament today, if such a thing existed.

Ewing's New World Plantations

His father was an accountant in Glasgow, specializing in winding up estates, especially those overseas in the West Indies. If he saw the potential to make money from them, he could acquire them himself, improve their turnover, and sell them for a profit. What a tremendous practical school of learning from which James Ewing received intimate knowledge of transatlantic estate-management. This ultimately led to him being a successful businessman and accountant specializing in the West Indies and, eventually, a leading West India merchant and sugar plantation owner. Through his uncle, Ralph Fisher, an absentee Jamaican sugar planter, James founded the business of James Ewing & Co. to trade under and was sole owner for many years. He was known by his peers for his independence of thought, word, and action. A true outspoken Glaswegian and Scotsman.

There had been more than one Ewing family member owning sugar planta-tions in Jamaica, Barbados, and St. Kitts for many decades already, with one Ewing uncle from whom James inherited an estate in Jamaica. He bought and merged plantations around the one he inherited and expanded their size by buying more surrounding land to create the one estate of some 26,000 acres— Caymanas. He quickly amassed a *vast* fortune at the height of sugar values.

James was an honest, canny Scots businessman and inherited tobacco plantations in Virginia from other relatives. Nothing more is heard of the tobacco estates after the Caymanas purchase, so we can assume he likely sold them.

James Ewing was not only well-heeled but considered by his peers a gentleman of his word. Trained in finance management and how to contain costs while maximizing profits and squeezing results from wound-up companies, he was a remarkably astute businessman.

Eventually, James took on two Scottish partners, like him, born in the 1770s: Kirkman Findlay and James Oswald. Each was also an MP for different City of Glasgow areas and heads of merchant houses and chambers of commerce. Each inherited their family businesses, and they formed a potent team.

James strongly supported free trade and contributed to the successful campaign to end the East India Company's business monopoly to the Indian sub-continent and the Far East. The first Glasgow ship independent of the East India Company reached Calcutta in 1816 while supporting the slave trade, for which James' plantations relied upon for labor until the 1840s. The shipment of slaves from Africa ended in the British colonies in 1807, but it did not stop slaves being shipped between islands, nor did it abolish the keeping of slaves already there or born into slavery.

During the American Civil War, many tobacco planters in Virginia were ruined by the war and the loss of slaves. Yet the merchants trading in sugar in the Caribbean were relatively untouched. As the bottom fell out of the tobacco market in America, James' sugar estate revenues were taking off in the Caribbean. Maybe this is when he lost or sold his tobacco plantations, as we do not hear about them hereafter.

Ewing became a Scottish politician as a Member of Parliament for Wareham and later Glasgow. He was the co-founding partner of the Provident Savings Bank in Glasgow (and deputy-governor). Over time, the bank grew across much of west Scotland. He was also a founder of the Glasgow Royal Exchange. When the building was constructed, he laid the foundation stone as chairman of the Subscriber's Committee. He was also chairman of the Glasgow Chamber of Commerce and a Fellow of the Royal Society, and he gave back to supporting the community from which he had sprung and where he'd learned to trade.

As an agent in Glasgow for the imports of his own sugar plantations in Jamaica and St. Kitts, James built the business through sheer effort, and his company grew at an unexpectedly fast rate. Some 120-plus years later, James' descendant, our modern-day Alec Hamilton, was to train in the same offices James Ewing set up. He'd learn how to manage the financial books, trade in the markets, and run a significant sugar estate.

In 1814 when James Ewing was thirty-nine, his father, Walter, died, leaving his house and estates in liferent[4] to James' mother, Margaret. James was visiting the plantations in Jamaica when his father died. After his father's death, the widowed Margaret did not enjoy living in her house in Glasgow, so she left Cathkin House and moved to Totness in Devon.

In 1815, James Ewing purchased what was described by many as "the most handsome" house in Glasgow, Crawford Mansion, at the head of Queen Street, which later held his famous rookery. Hence, he earned the nickname Craw-Ewing. He asked his mother to return from Devon and move in with him, so that as a single man he could be close to her. In those days before steam trains were the norm, it could take five to six days to travel from Glasgow to Devon by horse-drawn coach, with rests at coaching inns every night, but his mother did eventually move back to Glasgow to live with him. There is a lovely framed black and white sketch of the house with a silhouette of James Ewing imposed on it hanging in Alec's dining room at his home in Scotland.

In 1816, James was elected Dean of Guild at Glasgow University for two years, the university conferring on him an honorary degree in 1826. He was also to serve a second two-year term some years later.

The Philanthropist Reformer, and Slaver

In 1819, Ewing gifted £10,000 towards bursaries for university students who needed assistance (around £850,000 today, approximately US$ 1.1 million). In 1827, he founded The Ewing Gold Medal and presented the university with a gift of £100 to cast the medal, a prize for the best essay in Civil History. Today, 194 years after he established the award, the Ewing prizes are still awarded annually for the best essays on a prescribed historical subject, alternately in Medieval and Modern History.

---

4 For her use until her death

In the late 1820s, at a time when British public awareness of the true horrors of slavery had created disgust, James Ewing's cousin, Reverend Ralph Wardlaw, was a leading anti-slavery campaigner, and he publicly condemned Ewing's involvement in slavery. James Ewing knew he was swimming against the tide of public opinion yet seemed unmoved by the immorality of slavery and was still admired in the business community for his ability to make money.

On August 1, 1834, slavery ended officially in Jamaica after the bill was finally passed in the British Parliament. It could have been passed earlier, but most of the MPs with interests in slavery, including James Ewing, managed to get a clause tagged onto the bill that said that slaves had to work under the same conditions masked in terms of "apprenticeships" for another six years. As mentioned earlier, this period of apprenticeship collapsed after multiple-slave uprisings against such a provision, and freedom was won by all.

Ewing's well-publicized acts of charity and religious piety seem to have been highly selective. Here was his selective morality at work, being a leading light in caring for the poor and disadvantaged in Glasgow while working to keep on enslaving Africans in Jamaica to maintain a heightened revenue. By 1834 he had to face the freedom of his slaves, the payment of wages, and a reduced income. It was to be his son that brought in a humanitarian thought and care for the workforce at Caymanas and other estates that he inherited.

In 1822, James Ewing had built Dunoon Castle, the first property on that loch's shore. He was encouraged to stand for Parliament upon the death of King George IV in 1830, when he was already Lord Provost of Glasgow, and became MP for Glasgow, Renfrew, Dumbarton, and Rutherglen for seven years.

James Ewing Purchases the Strathleven Estate

On July 1, 1835, the deed of sale from Alec Hamilton's papers shows that Ewing bought the house and the 8,000-acre estate of Levenside, near Dumbarton, for £84,031 Sterling (equivalent in purchasing power to about £11 million today, or $15.4 million approximately). He later changed the name of the estate to Strathleven, the name it still holds today. The estate consisted of prime arable land and pastureland with multiple farms and a grand Palladian-style house built in 1700 right in the middle—one of the first Palladian-style houses built in Scotland. There is a picture of it in this book. The house was in terrible repair when he purchased it, but James sank a small fortune into entirely restoring the home to its original glory and made many improvements to the estate and its parkland, which took some years.

On James Ewing's sixtieth birthday in 1835, Parliament was dissolved when the Whig majority under Lord Melbourne called on King William IV (uncle of Queen Victoria) to form a government. The Duke of Wellington (retired from his distinguished military career and now a Member of Parliament) attempted to hold Parliament. However, he was insufficiently reformist, and Parliament was dissolved. Another general election called. James Ewing stood again as an independent MP but wasn't elected, and so ended his parliamentary political career.

James Ewing, who had become Lord Provost of Glasgow, was the last Provost of Glasgow to wear a full Victorian court dress. Court dress was required by all gentlemen holding government, civil service, and royal household offices. Different grades of uniform depicted one's official status and were prescribed in 1720 royal court guidelines. A gentlemen's hair, if extended, would be worn in a black silk bag resting on his neck. His shoes, black, could sport the most lavish buckles, often jeweled to show his wealth.

In 1836, James Ewing (at sixty-one) married Jane Tucker Crawford, the twenty-three-year-old daughter of James Crawford. Mr. Crawford owned one of the largest merchant businesses on the Clyde, with bases in Glasgow's Port.

By February 1836, James and his partner, William Mathieson, filed a claim for compensation for 586 slaves on five plantations in Jamaica (three in St. Anne's Parish, one in St. Thomas' Parish, and Caymanas Estate, his most significant estate, in St. Catherine Parish). They received a total of £9,328 from the British Government in compensation in the year 1837. It was equivalent in purchasing power today of just over £1 million (US $1.3 million approximately) for his freeing his slaves from bondage while compelling them to stay and be released from work in stages as apprentices on a wage. In "modern-day" money, this is around £2,218 per slave in compensation. This was when their purchase price was about $5,500 each. It's tragic to think that human life was worth no more. However, in slave-owners' eyes at emancipation, they now had substantial additional business costs because they had to pay wages to their workforce. This cost had not previously touched their profits and drove their future net income down dramatically. James had been a substantial slave owner, and although an absentee planter most of the time in Jamaica, he saw the abolition of slavery completed.

By 1838, his Glasgow townhouse, Crawford Mansion, was sold for £35,000 (£3.76 million in the "modern-day" terms) to the Edinburgh and Glasgow Railway Co, who built Queen Street station on the site where the house stood. The footprint of the house forms the solum of the station. In Scottish law, the solum is the ground area that lies inside the walls or foundations of a past building. James is said to have habitually endeavored to advance the country's national interest and always carried out his plans in the best interest of all classes of people, with a deep concern for the working class. Indeed, he was a generous benefactor of not just his alma mater university but of countless city charities for the working class. It was almost a contradictory behavior that he was a slave owner in Jamaica, though it is said that he looked out for his workforce in an unusually caring way.

Ewing was also appointed Convener of the Committee of the City Council to conduct the affairs of the High School of Glasgow. Under his guidance, they added subjects deemed to drive commerce and business into the curriculum, including mathematics and writing skills. He later wrote a *History of a Merchants' House* and was appointed president of Anderson University (today known as Strathclyde University). He became chairman of the Glasgow Marine Society and a director of the Glasgow Auxiliary Bible Society, the Magdalen Hospital, and the Glasgow Lunatic Asylum.

He sought to improve many government institutions, including Glasgow's central prison, Bridewell, and the town's hospitals and infirmaries, all of which had seen slight improvement since the 1700s. James fought for a new, much larger prison that enabled two prisoners in an adequately furnished room instead of the Bridewell to-date standards, holding anything from six to ten prisoners per cell, chained together, with poor sanitation and ventilation and virtually no furnishings.

Equally important to him was having female, not male, warders for the female prison wings. He even insisted that new and proper gaslight should light the prison common areas and courtyards.

James Ewing's Later Years

Together with Jane's lady's maid, James and Jane, who had not had any children by 1844, set off on a thirteen-month tour of the European continent, keeping in touch with James' business partner in James Ewing & Co, William Mathieson, in Glasgow, by very regular letters. These letters give an extraordinarily complete and fascinating account of their journey and observations of people, manufacturing, agriculture, and local history.

In James Ewing's *History of the Merchants' House*, he states that "the primary object of the Merchant's House, was the charity to its reduced members and their families." He also said, "It appears that the objects for which these mortifications' annual rent was destined divided themselves into three classes. First, for the support of the poor of different descriptions, secondly, for the payment of apprentice fees to destitute boys, and thirdly, for the education of young men at University"

The Merchants' House still today, I believe, distributes grants from the James Ewing Bequest, now combined with the James Buchanan Bequest. The funds continue to go to different purposes, such as The University of Strathclyde; Glasgow University for Scottish History and Russian Lectureship; the Glasgow Caledonian University; Glasgow School of Art; The Institute of Engineers and Shipbuilders; The Royal Academy of Music and Drama; and various hospitals and churches. In his last years of life, James was very generous with charitable donations.

The Passing Away of James Ewing

James Ewing died on November 29, 1853, just short of his seventy-eighth birthday, at a time when Britain and Russia were battling each other in the Crimean War. By now, running water in pipes, streetlights, and tramcars had been introduced to Glasgow homes and streets by the government—considerable advances in his lifetime. While he lived, the French and American revolutions had come and gone, and the British Industrial Revolution was well underway.

In his Last Will and Testament, James left £267,524 in financial capital, excluding property, to his nephew, Humphrey Crum. This inheritance was equivalent in purchasing power today to just shy of £33 million, or US$ 46.2 million. Plus, Humphrey was left Strathleven House and its estate of some

8,000 acres in Dumbartonshire in Scotland with self-sustaining, revenue-producing farms. He also inherited the 26,000 acres of sugar plantation on the Caymanas Estate in Jamaica, as well as an estate in St. Kitts and other holdings and companies. James had no children of his own; it all went to this eldest nephew, Humphrey Crum, on the condition that he added the name Ewing to his surname. So henceforth, Humphrey Crum was known as Humphrey Ewing Crum-Ewing. Humphrey was James Ewing's eldest sister's son; she had married a Crum. It was, however, a massive amount of wealth based on the back of sugar and tobacco planation slavery for most of James Ewing's, and his forefathers', management.

Here was a man who had made tremendous contributions to Glasgow's prosperity through his commercial empire when the city and its business community was growing as fast as its population. Much of Glasgow was built on the philanthropy of men who made their fortunes off the backs of slaves.

Humphrey Ewing Crum-Ewing Son of James

Humphrey (July 16, 1802–July 3, 1887) was born Humphrey Crum, the son of a Scottish Liberal politician, Alexander Crum the elder of Thornliebank, Renfrewshire. Humphrey had three younger brothers and a sister.

It is essential to review James Ewing's nephew, as it was his father and his direct descendants, not his Uncle James, who led to modern-day Alec Hamilton's great-great-grandfather inheriting the Ewing fortune.

Humphrey was educated at Glasgow College and in 1826 married Helen Dick, daughter of the Rev. John Dick of Greyfriars Sessions Church, Glasgow. They had five children, a little girl who died in infancy, another daughter, and three boys, including Alexander, who was to inherit Strathleven and Caymanas. One of their sons, another Humphrey Ewing Crum-Ewing, became a lieutenant colonel in the 3rd Lanark Regiment, and honorary colonel of the regiment. He and his fellow officers funded the formation of the Third Lanark Football Club, which was established in 1872.

After he inherited, Humphrey Ewing Crum-Ewing, as he now was known, did for some years shift to a heavier banana crop rotation in many of the sugar production fields, as not surprisingly, the cost of running plantations had raised and the value of sugar plantation lands had fallen.

Humphrey believed that if well managed, he could bring his plantations with their paid labor force to decent levels of profit, with proper care of the workforce. He put his money where his mouth was, and with prices low, purchased five sugar plantations in Guyana (known then as British Guiana), all sitting on the Demerara River (where the name for a style of sugar production came from). You will find them listed in the Guyanese Sugar Plantations in the Late Nineteenth Century record known as *The Argosy*, c. 1883. He also brought out engineers from Scotland to set up better land drainage to maximize production.

His workforce, interestingly, was made up of freed African slaves, local Indigenous people, and several indentured Indian servants, who were soon free of their bond. Between 1838 and 1920, nearly 240,000 people from India were brought to British Guiana as indentured servants, and over 13,500 Chinese, such Colonial British Indian Government support was given to Jamaica and others of its Caribbean possessions.

It is important to mention these Guiana investments, as they came down to Alec's mother's time when she became a Hamilton. Humphrey's five small plantations combined equaled 1,954 acres of land, and here he focused on producing sugar only, producing 3,300 hogshead a year (2,290 tons) with a labor force of 210 free people in total.

With her life use of Strathleven House, James Ewing's widow outlived her nephew, Humphrey Ewing Crum-Ewing, so he never lived on the fabulous estate. Humphrey and his wife originally had a house in Glasgow (20 Woodside Terrace, the author researched) and from 1868 rented the country estate of Mains House, now Kilpatrick. After the death of his uncle, he rented Ardencaple Castle in Helensburgh, Dumbartonshire, as his family seat. In time, Humphrey became chairman of the West Indian Association of Glasgow and a director of the Colonial Company of London.

During his semi-retirement, Queen Victoria made him Deputy Lieutenant of Dumbartonshire and her representative in the region from February 1874 until his death, aged eighty-four, in 1887. He was also a justice of the peace for four major Scottish areas: Dumbartonshire, Argyllshire, Lanarkshire, and Renfrewshire. An excellent, life-sized oil painting of this distinguished gentleman hangs in the dining room at Caymanas Great House in Jamaica today. A copy is reproduced in this book.

In April 1857, Humphrey stood unsuccessfully as an MP but was later successfully elected Member of Parliament for Paisley in November 1857.

Colonel Alexander Crum-Ewing

Alec's maternal great-grandfather was born in 1826 in Scotland, and while he was visiting his properties in Jamaica, died suddenly on December 30, 1912, during King Edward VII's reign. This Alexander was the first Crum-Ewing to live at Strathleven since his grandfather, James Ewing. He was modern-day's Alec Hamilton's maternal great-grandfather.

Alexander inherited the chairmanship of James Ewing & Co. and only took possession of Strathleven House when his great-uncle's widow died ten years later. Sometime before his death he sold the five sugar plantations in Guiana to the Booker Brothers and McConnell & Co.

Educated in England and at Glasgow University, he took an active interest in the West Indian business and Jamaican estates. As a result of the unfair continental bounty system that prevailed and created hefty sugar import tariffs to continental Europe (to protect the French, Portuguese, and Spanish sugar imports), he took 700 acres of the 26,000 acres of Caymanas sugar cane and replaced it with bananas to diversify his investments. At various times over the centuries, Ewings, Crum-Ewings, and Alec Hamilton himself have shifted production of some cane land to coconut palms or bananas, depending on crop values in global markets of their time.

Alexander's wife, Jane, was the only daughter of Admiral Hayes O'Grady of Erinagh House, County Clare in Ireland. Alexander and Jane had a daughter, Helen (born 1862), and a son (another), Humphrey Ewing Crum-Ewing (born 1866). Sadly, Alexander's wife died a few years later.

As an adult, Alexander Crum-Ewing first resided at Polmont Park in Falkirk, Scotland, where he was a keen follower to hounds. Afterward, he lived in Edinburgh for a couple of years. He then purchased the estate of Keppoch near Cardross, whose land he loved to farm and where he loved to hunt. It was a short-lived time of some seven years before he moved to Strathleven upon his aunt's death. After coming into possession of Strathleven, he disposed of most of the Keppoch estate, but he still did some farming there, retaining the home farm and most of the grasslands as his own. He was known to be active in county affairs and a keen volunteer in the local Territorial Force (the "modern-day" Territorial Army) as well as chairman of the County Licensing Court, vice-lieutenant of the county for nearly forty years, and Vice-Convener of the County Council. Added to his list of commitments was being honorary colonel of the 3rd Lanarkshire Rifles.

Putting this period into the context of the age he lived in, Humphrey had traveled through the Holy Land. He also saw the first troops during Queen Victoria's reign setting out for the Crimean War from the Turkish port of St. Ferapol. The famously patriotic but disastrous Charge of the Light-Brigade was to happen in October 1854, as was the fame of the nurse Florence Nightingale. She was the woman who forever changed nursing and sanitation standards in British hospitals and around the world.

In January 1867, Alexander and his brother, Humphrey Junior, had built and launched a 153-foot wooden, three-masted ocean-going barque, which they named *Strathleven*. Her maiden voyage was to Demerara on Guiana, setting sail from Glasgow on March 11, 1867, with general cargo and provisions.

Tragically, on only her second voyage, the vessel was to meet her end, wrecked on rocks at Heugh's Point, north of Float Bay near Demerara. She had been on her way back to Glasgow but was pushed off course by storm winds. Her shipment, which was lost, was mainly sugar, but with some rum. Fortunately, a lifeboat rescued all the crew. Sometime after this on a future visit to Guiana, Alexander's younger brother, Humphrey Junior, died suddenly while visiting the family's sugar plantations in Guiana; Humphrey was said to be a "fine, manly, hearty character."

One of the most frightening episodes in Alexander's life occurred in Jamaica on one of his frequent visits, during the earthquake that devastated the city of Kingston in 1907. He had traveled there with Sir Alfred Jones, having gone out to study the possibilities of cotton growing on his Jamaica estates.

In company with Messrs. Jones, Collings, Heaton, and the governor of the island, Sir James Swettenham (governor, September 30, 1904–1907), Alexander had left a building in Kingston where he'd attended a meeting just minutes before 3:30 p.m. on January 14, 1907. The first violent shock took place at this time, and the building collapsed, killing most who had remained inside, one imagines.

Many writers of that time considered this earthquake one of the deadliest in recorded history. From the quake or subsequent fires, which raged for over three days, every building in the capital was destroyed or severely damaged. Some 1,000 people died in the earthquake and fires, and approximately 10,000 were left homeless. A tsunami was reported shortly afterward on the north coast of Jamaica, with waves as high as eight feet, devastating many ports and fishing villages along the northeast and eastern parts of the island, with sea surges felt in Kingston, causing more damage to the city.

Alexander Crum-Ewing died on December 30, 1912 (often quoted as January 1913). On January 18, 1913, his obituary in the *London Times* was reprinted in Jamaica's national newspaper, *The Daily Gleaner*.

> "The death on December 30th, 1912, occurred in Jamaica during a visit from Strathleven in Dumbarton near Glasgow, of Mr. Alexander Crum-Ewing. He was the eldest son of the late Mr. Humphrey Ewing Crum-Ewing with Messrs. James Ewing & Co. of the West Indies. Until his death, he continued to hold significant interests in the West Indies. He was keenly interested in the Strathleven Estate upon inheriting it and devoted considerable attention to practical farming there. In politics, he was a Liberal until the introduction of the first Irish Home Rule. In addition to the Strathleven Estate in Scotland (and it's 8,000 acres) and the Caymanas Estate in Jamaica (and it's 26,000 acres), he left the capital of £881,000 (£103.2 million today, around $144.4 million)."

He had *nearly tripled* the amount of his inheritance and had the business acumen and luck of his uncle, but Alexander did so, using a paid workforce, which he managed and treated well. He also employed the use of modern machinery. His burial took place in Spanish Town in Jamaica, not too far from the Caymanas Estate. *The Daily Gleaner* reported the choir's enthusiasm as having been "quite remarkable." One choir member had walked thirteen miles from Kingston to Spanish Town to attend rehearsals, so important a figure to Jamaica was Alexander. Caymanas production and taxable earnings were essential to Jamaica's economy and government. Another mourner was reported as "walking from Shortwood," while many attending the funeral made their way from distant suburbs, and many workers came from the Caymanas estate itself.

Humphrey Crum-Ewing—Son of Colonel Alexander Crum-Ewing

This Humphrey was born in 1866 and died in 1946. In January 1912, he inherited his father's fortune mentioned above, along with Strathleven Estate and Caymanas Estate, the golden egg in the basket. He was modern-day Alec's maternal grandfather.

Humphrey and his wife had two children: their daughter, Constance Crum-Ewing (modern-day Alec's mother), who married Ian Bogle Hamilton, born in 1891, and a son, Alexander Crum-Ewing, born in late 1896. (The names Humphrey and Alexander literally alternated generation by generation in this family). They had bought a house in the New Forest outside London, in Lyndhurst, Hampshire, and mostly split their time between there and Jamaica. He stayed in Jamaica for much longer stretches at a time than his forefathers had but ensured that every summer he was at Strathleven, as his grandson Alec was to do at Lowood. Humphrey spent his time visiting his tenant farmers and reviewing the business accounts of James Ewing & Co, just as Alec would do in his time.

This Humphrey Crum-Ewing was known to have been very popular in Jamaica with his workers and appears to have been a considerate and caring employer. In the same way, his tenant farmers at Strathleven appear to have thought just as highly of him. He was enthusiastically asked to be the first honorary president of the Bonhill Parish Pipe Band, which formed in 1931 with his support. There are some lovely photos on file of the band on the front lawns of Strathleven House. Like his father, Humphrey became a Deputy Lord Lieutenant of Dumbartonshire.

As if setting the pace for his grandson Alec, not only did he spend every summer in Scotland (and a typical year spread between Hampshire, Jamaica, and Scotland), but he lived there full-time for his last few years, other than his annual visits to Scotland in the summer. Just as modern-day Alec Hamilton made his last visit to Scotland in the summer of 2018 and died in Jamaica in 2020, where he had lived since 1954, Humphrey made his last visit to Scotland in the summer of 1946 and went "home" to Jamaica where, suspecting his days were numbered, he chose to die. He passed away at Caymanas Park in November of that year.

Alexander Crum-Ewing (Another)

Humphrey's son, Alexander, was born in late 1896—his sister was modern-day Alec's mother, Constance. At the age of eighteen, young Alexander signed up to fight in World War One and joined the Seaforth Highlanders. He was tragically killed, unmarried and without an heir, in November of 1914 in the first few months of the war. Humphrey, now with no direct male heir, bequeathed his wealth and all his estates in Scotland and the West Indies, including Caymanas Estate in Jamaica, to his daughter, Constance Crum-Ewing, the future Mrs. Ian Bogle Hamilton.

James Ewing of Strathleven. Alec's maternal five times great-uncle and sugar plantation magnet. (PBA). Font of much of Alec Hamilton's wealth in Jamaica and Scotland.

Ewing coat of arms

James Ewing of Strathleven sculptured in a marble bust, which sat in Alec's Scottish home's inner-entry hall. (PBA)

Strathleven House, Dumbartonshire, Scotland. Originally with 8,400 acres and eight farms, purchased by James Ewing in 1830. Alec birthplace, 1932. (PBA).

Helen Crum-Ewing, née Dick (1792–1883). Humphrey Crum-Ewing's wife (CE).

Humphrey Crum, James Ewing's nephew, who became a Crum-Ewing to inherit his uncle's fortune and the Caymanas Estate in Jamaica in 1853. The painting of. Alec's maternal great-grandfather ,artist unknown sat in Alec's Caymanas House drawing room (WOP).

Chapter 8

SUGAR'S HISTORY AND THE CAYMANAS ESTATE.

The lives of both Alexander Hamiltons in this book were entwined with this crop. As we look at sugar's transformation, we can do so in both the colonization of Jamaica and the sugar industry's emergence there. This is essential to understand before talking about Jamaica's Caymanas Estate. The next chapter requires us to look at the foundation of African slavery, its emergence in the West Indies, in Nevis, and Jamaica in particular, and its eventual abolition in the British Caribbean. The early success of sugar production and slavery regrettably went hand in hand.

Caymanas Estate, Jamaica was modern-day Alec's life's work and legacy, and understanding the bigger picture of the estate's foundation and sugar production history keeps it in perspective. By the time Alec's maternal great-grandfather, Humphrey Crum-Ewing, inherited Caymanas in 1853, slavery had been abolished for nineteen years by the local British Governor's Bill of Abolition. Slaves first became "apprentices" for four years, still tied to their same masters on a part-wage approach. It was not a great success but did help the transition to freedom for slaves, for which the British government compensated planters.

Most previously enslaved people continued the same work on the same plantations but as free men and women with a government agreed minimum wage, food, and lodging. Their treatment changed dramatically, as harsh behavior gave workers the right to resign and walk away. For the first time, plantation owners' success depended not on forced work but on free people and how they treated them. On August 1, 1838, the law transitioned to total emancipation and unrestricted freedom for all former slaves in Jamaica.

The consolidation, growth, and success that James Ewing achieved at Caymanas Estate as a commercial business after emancipation is in part a testament to his adaptation of modern management techniques and machinery. Nevertheless, he had fought *not* to free slaves, and that we must not forget.

At the end of slavery, he did the right thing, although possibly reluctantly, we do not know—but his nephew had a more developed sense of care for his inherited free workforce and was the right man to build on that freedom and fair treatment.

Sugar First Appears

Sugar was first known from historical records to have been a crop in 8,000 BC on the South Pacific island of Papua New Guinea. Sugar later spread to "modern-day" Yemen, in the Middle East, which is about the size of Wyoming in America and twice the size of the UK. This new crop quickly appeared in Arabia, the Philippines, and India by 6,000 BC. By 600 BC, the ancient Greeks and Indian philosophers wrote about a new "medicine" called sugar and its use for common ailments, and by 1093, the Spanish had planted sugar in the Canary Islands.

Around AD 650, Arab nations found that you could form a sweet paste by mixing sugar with almonds, which we know today in Western culture as marzipan. The European Crusaders to the Holy Land brought sugar back to Europe for the wealthy from around AD 1099. At this time, the third son of William the Conqueror, Duke of Normandy, sat on the throne of England, and the Hamilton ancestors, the de Beaumont brothers, would have had their first taste of sugar.

On his second voyage to the Caribbean in 1493, Christopher Columbus brought sugarcane from the Canary Islands, where he'd first broken his journey on route to the Caribbean. With this voyage, Columbus intended to colonize and establish trading posts in various locations. Rather than just three ships, as on his first voyage, this time he sailed with seventeen ships and over a thousand men. This flotilla carried animals such as pigs, cattle, chickens, and horses to establish breeding in Columbus's colonies. He "discovered" Dominica, Guadalupe, Redondo, and Antigua, visited Puerto Rico, and "rediscovered" Hispaniola on this voyage. From there, he returned to Cuba and then Jamaica, landing on May 5, 1494. Each place he stopped he left sugarcane, animals, people, and guidance on how to grow cane crops and breed animal stock.

The Explosion of Sugarcane Production in the Caribbean

Thanks to Columbus's introduction, Jamaica's climate, flat savannah lands and mountain ridges, rainfall, sunshine, and fertile soil, Jamaica was ideal for sugar production. Much of the Caribbean echoed Jamaica's conditions. With the Arawak native Indian population forced into slavery, Jamaica's sugar industry commenced its journey in the 1600s towards its zenith in the 1700s. By the late 1600s, the Spanish had annihilated the local Indian population and began to import slaves from Africa.

Sugar production exploded with its rapidly growing demand in Europe and instability in tobacco prices in the early 1700s. As more and more Caribbean islands grew sugar, the availability of African slaves as a "free" source of production once purchased was a path already laid by the Portuguese and Spanish. When the British, Dutch, and French caught on to this new low-cost production source, sugar plantations sprang up at an even more rapid rate, not that they were all successful.

From the 1680s to the 1780s, Jamaica's slave population grew from some 3,500 to nearly 170,000. Nearly 75 percent of all slaves in Jamaica worked on sugar plantations. The European population, which rose in the same period from around 8,000 to 18,000, was made up of not just planters but also their families, overseers, engineers, and the civil and military government apparatus. By the 1780s, Jamaica was producing 36,000 tons of sugar a year. The average estate had grown dramatically since the late 1600s and was now 1,400 acres, and typically had over 200 slaves. Of course, many Jamaican sugar plantations were smaller, and as many more, like Caymanas Estate in the east and Galloway Plantation in the west, were much more significant. These vast estates and a few others were at 10,000–30,000 acres, held the most slaves, and produced the most significant contribution to tonnage sales and taxable income for Jamaica's exports.

Around 60 percent of all sugar plantation slaves by age and general strength worked in the cane fields, and 10 percent helped the skilled slaves in the mills and refining processes. A sizeable 25 percent of slaves were considered skilled laborers and handled the complex tasks in the mills and refining process under a professional production overseer. However, some of them were children too young to work, or those aging in the job who had light work around the slave quarters, and 5 percent were house servants.

The Sugar Production Process

Sugarcane is grown in tropical climates over a twelve to eighteen-month period. Whether you harvested sugarcane manually in the eighteenth and nineteenth centuries, or in modern times with sophisticated machinery for cutting and production, the cane is cut as close to the base as possible. The sugar is concentrated in the stalks. When sugarcane is gathered, it is stripped of its leaves and crushed or mashed to produce the juice and a fibrous byproduct, called *bagasse*, which is separated by straining. In the nineteenth century and earlier, this was aided by wind or watermills turning and "crushing stones," rather like a flour mill's flat stone. There are several photographs in this book of typical sugar plantation scenes. The juice crushed out of sugar cane was then heated and boiled in vats, and limestone was added. Impurities bind to limestone, which could be removed by filtration. Then the juice was transferred to evaporators to extract a syrup containing sugar crystals. In the 1700s, manual slave labor made this all happen.

Finally, centrifuge separated the sugar crystals from the syrup, and once dried and cooled, brown sugar crystals remained. This first boiling had the highest sugar content. A second boiling extracted a slightly bitter taste, and a third boiling delivered a dark syrup or molasses, known for its intense flavor.

Molasses

Molasses, sugar's residue, was important as the basis for hard liquor, primarily in rum distilling. Molasses was also used as a flavoring or in baking. It was a heavy load but was easy to transport in barrels and distribute inland from the coastal ports of America, England, Europe, and elsewhere. It was also a highly profitable byproduct of sugar production, and rum became the most common liquor in the Western world in the 1700s.

After Jamaica was captured by the British in 1655, rum became a staple of every British naval war vessel. The wind may have powered their warships, but rum powered its sailors. Every man aboard a British warship received a half pint of rum a day, as water could go stale on long voyages of months, so it was essential to the men's health! Hence the term, "a jolly sailor." Frequently, double the ration was issued as a reward when a ship had won a battle— the British Navy was Jamaica's single biggest customer for rum.

A Brief History of the Caymanas Estate Itself

There is an excellent early history and memoir on running the Caymanas Estate written by Humphrey Ewing Crum-Ewing, Alec's maternal grandfather. He wanted to leave a record for his daughter and her husband and their future heir, Alec Hamilton, to ensure Caymanas was managed as best as possible. He wrote this guide to the estate in 1944, two years before he died, when Alec Hamilton was twelve years old. Alec said it proved a treasure trove of references to review of how to run the estate. Summarizing the intent here enables us to understand not just how an emancipated workforce on a sugar plantation could run as a profitable business but also the guidance left behind that helped both Alec and his parents continue the inheritance.

In the 1800s, when Alec's maternal four times great-grandfather took over the running of Caymanas as an absent landlord, as all Alec's predecessors had been, workers in the fields still cut the cane by hand with cutlasses. Bullock (oxen) drawn carts pulled the cut cane to the mill and refining sheds and carted sugar and rum away for sale. Bullocks, horses, carts, men, wind or watermills, and refining machinery were the technology of their day. In this book. you'll find some old photos of these cane production processes from the field and transportation to the mill and factory.

Taylors Caymanas was bought in 1817 by James Ewing, and Humphrey Ewing bought Ellis Caymanas from the Dowager Lady Howard de Walden's trustees. These two estates, with their respective pens[5], Phoenix Park and Crawley, were amalgamated under Ewing's Caymanas. In 1912, the wooded mountain estates of Claremont and Prospect, contiguous to the other places, were bought by Alec's maternal grandfather. In addition to a little pastureland and logs, which were a valuable fuel source for the factory, they gained both banks of the Claremont or Ferry River, called Lower Downstream.

After his maternal grandfather had leased Dawkins Caymanas for nearly forty years, he bought it in 1920 from the executors of Colonel Gregory Dawkins of the Grenadier Guards. An officer and planter, he was well known in his day for the lawsuit over some military grievance he had against the HRH Prince George, the Duke of Cambridge, then Commander-In-Chief of the British Army. As a member of the British Royal family, grandson

---

5 A pen is an enclosure for livestock.

of King George III, and a cousin of Queen Victoria to be, Dawkins was a brave man to take the prince on. In 1924, Humphrey Ewing bought Lord Carrington and Abel Smith's "Cow Park," Farms 1 and 2, as all were adjoining his other Caymans properties. The whole was now combined under the name of Caymanas Estates at 26,000 acres. From James Ewing's forefathers down to Alec's father, they had assembled nine properties over four generations.

Originally there were sugar *factories* on all three Caymanas Estates. Of the Dawkins Works, nothing but some brick ruins were seen when Humphrey Ewing first visited Jamaica in January 1888. Today there is no sign of the Works at Ellis beyond the old mill. Taylor's Works ground the cane from all three estates, and a triple, vacuum pan, and centrifuge were installed in 1887, or possibly a year or two earlier—all state-of-the-art machinery in their day. The old estate factory's best effort was a crop of 1,730 tons of sugar and 470 puncheons of rum in 1925 under Humphrey Ewing, nearly ninety years after abolishing slavery. The estate was becoming one run with increasingly modern machinery added to by each generation. The workforce was paid a fair wage, and each successive Caymanas family owner felt honor-bound to take care of them all. From 1925, sugar production sadly dwindled to ninety-nine tons, with six puncheons of rum by 1931. The former Carrington lands were almost entirely in bananas by 1931—since 1899, this crop had been grown on the original Caymanas properties. While cane in the early thirties was reduced, banana cultivation had increased to 2,200 acres as a response to global market forces.

The years 1932 and 1933 marked the zenith of the banana industry in St. Catherine. From then onwards, Panama disease spread so quickly and created such havoc that it was decided that cane must again become the staple crop on the Caymanas Estates. To this end, Caymanas ordered a completely new factory from Mirrlees Watson Company Ltd., sugar machinery manufacturers based in Glasgow, Scotland.

Erection of the new engines commenced in 1934, but it was May 1936 before the new factory took over from the old. It is of some interest to observe that at the old factory, 830 tons of sugar was made at the cost of £15 a ton of cane, whereas the new factory produced 3,139 tons at £12.7 per ton. Caymanas reaped fifty-three tons to the acre. Humphrey Ewing noted that it also significantly reduced back-breaking physical work, which had to be the right choice for his workforce. The change from bananas to cane implemented at this time was rapid. By 1944, bananas covered only 270 acres, whereas earlier, 2,217 acres had been under banana crops on the ground. A planter always had to be ready to change what he planted to maximize revenue from his land according to market demands internationally.

Estate Manager/Overseer Max Henzell

The manager of Caymanas, hired by Alec's grandfather, Humphrey-Ewing, was now Royal Navy Lieutenant-Commander, Engineering, Mr. O. M. Henzell. He left the estate temporarily in 1940 for war duty (called up to serve in the navy) and oversaw the navy's quick-attack vessels, the MTBs (Motor Torpedo Boats). He led this highly specialized and highly effective new weapon throughout the North African Campaign and the D-Day landings on the French and Dutch coasts. If there is one thing in life to be learned, it's never to underestimate what someone has done in their life before you met them in a job they are doing in the present. Mr. Henzell (Junior) was still the estate manager when Alec took over in 1954, and before he retired, he helped show Alec the ropes of managing the estate.

When he went off to war, Henzel's place at Caymanas was filled temporarily by his father, Mr. L. I. Henzell, OBE of Antigua (Order of the British Empire). One of the most experienced factory experts during his interim assignment for his son, Mr. Henzell brought the manufacture of sugar at Caymanas to as near a state of perfection as the plant would permit. Neither did he neglect the agricultural side of his son's work. He had turned keenly to the cane cultivation, making drainage his chief concern, with what success may be judged by the progressive improvement in juice purity, as Humphrey Ewing remarked in his notes. Before the new "Henzell regime" at Caymanas, they had ground over eleven tons of cane to produce one ton of sugar. By 1944, after the four years the father had been at the estate, he needed only 8.49 tons of cane to make one ton of sugar. Henzell's son learned that you are never too experienced to learn new tricks from an old dog.

Every year at the end of cane-cutting season, Alec, like his predecessors, held a "crop-over party," as they call it. The party was a thank you from the estate owner to all the workers and their families at Caymanas, their suppliers and merchants, as the cropping season was over. Alec always invited Caymanas suppliers, shippers, and neighbors to join in the celebrations as well.

Prime Minister Norman Manley— and His Trust in Alec Hamilton

Prime Minister and Statesman Norman Manley, before, during, and after his premiership, came every year to the crop-over party at the Caymanas Estates as Alec's guest of honor. He commented in a speech to the gathered workers and guests one year that he saw Alec and Caymanas as a great example of how to take care of workers. Alec paid a decent wage and benefits and ensured safe and sound working conditions for his workers. He provided school and church and gave land for sports buildings and supported local villages. Norman Manley and Alec had formed strong respect for each other. One was a die-hard union man turned successful politician and statesmen, the other a sugar plantation owner and major employer in the area.

Talking to the union stewards at the Caymanas party another year, in the middle of their wage review with Alec for the Caymanas workers, the prime minister himself, an ex-union man, suggested that they accepted Alec's offer for the year-end wage review. He said he proposed this because it was a good, honest, and fair offer from a man who took care of them, and so they did. Norman Manley especially pointed out to the union chiefs Alec's genuine care for a worker's sick child or to make sure a worker was getting the medicine he needed.

At yet another crop-over celebration one year, Norman Manley told Alec that giving land as gifts for workers' families to have a church or building or a recreation center as he had been, were all actions the people would not forget, and he thanked him for showing other planters how to genuinely take care of their workforce. He commented that Alec was one of the few employers who saw the union as a partner to ensure his workforce was treated right and not as an enemy to fight.

Alec cared

The author listened to, watched, and sought answers to specific questions from people about Alec's role managing Caymanas, and many said of him that throughout his life they saw a consistent warmth of attitude towards his workforce. Alec's old pals John (the Caymanas vet) and wife Paddy, who attended each crop-over party, recalled how everyone, including Alec, had a rip-roaring time every year as they celebrated together. The workers knew that as a team if they made Caymanas successful, they'd all have a job to take care of their families in the year ahead, and they were first to thank Alec for how he took care of them all.

Alec looked back on the past and seemed to be more concerned that he had first taken good care of his workforce each year. Once he felt that they were okay, he knew they'd do good work and generate enough funds to run the estate and, yes, of course, cover his lifestyle, which was relatively modest in keeping with his heritage, most believed. Earlier in the book, we read how Alec was arm-twisted into selling a large parcel of his land to the government. What's important to mention is that Alec demanded that the government first set aside his workers' wages, redundancy pay, and pension funding before paying the balance to him for his land.

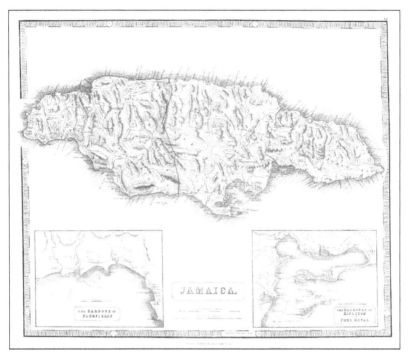

Antique map of Jamaica published in Liverpool, 1854, by George Philip & Son. Owned by the author. The inset bottom right is Kingston and Port Royal Harbor, and inland would be the Caymanas Estate Plantation. Bottom left, Savannah-la-Mar Harbor and inland would be access to multiple sugar plantations.

Rum filled barrels carted away for shipping, mid-1850's, Caymanas Park (WOP)

The "modern" Caymanas factory commenced production in May 1936 (WOP).

Caymanas Estate sugarcane fields today, a look unchanged for centuries (PBA).

The original Caymanas Estate overseer's (manager's) house in the 1880s (WOP).

The stone steps are all that are left of the original house today (PBA).

Chapter 9

SLAVERY AND A TYPICAL
TRIANGULAR SLAVE VOYAGE

Abraham Lincoln, the sixteenth President of the United States, in 1859 said: "Those who deny freedom to others deserve it not for themselves."

Slavery has been widespread since ancient times, regardless of color, creed, race, ethnicity, tribe, or country of origin of the enslaved or enslavers— for at least 5,500 years, there has been a trade in international human trafficking.

We cannot talk about either Alexander Hamilton, our book's two main characters, without talking about the region's history of slavery. The first Alexander was surrounded by it. The inheritance of the other was based on it. We must also acknowledge the elephant in the room today—the lingering resentment of slavery's history in the African American and Caribbean communities. It is understandable, and it hurts for so many.

When they touched on the topic some years ago, Alec Hamilton felt it essential that the author talk about this past abhorrent trade in human lives and not seek to avoid it for his sake. "We're obliged to look slavery in the face," he said. The extraordinary Nelson Mandela said, "I like friends who have independent minds because they tend to make you see problems from all angles."

The author sought to show all sides of a sensitive subject with no bias, nor create apologetic narratives for any either when conducting his research or writing. The author in South Africa had the honor of meeting some of President Mandela's former Ministers, who shared the same passion as the great man himself. A passion for stamping out what divides and pulling those of different color and ethnic backgrounds together to heal division and create one nation.

Many have commented to the author that Mandela would, today, be *utterly horrified* at the divide of color being exploited by many activists and politicians on both sides of the political divide. Exploitation rather than striving to shape understanding of the other, heal divisions, and create harmony between people of different skin and races as Mandela sought to achieve.

A Trans-Atlantic Slave-Ship Journey

Maybe the best way to understand such a voyage from England to Africa, Africa to the New World, and the New World back to England, is to share one actual example and follow such a voyage from multiple written records. The author chose the slave ship the *Juno*, the author having researched maritime, dock, and ship owner records on three continents.

The Juno, Sailing From Bristol, England Bound for the African Gold Coast, Jamaica & Home

The "Outward" Passage

The typical Outward Passage would take six weeks on average. Getting the ballast right for the lighter trading goods and for the human cargo of the Middle Passage was critical. That middle voyage's human load would still not be as heavy as that of the goods on the Homeward Passage to England. Sugar and rum in heavy barrels were surprisingly weighty.

The *Juno* was a slave ship owned by the Englishman John Fowler and was constructed in Bristol's shipyard, a critical English port, in 1762. She had a 182.3 standardized tonnage and four cannons mounted on her for self-defense, something not many slave ships had. Having studied extensive records and logs and researched data on this ship, we can follow the journey of its crew and the 300 slaves who were captured by African chiefs *intended* to be sold to the British.

Weathering sea storms relied heavily on getting the right balance of weight and distribution on the ship of its cargo, which changed on each voyage. The ballast you set out with and how you got rid of it before the return voyage to England was vital. Some might off-load in Africa, but most would need to be unloaded in the New World destination. Most slave ships setting sail from Bristol used their ballast from granite stone. Typically, these were four-foot cubes of granite, and a popular source to mine them was in Cornwall county, where the *Juno* most likely took it on board in Bristol.

The *Juno's* captain in May 1765 had his thirty-man crew pulled together and start readying his ship, checking her masts, rigging, sails, rudder, decking, and hatches, all while her hull was being checked inside and out as he loaded his ballast. He then began taking delivery of the trading goods he'd purchased in April and packed her non-perishables on board—her perishable foodstuffs, water, and beer would be loaded in the first week of June. The *Juno* was rigged to take 300 slaves once she had emptied her trading cargo at Fort William and had space for all provisions required to care for the crew and keep her human cargo investment alive. Depending on their size, slave ships could carry anywhere from 100 slaves to 600 in the case of large Spanish galleons converted for that purpose.

Popular trading items for most African chiefs were ironmongery tools like axes, saws, pots, pans, lead bars, and shot. Also on his trading list would be earthenware; bolts of cotton and ready-made cloth items; worsted material; caps; hats; and even chairs, sticks, umbrellas, and mirrors. Alcohol rapidly gained in popularity, as did tobacco. These were the "must have" items of the day in Africa, as were trinkets and beads. Medicine began to be valued too as Africans learned to trust it. All were valued goods to trade for slaves as, increasingly, was monetary coin.

The *Juno* would also be carrying goods for her European traders and soldiers stationed at the company's fort in the African port. The African fort would have requested some of the same items as above, plus guns and gunpowder and swords and cutlasses. European food provisions and wine and fortified wines such as Madeira, sherry, and brandy were all expected. Finally, the *Juno* would have been provisioned with food, drinking water, and beer for her crew, allowing some overage in case of delays through adverse trade winds. While water could go stale after too long exposed to excessive heat, beer would last longer.

The British Royal Trading Company, established by the Crown, controlled around eight fortified encampments along the Gold Coast of West Africa (now Ghana). Ashanti tribespeople were popular slave purchases for Jamaica. Fort William had become the main center of the British slave trade along the Gold Coast at the *Juno* voyage. Its castellated walls rose around forty feet above the Elmina River, on whose banks it sat, and she had defensive cannons on her battlements covering both inland and the river approaches.

She Sets Sail

The *Juno* set sail on her "outward passage" on June 7, 1765. Her owners appointed the captain (who oddly is not mentioned by name in any logs or manifests the author has seen), and she sailed to the recently constructed Fort William. It was completed in 1760 on the British-controlled section of the African Gold Coast. Dutch, Swedish, and Danish slave traders had all had some form of fort on this spot since the mid-1600s, as indeed the British had at one time. This was a more leisurely journey for the crew than the Middle Passage, and they could go about their duties without worrying about a human cargo.

The Juno Arrives Off The Western African Coast

She arrived in early September, three months later, and took double the average time to reach the river mouth and Fort William. A total of three months put her badly behind trading schedules (the slaves being lined up for her captain's purchase would have been sold on to others by now), and he risked unwelcome hurricanes on the latter part of her Middle Passage, which lay ahead. The ship was likely to meet heavy contrary trade winds and violent storms that could potentially damage a mast and sails, requiring slow running repairs at sea.

The captain could not sell his goods in trade, having missed his slot in African chiefs lined up by the company's agents to have 300-plus Ashanti ready for him six weeks ago. The company would now store his trading goods safely, under lock and key in the fort. His crew and company shipbuilders onshore would haul his boat up onto the riverbank and commence careening, cleaning, and mending the ship's hull as needed, and carrying out all necessary repairs, re-floating her, and converting her to take her human cargo. In the meantime, company agents had organized with local chiefs to acquire another 300 captives and deliver them as soon as possible.

It had all taken much longer than expected, and it would be two and a half months from arriving before his human cargo would be nearing Fort William. It was so late in the season; the chief could only muster around 250 slaves. Allowing for deaths on the route from up-country, the chief only saw 220 plus slaves arrive. He knew the company would select the best and drop the weak, but the best was in the buyer's eye. The chief wanted to cover all sales opportunities; unsold slaves could be taken back to his village or pushed into the next sale batch on the arrival of another slave-ship.

The Ashanti Slaves Arrive

The chief knew that the company would take his captives onto the fort grounds and manacle and chain them all to irons fitted on the walls. He knew they would spend a week or more feeding and watering them to build up their bodies' ability after an exhausting trek of possibly a hundred miles on foot, to have a chance at withstanding the grueling sea journey ahead. Slave ship owners were notorious for keeping their overhead costs to the bare minimum to increase their profit. Yet in time they realized the need to keep as many of their cargo alive as possible to maximize profits. Still, the conditions on board their transport for the next month or two would prove appalling, living often in storms in a mire of vomit and defecations of 120 other souls. They would have insufficient food, and their mere survival was in doubt as the faced an unknown future. Their mental anguish at the loss of family and home cannot be imagined.

With the slaves having arrived at the port, the captain and company representatives would start bartering the value of their goods by the slave's importance, arguing over every man, woman, and child, if any. How precious a commodity was the mirror the chief wanted versus the most muscular slaves the captain wished to buy as he attempted to weed out any who looked ill or diseased. Tragically, whether those not selected were the spouse or mother of another bought was of no concern to either the African chief or the ship's captain.

The slaves moved now into even greater heights of emotional shock and levels of exhaustion and stress as individually, they were being made to stand, often naked, and displayed and prodded and bargained for. They moved to anger or total despondency and fear of what lay ahead. Many of the men, warriors in their tribe, knew that if they did not try and escape and get their families out, once they got on that ship, they felt instinctively that they were never coming back. This was especially so if a man's wife or child suddenly was paraded or groped and prodded by a callous soldier, causing them to cry or collapse. Frequent desperate outbreaks of fighting would occur as male slaves did their best to break free and free their families. This generally ended in severe beatings for the men while their chains trapped them.

Time to Load Their Human Cargo

It was recorded that the captain only selected 180 slaves as good enough to purchase (from 300 he could carry); eventually, these poor souls, who would never see their homeland again, were loaded onto the slave ship. Many would lose family or friends on the voyage, or have their surviving family split up in Jamaica, never to see them again.

Plenty of slave ship records exist to show a similar amount of space allocated to each slave on the average British ship. Loading the slaves, the *Juno*'s crew would have to force their captives, struggling and resisting, down into the hold of the vessel. They were placed onto rows of bunks around six feet long (183 cm.) by three feet high (91 cm.) and three feet wide, between a base platform and the bunk above. The *Juno*'s slaves of 180 instead of the ship's maximum of 300 were at least somewhat better off, if such a comment can be made, and less crushed and confined. Some Spanish ships held 600 slaves and had a height between one bunk base and the person above of just sixteen inches (41 cm.). It is sickening just to imagine it.

Tall, strong, muscular men who were always the traders' ideal pick would genuinely be hard pressed to squeeze into such a space. Most men were usually chained in pairs (right leg to another's left leg) to stop them from attempting to escape or be free to attack the crew. However, women and children were generally granted more flexibility, although they would have been manacled in the iron wrist and leg cuffs. From the sixteenth century, all would more than likely been lying flat in platforms stacked in tiers. Unable to stand erect or turn over, many slaves died in this position of illness, scurvy, diarrhea, or other disease, and some of malnutrition. Captive slaves locked in the hold were given far less food and water than the crew and rarely any meat or poultry. They would spend most of their time in squalid conditions, and while British ships were maintained better than their Arab counterparts, breakouts of disease could occur. An utterly appalling way to treat human beings. Often husbands and fathers would give most of their meager food rations to their wife and children, and mothers to their children, in the hope that they at least may survive.

Out of 12 million African slaves who arrived in the New World over 400years (only 600,000 would ever land in America), 15 percent more of them (2.1 million) had died on British ships before arrival. Of the 14 million

African slaves that arrived in the Middle East and Muslim north Africa countries from the Arab slave trade, an appalling 75 *percent (42 million)* more had died on Arab ships before arrival. A total of 26 million Africans covering *both trades* survived their atrocious journey, but 44.12 million died before reaching their intended destination. The combination of those who arrived and those who died en route to Arabia or the New World was 70.12 million Africans who never saw their homeland again after being captured and surviving the journey from their village to the African coast, to be put on board slave vessels. At least another 12 percent of captives by African chiefs stolen to sell into slavery from other tribes died before reaching to coast to be sold to Europeans.

Interestingly, from harsh conditions and being obliged to sleep on deck (during freezing snows and burning tropical sun), occasional slave uprisings, and frequently harsh treatment by a ship's captain, some 20 percent of slave ship crew died on the triangular voyage too (on average six per ship's voyage).

The "Middle" Passage

The Juno Sets Sail For Jamaica

She commenced her "Middle Passage" in mid-December 1765 from the west coast of Africa. As she moved out into the ocean, she steered towards the wind, trimmed her sails, and as they filled and she gathered pace, she was on her way.

To place this period in history, just two weeks into her passage, on January 1, 1766, Prince Charles Edward Stuart (Bonnie Prince Charlie) became the new Stuart claimant to the throne of Scotland. In April, just before the *Juno* arrived in Jamaica, the first African slaves had been imported directly from Africa to Savannah, Georgia, and Spain had rounded up all ethnic Chinese in their colony of the Philippines and placed them in ghettoes.

Slave ship owners were notorious for keeping their overhead costs to the bare minimum to increase their profit. Yet in time they realized the need to keep as many of their cargo alive as possible to maximize profits. These conditions *did* improve considerably in the nineteenth century, as the British government introduced laws restricting the number of slaves per tonnage of the ship, with space allocated, and under required provisions in the Slave

Trade Act of 1788. It cut the number of slaves per ship by nearly a third, which intensified ship owners' worry about making a profit but enabled the slaves to survive in improved conditions.

On the *Juno*, conditions would likely be appalling. There were 300 African men and women who had to defecate, urinate, and vomit from seasickness in buckets, if available. Otherwise, where they stood or lay was all they could do due to the sheer dehumanizing, deprivation, and what must have been a horrific stench and foul air. Dehydration, dysentery, diarrhea, scurvy, and any diseases latent and carried with a slave would be rampant in such horrid conditions.

The slaves would be underfed, lacking in liquid, and lacking all basic hygiene. Hence, typically on British slave-ships, 15 percent died before they reached their destination. They were in worse conditions than an English peasant farmer kept his cattle. Slaves were usually given a ration of water and a boiled rice meal twice a day, including grains like cooked cornmeal or millet. Possibly there was added starch, like the common African yam or beans.

Everyone was brought up on deck once or twice a day, depending on the weather, for fresh air and exercise and a washing down with buckets of seawater hauled up from over the side of the ship. Some attempt was made to flush out the putrid human waste and vomit from the hull while the slaves were on deck.

The Juno Arrives in Jamaica

After a few contra winds, the *Juno* sailed along the south coast of Jamaica and eventually came round White House Bay. The captain would have recognized Crab Pond Point and Bluefield's Bay as he passed them. He knew he was very close and would shortly put into port Savannah-la-Mar in Westmoreland, Jamaica (southwest of the island), which he did on March 12, 1776. The *Juno* had taken two and a half months to arrive from the Gold Coast of Africa.

When the ship landed, the population of Jamaica was approximately 210,000, made up of 193,000 slaves, over 4,000 free people of color, and around 13,000 white Europeans.

From her original cargo of 180 slaves, with almost twice as much space below decks than usual, the port customs officer recorded her at the Savannah-la-Mar harbor as unloading all thirty crew but, tragically, only 160 slaves.

She had lost twenty of her African captives during the voyage. While that is better than the average British slave-ship Middle Passage loss of 15 percent, which would have been twenty-seven people, it is still twenty human lives lost. Speaking about a different voyage, some slaves were recorded as saying that the ones who died en-route "were the lucky ones who did not have to face a life of hard labor and never-ending toil"

We must remember that this was not only a massive trauma of mental anguish and life of slavery and hardship ahead, but their family left behind faced the trauma and loss of loved ones, never knowing if they were alive or dead.

The town of Savannah-la-Mar would have appeared to the crew as relatively new looking. It had only been built up over the last thirty-two years. A powerful hurricane had hit Jamaica in October 1744, and apart from damage in Kingston and Port Royal harbor, it had obliterated Savannah-la Mar. Eight warships and ninety-six merchant ships were wrecked, washed onto rocks, or left high and dry. This was an important slave entry port in Jamaica, as many of the sugar plantations were in the south, southwest, and central west of the island.

After customs had checked her crew and cargo, the captain began to unload his human cargo and then walked to Fort of Penn. Here they typically stayed for a few days or a week, manacled to iron shackles on the wall of the ground floor of the fort's internal square. They would have been given time to recover from the appalling journey and were likely fed relatively well for a few days to make them appear more appealing and alive.

Come the day of the next town slave market, they would have been washed and dried, then oiled, and then walked down in irons and chains to the slave auction, usually held near the courthouse. The captain would now sell them at the best price he could achieve. For those 160 Africans, a series of horrendous nightmares was behind them; they had lost family and friends, and they were weak and exhausted as they were sold one last time. Now they and faced an uncertain future, but one assured to be of twelve hours a day of hardship and toil. Their next nightmare had begun.

Preparing For The Voyage Home

The captain would have allowed his crew and himself time to rest and recuperate onshore. Then they'd commence the process of preparing his vessel for the return voyage. They would have to carefully offload his enormous weight in ballast—his myriad of Cornish granite stone blocks, which were ideal building blocks.

Just outside of the town of Savannah-la-Mar are numerous great houses built out of such building blocks. Up in the hills above the Galloway Sugar Plantation, Caledonia Great House was built from such granite blocks. Nothing in the New World could be wasted, and with tropical storms and hurricanes, these four-foot cubes of granite were perfect for building great plantation houses. Roofs might blow off, but the walls would stay. But many great houses that used the granite solely for the foundation and saved money building the house on top with wood might be destroyed.

Another use of these relatively uniform granite blocks was to build sea walls and early government buildings and courthouses, as well as army and naval barracks and forts.

The blocks were likely the foundations and steps of the old Overseas House at the Caymanas Estate, whose walls and roof were made of wood. Alec Hamilton's maternal grandparents and Ewing ancestors would have walked up and down those steps on their visits to the plantation from Scotland over the few hundred years in which the house stood. The granite stone steps are still there today and are all that are left of that house, as shown in a photograph in this book.

The ballast taken off, the *Juno* would now have been beached nearby and careened on her side while all necessary repairs were carried out. Her seams would be caulked and then she'd be turned on her other side and the same treatment given to the hull. Her rigging, sails, and masts would all have been attended to, and her hull would be flushed out of the putrid vomit, urine, and feces. She would be cleaned while she was refitted for her new, heavy cargo. Re-provisioned, she would have taken onboard a much heavier payload than her human one. Her cargo of sugar, rum, and molasses-filled barrels and other goods for the "homeward" passage voyage back to Bristol was ballast enough.

Just over a year before the *Juno* docked in Jamaica, on April 19, 1775, the American colonies commenced the War of Independence, seeking to break away from Great Britain. And just two years after she landed her cargo in Savannah-la-Mar, the entire port and town were destroyed in the 1780 hurricane. They were damaged again in another devastating hurricane that left virtually no building standing a few years later. Ready to go, the *Juno* gave notice to the customs authority that she was about to cast off, and she moved out of the harbor and set sail.

The "Homeward" Passage

The *Juno* departed from Savannah-la-Mar on April 24, 1776, for Bristol, England. Her crew of thirty, including her captain, would have been looking forward to getting home safely, and at least they had a home to go to and freedom.

She landed back in her home port on July 5, 1776, after a six-week passage from Jamaica—a total journey away from home of eleven months. This was three months longer than average, but not uncommon. Her crew and company dockworkers began unloading her cargo of sugar (often referred to as white gold), molasses, and rum. Desperate buyers for these highly in-demand commodities would have been eagerly awaiting their sale.

In the British regions of Wales and England alone, sugar consumption increased 2,000 *percent* during the 1700s, as did early dentistry, as records show.

After paying all costs for the ship and her journey, the purchase price of slaves and losses, all customs and overseas port taxes, and wages, the company would take out a profit share for themselves and any investors and start all over again with the residue funds. They would seek to buy iron ore goods and cotton and ready the ship and maybe a new crew for their next triangular trans-Atlantic voyage to deliver more slaves to British colonies and bring back to England more sugar and rum from which to make a fortune.

American Independence Declared

The Juno landed one day after a momentous world event was unfolding across the Atlantic Ocean. On July 4, 1776, the fledgling Continental Congress of the American colonies adopted and signed a document declaring their independence from Great Britain, a goal yet to be achieved.

The ship had landed just twenty-five-days before British Prime Minister, the Most Honorable Charles, Lord Watson-Wentworth K.G., 2nd Marquess of Rockingham, resigned on July 30 (his second non-consecutive term as prime minister). This is a vital link to the American story due to massive pressure from the British public over the outrage caused in the American colonies from a stamp duty the British government had imposed on them. This act contributed hugely to the colony's resolve to split away from the motherland and push its Declaration of Independence home. During this period, many slaves in Northern states chose to run away from their masters and plantations and flee to the Southern states.

True Emancipation in America – Was Another 99-years Away

True emancipation came to the entire new nation of the United States of America after the Civil War ended and the Confederate southern states capitulated and lost in May 1865. It took some months to enact, but in December 1865, emancipation became fact. All those enslaved in the whole of the new nation were finally free and released from bondage.

In 1865, there was a population of 34 million people in total across the new nation. This figure covered the soon to be nearly 4.49 million freed slaves, *which included* nearly 500,000 former slaves who had already been freed before emancipation. They were listed separately on the new nation's census. All those of African-descent were released at emancipation and accounted for 13.2 percent of the American population. Today, that community is 12.1 percent, according to the 2020 census, of 332 million total approximate population, so it remains similar.

Slaves Were Offered Reparations by President Abraham Lincoln

On January 12, the northern Union Army General Sherman had already accepted what was the final major Confederate Army surrender, having made a long march to the southern city where surrender to him was made. He knew the war was coming to an end in the months ahead. Last small pockets of southern army surrenders were occurring, while he and other Union leaders, including Secretary of War Edwin Stanton, gathered a group of twenty Black religious ministers in Savannah, Georgia. They had come forward as representatives of freed slaves across the southern states. The meeting took place in the high-ceilinged room in a corner of the second floor of Sherman's temporary headquarters, Green-Meldrim House in Savannah.

The new government of a United States of America, he said, was to provide shipment for all 4.49 million slaves to Africa, and settlements were to be established there to support their resettling as they found their way to their ancestral roots or made a new nation on the coast. More than 86 percent of the 4.49 million freed slaves were born on American soil, the *descendants* of slaves imported from Africa, and had no desire to go to a country they did not know, so they said no.

Sherman asked the leaders' key spokesman, the Rev. Garrison Frazier, a series of questions. The other slave representatives chose Frazier, as he was an eloquently spoken, sixty-seven-year-old imposing man of over six feet tall. Critically, Sherman's fourth question was: "State in what manner you would rather live, whether scattered among whites, or in colonies by yourselves?" He was asking what their people wanted in reparations for the loss of freedom, most having been born into slavery. Obviously, the idea of getting free passage back to Africa and support in settling a new state, a country virtually none of them knew, hadn't appealed to these African Americans, as less than 1 percent of the 4.49-million freed slaves took up the offer.

Frazier answered Sherman plainly when he said, "I would prefer to live by ourselves, for there is a prejudice against us in the South that will take years to get over." He went on to tell Sherman that what the freed slaves most wanted in reparations was land granted to each family so that they may build a home and grow crops and feed themselves as free people. Later they also asked that every family be given a mule to help them start tilling their land.

Emancipated Slaves Wanted Segregation

Sherman asked the other nineteen church leaders and representatives of the enslaved southern peoples present for their opinion. All but one agreed that *their people would want land to till themselves in Black-only communities*, not amongst whites, for the same reason Frazier had made plain.

Four days later, on January 16, 1865, General Sherman issued a "Special Field Order 15," empowered by President Lincoln, announcing that "every southern negro family (not individual, but family) would be granted forty acres (sixteen ha) of land of their own to till, to be established after finalizing the last pockets of civil war conclusion." What Sherman now offered was to set aside 400,000 acres of "confiscated" Confederate landowners' property for freed slave families. Sherman appointed Brigadier General Rufus Saxton to divide up the land, giving each family up to forty acres.

The 400,000 acres they could make claim to was to be within a clear designated area only, the "islands from Charleston, South Carolina, the abandoned rice fields along the rivers for thirty miles back from the sea, and the country bordering the St. John's River, Florida." They were "reserved and set apart for the settlement of negroes now made free by the acts of war and the proclamation of the President of the United States," Abraham Lincoln.

Sherman confirmed that Black communities would be allowed to govern themselves in segregation, away from white communities, as they had requested and as approved by the President. No freed slave could be happy with the past, but Lincoln hoped they would be pleased that what they asked for through their religious leaders was being granted: their chance to start a new life, free.

The effect in the south was like a lightning rod that crashed through the sound barrier. Despite that fact, one of the Black Baptist ministers in attendance, Ulysses Houston, lost no time waiting and almost immediately, in January or February, led his flock of 1,000 men, women, and children to the unoccupied Georgia island of Skidaway. This was several months before the formal freeing of slaves and before any land had been officially granted to Houston's flock.

However, tragically, President Lincoln, the first Republican President, was shot on April 14, 1865, and died the following day. He was succeeded by his Democrat vice president, Andrew Johnson. By 11:00 a.m. of April 15, Johnson was sworn in as the seventeenth President of the United States. President Johnson moved rapidly with sufficient backing from the Southern Democrat leaders, and clearly some Northern Union Republicans too, and sought to reverse and annul Sherman and Lincoln's wartime promises and proclamations.

Ulysses Houston's flock established a self-governing, segregated by choice, Black-only community and elected their first governor when they left Sherman's meeting in January. By Lincoln's assassination, many others had already started claiming their families' forty acres and began creating their Black-only communities. Some sources suggest the bulk of families had already staked their claims on the 400,000 acres and were requesting plots to be deeded to them.

A Reparations Solution Found – And Reneged On

However, President Andrew Johnson pushed legislation through the new government of the USA that rescinded and annulled Lincoln and Sherman's declaration. All land deeded to black families and those being prepared to be granted to former slave families was cancelled by federal directive. The Southern state Democrat party legislators were quick to evict the former slaves and hand back the land to its pre-Civil War Confederate owners right across the south. Some Black communities did maintain control of their land in areas no one else truly wanted, and some under Johnson's earlier, Homesteading laws were granted, and Black land ownership grew at a rapid rate in one state, Mississippi, during the late 1800s, as they claimed low-lying flood lands that no one else wanted. By 1910, former slave families owned 15 million acres of land (6.1 million ha). Tragically, a massive amount of this land ownership was lost in the Wall Street Crash of 1929 that devastated the American economy, as it was by as many or more white families. Several commentators and race relations experts remark on how different race relations in America would be today if the southern land distribution to the former slave families had been completed and left in place.

NOTES:

The Abolition of Slavery Around the World

Ahead of the pack, the Danish ended slavery in 1792. Then it was Sweden by 1813, Mexico in 1829, and Mexican Texas in 1830. Great Britain followed in 1833, France by 1848, Ecuador in 1851, and Argentina in 1853. Peru and Venezuela ended slavery in 1854. Egypt, India, Pakistan, Bangladesh, and Nepal, once they came under the rule of the British Raj, ended slavery in 1857. The Dutch and Belgians did in 1863, except for the Dutch colonies of Indonesia, where it ended in 1860. Russia ended slavery in 1861, and America by 1865. Spain emancipated slaves in stages by 1867, and Portugal by 1869. Its colony of Brazil, by now independent, waited until 1888. Japan was in 1871, the Ottoman Empire ended slavery, in stages, by 1882, and Cambodia ended slavery in 1884. The On the same day it became a newly annexed territory of the USA, Hawaii emancipated all slaves and indentured peoples in June 1900. Thailand had not effectively ended slavery until 1905. Malaysia did in 1915, with Burma and the Philippines around the same time. China officially ended slavery in 1910, but not in reality until 1940 man believe.

The US Census

By the 2020 US Census, 57.8 percent of Americans identified as white only, and 12.1 percent identified themselves as Black only, with Hispanics making up 18.7 percent of all Americans (over 50% more than African Americans), and 7.2 percent identified as Asian, the fastest growing racial group in America today out of its approximate 332 million population. Nearly 58 percent of Americans are white, down from 63% in earlier census.

The 2014 DNA study by the respected genetic analysts at 23andMe of over 500,000 Americans showed that the average African American has 24 percent European or white DNA, and the average white American has 3.5 percent African DNA.

Arab Slave-Trade of Africans & of White People

The author's research covered multiple groups of subjects. From the forgotten Arab slave trade of Africans to the Middle East and North Africa before and during trans-Atlantic trade, it saw *far greater numbers* of Africans enslaved in Muslim countries than the New World, around 14% more. The earlier Muslim slave trade saw twice as many white Europeans enslaved than the 12.1 million black Africans enslaved in the New World.

The Long-Established African Slave Trade by African Chiefs

African kings and chiefs engaged in slavery and held regular slave markets 5,500-years before the New World trade. African rulers actively participated in the New World and Middle East slave trades, seeing more incredible wealth. When Britain and France, for example, outlawed slavery across their colonies, some African rulers pushed to keep the New World slave trade due to enormous sums of money they were making, as the author's research evidence showed. Facts, not attempts to lessen the Christian and Muslim world trades in slaves.

Research papers also cover native Latin American Indians who came to Jamaica 5,000 years before the Spanish enslaved them. Papers cover later Indian tribes that migrated from Latin America to Jamaica long before the Spanish. Those newer tribes were forced into slavery by the original Indian tribes! When the Spanish took Jamaica, they enslaved every Indian tribe they found. There are research papers, too, on Native American Indian's enslaving rival American tribespeople and enslaving escaped African slaves too.

Additional sources written about from academic and historical data:
U.S. Census Bureau: Variation by Population Characteristics
Sepia Orbignya research papers
UN statements on enslaved people today
UNHRC and human rights reports
UN Association at UCLA
Somerset v. Stewart—UK Judicial reports
Human Rights Watchdogs
There are twenty-nine research papers written by the author on slavery.

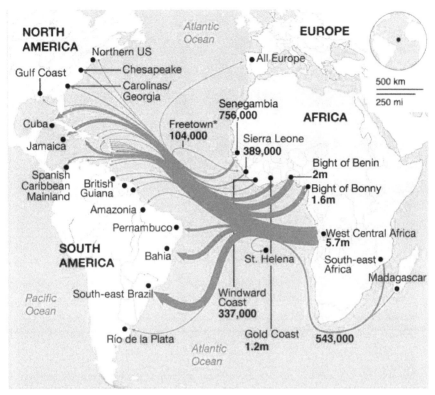

The land boundaries shown on this map are those understood in the year 1750. The source of both the map and data is *Slave Voyages,* created by the BBC and made available to the public on BBC News—Africa blog. This blog says that 104,000 freed African slaves returned to Africa. 12.5 million Africans were enslaved by the trans-Atlantic trade in total over 300 years in the Americas and the Caribbean. Most academic research lists the number as 12 million now.

Arab slave traders moving captives to a seaport for transportation c.1680 (NCA).

A CNN report, 2020. Libya, on the outskirts of the capital, Tripoli. Very young Nigerian African girls, teenagers, and women, it appears, being herded to the slave market by their Libyan Arab hosts to be sold (CC).

Emancipation Day, Celebration Banquet for all those freed from slavery at the Dawkins Caymanas Estate, Jamaica, August 2, 1838 (NCA).

Caribbean sugarcane cutting by hand in the 1700s (NCA).

A sugar-plantation boiling house like those in James Ewing's time
before emancipation and modernization (NCA).

Chapter 10

MODERN-DAY ALEXANDER HAMILTON:
BIRTH TO ARMY DAYS

The Second of This Book's Two Apples

Raised in a Palladian house, Alexander Vereker Hamilton was born on November 1, 1932, at Strathleven House in Dumbartonshire, Scotland (his maternal Ewing family seat). He was a scion of the Westbrook and Elrick branch of the Hamiltons. Alec was nearly eighty-eight years of age when he sadly passed away in Jamaica on Easter Sunday, April 12, 2020.

Alexander, Alec to family and friends, was born with an ancestry of 747 years of Hamilton-named lineage and shared the same ancestor with Alexander Hamilton, a Founding Father of America. This Scotsman descended directly in the mail bloodline from the first Norman Earl of Leicester, who fought with William the Conqueror in 1066, and from a Viking earl born 1,052 years before his birth. At the age of twenty-one, he inherited one of the most extensive sugar plantations in Jamaica, and from 1954 onward, he made it his life's work and Jamaica his home.

While slavery had ended in Jamaica in his maternal great-grandfather's time, some 116 years before he arrived in Jamaica, he was painfully aware of that past. He was proud that his maternal grandfather and parents had sought to build on those freedoms for all and improve their workforce's lot, one generation after the other. He approached his leadership of Caymanas as a man filled with business and common sense, a man with the common touch who treated all his employees as he would anyone else. He was a man who spoke softly and kindly and who, with his mother's full support, gifted much of his land to employees and for his workers' and nearby villages' use. He wanted to enhance their lives and give back. Much of his land went to the people of Jamaica to create housing estates for an ever-growing capital city. He will always be remembered as the man who sold land that enabled one of Jamaica's most followed sports, horse racing, to build its new state of the art course on his former lands, Caymanas Park Racetrack.

Sharing several of Alec's childhood memories gives us a sense of what early experiences influenced the man as his life and times unfolded. These early memories stayed with him over and above everything else that happened in his life, so powerful were they. They sliced through wars, personal and country tragedies, and life's general ups and downs over nearly nine decades from the twentieth to the twenty-first centuries. These stories enable a sense of his childhood and young adult years as he saw them, in a bygone era of both Scotland and Jamaica. With Alec leaving this world last year, the stories he shared firsthand with the author become unrepeatable opportunities for those who knew him in other parts of his life or did not live in those years. It opens the door to understanding a little of how he was raised and what events and people influenced him.

Alec's Place Birth

Strathleven House was one of, if not the first, grand Palladian-style houses in Scotland, built in 1717 for William Cochrane, the Earl of Dundonald's son. In 1677, William had acquired the estate and lands where a fortified tower-house had sat from 1465. The tower-house was removed to build this splendid, Palladian-style house on the same spot. Today, the house is the offices of The Scottish Buildings Historical Trust. The historic and stunning parkland and farms of some 8,000 acres, which had surrounded the house in Alec's childhood days, are now an industrial estate with countless factories, businesses, and warehouses. Fully restored, the house now sits in the center of this manufacturing estate like a beacon of more genteel and harmonious days when it sat in the center of a picturesque landscape.

By 1830, having changed hands twice, the estate was purchased by James Ewing, Alec's four times maternal great-uncle. For James, it was the visual announcement that he'd arrived as a West Indies sugar baron and American tobacco merchant and was somebody of great import in the very class-conscious Georgian era of British society. He was part of the nouveau riche, as the aristocracy would have viewed him, but they would pay attention to him in a world rapidly changing. As more and more people demanded access to sugar, production increased, and James Ewing made an absolute fortune. It was a level of wealth that came on the backs of slaves, something those who enjoyed this wonderful, sweet sugar did not stop to think about.

The estate was still known as Levenside when James bought it (after the

River Leven that flowed through its grounds). It was only in 1836, after he'd married, that James changed the estate name to Strathleven. Strath is a term in Scotland depicting a wide valley, hence Strathleven depicts the wide valley through which the Leven River runs, as Strathclyde city is the wide valley through which the Clyde River runs.

Alec's maternal grandparents lived grandly at Strathleven House with, in their day a butler, cooks, maids, gardeners, grooms, nannies, shepherds, and tenant farmers. Some of the antique furniture from Strathleven House landed up at Alec's current house on the Scottish borders.

The Strathleven House library formed Alec's library at Lowood House, inherited from his parents. A few years before Alec's death, Scottish Government Archives cataloged all family documents and materials at Lowood House. There are photos of the Strathleven House and estate at the end of this chapter.

Memories of an Age Gone By

Recollecting one's life is not an easy matter. It is not always easy to jump to another era, especially if it is many decades ago, unless our memory is jogged, sometimes by others. Alec faced with patience a list of prepared questions put gently to a man in his late eighties. Over some weeks, an interview pattern in both Scotland and Jamaica emerged to suit Alec's comfort level and age, over a visit twice to each home over two years. In the end, two hours each morning and two each afternoon found a balance with Alec and allowed him to "rest and recover from your endless questions," as he once said to the author with a grin.

Once both Alec and author figured out that he needed two to three minutes of silence after each question being posed, as they were moments of silent reflection, not an inability to remember, they plowed on endlessly thereafter. Inevitably, the longer they spent together, the more relaxed and open Alec was with his answers to questions on any topic. Given time to reflect, his answers sharing his inner thoughts formed with ease.

Occasionally, to help him recall an event that was momentarily eluding him, numerous photos of people or events that matched questions about his life were shown to him. Such images proved invaluable during these rare moments when Alec drew a blank. Whenever a photo was presented to him and enquired about, he was off like a shot, regaling the author with who was in the picture, where it was taken, and what the event was. Each turned a key that almost instantly unlocked a door to Alec's memory.

Here was a man in his twilight years, who still had good recall, even if it had to be prodded occasionally. He had led a full and hectic life, and as a young Scot, he'd served his nation in war, and he'd inherited a substantial business empire with land, agriculture, and people to manage on two continents. He worked professionally and diligently but did so with calm and enthusiasm. He took to Jamaica, its people, and culture like a duck to water, and it was home for sixty-six years of his life. The Jamaican people reciprocated his kindness and the tolerance he showed others.

Fun Childhood Memories of Strathleven

Alec loved playing in the seemingly never-ending park-like grounds of Strathleven or wandering across its farms—there were 8,000 acres in all to get lost in. Or he could just ramble around the big house itself. In visiting the house, as you can today, one steps back into *Downton Abbey*-style days with grand entertaining rooms, fine plasterwork, high ceilings, intricately carved wooden balustrades, massive solid mahogany doors, and, below stairs, a warren of corridors in the working part of the house.

After they were bathed and dressed for bed at the end of a long, fun day, the children's nanny would bring them down to the drawing room to say goodnight to their parents each evening. Nanny and the nursery world Alec lived in when very young were memories as clear as day for him all these decades later. He'd often scuttle down the grand staircase from his bedroom and then slip unnoticed from the entry hall. Then equally as fast, before he was spotted, he slipped through the door into the stairwell that led to the servants' area downstairs. He'd then slide into the great kitchen in a hurry, and sitting in front of the black, steel ovens, be treated to hot oak cakes by Mrs. Heggie, the family's cook. Mrs. Heggie had been with the family forever and would always greet Alec with a warm, motherly smile and a hug and then pass him whatever freshly baked treats she had.

Mrs. Heggie always whispered to Alec not to tell anyone she'd given him treats. Of course, that made them all the sweeter—to have forbidden food-stuffs, he told me. That kitchen at the restored Strathleven House still exists today, and when you stand there, if you can do so one day, Alec's story will fully come to life. When you stand in front of that black, cast-iron cooking range from the late 1800s, you can close your eyes and, in a moment, hear the hustle and bustle of a nineteenth-century kitchen and smell the aroma of fresh oatcakes cooking. The in their day state-of-the-art cast-iron ovens are still there with their hob tops and bread oven.

There was a broad strip of lawn right along the front of the big house, which is still there today, and it had two lion statues guarding the driveway entrances. Alec also vividly recalled what were to him giant statues of Diana the Huntress and Apollo. The statues are no longer there, and Alec wondered where they had ended up. He thought they had possibly disappeared along with the missing Hamilton Palace staircase that had been purchased and put into Strathleven House when the Hamilton Palace was collapsing.

Stories Told to Alec

Some of Alec's most cherished childhood memories were visits from his famous great-uncle, General Sir Ian Hamilton. "We were not close," Alec said, "but goodness did I look forward to his visits. I hung on his every word, and no matter how many questions we children asked him, he took time to answer them." He was Alec and the family's living hero.

Sir Ian was always very good with the children, especially the boys, who were excited by his illustrious and international reputation as a military leader and soldier of the Empire, which was by Alec's day fading slowly away. No one they knew had anyone in their family who had a relative with such a distinguished military career stretching from the Second Afghan and both Boer Wars to World War One. Alec remembered when he first heard that his great-uncle had received prestigious Sovereign Orders; he felt terribly proud of his great-uncle.

General Sir Ian Hamilton was a living legend in his own time, to none more so than his great-nephew Alec, his siblings, and his school chums. Sir Ian was on personal terms with the famous military and political figures of his day in Britain, which made him doubly impressive to schoolboys. He had been friends with military giants like General Gordon of Khartoum and Lord Kitchener; with the literary giant Rudyard Kipling; and a lifetime friend of the soldier, journalist, and eventual Prime Minister of the United Kingdom,

Sir Winston Churchill. All these men were boyhood heroes to Alec and his parents' generation. They were the stuff of legends in the fading days of the British Empire and before World War One would consume the world in war.

Alec's Memory of His Great-Uncle

Alec might be one of the few people alive who had first-hand encounters with this legend in the family, very personal experiences from time spent in that great man's company. Sir Ian was uncommonly kind and not stuffy or commanding but gently spoken. Alec said, "We were all immensely proud of him." Once, when Alec lost the two shillings Sir Ian had gifted him, Big Ian, as the family called him, replaced it without a second thought. He often played games with the children, throwing cushions, climbing trees, or scrambling under tables and chairs to chase them, and generally amusing them with his antics. Such behavior put this great war hero in another light as a happy family elder. Not having had a son of his own, he enjoyed romping around on the floor with his nephews.

Alec remembered the vast parties Sir Ian threw, and how at his birthday parties, he'd have masses of family and friends. "We were sat down separately at dinner parties," Alec recalled, "which suited us." He always came to check on the children and would make some humorous remark, which left them all in stitches and made them feel grown-up. Sir Ian was a very distinguished-looking man, every inch (no pun intended) the army general. In his mid-teens, before Big Ian died, Alec attended several large cocktail parties Big Ian threw at his home. After a big party, a select group of friends and family then stayed on for a dinner party to celebrate his birthday each year.

Childhood Memories

One of Alec's best friends as a child was Bill Findlay; their families were close. Strathleven was very near to Loch Lomond. On the far side of the loch sat Boturich Castle in Balloch, Dumbartonshire, on the loch banks; Bill's family owned it at the time, and it is where Bill was born. Interviewing Bill, a second time at his home in Dumbartonshire, the author was able to view his family's castle from the loch, which remains a stunning sight. Bill and his delightful wife, Delia, are charming people, and the friendship between Alec and Bill was strong as ever it was.

Alec's family didn't know Alec to be very academic; hence, before going off to boarding school, he was first schooled at home in Strathleven by a senior governess. She had a reputation for being an expert at getting backward children ready to cope with boarding school year-one learning. A neighbor's son was given the offer to share Alec's new governess. He was a few years older than Alec and his name was Michael Toynbee. Alec's siblings, Mary and Helen also formed part of the governess' class. Michael and Alec were great friends, and living in a nearby estates, they saw each other often. They called their governess Tortoise, as she supposedly looked rather like one, and "She taught us all together," Alec's sister Helen confirmed.

Alec's prep school headmaster was a Mr. Wickham, who was a very, very nice man and mad on trout fishing—as was Alec. Mr. Wickham asked Alec one day what he would like to do best on a terrible, pouring wet day, and Alec replied, "Go fishing." He then was asked what he would like to do best on a good day, and he replied, "Go fishing," which went down very well with Mr. Wickham.

Off to Boarding School

After the forced sale of Strathleven to the Scottish Board of Trade, the family took a house called Winn's, near Lingfield in Surrey, England, in 1949. They were to also buy the Lowood Estate in Melrose, south of Edinburgh, with the proceeds of Strathleven when the court cases brought by the church, claiming they were promised 80 percent of any sale of James Ewing's will, were over.   Alec's father had a growing architectural practice and some major commissions in London, so moving nearby to Surrey enabled him to build his practice. Alec was already at boarding school with Bill Findlay by then, a school chosen because they wished to have him not too far. Ian, Alec's younger brother was born at this house in 1938. It must have been a very unsettling time in Alec's life. He and his family had been forced out of the only home he knew, yet boarding school would have given him the stability of constant surroundings, friendships, and routine—and his oldest pal, Bill, was with him.

After attending the Twyford Preparatory boarding school in Hampshire, Alec and Bill Findlay started at Canford Public School near Wimborne-Minster in Dorset. Canford was a private boarding school for boys only at the time. For American readers who may not be aware, a "public school" in the United Kingdom means it is a fee-paying private school, not a free government school as in America. Canford was well known for its athletic success, especially for its rugby and cricket teams, in Alec and Bill's day.

Bill and Alec landed in the same dormitory in Beaufort House and started at Canford School in the September term of 1946, when they were both around age fourteen. In January, the housemaster turned off the heating, saying they didn't need it, and Alec said he suddenly felt freezing just remembering it. He had no winter clothes at school and was told it was character building, and he ought to find his British stiff upper lip.

After World War One, there was continued austerity of rationing under the new government, with food and coal shortages for heating. It was not that Canford was failing to heat the school to save money; there were regularly no heating supplies to be had. As Secretary of State for the Government, Ernest Bevin said at the time, "We're a country surrounded by fish and built on coal, and only a genius could be short of both!"

Alec enjoyed his school days, and while not brilliant academically, he did okay. He played rugby and cricket at school, and while not gifted at either, he said he enjoyed them both. Alec liked making things and loved getting home to Scotland to shoot and fish— his passions then and for the rest of his life.

Alec said the annual family trip up to Caithness on Scotland's northern tip was always the highlight of each year. He continued the yearly tradition from 1955 up to 2019 (pre-Covid pandemic lockdown, in what was to be his last visit to Caithness and Scotland). Erica, Alec's wife, had feared this 2019 trip might be Alec's final one, as he was increasingly ill, and luckily, she ensured that all his family attended to make it unique. In past years, much of the family spent their time shooting on their grouse moor, sea or loch fishing, and lobster and crab potting from a small boat. Alec recalled that picnics, whether sunshine or bitter cold, were always de-rigueur to take part in for all.

Looking back to Caithness visits from childhood, Alec made a deeply felt statement when he said, "We forever take it for granted, but goodness, it's a luxury to be outdoors. To be with family, to have togetherness. We took part in sports together, went fishing, and were keen to see what we'd caught in the lobster and crab pots." In Caithness, they either were outside doing all these things, or they were all cooking and eating together, laughing, chatting, or just sleeping.

Canford School

Alec and Bill agreed with a chuckle that neither of them was academically minded, and their parents knew that likely precluded them from getting into Eton or Harrow or the like. They knew that themselves already, Bill said, but they had a strong bond together because they were alike in personality and academic ability. "We pair of pals" (as Bill described them) "skidded along with middle C school grades all the time, and we became very artful at shooting a line that sounded like we knew what we had learned, even if we had not."

The pals were two of three Scots in their boarding school, including a boy named Malcolm, who became great friends with the two of them. Alec said Malcolm always adopted rather grand social airs, suggesting to those who did not know him that he came from a very, very noble Scottish family. "It was just Malcolm, and we accepted that he was still a good pal." One year Malcolm said to a group of boys that his parents could not make speech day, as they would be at Holyrood Palace in Scotland for a garden party with the queen. With a nonchalant air, Alec calmly replied, "Oh, my parents were invited by the queen too but have chosen to attend our speech-day instead." Bill commented, "Now that's panache!"

The Notorious Cannon Club

While Alec and Bill may not have distinguished themselves scholastically, they created a legend in its day—the infamous, the notorious, "Cannon Club." On a lathe in the school workshops, they had made a tiny brass cannon, in every detail faithful to the old-fashioned cannon of the 1600s. In the metal workshop, the cannon was bored to take a regular English shotgun cartridge. With neither metal nor woodworking master knowing what they were making in the other class, they couldn't put two and two together, the boys reasoned. They fashioned a block of wood for the cannon to be placed in and hold it steady. To ensure that this assembly didn't fly backward at high speed and hit someone when they fired the cannon, they put nails in the woodblock's base, facing back from the bullet's exit at a 45-degree angle. When the cannon was being readied for firing, the boys planned to push the block backward while pressing down so that the nails would dig into the earth even more with the recoil upon firing. The whole thing had been very carefully planned, Bill said.

They had been hatching their plan for some months and were very careful to keep it secret. When returning from their next term break, part of their private plans required Alec to bring back with him several gun cartridges. Bill said, "We'd worked out that we could remove the gunpowder from a cartridge and use it in the brass cannon chamber to light with a fuse and reproduce a true cannon-firing experience." It's just as well they hadn't met up with a descendent of Guy Fawkes, or the boys may have had grander thoughts! More on that for those non-British readers can be found under the notes at the end of this chapter.

The question was, Alec said, how to get the cartridges back down from Scotland, into school, and stored unnoticed. Eventually, he came up with the idea of hiding them in jars of guava jelly (a jam or preserve made in Jamaica). Luckily, a box of guava jelly had been brought back from Jamaica on his parents' last trip. All Alec had to do, said Bill with a boyish grin, was to take out a soup spoon of jelly from each jar to make room, push one cartridge into each pot, seal the lid, and pop it back into the box of twelve jars. Down to school with Alec went the box of guava jelly jars, and he then stored them in the "tuck" room (inside a mini trunk with a lock for children at boarding school to "tuck" away candy and goodies), and there they innocently sat until the boys were ready on the very next weekend. "Goodness knows what would have happened if there had been a fire in the tuck room!" Alec said.

Delighted with their creation, the boys snuck off the very next weekend up onto Canford Heath, a little above the school and not far away. They placed a shotgun cartridge in the cannon's chamber and wadding in front of it. Then, to act as a fuse, they took out some of the gunpowder from a second cartridge to create a trail from the chamber, out of the hole in the top of the cannon and across the top. They had prepared everything to plan and laid the trail of gunpowder ready to light the fuse and jump way back out of the way.

Either someone snitched or had overheard plans and ratted the boys to a school master. The boys, excited and keen to see their hard, creative work succeed, lit the cannon's gunpowder trail and stood way back for safety. It fired brilliantly but straight into the earth a little way off, and to their shock, at that very moment of triumph, a schoolmaster appeared on the heath, running towards them and shouting, his arms flailing. They had been caught red-handed. They got a jolly good telling off on the heath, were put on report, and faced detention. They got a good ticking off from their housemaster too and lectured on how dangerous it was to play with live ammunition and gunpowder.

Two Determined Little Gunsmiths

The cannon itself had not been confiscated, nor had Alec owned up to having more gun cartridges still hidden unnoticed in guava-jelly pots. Alec and Bill waited a few weeks for the furor of their crime to calm down and begin to fade from everyone else's memory. The occasion arrived when the boys thought it safe, and off they slunk to their house common room on the weekend. They checked no one was about, closed the door, and prepared to fire the cannon indoors to see how far a cartridge would go through a book! What a pair they were—but Lady Luck wasn't with them again this day. Alec pulled out two-gun cartridges he'd removed from guava pots, placed one in the cannon, and as before, broke one open to create their line of gunpowder fuse. The coast was clear, Bill had whispered to Alec, and then he returned to join him as the gun was fired. A brief chat to ensure they agreed that all was set up well, the book was placed in the cannon's direct line of fire, Alec lit the match, and just before they lit the fuse, the door to the common room burst open and in strode a master who screamed, "What on earth are you two doing?"

The schoolmaster who had caught them in the act in the common room, instigated a search of their dormitory and their lockers for any other cartridges. Still, no one thought to look in the guava jelly jar box, so he found none. The boys did not get into additional trouble, and Alec jokingly commented that this could have been the start of an early career in smuggling.

This was the sad end of the "Cannon Club," as apart from getting a jolly good telling off, being put on the report to the headmaster, and getting the incident reported to parents, the cannon was confiscated. It was returned to Alec at term end, with clear instructions to take it home and *not* bring it back to school. That cannon always sat on the fireplace hearth in Alec's study in his home in Scotland, a prized trophy and memory of fun school days.

The "Bobby Sox" Ball

Alec remembered what great fun they had in 1948 when he was sixteen and Bill's parents gave him a "Bobby Sox" Ball at their castle home during school vacation. "Bobby Sox" were all the rage at the time, and pop music was wildly popular in America. Bill's parents intended that Bill and his pals, like Alec, all away at boarding school most the year, could meet girls of their age from other good families in a chaperoned environment.

In their final year at Canford, Bill became a prefect and had single lodgings. In contrast, Alec said with a slightly cheeky grin, "I was too irresponsible to be a prefect!" As if to prove his point, Alec shared the story of how he made a bet with fellow pupil Tony Nutt, wagering the considerable amount of £5 (worth around £57, or US $70 today). It happened one evening before it was dormitory lights out, and he dared Tony to escape school unnoticed and run through the nearby town of Wimborne, naked. Good sport, Tony did, Alec said, watched by some of the boys as witnesses. "I paid up," Alec reported.

They spent much time in the common room, and Alec and Bill had fond memories of these moments. The school refectory food at this post-war period was dreadful, they agreed. The cook left the eyes in the potatoes, the freshness of meat was questionable, and the only meal Alec enjoyed was deep-fried cod in batter. School for Alec was always inadequately warm in the winter and the food appalling.

A Deer Takes its Revenge

When Alec was on the last days of his summer recess from school up at the family home in Scotland, his sister Helen had been deer stalking up at Caithness on the family moor. She decided to post a pair of venison legs to the house at Lowood. Alec collected them from the local railway station and gave them to their cook, who made a delicious venison stew with one leg. Shortly afterward, his parents brought Bill across from Dumbartonshire, and they were off on the train together from Edinburgh down to King's Cross, connecting to Dorset and back to school.

Only a couple of days after returning to school, a parcel was delivered for Alec. Thinking of the idea too late to send the other leg of venison back to school with Alec, the cook got permission to post it to Alec at school so that he and his friends could enjoy it. Alec wasn't sure what to do with it when on the Wednesday it appeared at school in an oblong box, and no one knew what it was. From evening until it could be decided on the weekend what to do with it, Alec stuck it in his locker and hoped one of the school cooks could do him a huge favor cook it for him to enjoy with his pals. Just two days later, Alec woke up with the flu and went to the San (the school nurse) in her sanitorium. That same Friday, he was admitted to her mini-sick ward for three days. San expected to discharge him Monday morning for school.

Alec, consumed with the flu, forgot all about the raw venison leg in his locker. Bill got a message to him Sunday afternoon to ask if he had any idea what the stink was coming from his locker. When Alec had recovered sufficiently to be sent back to his dorm, he sadly had to throw away the venison, as it had gone off.

Alec would sometimes go to Winn's, the Surrey family home, during the Easter term breaks, where his local boyhood friend Michael Toynbee and his sister Jane were always pleased to have him back in the area. The Toynbee family seat was at Scarborough Castle in Kent, not far away from where both families often went on vacation.

Caithness Memories

The house, properties, and grouse moors in the Caithness region of Scotland had belonged to Alec's grandfather and were by this time in the hands of his parents, and later they were endowed to his elder sister, Helen.

One of Alec's grandfather's houses on their lands was called Castle Hill in Scotland's northeast reaches by Caithness. He also owned the nearby Sackville Moor and Sackville House, which he renovated after it burnt down. The house sat majestically between Castle Hill and Kelso. Alec said that Sackville House is now a ruin, but the family still hangs out there when shooting on the moor. For his grandfather, it was all about the shooting season and the excellent grouse and snipe shooting inland from the house on the coast, where it sat along a six-mile sand beach. The local farm and peat wetlands on the Sackville estate were also ideal conditions for snipe, a small, fast bird requiring the skill of excellent "shots."

During the immediate post-war period, parcels and hampers were regularly sent down from Caithness to Winn's when the family was still living there before Lowood was purchased near Melrose. Alec would often go with his father to Lingfield station near Winn's to collect them. Typically, they'd be full of items in very short supply in the south, such as duck, geese, grouse, partridge, sides of ham and legs of lamb or venison, and vegetables of every kind, topped off with beautiful cheeses. Alec recalled how lucky they were to have such goods sent to them during strict rationing of goods in shops.

Alec's First Pair of Shotguns

When aged fourteen in 1945, his grandfather gave him a pair of John Dickson & Son round action shotguns as a gift, which he still had at his home in Scotland when he passed in Jamaica last year. His mother, he said, had a "John Dickson" 16 bore gun, his father a 20 bore. That gunsmith was established in 1820 in Edinburgh and was favored in Alec's grandfather's day amongst Scots. They still produce fine guns today. Alec's grandfather would take him to camp out in the old Sackville House ruins to teach him snipe shooting, which requires fundamental first-class shooting skills, as snipe are truly fast in flight. It is not like duck flighting, when the silly things go around in a slow circle back to the pond where beaters flag them up.

For Alec at Caithness as a child, being taken up to the top of the lighthouse was just brilliant. Likewise, taking a lunch of jugged hare or a beef stew was an exciting memory and experience. So was taking the boat out to set lobster pots, and a day or two later, seeing them in those wicker traps, retrieving them, and carrying them back home for another type of pot.

After the Second World War, the Hamilton family sold Castle Hill House in Caithness, and another house there, Horseback, was acquired.

The Girlfriend, the Farewell Ball, and The Army

Schooldays now behind them, Alec and Bill somehow survived their various antics. Before they went their separate ways for National Service, Bill had a big party at his family home, Boturich Castle. The ball was, in fact, a joint party for himself and his brother David. All their Scottish pals and those from school came, and family friends such as Alec and girls of their age, such as Delia Chance, who later became Bill's wife. Bill said that the best-looking girls always followed Alec. They all fell for this tall, handsome young man who had great charm and a heart-melting smile, he recalled. They were like bees to a honeypot, and Alec was the honey.

Alice Delhalla (who had a Swiss father who was a pastor) was Alec's girlfriend at the time, and her aunt married Bill's uncle. Alice was, Bill said, "totally head over heels in love with Alec and was quite a stunner."

Alec gave Alice full marks for her behavior when she stayed as a guest of Bill's parents at Boturich Castle. Alec and Alice agreed unofficially and in private to get married but would not tell anyone yet. They decided that he should do his National Army Service first and then formally ask her father for her hand in marriage when he came back. Also at the ball was Sarah Platt. The Platts were nearby neighbors of the Hamiltons, and all knew each other well from childhood. Bill first met Sarah at a Hunt Ball in the area, and her family was great friends of the Hamiltons and Bill's family. Bill said it was evident that Sarah was very keen on Alec also, but Bill had a £5 bet with another pal that Alec would marry Alice!

Preparing for Military National Service

World War One had ended in Europe in May 1945 when Alec was still at school, and with the Japanese surrender in Asia in September of that same year, conscription into the British Armed Services ended. Conscription has happened over the centuries in different formats in Great Britain and many other countries.

The British government brought into being the National Service Act of 1948 with the outbreak of the Chinese Communist uprising in Malaya (the "modern-day" separate nations of Malaysia and Singapore). In the beginning, it required eighteen months of service. By October 1950, this changed to a minimum of two years of military service; the British supported the Americans in the Korean War at this time also. Britain used National Service troops in multiple conflicts that had erupted post-World War One, including Malaya and Korea, the Cyprus Emergency, and the Mau-Mau uprising in Kenya. The final use of the British National Service was in the Suez Crisis in Egypt in 1956. National Servicemen who demonstrated promise could be commissioned as military officers.

Alec had left school in July 1950, and sometime afterward, formerly applied to the War Office Selection Board (WOSB) for officer training at Fort George near Liverpool in England. He was accepted for the short six-week course, entered as a subaltern, and graduated as a lieutenant. The army conducted the training at Eaton Hall, which was the home of the Duke of Westmoreland.

Second Lieutenant Alexander Hamilton

Second lieutenant is the rank held on commissioning into the British Army from the Royal Military Academy Sandhurst. It is generally retained for one to two years. During their time as second lieutenant, officers complete unique arms training relevant to their corps. After training is complete, they lead up to thirty soldiers in a platoon or troop, both in training and operations. Alec made great pals with fellow officers while at Eaton Hall, and they often, on days off, went into the nearby city of Chester and occasionally traveled farther up to Inverness in Scotland.

As a second lieutenant upon graduating, Alec would be responsible for a platoon of up to thirty soldiers, even though a young man just out of school.

The training was not for the faint-hearted, Alec recalled, and the sergeant major worked them hard. He reminded them that they had been selected for officer training, and officers he would make them. They had to take part in endless drills, marches, and maneuvers while carrying heavy backpacks and machine guns. Exhausted, they had to fire their weapons when commanded and run on-the-spot repairs when guns jammed. Coming ashore with a wet gun was not acceptable.

They learned leadership skills, surveillance, and map reading, and they had to take boats out to sea and navigate preset destinations. Suddenly, they might all be told "everybody overboard," and off the side of the ship each went into the cold water, carrying their packs and a heavy machine gun held above their heads. Somehow, they had to swim and stagger ashore with this load. "If your weapon got wet, you went on the report," Alec said.

They were drilled endlessly on the parade ground to march in unison and time with each other, and they learned the importance of this soldiering discipline. The sergeant major gave no quarter to errors and bawled them out, yet when they graduated, he became to most of them a dear friend whom they'd never forget.

While he could no longer remember the man's family name, Alec said that his best pal in training was a chap called Gillespie. He hoped to join the Gordon Highlanders, too, as Alex did.

Graduating, Alec returned to Lowood in Scotland and applied to the war office to be assigned to and remain with the Gordon Highlanders. Big Ian spoke to the regimental colonel and his pals in the war office on his great-nephew's behalf. Alec was duly assigned to the Gordon Highlanders. A proud moment for him, Alec said. Bill was also selected for officer training but at a different location and served his national service in a guard's regiment. Gillespie was accepted into the Gordon Highlanders too.

As he was not from a well-to-do family, as a gift, Alec's father, at Alec's request, bought Gillespie his entire officer's uniform—two sets, right down to his kilts, sporrans, dagger, and his mess uniforms too. The regiment's famous socks were a red and black dice pattern, colors for her Highlanders that Queen Victoria had chosen herself.

At this exact moment in time, his mother told Alec that if he wanted to inherit the Caymanas Estate in Jamaica, it would be his. However, it was on the condition that he was willing, after his two-year national service, to move full-time to Jamaica and manage in situ. If so, she would leave it to him in her will. If he did not want to move to Jamaica and manage it himself, she would sell the estate. Alec told her that he would happily reside permanently in Jamaica and become its first resident owner/manager in 300-plus years of it being in her family's possession. So it was to be then. Alec, of course, had joined the family on many a summer visit to the estate to check out how the business was running and have a vacation, so he knew it well. He'd fallen in love with Jamaica a long time ago.

Off to Malaya and The Sea Journey Out

The Malayan Conflict, as it was known, stretched from 1948 to 1956. From 1951 until 1954, the Gordon Highlanders fought an exhausting but influential contributory role in the war against the Chinese Communist-backed insurgents in Malaya's jungles. Encouraged by China's Communist Party, the insurgency against British colonial rule had broken out in Malaya. The same Chinese people Britain had helped train during the recently finished World War One to defend their nation and Britain's colonies in the Far East were the same men who turned on their colonial masters to train Malayans to fight the British. In the first years of the "Emergency," as the Malayan conflict became known, the terrorist groups had several victories. They killed hundreds of civilians and members of the security forces. The actions of these terrorists created opposition from groups within the Malayan population who had aided British troops against the Communists. Britain encouraged this local support by promising an independent Malaya.

Alec was to be posted to Malaya as it then was. It is now split into Malaysia, with its mainly Muslim Malay race, and the island tip, Singapore, with its primarily Chinese race. Alec was shipped off with his regiment by train from Aberdeen in Scotland to the English port of Liverpool. This was their first stop on their long journey to Malaya. A troopship then took them from Liverpool to Singapore via a long voyage. The trip's final leg was over 9,500 miles and would take around four to six weeks, depending on the weather.

A regiment like Alec's might hold around 650 soldiers, and those with more than one unit of this size are referred to as a battalion, whose units comprise three or more companies of similar size at the time, Alec said. In Alec's case, his regiment companies were made up of multiple platoons, twelve men strong, and a commander. He had twelve men under his command when he left England on his troopship, nine of which he saw freely every day, and then there were, of course, his three jailbirds to manage.

During this sea journey, three of Alec's platoon were under close arrest—two held for physical abuse misdemeanors. A third chap had jumped two troopships before being clapped in irons and placed on Alec's ship under his guard and command. When traveling from Aberdeen to Perth in Scotland, this soldier ran off again after boarding the train and was later captured again. When his train got to Perth, his entire family was there, demanding he not be forced to join the insurgent wars. They pleaded to no avail that he be released and allowed to go home. He was not released. He escaped again between Perth and Liverpool; hence he was now a prisoner forced into his assignment to Singapore under strict guard.

The boat, he recalled, stopped in Casablanca on the coast of Morocco then went through the Med and Suez Canal and around the Cape of Good Hope off South Africa. They would then stay in Aden, go across the Indian Ocean, stop in Bombay in India, then stop in Calcutta and on to Singapore. Each stop was to take on fuel, water, and provisions for the crew and troops. It also allowed some respite from the long voyage at sea for non-sailors. Alec recalled his fascination with every place and culture he saw.

Suez Canal Explosions

Alec recalls passing through the Suez Canal one morning, eating breakfast in the officer's mess, when a massive explosion outside blew off some of the ship's portholes from the mess bulkhead. It saw his plate fly up in the air, scattering his bacon and eggs, and all confusion momentarily reigned. Everyone except old, seasoned officers hit the deck, only to discover that it was a battery of British gunners who were firing a farewell salute to them as they passed—to every new officer and soldier's embarrassment. The salute gun fired four volleys, all blanks, but just twenty feet from the side of their ship. As the Suez Canal is narrow, all thought they were under fire, which proved an early lesson in the sounds and surprises of combat and keeping one's cool in all circumstances.

Alec made time to interview and get to know his platoon members one by one and as a team during the long Malaya-bound voyage and at each refueling and provision stop. He'd listen to their experiences and concerns, praise and reassure his men. He also made time to read his officer's manuals in order to do things literally by the book.

Arriving at Singapore

Eventually, they arrived in Singapore in the massive tropical heat and humidity of the summer. Another Gordon Highlanders officer accompanied Alec with his nine soldiers and three men under arrest until they reached their destination, a Captain Finlay Sheriff from Edinburgh. Finlay informed Alec that his regiment had already left for the Malayan hills the day before and that Alec and his men must join them without delay. They went by train first thing in the morning to join his regiment upcountry. Finlay also advised Alec that communist insurgents had killed the last platoon lieutenant for Alec's assigned station and that Alec would be replacing him. Alec swallowed hard but thought, *Goodness.*

As you can imagine, he said, "I was not filled with confidence but with angst," knowing that he was being assigned to protect the same rubber plantation where his predecessor had just been killed. Anyone who worked for the British and the British themselves, as well as planters, local Malays, or soldiers, were fair game to the enemy.

Alec's predecessor had headed up the road towards the plantation when he and his men were attacked. Generally, the patrol's riskiest period was walking through the narrow streets of villages or down narrow roads with heavy jungle cover on either side, where the enemy could quickly spring an ambush. As this previous platoon and officer approached hidden enemy dugouts, the insurgents had popped up from them, opened fire with a machine gun, and killed the lieutenant and almost his entire platoon.

Alec and his men journeyed on towards their destination, all the while acclimatizing to the heat and constant humidity.

Finally, Mainland Malaya (Today's Malaysia)

Setting off by train from the Port of Singapore, Alec and his men headed up into Malaya, the train tracks winding through the jungle. Alec and his twelve British soldiers, most of whom had not experienced the wild, hot, and humid jungles of Asia, were facing multiple experiences all at once.

The Malaya jungle regions tend to be excessively hot, with typically around 80 percent humidity, and in the 1950s, a fair amount of danger from its inhabitants. The jungle and the edges of villages and cleared acres, like rubber plantations, would be rife with mosquitoes and the debilitating illness, at best, or death from malaria and dengue fever they potentially offered.

In the 1950s, snakes, from python who could wrap you in their death squeeze in your sleep (as Alec's soldiers feared) to thirty-five types of venomous snakes, abounded. Some 450 species of spiders waited for you, although not all were harmful to humans. But all were small and hard to spot—so smart people kept one eye looking upward for spiders' webs, and the other eye looking down for snakes on the ground. The wild Malayan tiger was still about in decent numbers in these times, as were brown bears, wild pigs, and the rare rhinoceros in some Malaya regions.

Into this environment Alec and his men eventually arrived. After a cross-country road trip in army trucks from the nearest rail station to the village and plantation, they settled into their barracks and accommodation in Tappa. Alec instructed his men to get to know the villagers over the days ahead. He made it a point to see the village imam (Muslim holy leader), who he knew was crucial to making a good relationship with the village's people. They struck up an instant friendship. The imam was glad that the British had so quickly sent reinforcements to protect his people after the murder of Alec's predecessor and his men. Alec was fascinated to learn about Malay and Muslim culture, the village surroundings' strengths and weaknesses, and the access roads and tracks emerging from the jungle.

He drilled his men, ensured that they were alert 24/7, and worked hard to ensure every man sought to build rapport with the locals to encourage them to flag any suspicious characters or potential communist informants. Alec discussed with his men tactical team reactions to different types and strengths of attack at their base or on patrol, and how and who would do what.

First Skirmish With The Enemy

It was to be his only brush in battle with the enemy. One morning, the imam asked to see Alec. He warned him that rumors were afoot in the village that insurgents were heading their way. The imam understood the insurgents' goal was to steal food and money from the villagers and try to kill more British soldiers. He said the insurgents knew that British reinforcements had arrived at the village and were already patrolling the area. Alec thought that they would most likely use the same approach road to the town as he had, and the imam agreed, so Alec armed his men, shared his plan secretly with them, and they immediately commenced their defenses. By mid-afternoon, Alec quietly took seven of his men around the outside of the village. He determined to give the place a wide berth so as not to be detected by anyone. He was concerned that there was a communist spy in the village who'd give their location away. He left his other five men at their base to defend it and the plantation in case of a surprise attack there at the same time.

Under cover of the dense jungle that the village's approach road gave, he led his men to the upper part of the approach road, out of sight of the town. He'd set off in the opposite direction when leaving the village to hide his real destination, which was the very same spot where the insurgents had murdered his predecessor and men. Alec decided to use the still in situ trenches dug by the communists, and he and his men hid and camouflaged themselves.

Sure enough, at twilight, as darkness began to fall, insurgents were spotted by his scout hiding a mile up the track. The scout quickly made his way back, unseen, to warn Alec. The insurgents, he said, were way in the distance, approaching on the same road, and maybe ten minutes away from coming into view. Alec and his men removed their weapons' safety catches, and each ensured that they were well camouflaged in the trenches. Alec issued instructions at a whisper that no one fired under any circumstances until he did. No matter how close the enemy appeared, they were to hold fire and wait for him to choose the best moment to open fire. All acknowledged his order. The men's weapons included submachine guns and a sizeable tripod-mounted machine gun, rifles, and handguns.

Dogs from a not-too-distant vegetable field on the approaching track started to bark, giving Alec an early warning. Five minutes later, hearing the insurgents' chatting voices approaching closer, dogs in their village started to yelp. The tension Alec and his men felt was high, as they had no idea how many insurgents were coming, and they might be overwhelmed. They all peered into the darkness, wanting to catch the first glimpse of the enemy. Alec needed to gauge the enemy's strength before he sprung his surprise attack, only once they were literally upon them. He could hear the insurgents chatting now and could, through his camouflage, see them walking calmly towards them on the road. But as darkness had almost completely fallen, they were not yet close enough for him to see how many might be stretched out in a line

Suddenly and without warning, one of his men, whose nerves had got the better of him, sprung out of his trench and fired his machine gun. He let loose two magazines while shouting, "There they are, sir; there's the bastards!" A gunfight ensued, and all the insurgents were killed but for one who got away. None of Alec's men were injured, and during his time stationed in that village, the communists made no further attacks on Alec's station. Whether due to a retreating insurgency campaign or the robust repelling of the episode, it was to be Alec's only brush under fire with the enemy in Malaya or anywhere else in war conditions.

Alice Breaks Their Informal Engagement

Alice corresponded with Alec throughout his two years of military service in Malaya. Despite postal delays to and from remote outposts, their letters eventually arrived at each other's destinations. They did manage to keep up a good correspondence, even with these delivery difficulties.

Alec said that in his final months out in the East, both he and Alice began to realize that they were drifting apart; absence wasn't making the heart grow fonder, and their letters were getting a little less romantic and more about day-to-day occurrences between old friends. Alice finally wrote to Alec to say that she was dating Peter Worthing and could not remain faithful. She wanted to end their informal commitment to each other.

Alec thought it odd, as he knew Peter relatively well, and Alice had always said before that Peter Worthing was a friend but quite dull and boring. Nevertheless, Alec wrote back to her and said that he understood and that he willingly released her from their informal commitment and wished her well with Peter. I am sure while having already felt the pangs of love ebb, he was nevertheless disappointed and a little sad at being gently dumped, and he did not remember hearing from her again. His first real love had gently filtered away.

Heading to Jamaica to Embrace His Destiny

The insurgency was over for Alec and his platoon, who all survived and were on their way home in what Alec thought might be the late summer of 1952.

The whole family was proud of Alec having gone off to Malaya to do his bit for King and Country. They were especially delighted that he served in "the family" regiment of the Gordon Highlanders. Alec had enjoyed the authority and leadership role as an officer. If he had not had Caymanas Estate in Jamaica to go to afterward, he would have stayed in the army, he said. The army had implored him to do so too, as the regimental colonel saw in him a great future as a senior officer, already of a respected standing and valor.

Senior officers noted his skill at interrogating prisoners with an excellent questioning technique, and they were impressed by him. His peers said he was good at getting information out of the enemy by treating them with simple good manners and conversation. They said he never raised his voice or showed anger. This left the Malay highly respectful of him.

A calm and gentlemanly line of questions to prisoners slowly relaxed them and reeled them in. Alec treated all with respect and never lost his temper. This self-confidence and ease in authority formed him, his character, and his leadership style at quite a young age. This must have helped prepare him well to lead the large workforce of what was one of the largest estates in Jamaica, as we know.

His army days over, Alec made his way back to sunny Scotland to prepare for his destiny. He was first to attend business management, marketing, and financial training there at James Ewing & Co.'s maternal family firm in Glasgow.

NOTES:

Some sources of data:
UK Office National Statistics, monetary values and inflation rates over time.
The Scottish Historic Buildings Trust.
UK National Army Military Records.
The Malaya Emergency, UK government National Archives.
The Gordon Highlanders Archives.

A more detailed *paper* is available on Caithness and the World War One Imperial German Naval fleet that was taken there as part of the capitulation by Germany, and what happened to it.

The Dovecote at Strathleven
House, Dumbartonshire,
Where Alec Hamilton was born
in 1932 (PBA).

Farming in Scotland in the 1930s; tractors were emerging too (NCA).

A teen Alec in Hamilton tartan kilt with his siblings: Helen, Ian, and Mary (WOP).

Alec, aged thirteen, caught his first twelve-pound salmon on the family's 1.5 miles of the Tweed. Five years later, he's in his Gordon Highlanders Army Officer's mess kit (WOP).

The Gordon Highlanders Regiment
2nd Lieutenant Alexander (Alec) Vereker Hamilton (WOP).

Alec's Malaya Campaign, 1950–1952. A roadside ditch tactic that Alec Hamilton and his men used to lay in wait for communist insurgents (WOP).

Chapter 11

LIFE AS A PLANTATION OWNER, CHANGES AND CHALLENGES

Preparing for a Planter's Life

As he looked at the photo of himself in his army officer's mess uniform, it seemed to Alec like only yesterday that he had enlisted in the Gordon Highlanders regiment. In the photo, which is in the book, he was wearing a handsome cutaway, white regimental evening jacket, black bow tie, and regimental kilt and sporran. Yet here he was some sixty-five years later, with distinguished national military service behind him, mentioned in dispatches, and a lifetime of service to Caymanas Estate, Jamaica, and the people of Jamaica. "Where did the time go?" he asked.

Back home in Scotland, his duty to King and Country behind him, Alec joined the family's holding company in Glasgow, the James Ewing & Co., and trained in accounting, trading, marketing, and business estate management. That was the agreement he'd made with his mother before commencing his national military service. He accepted the Caymanas Estate and ran it firsthand, living in Jamaica.

Alec began overseeing Caymanas Estate's 26,000-acre sugar estate in 1954, but it became much smaller by the time he died in April 2020. Over those years, he was obliged to make land sales to the government for housing and infrastructure projects, and he sold land to create the national racecourse, a golf course, and a polo club and grounds. In the end, such strategic moves kept an equilibrium and profitable state of land and production, enabling Caymanas Estate to survive. Alec's declining health in his last few years saw his wife, Erica, step up and assist in running the estate with support from the Factor (accountant) and Alec's eldest son Johnny Hamilton, who would take over the estate management one day.

Sheila's Memories of Alec's Preparation

Sheila Lyle (née McNeil) is a Scottish lass now in her nineties and was the de facto company secretary of James Ewing & Co.'s Glasgow offices. Around

1990, in her late sixties, she retired after having commenced with the firm on September 7, 1942, forty-eight years earlier. Dates, people, places, and situations come to mind for Sheila in an instant. Talking with her, people are stunned at how razor-sharp her mind is. She was at the business's Scottish headquarters for the first thirty-seven years of Alec's time at Caymanas Park.

Sheila was an extraordinary woman who knew the entire business inside out and was an encyclopedia of what had been done. She knew when and why, its cost, and its purpose. Sheila knew what had worked, what had not, and why, in both the business and the plantation. She knew all the firm's trading partners and suppliers, and they all went through her as a filter. Sheila was there on Alec's first day of training. With a memory like an elephant, this remarkable woman proved a treasure trove of information and dates to the author. An answer to any question was delivered without the slightest hesitation.

When Sheila had joined the family firm of James Ewing & Co., Alec was aged ten. One of her first tasks was to collect rents from the farmers and tenants of the family's Scottish Strathleven Estate and the family-owned estates in Jamaica, Nevis, St. Kitts, British Guyana, and Cayman. The James Ewing & Co. interests were looked after by these offices in Glasgow and their factors McClellan-Kerr & Company, representatives on each island, and their plantation overseers.

One of Sheila's endearing memories was the aroma of fine whiskey stored in barrels in the building's cellars on the floor below her office, a true Scottish lass indeed. Alec's oldest pal, Bill Findlay, had done some business training with James Ewing & Co. at one stage as well. Bill remembered this only too well. He felt that it was excellent training and said he'd gotten to understand a little of the sugar business to which his best friend would dedicate his life.

Each day Alec would drive into Glasgow from Strathleven House in a black, open-top Austin sports car, and Bill recalled, "Do you know, virtually every girl who met him or just saw him whiz by fell in love with him? Alec was damn good looking, and it seemed that no girl could fail to swoon over him."

After Alec's first full year managing the estate, Sheila recalls his mother asking her how she thought Alec was doing. She was able to say with hand on heart that he was doing exceptionally well and was so easy to get on with—so professional, polite, and efficient. She said that Alec always put everyone at ease with his calm, soft-spoken voice, warm smile, and lively sense of humor, and she added that the financial books were doing well also.

On average, Alec went back to Scotland every year for a three-month vacation and "home office" meetings and reviews. This is a practice he followed most years from 1955 onwards. A fair amount of time was spent reviewing the business management and trading results in Sheila's offices with her, her colleagues, and the factor.

Taking Over The Caymanas Estate

Alec went out to Jamaica from the family's estate in Melrose, Scotland, in March 1954, his twenty-first birthday having been just four months earlier. The estate, Jamaica, and its people became his lifetime passion and love.

By now, Alec had a sound understanding of managing a plantation business and its workforce. He'd studied and gained solid knowledge of the sugar industry inside and out. He learned how to spot bookkeeping scams and stock pilfering and understand the shipping and sales processes. He was educated in the keys to driving revenues to the bottom line and building a return on investment to the owning company by taking care of his employees first. Practically, he learned how to manage a significant, multi-million-dollar business and revenue producer for Jamaica through its then-sizeable export tax contributions. The theory was complete, and it was soon time to put it into practice and commence the fulfilling of his destiny.

In 1955, the then Chief Minister of Jamaica (the precursor of the title of Prime Minister after Jamaica's Independence), Norman Manley, made a statement regarding the Caymanas Estate, as was reported in *The Daily Gleaner* newspaper (found from research): "One of the most significant financial contributors to the Jamaican economy, on whose annual business results are indicated Jamaica's economic rising or falling, are the annual reports of the Caymanas Park Estate."

Sir Alexander Bustamante, a future first prime minister of Jamaica, was an exceptional man who enabled Jamaica's transition successfully to freedom and independence. He was a founding member of the People's National Party (PNP) and split away to form the Jamaica Labor party, the JLP, and spoke well of Alec.

The Daily Gleaner newspaper articles spoke highly of both the Caymanas estate and Alec's evident success in his first year of management. That Jamaica's government could best predict the nation's financial year ahead based on how Alec's estate prospered says much about the estate's economic success and the revenues it raised in taxes, which helped fund government infrastructure growth. Such funding towards running the country and its infrastructure came to a great degree from all the significant estates in Jamaica, whether by sugar, citrus, iron ore, or bananas. When Alec took over the estate's running from his parents, it continued to prosper in a climate of lowering global sugar prices.

A newspaper photo of Alexander Bustamante and Alec is in the book—Bustamante was a man Alec greatly admired. Bustamante's knowledge and Norman Manley's skills as prime ministers were lost on Norman's son when he became prime minister, Alec had remarked.

As prime minister of Jamaica for the PNP party, Oliver Clarke once commented that Michael Manley, Norman Manley's son, was accountable for the country's virtual bankruptcy. His democratic socialism experiment led the nation down a rapid path of economic failure, which resulted in massive unemployment, rising inflation, and alarming levels of violence.

Michael Manley's policy of strong-arming owners into selling their land at the lowest rate no doubt and, in some cases, exchanging it for land bonds resulted in a massive loss of production across multiple industry sectors. This was the world that Alec Hamilton saw arise nearly two decades after arriving in Jamaica. Export tax revenues plummeted under Michael Manley, and the nation's defunding infrastructure created a mess. It led to Jamaica's calling in the IMF (International Monetary Fund) to bail them out.

"Many today choose to forget the damage that man did to Jamaica and its economy," Alec said to the author. There are generations of Jamaicans born after the Manley years of economic disaster who never experienced its failure. In recent years, when the then-PNP government was waning in the opinion polls ahead of the election (that it lost), Alec added that Portia Simpson-Miller, in her last months as PM, suddenly 'dragged Manley out of a cupboard, metaphorically speaking. They dusted his image off, hailed him as the people's unblemished hero, and ignored his accountability for the economic failure and bankrupting of the nation.'

Giving Back

In the late 1950s, Alec, with his mother's blessing, generously donated numerous parcels of land from the Caymanas Estate to local communities and for his workforce's use. He felt it was the right thing to do. Alec may have had nothing to do with slavery nearly 120-years before; however, he believed that he had a duty to do the right thing for his people and, in his way, make reparations for the past. His mother agreed with his generosity of spirit. The multiple acreages of Caymanas land gifts from the Hamiltons went to build a school here, a church there, sporting clubhouses, and cricket pitches. Often Alec made cash donations, quietly, for various local projects.

This is genuine philanthropy and taking care of people and communities who have given their working lives to Caymanas.

> "It is not just about paying a going wage and taking care of your workers, it is about recognizing each as an individual who matters, and helping their communities," Alec commented.

In this, Alec demonstrated for all to see how you take care of your workforce. He knew that genuinely caring for his people made loyal workers, which was also common business sense. He gained a reputation for always lending a listening ear to anyone who had an issue or was upset about something.

Memories of a Life at Caymanas

Alec, like his parents and maternal grandfather, proved to be an incredibly fair and kind employer, aware of the past and the need to use their privilege today to help the local workforce's families and communities.

Alec lived and worked at the Caymanas Estate from when he first stepped on Jamaica soil, aged twenty-one, until he sadly left this world. Sixty-six years of memories and stories from so many who knew him are not just stories of one man but also stories of Jamaica and Jamaica's past. Tales of a bygone age from the mid-fifties onward enable you, the reader, to sense the Jamaica of recent history and get a sense of the life of modern-day Alec Hamilton.

Living so far from town was seen as living in the bush in the 1950s. Caymanas was way out in the middle of nowhere and too far to pay a quick visit for lunch from Kingston's capital city, for example. The roads were minor and winding country ones, not the fast highways that now take you right past Caymanas in a flash driving out from Kingston. At first, Alec was a bachelor on his own when he relocated to Jamaica, with no family or friends nearby. Everyone worried that it could be too lonely and asked him if he feared getting robbed, living so remotely.

As they grew and expanded to accommodate more and more country folk seeking work in the burgeoning capital city, the outer Kingston suburbs, and the very poor shantytown of "Sufferer's Heights" had gotten closer and closer to the Caymanas Estate. However, Alec had a good relationship with his nearest neighbor, as he seemed to create with most people. He helped people out in the "Heights," as we'll see later.

Caymanas Golf & Country Club

During Alec's early years at Caymanas, with his mother still gently guiding him, they leased 116-acres of land to a Canadian and Jamaican business consortium for an eighteen-hole, par-72 golf course and golf club development, all later sold to their operators. It was to be designed by the famous Canadian architect, Howard Watson. The club opened for play in 1958, four years after Alec had taken over Caymanas. Alec intended to earn a stable annual income from the land leasing rights when sugar prices were low and not showing long-term recovery signs. Alternative revenue streams to keep the estate profitable are a must in any changing market. Later, the Jamaican government acquired the land and took ownership of the leases and golf course.

The golf club became a top-class, well-maintained course with a high-standard and excellent clubhouse service and cuisine. Yet by March 2017, it looked run-down, tired, and underutilized. The government then sold the Caymanas Golf & Country Club lock, stock, and barrel to a private investment group effective April 1, 2017. Alec felt that this was a good thing and hoped to see an injection of capital to raise the course and clubhouse standards to their earlier prototypes. He also thought it was good timing for the government to sell and utilize its investment for the people's projects.

Caymanas House's entry road is just after the golf club's 24/7 staffed security gate and across a fairway. The journey from the club's entrance gate takes you across a corner of the eighteen-hole golf course and up through a winding country road, creating a great sense of arrival to the house. Guests will have driven along its tree and hedge-lined road uphill to the property's main entrance gates. If they have a keen eye, guests will notice the estate's private aircraft runway while driving up as was until a few years ago. Now it's in a bad enough state of disrepair; even the drug lords of past years wouldn't dare attempt to land and drop off their merchandise. "It mash-up," as a crop worker at Caymanas Estate said. Time has broken the runways slabbing, with many chunks sticking up in the air, making it impossible to land.

The Creation of the National Horseracing Track

Over earlier decades, various companies established and ran a racetrack at Caymanas, leasing 196 acres of land for plant and track facilities from the Hamiltons. Sadly, against a backdrop of several such companies failing to make the racetrack a going concern, the government of the day was smart enough to see its long-term ability to make money and stepped in to buy the leases. Potentially it was a highly lucrative business that would generate tax income for government coffers, as every chance is taxed. As a growing number of Jamaicans enjoyed a little flutter, they could place a small bet, dreaming of wealth. It was a way of raising money to invest in Jamaica's infrastructure to benefit Jamaica's people. After that, the PNP government under Michael Manley announced that they'd formed 1989 Caymanas Track Limited, with government and private investors investing in a revamped track, facilities, and public areas.

That company, part-owned by the government, leased from the government the 196 acres of Caymanas. That included its plant, land, track, and brand new, state-of-the-art horse racing facilities. It generated employment for some 12,000 people with jockeys, managers and owners, breeders and grooms, bookmakers, track and grounds-staff, administrative, and catering staff. Today, it employs over 20,000 people.

The new company investment included a then-state-of-the-art, multi-million-dollar totalizer system, the latest bet-claiming system, an off-track betting system, an electronic audio-visual network for betting shops, and massive viewing screens at the track. The government had made an intelligent move. It indeed was to prove an excellent income stream to help pay for Jamaican infrastructure growth, as I am sure it remains today.

Alec's Reputation Proceeded Him

Alec was still known as the man who owned Caymanas Estate and an admired racehorse owner. Whenever he arrived at the Caymanas track, as he frequently did, he was spotted by one and all and held in good esteem. People asked him how he was or asked others to make way for him as their respected racing elder.

Frequently heard was the cry, "Move na, ya na see it Masser Hamilton a coming?" Security guards immediately welcomed him as he slipped into the horse owners' entrance, jumping ahead to open the gate for him. All the trainers knew who he was and teased him that their horse would beat him today. His son Johnny frequently escorted his father to the races and has a passion for racing too, it seems. Johnny has become well known by all the trainers, jockeys, and staff at the track, so the family heritage at Caymanas continues.

Alec's passion for breeding and racing horses always brought him to life when he walked through the owners' entrance. When I walked with him in the trainers' and owners' enclosure behind the scenes, he moved at a jaunty pace across the paddock to the stands after he had checked out his horse running in the next race. People invited to join him as his guests for the day had a problem keeping up with him. His usual, slow, cautious walk broke into a trot so that even a teenager had to quicken their pace to keep up with him! When he arrived in the stands, acknowledging many well-wishers' comments, he was focused on the next race and his horse. Every regular punter having placed their bet turned around and shouted greetings as soon as they spotted him.

'How ya doing, Masser Hamilton?' or 'Who gwan win today, Sar, tell me na, whom ya say gwan win today?'

Socialist Government Experiments

The socialist People's National Party (PNP) government, under Michael Manley as prime minister of Jamaica, served the nation twice. After his disastrous economic policies collapsed Jamaica's economy the second time, as many said, he lost a landslide victory to the opposition party. To be fair to Manley, it did not help him that the world oil price had risen ten times during his terms of office. However, his socialist policies most commentators agree helped drive the economy into an abyss.

The businesspeople and professional talent who feared a Communist state in the making as Manley became closer and closer to Fidel Castro in Cuba, accepting Cuban assistance with teachers, doctors, and military advisors, fled Jamaica in the 1970s. The loss of so much business leadership talent caused many companies to close at the same time, which led to a massive 30 percent unemployment rate in Jamaica.

"Manley promised the people utopia, and how can you blame the people for wanting a promised land of milk and honey" Alec said, but it never came, and in the end, the working Jamaican was worse off. It has taken decades to come back, and there are still struggles. These past successful, well-run industries raised a significant part of the funding government needed through business and export taxation to fund hospitals and police, firemen, road infrastructure, government employees, housing, the army, and employment projects. Suddenly, the vehicle of the state was running on empty. Poverty and crime soared, academics evidence.

As Margaret Thatcher, the United Kingdom's Conservative prime minister from 1979–1990, famously said,

"Socialism Is Fine Until You Run Out Of Other People's Money."

For the Hamiltons, this was a moment of déjà vu. For Alec in Jamaica in 1972, painful memories of his family's Scottish Strathleven Estate's compulsory purchase in 1947 by the Scottish Board of Trade loomed. One day, in front of everyone present at a PNP rally event held on Caymanas Estate land that Alec went down to listen to, Manley proclaimed that:

"Alexander Hamilton has 'gifted' 1,600 acres of land on the Caymanas estate to Jamaica's government for the people." All loudly cheered, and many shouted out. Alec recalled that "Alec, him a true Jamaican, a man of the people."

Knowing nothing about this, Alec decided it best to say nothing at the rally of his supposedly "gifting" land to the government. The next day Alec set about negotiating the best price possible for the acreage behind the scenes with his accountants, and he did get paid for it. If it helped Jamaica's ordinary people, then he traded that land away willingly, albeit probably below what it was worth. The Manley government often pressured land purchase but never stole it, as happened in some African countries. Alec certainly wanted to see life improve for the ordinary Jamaican and was very much a champion of the people in his way. He received recognition for his contributions to Jamaica and its people and cared deeply about his workforce and the average Jamaican.

Burglary

As it can be for too many, coping with burglary is a common way of life in Jamaica. Relating one of many stories Alec shared on burglary shows us a little of his character firsthand.

It occurred when his parents visited Jamaica, as they did most years. He'd regularly take his mother shopping in Kingston and had on this day. They came back from shopping, and his mother went into her bedroom and threw her handbag and shopping bags down onto the bed. A little later, she went back into the bedroom to pick up something or other, opened the door, and found a man trying to conceal himself behind the door!

Straightaway and in a cross voice she said, "What the devil are you doing here? Go on, get the hell out of here, go on, get the hell out!" That's just what he wanted to hear, and he scampered out through the French doors onto the veranda and down the drive as fast as his legs could carry him. Agnes, the cook at Caymanas House in Alec's early days, heard all the commotion. She shouted out loudly to the Hamiltons from the kitchen in a good Jamaican patois voice that the burglar must have taken something, and they should stop him. Sure enough, when Alec's mother looked inside her handbag, she saw that her money purse was gone, so he had taken something.

"Watchie," the watchman (a classic Jamaican nickname for a watchman), usually stayed the day at Windsor, Max Henzel's cottage nearby. Max was the plantation/estate manager, and Windsor Cottage was his home. As luck would have it, at the very moment the thief was running down the hill, Watchie was coming up, and he heard Agnes shouting to stop him. Watchie duly stopped the burglar. Although Alec doesn't think Watchie had ever used it, he always carried a single-barreled shotgun, which may have enticed the burglar not to run.

The man was so afraid of Watchie with his shotgun that he timidly marched back up the drive ahead of him, protesting his innocence all the way. Agnes searched him, but he appeared to have nothing on him and kept protesting that he hadn't stolen anything. Agnes pointed to his calf-length boots and made him take them off. Out came dollar bills he had stolen from Alec's mother's purse —which he only then confessed to stealing, taken the dollars and thrown the purse in the bushes when running down the hill

The sad thing was that he was a poor ex-sailor, and he had been let out of prison that day, having served something like five years in the Spanish Town goal. No one he knew would help him, and he said he felt desperate to feed his children. Alec had taken the time to ask him and saw the man's genuine distress over caring for his children. He believed the man's plight. Harking back to his military days in Malaya, he had retrieved the story from the man by his kind nature. He continually displayed support for the poor, and he told the thief to keep the money for his family.

However, theft is theft for the police, and by now they'd arrived, summoned by the staff, and had taken witness statements. The officer listened to Alec's request for clemency. However, the police knew the man as a well-known thief, always in and out of prison. They were clear that they had to arrest him, and at his subsequent trial, the magistrate sent him back to prison, despite Alec's request for clemency. That was one of the few times Alec was glad to say that he had been robbed, as the police, as a concession to Alec's plea, allowed the man to keep the money Alec gave him, providing they ensured it went to his wife and children. There are other not too dissimilar stories available to the family via the author.

Jamaican Obeah

A construction supervisor from England, George Pierce, came out to Caymanas to supervise the work and ensure it was being done correctly and to Jamaican building code. Here he was, George, some days or weeks later, sitting at midday on the roof before starting his rounds. The workmen, who had done an excellent job, were educating him in Jamaican folk law.

Having put back the tiles, the men wanted to make quite sure that *duppies* (Jamaican patois for ghosts) didn't get into or under the roof titles and slip into the house. Some of the men sitting near him on the top explained what was needed. They had to slaughter a cockerel and required white rum for the ceremony. Sitting under the hot sun, he looked down and saw his carpenter looking up at him from down below.

George saw that the carpenter was carrying a glass, which contained the white rum mixed with cockerel's blood. He could see the blood trickling down the outside of the glass. The carpenter instructed him that he'd have to drink some and sprinkle the rest across the roof. Poor George … he must have thought up some excuse, because he couldn't drink the rum and announced that he wouldn't take any white rum and cockerel's blood at midday on any roof. A compromise was worked out, as Alec has never had duppies in the house since, and all's been well, fingers crossed.

(See this chapter's footnote on Obeah for those who wish to learn a little more.)

The Duppy Tree

One thing leads to another, and Alec was talking about duppies and remembered an old cotton tree they had to take down when the roof was being built and George was visiting. Duppies like to live in or under cotton trees. There was a lovely big cotton tree on the old road to Caymanas Bay on the plantation's perimeter, down by the old sugar factory, right on the roadside, embedded in the curbstones and under the road itself. It was becoming quite dangerous as it was rotting, its branches were falling off, and its enormous roots digging under and lifting the road. So Max Henzell (the estate manager) decreed, "Well, we're just going to have to bring it down, chop it down," he told the overseer. "C'mon, get the men; let's chop it down."

The men nearly freaked out in panic and shouted that they'd have to ask God if they could do that. When Max asked what that entailed, he was told they'd need white rum, cassava, breadfruit, Johnnycake, and all kinds of other things to put around the tree. The Jamaican Johnnycake, or journey cake, had to be made too, and sure enough, all the workmen who were to be involved in cutting the old cotton tree down had to gather. A ceremony to appease the duppies from losing their home and haunting the workmen forever had to be performed. The service would be carried out in the evening and overnight. The men went off to get the necessary provisions and settled in for the evening.

Max returned to the cotton tree in the morning, and surprise, rum, Johnnycakes, and cassava were all gone! So Max asked the workers to get back to work and cut the tree down. At this point, there was a crack of lightning and thunder, and it started to pour rain, and the men, in unison, told poor Max that it was a bad sign from God, and they couldn't cut down the tree that day. This happened for another two days repeating preparations with one excuse or another.

The following day, Max returned yet again and made clear in a slightly angry voice, "Right, come on now, there's nothing to stop you from cutting down this tree." With their axes and big saws, the workmen got up, put their tools down near the tree, gathered around it, forming a complete circle, and joined hands. They recited a chant, asking God not to blame them for cutting down the tree, since the manager was making them do it. To make sure God was clear on who was responsible, they pointed out the house up the hill where Max lived. They then went around the tree singing a little folk chant, and eventually they got to work to cut down the old cotton tree.

Max went back home for breakfast and the rest of the morning, but he felt like the wrath of God had hit him. He had never, ever felt so ill in his life. He wondered if Cookie had put something in his breakfast, but he forced himself to get up at lunchtime to show his workers that nothing was wrong, and he went out into the yard to check the tree. Alec smilingly shared this experience with the newcomer. You must always ask the duppies' permission, you know," he said. "You mustn't get cross with the duppies."

Memories of Alec's Arrival in Jamaica, From Others

When Alec arrived in Jamaica, one of the first people he met, who happened to be almost his age, was the Caymanas vet, John Masterton, and his wife, Paddy. John and Alec quickly became great pals, and John became Alec's oldest friend in Jamaica, and is now about ninety, I believe. Alec and John got together whenever they could. John sat for many years on the Board of Directors of the Caymanas Estate, a seat now occupied with both John and Alec's pride by John's son. In Alec's first week in Jamaica, John remembers Alec's mother asking him to look out for him and introduce him to the right people. After all, unlike John, Alec did not know a single person in Jamaica when he arrived, other than a handful he'd met on vacation visits … not that John had been there much longer.

Alec astonished them all at just how quickly he adjusted to the tropics, the way of life at Caymanas, and the Jamaican workforce. John felt that the man just had a way with people, even handling squatters on Caymanas land. He treated everyone with dignity and respect, as he had done with his communist insurgent prisoners in Malaya when serving in the army there. Black or white, or any race, it did not impact him or his attitude to people.

For Alec, squatters would move, but many knew that they would not have moved for anyone else; they'd kick up a stink and refuse and cause damage.

John had his veterinary surgery in Spanish Town, close to the Caymanas Estate, and looked after all the Caymanas Estate's livestock, from cattle to horses, especially the prized and highly valuable racehorses, domestic animals, and poultry stock.

Most people described Max as having been an excellent manager of Caymanas and very efficient. He had a reputation, though, for a very explosive temper that few could handle. His leadership approach was the opposite of Alec's. John recognized how quickly the Caymanas workforce took to Alec because he was a soft-spoken "gentleman" who treated his workers as equals from day one. Alec didn't bark orders at his staff or workforce in the old management style. He politely asked a field worker in a familiar, pleasant voice if they would do something for him. He was never afraid to roll up his sleeves and start the work himself. This usually brought hesitant workers, not to be shamed by the owner doing it.

Alec, most agreed, seemed to be the first and only man to cope with Max's frequent temper outbursts, even against Alec himself, as the owner and Max's boss. Max was a fearsome presence to many, including John. John recalled that Alec seemed to instinctively know how to absorb Max's quick temper and then focus on what mattered. Max would calm down and get on with what Alec wanted.

Turning Employee Concerns Into Solutions

Alec always asked his workers when he was out in the field, the factory, or office where they lived and how their family was, and he remembered anything untoward. The key was that he always remembered every person's name and used it too. This went down well, making it clear by this one simple act that the person was an individual, not a worker lost among many. They knew that their employer and owner of their workplace believed they were important too; he respected them, as he showed that he cared about each person.

It was part of his success and why the respect he gave his people flowed back to him in a significant way. He'd offer to help workers' families when needed and instruct someone to determine how he could help. He'd remember two weeks later having asked about a sick child and enquire how they were doing.

When workers in any business or company today feel respected and as if they matter, you'll find a happy workforce who'll go the extra mile—nothing has changed over millennia.

Close to Caymanas was the central squatter township mentioned earlier, "Sufferers Heights," situated on the outskirts of Spanish Town. It has since been named Windsor Heights, and I do not know what size it was in the 1960s when people started to build huts and claim squatters' rights to the hillside, but it is now some 280 acres of homes for those living there. At least 15,000 families are known to declare it as their home, with just 1,250 plots. It was many times that number in the 1970s, but neither John nor Alec could remember its size then.

The next thing John knew, Alec had gone up to Sufferers Heights to visit one of his workers who had a very sick child. He went to take some medicine he had purchased for the child and to see if he could do anything else for his worker's family. People were shocked to hear this, as it was deemed *very* dangerous for any stranger to go there, let alone a white man.

Alec had gone up there many times, John found out, to check on his people and their families. It turns out that his workers who lived up there made sure that all knew who Alec was, that he was a good man, and that no one touched him. Anyone else, they all agreed, would have been attacked, robbed, and possibly killed. This tells us what we need to know about Alec Hamilton as a leader, employer, and person. How blessed all who have known him felt about working with him.

The Flame That Attracted The Moths

It wasn't just in Scotland, but now in Jamaica too Alec has been described as like a bright light at night, which attracted the most beautiful women anywhere we went. They were like moths to a flame, and they moved involuntarily towards Alec, "which could be very off-putting to a fella with him, who'd feel left to one side," as his oldest friend in Jamaica, said of Alec. He did nothing but walk into a room. There he was, surrounded immediately by the prettiest women.

A photo of the newly arrived Alec in Jamaica, sitting at a desk in the Caymanas Estate office, is at the end of this chapter. God blessed him with a kind manner, a cheerful personality, and a winning smile. To top it all, he was well-educated and raised as a gentleman—and his time in the army and years in Jamaica gave him street smarts. As they say in Jamaica, he had *broughtupsy*."

The Catch of The Season

That Alec had inherited wealth and one of the most extensive plantations in Jamaica at the time, was the icing on the cake to all of Jamaica's eligible young society ladies. The mothers of available daughters would have been busy arranging *chance* meetings and sending out invitations to lunch or supper.

Alec was a great catch for some unmarried young woman, and word got back to Great Britain too, so that the "fishing fleet" coming out to Jamaica that season was alerted. The fishing fleet was a colonial term for a group of young society ladies with blue-blooded backgrounds landing ashore overseas hoping to catch a suitable and potential husband in their net. Many families would pay their eligible young daughters' costs and arrange for them to stay with friends or friends of friends in Jamaica, for example, for "the season." There were many single, well-to-do, or high-flying government or British military men right across the British colonies from which a gal could land a husband in her net. The gals would take passage to the colonies from the 1700s through to the 1950s-1960s, making the sea voyage (and later flights of course) out to Hong Kong, Singapore, Sri Lanka, India, Kenya, Jamaica, Barbados, and numerous other territories, hoping to "catch" a wealthy husband.

For many, the fishing fleet gave a young bachelor stationed overseas a once-a-year opportunity to find the right woman from his homeland of the right pedigree and settle down. Today, young women would likely have called Alec good eye candy. Every eligible Jamaican debutante's mother probably had her eye on him too and aimed to get his attention before the fishing fleet arrived. In the end, it was the daughter of old family neighbors near his home in Scotland who captured Alec's attention. He'd known her growing up, of course, and when she visited Jamaica with Alec's sister in 1958, he was smitten—but more anon.

Horse Racing and Breeding

When Alec first started racehorse training with the stables at Dawkins Caymanas, John Cliggott and his wife, Eileen, came out with a stallion from the UK, Mountain Music, and four or five broodmares. Alec set up a little training establishment there and bred horses.

There was a long cane interval; it was just about a mile in length with a slight incline of land upward over that stretch. A beautiful smile that the horses could gallop up, Alec reckoned. They harrowed it and the cross interval, going down to the pump house on the lagoon, and just at that section was about six furlongs from the Caymanas Bay end. Alec erected a stand there, a raised wooden platform, from which you could get to see the horses coming thundering up the track towards you. It gave Alec some idea of what time the horses were doing with six furlongs. The horse and jockey would pull up, turn around, walk back towards the cross-interval, and down to Dawkins Caymanas and home.

One afternoon at races in 2015, Alec's horse Charlotte Russe pulled herself up to a complete halt in the middle of the big annual Derby Day race! The entire grandstand was aghast. Everybody had said before the race that they thought Alec had got a Derby winner and couldn't fail to win. Sure enough, she started as the hot favorite to win, but when she got to the second bend past the clubhouse for the first time, she just dug her toes in, and *nothing* the jockey attempted made any difference—she was not going another yard. The rest of the field went on, and she took no part in the Derby. Alec was beside himself to discover what on earth had happened.

With Alec's team so very disappointed, a local man ran up to Eileen Cliggott, the trainer, and shared his belief that the cause of this unbelievable event was that a duppy lived nearby and that he'd need white rum and a white cockerel to get rid of it. Thinking back to the duppies under the old cotton tree, Alec must have reflected that it always seemed to need a white cockerel and white rum. Still, his people procured the necessary items, as Alec *never* ignored advice when it came to duppies.

Some rites were performed over at the racetrack and at the racetrack's corner by an Obeah man. Alec told them to start Charlotte Russe again, and nothing else would happen. A few weeks later was the Jamaican St. Leger Race, so they had their horse Princess in that race, hoping that the Obeah man had excised the evil spirits that had upset the horse. Amazingly, there was no trouble at all; the horse sailed around the duppy bend without flinching and won St. Leger quite easily. But St. Leger's not the Derby, and Alec often said that he still had to win a Derby. But it just shows you, Alec emphasized, that you've got to have the duppies on your side in Jamaica, so don't knock them or Obeah.

Success With the Racing Stables

One of Alec's Caymanas stables' first horses to do anything in the winning stakes was Compound Girl. Alec had needed some mules for the estate, and Bill Knowles had gone down to Mountainside, a good mule-breeding county, and bought four or five mules for him. But in the package (a take-one-take-all deal from the buyer), he acquired a three-year-old horse, an unraced filly.

Alec thought he'd have a little bit of fun and see if she could win a race. They put the horse in training, which was frowned upon by Max Henzell, the overseer. He thought it was all an enormous waste of time and an even bigger waste of money to train this "scrap of a horse," as he called it.

Nevertheless, the horse was put into the running at "Little Ascot" at the Caymanas Park racetrack in June that year. That same evening, the queen's birthday cocktail party was given by the governor-general at King's House in Kingston, the capital. Everybody invited was expected to go and have drinks and raise a loyal toast to the queen. It was the "done thing," and thankfully still is.

First, though, Alec went off, to Little Ascot to watch his "scrap of a horse," which had gone and won the race! Alec dashed back home, got changed, and went on to the party. Max was at King's House too. With a smirk of "knowing" that indeed, he had been right, Max teasingly asked Alec if his horse "ran dead last."

Alec was delighted to say that the filly had won her first race, first time out, and a large margin.

At this point, to Alec's surprise, Max jumped for joy and skipped around the ensemble of guests, asking everyone with great glee if they had heard that "our" horse had won. Suddenly, from being an enormous waste of time and money, it was "our" horse! A genuine rag to riches equine story. Max held the Caymanas Racing Stables in his heart with pride, and any success became "ours" because he was so much a part of the estate as anyone else was and proud of every horse's success.

A Chance Investment Paid Off

Alec had one of the quickest returns on his money with a horse that John Cliggott was training for its owner, a filly named Krakoush. John was preparing her for the Jamaica Turf Club. She was quite a nice, imported filly and stayed a bit of a distance, and she was running at Little Ascot. In about the sixth race, Alec went down to the holding ring, and John told him that he thought the horse was doing very well and that it might win that day. Alec liked this mare and wondered if John thought the owner might sell it. John said he'd ask when he next saw the owner, a Mr. Armond.

Alec went back up into the stands and some way off happened to see Mr. Armond, whom he'd met before. He went straight up to him then and there and asked him if his horse was for sale. Mr. Armond was willing to sell any horse for the right price. Alec negotiated a deal for £600 for her and shook hands to close the deal. (Today, that's worth just under £17,000, or US $22,000.)

Alec went straight to the race stewards and explained that he'd just bought this horse and had the transfer of sale document signed by the seller (he'd come prepared). He asked if he might run it in the next race. The stewards looked at their watches, wondering how Alec could get the horse ready in time, since, as they reminded him, it had to be in approved Hamilton racing colors. Alex had his trainer get Krakoush ready quickly, found one of their jockeys, and move out.

In about the sixth or seventh race, Krakoush came out, ridden by Mr. Binns, Alec's stable jockey and part-time barman. While not a fantastic jockey to date, in Alec's opinion, he was a jolly nice man, who was undoubtedly loyal to the Hamilton stable. Alec thought he deserved a chance to show himself.

Brilliantly, and to everyone's astonishment, Krakoush and Binns duly won! Alec got a quick return on his six-hundred-pound purchase with the race winnings, I'm sure to Mr. Armond's shock. Anyone in the horse business will tell you that you either have an eye for spotting the right talent or you don't, and Madame Luck is sometimes with you.

The Art of Leadership Listening

When Alec first started working at Caymanas in 1954, Joe McCorry was the field superintendent (sugarcane fields), and Max Henzell was the estate manager for Alec's parents. They thought that Max was a tremendous manager and an excellent engineer. They saw him as one of the best sugar engineers in the West Indies who was doing a massive land reclamation. He brought reclaimed land into quality sugarcane production. He had improved the factory and distillery, which led to making the estate profitable. What a great mentor for Alec as he commenced taking over Caymanas.

Alec knew he owed much of what he'd learned in those early years to Max. One of the main things was that, during the harvest, you met at least at 5:45 a.m. down at the factory, having got up and 5:00 a.m. They would get to see the night workers going off and the morning shift coming on. The men could see them, answer questions on how their work went, and Alec could find out if all the equipment was working well. They could ask the chief engineer if he was planning any stops for the next day and look at the factory figures and account updates. Joe, Max, and Alec would always hop into the Jeep and drive around all the cutting gangs in the fields to check on work, men, and production. They usually had three reaping crews in those days: one at Caymanas, one down in Lawn, at Ferry, and one over at Cumberland Pen.

They would visit them all, not always going the same way around but turning up at slightly different times in the morning. Alec continued this routine all his working life at Caymanas whenever it was cane-cutting season, to whatever sugar fields had been not taken over by the government or leased out.

It was good to be out early—Alec had time to see projects that were happening. It was invaluable to be with the field superintendent, to discuss replanting, putting in new drains, putting in pumps, putting in crossings, or whatever he spotted was needed. They'd visit all the cutting gangs, giving them their daily quota of how much cane was expected to come in from that gang. After Max had left and Alec become known to his workers as manager, Alec also had a chance to see if the workers wanted to raise any work or personal concerns. The workers had learned that he always welcomed their raising matters with him and always sought to solve problems, work or private, as best he could. This, combined with taking time to get to know every worker's name and family situation, made for what I call outstanding leadership.

If workers had any grievance or personal problem, they would be able to deal with it then and there. They knew they could stop and come and talk with "Manager." Alec mentioned several times that his workforce called him Manager, which meant more to him than being known as the owner of the plantation. They'd often stop him and explain all kinds of things. Maybe there was a death in the family, and they wanted a burial site gifted by Alec, or they wanted a loan to help with the funeral.

Max, when he was the manager, did have a bad temper at times. He would curse and swear at the workers in the most frightful manner that had, at first, surprised Alec. However, the workers would laugh. If he swore at them, they knew their jobs would be safe—as he couldn't turn around and fire them if he'd cussed them off. It was when Max looked at them and, in a calm, quiet voice told them, "You're fired!" without losing his temper that they knew that there was not much point in protesting. They were fired. They'd likely had numerous warnings about whatever it was they repeatedly had done wrong.

In 1983, Alec decided, after all the traumatic and violent gun-filled events of the previous decade in Jamaica, and an unsettling future, to sell around 23,000 plus acres of Caymanas to the government. He negotiated with Prime Minister Edward Seaga, leader of the JNP, the Jamaican National Party. He made a good sale of different parts, and the government leased much of the sugarcane to other planters to manage for them and produce income for government projects.

By the time of Alec's death on Easter Sunday, April 2020, Caymanas Park Estate was now down to around 700 from his inherited 26,000 acres.

NOTES:

Sources:
The Daily Gleaner, Jamaica's first national newspaper, and their library archives. The Scottish and British Chambers of Commerce Company Registration files, Jamaica National Archives and Parish records. The Ewing company, and Hamilton family archives.

Jamaican Obeah

Obeah can be described as a folklore approach to mystical healing with centuries-old ceremonial rituals and natural remedies. Those born with *the gift* to communicate with the spirit world can cast spells and bring forth evil spirits for those who do wrong. Obeah first arrived in Jamaica when African slaves came and were derived from merging several West African shamanic teachings and practices with those of the Igbo tribe of Nigeria. You can find the folklore practiced in various forms across the Caribbean. Today it is less followed by younger Jamaicans but is still part of Jamaican life for many.

An "Obeah" man or woman is believed to be born with the ability to develop and harness their powers. The first records of Obeah in Jamaica appear in the accounts of a Maroon (slaves released into Jamaica's hills when the English captured Jamaica from the Spanish) during a rebellion that arose in the 1700s. Obeah became an essential part of the slaves' distinct cultural identity and a symbol of defiance to their masters.

The Jamaican Johnnycake

This food item is also called journey cake: a small, round, fried dumpling; it is the perfect accompaniment in Jamaica with any meal or on their own. It's believed that Jamaica inherited the custom of frying dough, which is evident throughout the Caribbean today, from the American Indian Tribes.

Alec's Stories and Memories of Caymans

There were *many, many* more available, but not all were able to stay in the final edit of the book, and they deserve a booklet of their own. The author has a full version of 'all' those stories for Alec's immediate family.

Jamaican Patois

Some people spoke to Alec in the local and the lovely Jamaican patois dialect; some of those phrases have been placed in the book just as they sound phonetical. It allows you to read and celebrate the dialect. To have sought to correct them and write them in formal English would be somewhat condescending.

In the hills above the plantation stood the modern Caymanas House, designed and built by Alec's father; an original sketch drawn by him in 1940 (wop).

The house today with a second story added by Alec when children appeared on the scene in the 1960s—a drone shot taken by his nephew Felix Hamilton (Ian's son) on Xmas Day 2019 (wop).

Caymanas Estate land stretched just under 41 sq. miles (105.2 sq km) from the Blue Mountains on the left to the ocean on its right. The sugar fields straight ahead are viewed from the long verandah of the house (PBA).

Alexander (Alec) Hamilton arrived in Jamaica owning the Caymanas Estate. He was one of the most eligible bachelors in Jamaica at the time, aged twenty-one in 1954 (WOP).

Portrait by Basia Kaczmarowska-Hamilton.
Alexander Vereker Hamilton, in 2003 used as a reverse image in sepia on the book's front cover (WOP).

Alec, post-lunch at the iconic Strawberry Hill Hotel up in the Blue Mountains of Jamaica, late 2017. Owned by Chris Blackwell (Bob Marley's producer) and managed up-to Covid by the author's old friend, Dianna Marley (PBA).

Alec's oldest friend in Jamaica from the day he arrived at Caymanas Park in 1954, John Masterton, now ninety-three. John had only recently come from the UK and was hired as a veterinary surgeon for the Caymanas Estate (PBA).

Chapter 12

ALEC'S JOY: HIS FAMILY AND FAVORITE MEMORIES

A Visit From Sarah in Scotland

Sarah Platt's visit to Jamaica from Scotland, accompanying Alec's sister Helen in 1958, rejuvenated a lifelong friendship and stirred love. The Hamilton and Platt families were great friends in Scotland and near neighbors, and with her extended stay in Jamaica, Alec realized that his childhood friendship had turned to love.

Sarah's mother was a Mackenzie, and her father had sadly been killed in the Second World War. Her elder brother, Alistair, was like a brother and father figure to Sarah, Alec felt. Alistair loved his sister very much and thoroughly enjoyed Alec's company. He remained a great friend to Alec until his death. The Platt family home was Muirhouselaw, in St. Boswell's, very close to Alec's family's Melrose Scottish estate.

After Helen and Sarah visited Jamaica, Sarah and Alec kept up a close correspondence, as absence made the heart grow fonder. Alec flew to Scotland and went with Helen to Edinburgh. Sarah, as expected, was there. Helen and Alec invited Sarah to a shooting party lunch at Lowood the following week. Alec was walking back to Lowood from the shoot, for lunch with Helen, and unbeknown to him, Sarah had already arrived at Lowood. Mrs. Hamilton Senior didn't realize Alec had invited Sarah for lunch and offered her a drink. She then wished her farewell and apologized that she had to get organized for a shooting lunch she was hosting, so poor Sarah, somewhat embarrassed, left.

Alec was mortified when he arrived back at Lowood and heard of Sarah's visit and polite dismissal and drove at high speed from Lowood to Sarah's family home in Boswell to apologize to his love for the misunderstanding. He used a local Scottish expression for his reaction: "I moved like a whore before a policeman!"

Mrs. Mackenzie (Sarah's mother) was somewhat of a socialite and a highly hospitable lady, always throwing fabulous dinner and lunch parties. She laughed the whole thing off when Alec explained why he'd come to see Sarah. A week later, Alec heard that Sarah went down to London. A plan hatched, and he followed her. When in London, Sarah stayed at a flat (apartment) she shared with a couple of girlfriends in Lowndes Square, just off Sloane Street. Alec proposed to her that same evening, and she accepted. He remembered the evening with a warm smile as his mind momentarily drifted to that very moment. They went straight out for dinner to celebrate, a sparkling engagement ring on Sarah's finger.

The following year after Alec's marriage proposal, on November 5, 1960, Alec and Sarah got married in Scotland at the Merton Parish Church. It nearly didn't happen, as on the preceding Monday, October 31, driving back together from their last shopping trip, Alec was going a tad fast, he admitted, when the car skidded in a heavy fog on a hill. The vehicle crashed into a ditch on the side of the road. Thank goodness there were no severe injuries, but Sarah had nasty bruises to both knees and a cut on one corner of an eye. She narrowly missed losing her sight, the local newspaper reported of the accident. However, the powder puff must have been at work on the big day, as written in the newspaper article, as no one could see the cut.

Sarah's brother, Alistair, had flown back from Kenya the week before, just in time to give his sister away at the altar. He had been in Kenya for some months studying farming techniques, which created innovative new ideas.

Alec turned twenty-eight four days before the wedding, on November 1, seven years after he had made his life permanently in Jamaica. The Scottish media commented on the bridesmaids' dresses and the pageboys in kilts, all looking rather lovely amongst the 250 guests attending the wedding. Alec arrived at the church with his younger brother, Ian, as his best man.

The Honeymoon and Life at Caymanas

The newlywed Mr. and Mrs. Alexander Hamilton spent their honeymoon in New York City, Mexico City, and Acapulco, on the Mexican coast, before returning to Jamaica to start their married life in Caymanas. When in New York, they stayed as guests in the home of the Rockefellers, through their friend Charmaine's introduction. Charmaine had been one of Sarah's flat mates, who went around the world on her own in the 1950s, which for a young, well-born lady just was not done. But she was one of life's free spirits and made of solid stuff. On her first round-trip, the Rockefellers had hosted her stay in their home, and she'd kindly asked them to invite Alec.

They returned from their honeymoon straight to Caymanas Estate, and sure enough, their first married Christmas was upon them very soon. One day, Alec came back up from the office, and Sarah proudly announced that she had bought the Christmas turkey. Alec asked if she had been to Kingston to the butcher. "Oh no, an old lady came with a turkey on a string, walking all the way up the hill!"

Taken aback when the old lady had arrived at the house, Sarah had asked Agnes what she was to do, and Agnes told Sarah that squire would always buy a turkey from this lady, who was very nice. So Sarah bought it. Alec had never bought a turkey from this lady before but had always had a lovely, big, fat, juicy imported one. Certainly not the kind of scraggly one that had walked from Kingston to his house, as he explained to poor Sarah, who had probably been horrified thinking Alec, as a bachelor, had always chosen a scraggy turkey from this old lady at Christmas. In due course, the cook prepared the turkey for Christmas.

"Well, all I can tell you is that it was the toughest Christmas turkey I'd have ever eaten, and I don't want to have another one that's walked up the hill, ever again," Alec recalled. So that was poor Sarah, egged on by Agnes to buy the turkey, and their first married Christmas turkey luncheon a bit of a flop—but lesson learned and Agnes a little embarrassed.

Helen recalled that Sarah was, of course, a local lass from their youth when the Hamiltons were in Lowood, in Scotland, with her family living close by. Sarah and Alec, even as teenagers, had done everything together and were great pals, with Sarah willing to have a go at everything. Sarah enjoyed being with Hamilton family members. She was highly sociable and enjoyed parties, although many didn't see her as overly sporty. After their marriage, Sarah got on well with Jamaicans, and she and Alec played golf and tennis together.

The Smoked Salmon Incident

While looking back on Agnes' time devoted to him and his family as their cook, Alec remembered that one year, he'd come back from his annual Scottish holiday and brought back a lovely side of smoked salmon. He had caught the salmon on the family's stretch of the Tweed River at Lowood, and his farmer had smoked it for him. When back home in Jamaica, Alec put it straight into the fridge

The next day he went down early to the office to see that everything was all right, and when he came back for supper, he asked Agnes what she had found for supper. She told him she'd cooked up a little bit of the fish he'd brought back from Scotland in "a lovely white sauce." Stunned momentarily into silence, one can imagine, Alex was duly served smoked salmon, all chopped up into little bits, in a very lovely white sauce for supper. He admitted to Agnes that it was very, very good but he had to tell her (holding his breath) that the fish was an exceptional *smoked* salmon and meant to be served cold in thin slices as it was.

In an educating, calm tone of voice, he explained to poor Agnes that when he brought something back and put it in the fridge next time, she mustn't use it unless she asked him first. He explained that this Scottish smoked fish was an extraordinary thing for special occasions and is *never* cooked. He realized that he had not explained what smoked salmon was, so he could not be cross with Agnes in the end—it was a learning experience. She was very sorry and said she'd never do it again.

Agnes Passes Away

Dear Agnes, she had to go to the hospital with an awful growth on her ankle in later life, which never seemed to get better. It turned out that it had formed into a melanoma, and in time, despite all the care and hospital treatment Alec ensured she had at whatever the cost, his dear Agnes died. Alec recalled being heartbroken, as he'd grown to love and trust Agnes and valued her loyalty over so many years, not to mention his love of her cooking.

Agnes was going to be buried down in St. Elizabeth, her home county in southwest Jamaica, and her brother, a nice man and a sergeant in the police force, had taken control of everything. Sarah and Alec and all the maids and house staff went down for Agnes' funeral. It was at Mountainside, Alec believed.

They set out, and after they had gone over Spur Tree Hill and downhill, it started to pour with rain. Buckets of rain were coming down, so they were rather late when they got to the church and got soaking wet clambering out of the cars and rushing inside. The service had already started, so they crept in quietly and sat at the back.

The minister jumped up and announced to the congregation, "Oh, nice to have Mr. And Mrs. Hamilton here, and we'll ask Mr. Hamilton to say a few words after the singing of the next hymn." Unprepared he might have been, but he wasn't going to get away without saying something, and he truly loved and would miss Agnes, so Alec quickly put on his thinking cap. During the following hymn, the heavens opened over Mountainside with such a deluge of rain that they couldn't hear themselves think, as the church had a tin roof. The rain hit the galvanized metal with a deafening sound. Everyone just went on singing, but even louder.

The Lord Heard Alec

Alec was eventually called up to say a few words from near the altar. Well, here was Agnes, lying in an open coffin, right up next to the altar with what seemed like a thousand-watt spotlight hanging just above her, so you can imagine that poor Agnes was gradually cooking. Alec stood beside her coffin and shared some personal words about what Agnes meant to him and his family and recalled for the congregation that Agnes had always gone down to St. Elizabeth for her holidays.

He told everyone that every time she went back home, she would say the same thing: "Oh, we did have a lovely rain, a lovely rain." She loved the rain, and she had always felt it was so suitable for the garden. He added that Agnes would love this day of her funeral because it was such a lovely rain. "Dear Agnes, is no longer with us in the body," he said, looking with compassion at her family, "but I'm quite certain that she's here in spirit."

The *very second* the words left Alec's lips, there was a flash of lightning that illuminated the whole church. Then came an enormous and deafening crack of thunder, instantly followed by the shrill, explosive sound of glass breaking and shattering all over the coffin.

Everybody looked in stunned awe at Alec and stood up at *God's message,* saying, "Amen, praise the Lord, the Lord has spoken, Amen." Alec quickly sat down - many of the older folk thought he'd called on the spirit of Agnes, who had answered in no uncertain terms. Many thought Alec must be a white Obeah man, and they indeed were in awe of his spiritual powers to have called God as his witness.

As everyone left the church, they saw that lightning had also hit the hen coop just outside, and it had killed twenty-three chickens. When they saw the dead chickens, they looked upon Alec with open mouths. To several older ladies that day, Alec was the hand of God—and all fell silent and reverent around him. What's more, the rain had filled Agnes' grave to overflowing with water, someone called out.

It was no good putting poor Agnes in the water, so all took cover as the rains continued in a deluge. Plenty of hot chicken-cock-soup and mannish water was being served at the Wake. The mannish water was *generously* laced with rum … to keep the cold out, of course. Meanwhile, as the rains let up, graveyard workers and family got buckets and began to bail out the grave, and eventually her family got dear Agnes buried and covered in before the next rainstorm came. Sarah and Alec then made a polite exit, saying their goodbyes to family before that next heavy downpour. They gave a lift to drop off three of their staff at their family homes on the way back to Caymanas: Dell, Tulah, and Elizabeth.

Alec remarked that he would greatly miss Agnes, who had been so loyal.

The Man Who Fell From The Sky

A few years later, the Caymanas House roof saw another incident when the Jamaica Defense Force (JDF) gave their recruits parachute lessons. It did not end well for Alec's rooftop, but it is a Charlie Chaplin-type farce, as his recollection of the day's events makes clear.

The JDF had a British instructor out from England to conduct the training, and they'd asked to borrow the Caymanas Estate airstrip. From the ground, people could see the little planes, after the take-off, circle and climb higher and higher. Then I suppose somebody was given a push, and out came the parachutists. They were meant to land on a wide-open field at Caymanas. However, they got blown off course, and one of them came crashing down into a tree just down the drive from Caymanas House. The poor man was swinging from the top of this giant tree, shouting, "Help! Help! Get me down!"

Another parachutist was falling towards the house, but Sarah was watching from home and couldn't quite see through the trees in her line of sight. She ran outside to see where the chap was going to land, and suddenly, there was an *almighty* crash overhead, and the fellow went straight through the roof of the house. Luckily, his sturdy boots went through first and dropped him into the children's bathroom upstairs. Sarah, shocked, shouted out, "Are you all, right?" Hearing no reply, she shouted even louder, "Are you all-right?"

She feared the worse, as the seriousness of the situation quickly sunk in. There wasn't a sound, not a whisper. Then a little head popped up over the roof's parapet, with its crash helmet on, slowly and somewhat gingerly—still with his earplugs well and truly embedded in both ears. Sarah realized that the poor man had not heard her calling him, but thankfully he *seemed* okay. She suspected that he felt a little embarrassed and dreaded the telling-off from his superior officer when he returned to barracks.

It seemed that the airman had had a lucky escape and was without injury. However, there was now a big hole in the house roof, which they had to get repaired, if for no other reason than the massive damage that could follow an excellent Jamaican rain. Alec sent the bill to the JDF for settlement but was taken aback by their reply: "No, no, that's not our problem. Maybe the soldier should pay; he's the one that caused the damage!" Alec was furious, and no matter to whom he addressed the issue, they turned their backs on dealing with it. It was a very long time ago, but by Alec's death some forty years later, the JDF would appear to *still* owe the money for the Caymanas House roof repairs!

He's One of Us

On another occasion, Alec and Sarah were in their Land Rover, driving some friends over to Kingston. He was obliged to go via Sligoville, still in St. Catherine, about thirteen miles northeast of Caymanas Estate, as Bog Walk Gorge was closed to all traffic. That meant going up and down and around hill bends to pass through Sligoville. There was an awful lot of traffic on the road, which was moving just a few yards at a time. All the cars were going slowly, and at a stop-and-start pace.

They happened to stop at one place, and there was a van coming up on the outside "created" lane. It was full of Jamaican "Dreads" (as they called themselves), all with heavy gold bling around their necks—the "gold chain brigade," as Alec referred to them. In Jamaica, the sixties saw this copying of the movement that had started in America: the young men wore huge gold chains. These guys stopped their vehicle alongside Alec's, and they all just glared at Alec, Sarah, and their friends in a most threatening, silent, and almost sinister way. In a very menacing voice, the driver of the Dreads said to Alec, "Hah! You don't like Black men, do you?"

Alec, as is his way, replied, "No, I don't like Black men at all—but I love Black women!" At which point, the entire car of Dreads burst into laughter.

The guy who had made the challenging comment to Alec gave him a high five through their open car windows and gave Alec a great compliment. He said, "Yeah, man, you one of us," and they parted friends, everyone laughing, though Alec's friends were sighing in relief. That was so Alec; he had zero color or economic prejudice. He either liked you or didn't, and he defused anger with either silence or humor, more of the former in his latter days.

Mr. Henry's Wedding

Alec will never forget a particular employee's speech at the wedding of Henry, the barman at the Caymanas club.

Henry already had four or five children (although Alec wasn't sure if they were by his bride-to-be or other women). They were all made pageboys and bridesmaids, to their great joy. There was a large wedding reception at the Caymanas Community Club afterward, which Alec had built, and all sat around drinking and chatting. Mr. Cole, who was the chief clerk in the Caymanas office, acted as master of ceremonies.

Mr. Cole made a speech addressed to the bride and bridegroom's parents. Alec was unsure what was happening, as he didn't see any older people at the family table. It was the most extraordinary speech because Mr. Cole started by saying, "Now the bridegroom's father … oh, he is deceased. The bridegroom's mother … oh, she passed away some years ago too. The bride's father is no longer with us in this world, and the bride's mother was a sad woman when her daughter became a mother before she became a bride! But I'm happy that she can now die in peace because her daughter is now a bride and a mother."

The entire room collapsed, laughing. Alec, with all the guests, lifted their glasses of Porto Puno and drank to the couple's happiness. "I'm glad to say Henry is still with us," Alec remarked when he told me about it, "and gravitated from being a barman to working with the horses. He is generally down with Mr. T. Chung and now in charge of many horses and is a right-hand man to the trainer. He made his homemade fruit wine with port wine, sugar, raisins, and yeast. Puno is a makeshift mixture. It is not too uncommon for some unplanned recipes to create the perfect bacteria for botulism food poisoning! So be careful if you want to have a go at making your own Puno."

Alec's Daughter's Wedding

Alec's darling daughter, Laura, chose to marry in the garden at Caymanas Great House many years later. Alec had shown in comments he'd made at various times that he adored his daughter, just as he was equally proud of his two sons. That was a wonderful occasion, many recalled. Laura and her husband-to-be, Lionel Mill, were married by the district registrar, who came up to Caymanas for the ceremony. The wedding rites were blessed by Canon Thomas, from Kingston Cathedral. Family and friends from all around the island, and indeed the world, came. Alec invited the estate's entire workforce to go to the wedding and enjoy the day too.

The event went on late into the night, and Alec remembered on the following Monday, down at the office, that the plumber, Mando, was still looking a bit worse for wear. Alec asked Mando if he had enjoyed the wedding or if he'd had too much rum. Mando replied that he loved it but was just sad that Alec didn't have two more daughters needing to marry. Jamaica's Appleton Estate Rum took a good *licking* that weekend, as Jamaicans would say.

Payroll Heist Once, Payroll Heist Twice

After an earlier payroll heist when a gang stopped the accountant's car on the way back from the bank, they stole the entire payroll of Caymanas; luckily, Alec was insured.

One Thursday night a couple of years later, Caymanas had a new payroll routine, ready for distribution on Friday. But an insider it was suspected must have leaked the news about when they'd have all the cash in one place. The first Alec heard about his second payroll robbery was early on a Friday morning when they rung him from the office, saying in a broad patois accent, "Everybody held up last night! Everybody held up, all the office ransacked, the whole safe broken into, everything gone."

Alec went down to find out what had happened. They had a lovely big safe in the office with solid steel doors. The office was a wooden building with an upstairs, and the safe was built into the walls up there. But the night before, shooters had presumably slipped into the office compound late afternoon and hidden. They had captured the watchman at the gate and made him open the factory workshop. They had carried out acetylene torches, the gas bottles, tied up and gagged the poor watchman and his helper, and set to work trying to burn open the safe with the acetylene torches. This took them a long, long time, and there were so many sparks spitting onto the floor that they started to smoke and burn. The watchman, trussed and tied up, was dragged through the fire by the robbers so that his body would put out the flames. When they finally got it open, there were the envelopes for all the workers on the estate, nicely bundled up in groups—so much money.

In the safe too were several old Estate guns that weren't of any use—single-barreled ones that needed repair and were waiting to go, and Alec thought a couple of revolvers were in there as well. More important to Alec was one of his pairs of Dixon twelve-bore shotguns in top working condition, a gift from his grandfather back when he was a teenager. Alec kept one in Scotland for when he went over there and did some grouse shooting, and he kept the other locked in this safe to shoot the odd duck or pigeon, if he was lucky.

A Roadside Robbery

"However scary the *Daily Gleaner* newspaper headlines about robbery may be, one always is optimistic and believes, well, it's not going to happen to me," Alec reminisced. "Well, it comes home to everybody eventually in Jamaica." There was the time when Alec and Sarah's son, Johnny, had been asked to participate in a music video. The production team would shoot it out near Bull Bay somewhere, and Johnny asked his friends—Mark Jefferson, Mark's brother Andy, and Andy's girlfriend—to join him in the car.

The four of them set off to see if they could find the film location. They stopped, asked for directions here and there, and ended up coming back through the same local district.

Two youths, who Johnny recalled looked like they were all "ganja'd up" (high on marijuana), were standing in the middle of the road with guns. Johnny had already started to slow down, and one shouted, "Stop, stop, want your money!" Johnny didn't have a chance to drive around them and speed away, so he slowed down even more. As he did so, one "Yute" without warning opened fire at Johnny's car. With a boom, boom, boom sound, bullets smashed through the windshield of the vehicle, Johnny recalled, and the four of them must have dived for cover in fear for their lives. Before Johnny knew what was happening, a gunman had run up to his driver's door, pointing his gun at Johnny through the open window while the vehicle was still in motion.

Another robber, matching the car's pace, dashed his arm to the steering wheel and grabbed the keys from the car ignition. The car came to a stop. "Everybody out; we want all your money," the robber shouted while waving his gun.

While the gunman told Johnny to turn all his pockets inside out, he found a few one-dollar bills and nothing more. Meanwhile, the gunman on the other side had got Mark Jefferson out of the front passenger seat and had him turn his pockets out—he had just one dollar in his pocket. Andy and his girlfriend remained in the back seat and dared not move. Then the gunman, now standing about a yard from Mark's face, pointed his gun at Mark's chest and, looking down at Mark's left hand, shouted, "All right, give me your ring, your ring." Even though the friends had decided that they'd do whatever the gunmen told them, when it came to it, Mark said in a good Jamaica patois, "Lord, man, that ring was given to me by my father; it's an heirloom. It's the only thing I had left to me by my father."

Tragedy Struck - A Fatal Shooting

Without warning, there was an ear-piercing bang at close quarters. The gunman standing by Mark had just pulled the trigger and shot him straight through the chest. Mark gasped, shouting, "Christ, man, he shot me," and collapsed to the ground, blood pouring everywhere. He was choking and coughing up blood, which must have been such a scary and horrid sight for his friends.

Johnny kept his cool, jumped out of the car, and rushed around to Mark and the gunman, shouting, "Christ, man, look what you have done! You shot the man!" He told them to help him get Mark into the car to get him to the hospital. "Come on, where are the f----g car keys? Give me the car keys," Johnny demanded. Johnny drove everyone to the hospital at break-neck speed, leaving the two robbers on the road to getaway. He kept reassuring Mark that he would be okay. Johnny was brave and lucky to get everyone else out without being shot, because it typically happens, Alec noted.

Johnny had a radio walkie-talkie connected to the office and called Alec. He begged Alec to find Mark's wife and get her to meet them there, as it didn't look good. He added that he hoped to get Mark to the hospital in twenty minutes or so. Alec was shaken and had to rush to the telephone back at the office to make one of the awful telephone calls of his life. Before he could make that call, Johnny called back on the walkie-talkie to say through tears, "I'm afraid it's all over for Mark; tell his wife he's gone." Poor Mark didn't stand a chance; he was shot straight through the chest at point-blank range. Sadly, everyone in Jamaica knows at least one person who similarly lost family or friends in the 1970s and 80s. For Mark's wife, who was expecting a child, it was the most terrible thing of all. It was news that no one ever wanted to hear. Alec and the author shared their hope that Mark's wife in time came to terms with her grief, and maybe remarried and found happiness again, and that their child would later hear about their brave father. The next day when they looked at the car, Johnny and Alec saw that one bullet from the first few fired at the car came right through the middle height of the windshield and was lodged in his seat. How it missed him is amazing, yet Johnny's only concern was losing his friend, Mark. It greatly upset him for years to come.

Losing His Darling Sarah

The economic collapse of Jamaica made those who had income, and Helen, Alec's sister, noted how tragic it was for them in 2001, primarily for Alec and his children, to lose Sarah to such a debilitating motor neuron disease, an affliction of the brain and spinal cord. Alec's sister-in-law, Basia Hamilton, the artist, commented that Alec was very, very good with Sarah and supported her totally through such difficult times. She was being treated in Scotland, and Alec had built a small indoor swimming pool with jet-propelled water flow for her, as the doctor felt it would help her muscles.

When Sarah asked for one last visit in Jamaica, Alec had all the necessary medical equipment installed in the house in Jamaica and took her back out there. He tended to her and always cared for her, refusing full-time nurses. Sarah's family, the Platts, and Helen felt Alec gave her all the support and love she needed. Sarah's brother, Alistair, remarked that he would never forget Alec's total dedication and devotion to his sister and that he would remain forever grateful to him. It took years for Alex to partially recover from his loss.

Alec's Siblings

Mary

Mary Constance Monteith Hamilton was Alec and his sibling's eldest sister, born on November 11, 1925. She married in 1953, four days after the coronation of the present Queen of England, and had two sons, born in 1956 and 1958. She was a highly social woman by all accounts; she hunted, entertained, and eventually moved to Ireland with her husband to live in Wexford and Limerick. Her husband, Teddy, who was twenty years older than Mary, sadly became an alcoholic.

Mary died in 1984 at just fifty-nine years of age. Much of her life apart from them has left her siblings with limited memories of her, and "it's not easy to recall events from so long ago when we are much older now," Alec recalled.

Before Ian was born, Mary entered less into the same things that Helen and Alec did, being older. They'd walk down to the walled garden together near the big house. Here they would deadhead the dahlias, put them in old flowerpots, pat it all down with sand, turn it out, and have competitions to build a giant castle. They would visit Mrs. Heggie, the cooks, cottage. She always had masses of scones and biscuits (cookies) and all sorts of goodies for them to enjoy,

Helen

Helen Bogle Hamilton was born on September 21, 1930, a couple of years ahead of Alec. Their younger brother, Ian, recalls that Mary and Helen were very keen on horses and often went out hunting. As he was very young, he doesn't remember much about their early days, though, since they both went off to boarding school and were only home for short periods of the year.

Helen recalled there was supposed to be a "witches' mound" just in front of Strathleven House, and it used to be inhabited by black rabbits. An ancient yew tree, hundreds of years old, stood by the witches' mound. "It's funny how specific visual memories pop back to us even seventy years later," she said.

Helen also shared the memory that at Strathleven, there was a wing for the nursery, and from it, one door went into a small sitting room, and another went to the tiled hall below stairs. Another door led to yet another wing beyond that. From the nursery, flying through one door and room to another made an incredible racetrack for the children. Until caught, they would tear around and open all the doors and bicycle as hard as they could along this "racetrack" until any adult saw them. Alec suspected it was Nanny most of the time.

When they were old enough and were taught to shoot, Helen and Alec did so with a 22 caliber, and shooting was something of a bond between them. The family's Blackadder Chapel was at the bottom of the house, below ground. The chapel had the same name as an area of the nave in Glasgow Cathedral called after Robert Blackadder—the cathedral's first archbishop, not a character played by Mr. Bean.

A chap called Andrew ran the Ewing offices in Glasgow when Alec and his sisters were youngsters. Andrew would tell the children about the ships going out to Jamaica with what supplies or equipment for Caymanas. He'd also regale them with how much sugar they were bringing back from Caymanas to the UK. It is from these early tales of seafaring adventures and Jamaican plantation stories that Alec must have been fascinated, without realizing that this would become his life's work one day. Until recent years, when his memory started to slide, he was a justice of the peace, always willing to help people brought before the bench (the local court) in Jamaica to try to get them help. He always contributed to a few preferred charities and latterly also to motor neuron disease charities, for obvious reasons.

Helen said of Alec that how he handled his cancer conveyed how he faced life.

He was very stoic about it and never complained, never explained … taking a leaf out of the queen's book. He was also known for being very loyal to family and friends, and once he gave his word, it was never to be broken.

Ian

Ian Crum Ewing Hamilton is the youngest of the four siblings, born in 1938, and has visited Jamaica for vacations often over the last sixty-plus years since Alec made it his permanent home. He enjoyed visiting and staying with Alec and his family, and sometimes he stayed with old friends who lived on the island. One such friend who lived on the north coast was Lady Sarah Spencer-Churchill, the 10th Duke of Marlborough's daughter.

Ian was destined to meet, fall madly in love with, and marry the now internationally famous portrait artist, Basia Kaczmarowska, born in Poland. She graduated from the Academy of Art in Gdansk, Poland, then studied at the Academia di Belle Venice and Rome. She specializes in portraits in oil and pastels and has painted anyone who is anyone.

When Basia first met Alec, she loved his consistently positive approach to life and his kindness; she said his service to strangers and his gentle way of speaking to people was exceptional. Basia and Ian have two marvelous sons, Maximillian (Max) and Felix, both young men now.

In the early 1970s, Ian lived in Newbury, England, where he owned a horse stud farm for several years and had a passion for backgammon. Ian eventually sold the stud farm and bought a lovely property in a nearby village. It is a village of just over 2,000 people. Famous past residents were Henry St John, 1st Viscount Bolingbroke, and in the 1800s George Palmer, founding partner of the world-famous British biscuit (cookie) company, Huntley & Palmer.

Talking about his brother, Ian said that he always felt that Alec had an excellent rapport with their parents and got on so well together, but then he does with most people.

As a leading architect himself, Alec and Ian's father was a little saddened that neither of his sons wanted to do architecture. Ian is only sorry that his father didn't live to see his grandson, Max, become an architect. Ian felt that overall, growing up they were a peaceful, happy family; he never remembers any great upsets or fights, although he was sure there must have been little ones.

When Alec first went off to boarding school, Ian was born, so it wasn't until much later in life that they would spend more than just summer vacations or Christmas together. Consequently, Ian did not have an opportunity to spend more time with Alec growing up.

Ian himself went to the same prep school as Alec, Twyford, and remembers that World War Two ended when Alec was eight. He has vivid memories that before the war ended, when they were in their house in Surrey, a doodle-bug German rocket bomb landed not too far from them on an asylum for the insane, with much loss of life. Many of their own homes' windows were blown out by the force of the blast, something Ian never forgot.

Both Ian and Alec caught the gardening bug from their mother, and at their childhood home in Surrey, Ian was given a small strip of garden to care for himself. He recalled how he'd managed to be given a strip at school too. To this day, Ian loves getting into the garden. Alec, when at Lowood, could often be found pottering around the garden first thing in the morning after breakfast and would always have a bag of breadcrumbs and feed all manner of birds. "Have you have ever noticed," Alec once remarked, "how in any country, wild birds, like most domestic pets, seem to have a built-in clock? If you go out each morning to feed wild birds at a set time, they soon learn to be there waiting for you." The author watched Alec several times prove his point.

Basia remembered that after wedding Ian, they visited Alec and Sarah at Lowood, and Sarah served a most beautiful afternoon tea while Alec was out fishing on the banks of his stretch of the River Tweed. He managed to catch a rather lovely twelve-pound salmon, and Basia asked him why he'd struggled for two hours to catch a fish on a hook. Why not just use a big net and scoop one up? Alec was much amused by the comment and rolled his eyes at a non-fisherman's view, Basia recalled.

The Annual Ritual of Caithness

Ian from childhood, and Basia since their marriage, loved being part of the annual Hamilton clan migration mentioned earlier, joining Alec, and their sisters and families each year up at Mary's house in Caithness, at the very tip of Scotland. As Basia commented, "It is de-riguer, you have to go, and everyone's children come too, but goodness, how we loved our time there with Alec, Erica, and the family these last few years." They all had a magical time, loved having picnics and enjoyed each other's company. Team meal preparation, cooking and eating, seems to come across as a fond memory of everyone that attended these pure family get-togethers.

Alec and Helen, in younger times, would both go out shooting and stag hunting on Helen's moor and were, Basia described, very, very close with each other as friends, not just siblings. Alec's oldest friend, Bill Findlay, and his wife, Delia, often joined these annual family retreats too and were considered by Alec and all the family as simply their family too. In 2018, Alec made his last visit to Caithness. He was rather too poorly in 2019 to travel from Jamaica and, sadly, Covid happened and then his death in Jamaica in the spring of 2020—before the annual pilgrimage to the northernmost point of Scotland.

Basia had always enjoyed going to the church at Dunnet Head every Sunday morning up at Caithness when the "tribe" made its annual pilgrimage. The Hamilton family has their pew in the church there. As HM the late Queen Elizabeth, the Queen Mother, lived close by, they always met up at church on Sunday morning with her during HM's visits at the same time. Over the years, there have been numerous occasions when Her Majesty dined at the Hamilton's and the Hamilton's at HM's Castle of Mey, also in Caithness. In her studio in London, Basia was honored to paint HM the Queen Mother's portrait many years later. You can find an image of Basia painting Her Majesty at the end of this chapter.

In describing his brother, Ian felt that Alec had brilliantly led his workforce with a valued, old-style paternal leadership and respected them in both Scotland and Jamaica. He described his older brother as one of life's genuinely kind people; he had honest love for his friends and family, would have done anything for them, and often did. He was very loyal and had each family member's back when it came down to any problem. "Alec was a decent man. The word 'worthy' isn't always applicable to everyone, but Alec earns that word." Ian recalled that the Caymanas overseer, Max Henzell, before he retired, always envied Alec, as his workforce so valued Alec because he had what we'd call today, the "common touch."

Ian added that "If we're honest, we're a stubborn family of individuals, you know. Mary was, Helen was, Alec certainly was, and Alec's three children all have the stubborn Hamilton streak, as I do too." When people can humorously mock themselves, you know they're terrific people, and if we cannot laugh at ourselves or our friends teasing us, then shame on us. Ian is one of life's genuine no-nonsense people whom the author enjoyed interviewing for this book, as he did his highly entertaining wife, Basia.

The Family's Renowned Portrait Artist

A handful of Basia's portrait sitters have included: His Holiness Pope John Paul II; president and Nobel Prize winner, Lech Walesa of Poland; HM Queen Elizabeth, the Queen Mother; HRH Princess Anne, the Princess Royal; HRH the Duke of Kent; HRH Princess Alexandra; their Royal Highnesses, the Princesses Beatrice and Eugenie; the Duchess of York; HRH the Maharaja of Jodhpur; the late Marquess of Bath; the Hon. Nicola Crosswell-Muir—the list goes on and on.

Anybody who's anybody on several continents has sat in front of Basia's easel and paintbrush. Basia was presented with the Polish Order of Merit for her unstinting work in promoting Polish culture and art and is a past chair of the Polish Club in London's Kensington. When Basia works at her portrait art, she says that she likes to draw like a hungry tigress and lives on only Kit Kat chocolate bars (yummy) and the odd cake she makes before painting. Many have commented that it's an honor to have Basia paint them, but what they most looked forward to, was being able to taste her legendary chocolate cake.

Erica Downer

Erica had been born and raised in Jamaica to British parents, her father, a church minister. She was given a first-class education, had a happy and enjoyable upbringing, and in time became part of Alec's circle of friends.

She had married a man she was truly in love with, helped and supported him as he grew his small air conditioning agency business in Jamaica with enormous energy and hard work, and made it into a nationwide one. Later, he bought a tired, has-been hotel resort in Montego Bay and turned it into an all-inclusive smart hotel, the first of what this dynamic businessman turned into the world-known-brand Sandals Hotel & Resorts chain. Gordon "Butch" Stewart, her first husband, shared the joys of having two sons together: Robert "Bobby," their eldest, and then Jonathan.

Over the years Erica turned a blind eye to several of her husband's *discreet* affairs with other women, she said, as she loved him and their boys. Tragically, their youngest son, Jonathan, when just twenty-four years old, died in a car accident in Miami in 1989. "Butch" recalled the incident in a 2008 newspaper interview, saying, "For two months after he died, I was useless, and after that, I was running on remote control. Things were a blur. It's every parent's nightmare."

When Butch later engaged in a more public extra-marital affair, it was time to bring an end to an otherwise harmonious marriage Erica felt. It was a very amicable uncoupling because they still truly liked and respected each other. Erica commented that these things can happen. They set an example few follow by remaining good pals forever afterwards, with no acrimony, and were each a devoted parent to Bobby. Butch had always remained kind and generous to Erica, she recalled, right through to his tragic death in January 2021. She reflected on how she believed that she always got on with Butch's subsequent wives and likes all his children. She knew how proud Butch was of all eight of his children and his numerous grandchildren and great-grandchildren and felt his death a tragic loss to all of them.

Being wooed somewhat on the rebound from Butch, all be it some years later, Erica eventually married again to a Mr. Downer. Apart from a great son, Edward, whom she loves dearly, the marriage became an unhappy and fractious one over time, pole opposite to her happy and loving marriage with Butch. Often people feel trapped and embarrassed to walk away from a marriage that breaks, and in their eyes, they don't want to be seen as a failure. Her initial hesitation evolved into her being desperately unhappy, she said. Sadly, the marriage turned somewhat unpalatable and ended with divorce. That was that as far as Erica was concerned, she did not imagine she would fall in love with anyone again, had a wonderful circle of friends and had her two boys to dote on, Bobby and Edward as they made their own lives.

Alec's Circle of Friends

Alec, like Erica, did not think he would find love again after losing Sarah and didn't wish to. Erica had often met Alec in similar social circles over the six years since Sarah had died and got on very well, simply as good pals, during and after her Downer marriage. So, it was not unusual to find them quite innocently in each other's company at major social events, art exhibitions, or pals' dinner parties.

After Sarah's death, Alec told the author that Erica was one of the friends who just instinctively knew what to say to bring comfort, when to listen when to share a thought on coping with the down moments, and when to leave him alone. She wasn't demanding or needy was his phrase. Alec said they just seemed to gravitate more frequently to being in each other's company and shared their ups and downs in life (No "Downer" pun intended). Slowly they both began to feel more than friendship and a genuine love growing. Reversing the oft-heard saying, Alec said that he suspected that it was a case of 'twice bitten, now shy for Erica.' She didn't see marriage on the horizon. People noticed that they gave great solace to each other, seemed happiest whenever in the other's company, and had become more than friends.

Alec's brother Ian always felt he said that 'Erica truly helped Alec cope with his loss, to come to terms with the tragedy of losing Sarah and rediscover a reason for going on. She showed him great empathy. More than friendship began to blossom slowly over a few years, and both were a little unsure and hesitant when they began to feel they had found true love again.'

Alec Proposed Marriage

Two years later, some *eight years after* Alec lost Sarah, Erica was surprised when Alec proposed marriage to her, but she just knew it was right for them both—they were happiest in each other's company.

Erica's life encompasses her love of painting, having been a wife to Alec, a mother to her two sons, and a businesswoman who for a couple of years contributed to the running of Alec's two estates, the farm, and plantation. She kept an eye on all their employees on both estates as Alec aged and became a little less engaged in the business day-to-day. Somehow, she manages to find time to lead an active social life in Jamaica and Scotland. In Alec's last few years, she took care of his medical issues and ensured he got the best hospital treatment, flying him to wherever he needed to be for the best care.

Ian commented that Erica was constantly checking to ensure Lowood and Caymanas were being run in Alec's children's best interests; as Alec got older and less able to be involved, his memory began to slip. Erica stepped into the breach acting with an extraordinary level of transparency, a genuinely honorable woman, Ian said.

That Annual Visit to Scotland

It always started with Alec and Erica arriving at their home on the River Tweed's banks in Scotland for the same three summer months each year, and every morning's routine was similar for Alec. Their marvelous cook/ housekeeper, Hilary, would have oatcakes and all sorts of things baking in the oven and oatmeal porridge bubbling away on the Aga top. Even in his eighties, Alec's childhood taste for them remained, and they both were still an essential start to his day in Scotland. He loved oatcakes and oatmeal porridge; always with full-fat-cream, he'd generously pour himself until his porridge was awash with it.

When he wasn't in Scotland, he still liked his oatmeal porridge; regardless of where he was in the world, it was part of his go-to breakfast routine. Guests staying at his home in Jamaica would find porridge on the menu at breakfast there too. He was a Scotsman by birth, a Jamaican in how he lived his life, with a hint of Scotsman by habit, so it should be no surprise.

As guests left their bedrooms at Lowood House to come downstairs for breakfast, the aroma of Hilary's oatcakes baking meant that they simply had to follow the aromatic trail that led to the kitchen, and there was the round family breakfast table in a curved bay window overlooking the River Tweed. The river flowed and lurched along at quite a speed, the grassy banks waving in the wind, birds flitting from tree to tree. This is Scotland at its best.

Like many older couples, Alec and Erica spent most of their time quietly doing their own thing while together, in loving conversation or teasing each other. There was the odd irritation as in all marriages, but they shared a dry and wicked sense of humor. Ian said that "Erica put Alec's health, wellbeing, and medical care first." His ongoing trials with cancer were tough for Alec, Erica, and his family to face. Having chunks of your face, nose, and ears removed, replaced, and reformed from the skin taken from elsewhere on your body is not for the faint-hearted. Getting old is not for sissies!

Getting old and ill as a person's memory begins to flag is not easy for anyone or those close to them. Alec was still the same; he still liked excellent company and retained his sense of humor. He loved to look back on his life and reminisce, and on many occasions in Jamaica, the author found him looking back at old photo albums and reading his old diaries and game record books. Remembering a particularly fun week of grouse shooting in Scotland, or a particular memory of catching yet another twelve-pound salmon on his stretch of the River Tweed. Alec recorded significant events in diary notes every day of his life in little hand sized books, even if it was one comment.

Loss, and Upheaval of Erica's World

Butch dying, nine months after Alec, came, Erica said, as a double blow. She found herself wanting to be alone and withdrew into frequent moments of melancholy for months and months. After her father and sons, the two men she loved most in her life, had both died in the space of months.

Erica has come to terms without Alec in her life; it has also meant upheaval in her surroundings and homes. Few not faced with such tremendous change occurring all at once are unlikely to understand the enormity of such a period in another person's life. With Lowood sold in 2018, handing over to the local Scottish government by April 2022, his children felt obliged to auction its contents which their Trust did in October 2021. Erica had to spend time in Scotland in 2021, removing her personal items and clothing and deciding what to do with them, as she would no longer be able to call Scotland a place where she had a home. Later in the year, she had to do the same at Caymanas House in Jamaica, as the estate reverted to Alec's children's Trust, who had decided to lease the house out.

Fortunately for Erica, she had maintained her private homes entirely at her own expense throughout her marriage, homes which she owned before her wedding. One of Erica's two homes is a modest townhouse in the capital of the island, Kingston, and the other out at Discovery Bay, a town in the parish of St. Ann. Erica felt blessed to have had homes to go to and two sons who wrapped their arms around her and helped her through her loss, grief, and tumultuous change with the houses she called home, no longer hers to live in with Alec's passing. She was also terribly grateful to Alec's children, who enabled her to slowly take her time to withdraw from her life that was no longer to be hers.

Alec's Children

Laura, Johnny, and William, Alec, and Sarah's children, were all born and raised in Jamaica, a country they love and cherish, and were all educated, in part, at boarding schools in Great Britain. Every year they whole family decamped to Scotland and the children enjoyed their family homes in Scotland, their wider family and heritage.

While Johnny has always lived in Jamaica, Laura now lives with her husband and children in Surrey, England. William lives with his wife and children in Edinburgh, Scotland, very close to the Lowood Estate, which is just forty-five minutes to the south. All of Alec's property, estates, capital investments, and belongings are held in trust for his three children to share, other than bequests made to a few others. Johnny was destined to take over the running of the Caymanas Estate in Jamaica for the trust, William the Lowood Estate in Scotland, and Laura the unique beachfront property on Jamaica's north coast.

John (Johnny) Alexander Hamilton was born in 1963. After going off to boarding school in England, Johnny studied farming (for a future at Caymanas) and returned to Jamaica. When home, he followed his passion for creating bamboo furniture, having fallen in love with the concept when visiting Thailand. Johnny launched his company, *Original Bamboo Furniture*, in 1990 from a factory built on the Caymanas Estate, creating sustainable, stock designer bamboo furniture. You can see an example of Johnny's sofas and chairs in many Jamaican homes and some hotels. He has several lovely children and has the vivacious Janet Brown, with whom he has happily shared his life with for many years now. Alexander was born in 1990, Jonah in 2006, and the adorable Neya, born in 2013 to Janet and himself.

Laura Constance Mill (née Hamilton) came next into Alec and Sarah's life, born in 1964 in Jamaica. She was schooled in England and after some years of 'discovering herself,' as she describes her early adulthood, she met and married Lionel Mill, from England. Their wedding took place at home at the Caymanas Estate in Jamaica. They now live in Surrey, England. As they say, Lionel is something in the city, and Laura is a successful artist and designer of stunning fabrics and ceramics. Laura and Lionel have three children: Poppy born in 2000; Bogle, born in 2001 (an old family name linked to the Hamiltons); and Monteith (another oft used name by the Hamiltons), born in 2004. In 2008, 'Laura Hamilton' set up her company, *Bird in the Hand*, in Hackney, London. Her online division ships her sought after products globally.

William Vereker Hamilton was born in Jamaica in 1969 and went off to boarding school in the UK, too. He was sent off relatively early at just six years of age, and one stark memory of his first winter in England after Jamaica was that he had blankets but oddly no sheets at school. As you'll remember, Alec had a similar stark memory of his boarding school of constantly being cold in British winters. Later in life, William married the lovely Veronica Piccolo. They have two children, Amelie, born in 2006, who is growing up so fast, and little Pablo, born in 2013. Pablo is an energetic and free-minded spirit, and the author much enjoyed meeting them in Scotland a couple of times. From his home in Edinburgh, William runs a successful Airbnb business.

The Lowood Driveway

As the book draws to a close, talking about the sense of arrival at Alec's Scottish home is an excellent way to ease towards the end of his life and times, as the sense of arrival and departure at Lowood House is quite extraordinary.

As you pop through the estates main entrance's stone gated pillars, you pass the old 'wee' Gate Lodge on your right, which hangs aside the river, and stroll towards the house along a half a mile of private, gently winding road. Trees abound, acres of unending fields unfold before you, and there's the smell of fresh grass. Occasionally dotted here and there stand, like tall sentinels of nature on guard duty of this ancient land, one-hundred-year-old trees sprinkled across the fields in all their splendor. It is a view straight out of a Constable or Turner painting. Several individual trees have girths that would make an elephant proud. It is just idyllic, especially as the rare herd of Jacob sheep appears, grazing on the verdant grassland between you and the River Tweed, and as rare, the belted Galloway cattle who wander across the fields on your left.

Slowly in the distance, the house begins to investigate your sighting of it, as it gradually looms into view through large trees obscuring it from the drive at first. As the grey stone walls peep at you from behind tree lines, it is as if the house is sizing up whether you are a welcome visitor or not. The River Tweed appears on your right again as you continue along the drive and grazing fields to your left – suddenly, you can hear the sound of rushing water and the rustling of leaves in the trees as the bank of the River Tweed is closer to the house now. The site, the sounds, the fragrances in the air, the wind rustling, the grass on the river bans waving, align to create a most extraordinary moment for any visitor.

Alec used to love taking this walk in his younger days. He said one of his favorite things about Lowood was that every season brought a different walk experience down that same long drive. Erica wrote a lovely poem a few years ago for Alec to bring back those memories for him, which is reproduced at the end of the chapter under Notes.

Looking Back on His Life

Alec reflected for a few moments after being asked by the author to look back on his life and summarize what he was most proud of achieving. He said that his greatest joys were his family and friends and having accomplished marriages to two women he had loved (which brought a chuckle from him at the sound of the phrase). He felt blessed to have inherited and lived on the Caymanas Estate in Jamaica and the Lowood Estate in Scotland. Alec added that, while he, like all of us, has made mistakes and has some regrets, overall, he felt good about his achievements. He said, of course, "my three children are my most outstanding achievement and my life's legacy, and my grandchildren as I am so proud of them. When I go one day, it will be with a sense that I have led a full life." The author has felt blessed to know Alec and his life in its entirety and admires the man's integrity and achievements.

Losing Alec

In 2017, the prime minister of Jamaica, Andrew Holness (JLP), paid Alec a lifetime achievement honor and bestowed upon him the Prime Minister's Order of Distinction, Jamaica (OD). It was granted for services to Jamaican horse racing.

Alec loved life, loved his family, loved his friends, and loved the land he inherited in both Scotland and Jamaica. Above all he loved Jamaica and its people from the moment he set foot on it until he died on it.

So it was that sixty-six-years after arriving in Jamaica, this son of Scotland, scion of the Hamiltons of Westport & Elrick, Alexander Vereker Hamilton, justice of the peace, commander of the Order of Jamaica, passed away on Easter Sunday, April 12, 2020. Alec was a legend in his own time in the horse racing world of Jamaica and for his Brahman cattle breeding there. He will be remembered in Scotland for his ardent breeding of and supplying others with the rare, belted Galloway cattle and the equally rare Jacob sheep. People will recall a passionate country sportsman and, above all else, a man who has left footprints in the sands of time that his family can follow.

The author began chapter one you may recall with the following quote:

> *You can't go back and change the beginning, but you can start where you are and change the end.* C. S. Lewis.

Well Alec wrote the ending to his own story by how he lived his life and by his deeds, which are carved for all time in his branch of Hamilton family folk law. This book in part preserves the memory of this Hamilton for all to know.

The following poem by Erica Hamilton of the driveway at Lowood House, in Scotland, was dedicated to her husband, Alec.

A Walk Down the Drive.

Near the town, but secret, Lowood lies,
Serene and beautiful beside the rushing Tweed.   ·
The woodland golden spires to misty skies,
The parkland, where the curious Belties feed.

The teeny lodge, the tunnel 'neath the trees,
A bank of yellow primrose in the spring.
But soon, the tangled undergrowth will freeze,
In wind and frost that winter's hands will bring.

Further on the grassy mossy lochan,
Where Belties drink and deer, wildfowl abound.
The fox's hole in woods that gently beckon,
Stop, listen; you will not hear a sound.

At last, the robust and tall guardian boles,
Before the looming house, both old and grey.
The sweeping lawn provides a home for moles,
All space for grandchildren to play.

© Erica Hamilton.

The Authors Farewell

Goodbye, Alec, and until we meet again, God bless.

Alec and Sarah (née Platt) and Alec's brother, Ian, at the Jamaican Governor-General Sir Kenneth Blackburn's party, King's House, Jamaica (WOP).

Alec's wedding in Scotland to fellow Dumbartonshire Scot, Sarah Platt (WOP).

Alec and Sarah and their first two children, Johnny, and Laura, at Lowood, the Scottish estate Alec inherited from his parents (WOP).

Ian Crum Ewing Hamilton, younger brother of Alec Hamilton. Portrait painted by his wife, Basia Kaczmarowska Hamilton (WOP).

Barbara (Basia) Kaczmarowska-Hamilton, Ian's wife, and portrait painter, seen here painting her late Majesty Queen Elizabeth, the Queen Mother (WOP).

Alexander and Erica Hamilton, love, and another wedding for both (WOP).

Alec's oldest friend from childhood, Bill Findlay, now eighty-eight. He was born in the family's Boturich Castle on the banks of Loch Lomond, Scotland (PBA).

Alec reading an old estate game fishing book at home in Scotland, 2017 (PBA).

Lowood House sits on a mile and a half of the famous River Tweed (PBA). Lowood House, Alec & Erica Hamiltons Scottish home, and it's rear lawns. (WOP).

One of the famous and rare belted Galloway cattle at Lowood. A herd bought by General Sir Ian Hamilton from Sir Winston Churchill, inherited by his nephew Ian and then by his daughter, Helen, and Alec on their two nearby estates (PBA).

Equally rare Jacob sheep bred by Alec at his Scottish estate, whose horns make them look like goats to many (PBA).

About the Author

The author, photographed by Becky Elizabeth Photography, the USA.

Robert Gary Dodds is known as someone who has a quick wit and a sense of humor. As a published author, he is evolving into a serious writer of biographies and historical research, as we hope you will agree. He is highly adept at assessing and reading people and asking intuitive questions that uncover the facts that have made great stories for this book.

Born in England of earlier Scottish and Cornish heritage, his wife of 43-years is from one of Jamaica's old families with Scottish roots, the Harvey family. He retains extensive contacts globally and has worked with charities wherever he and his family have lived. He currently sits on the Global Advisory Council of the Akilah Women's Institute of Rwanda.

The author is at ease in almost all cultures, having lived in Europe, the Middle East & Africa, Asia Pacific, and North America, and he's conducted consulting work in the West Indies and Latin America. This is a man equally at home in Qatar's empty desert quarter with Bedouin tribespeople or the lush Blue Mountains of Jamaica with old friends. He loves nothing better than being with friends or family, especially his grandchildren, children, wife, and three miniature schnauzers in North Carolina. They retired from their international careers in December 2014.

Robert Gary Dodds—Author ™

The Books Dedication

I am delighted to dedicate this book to the greatest blessings in my and my wife's lives—our grandchildren: our grandsons, Kai, and Charlie Shimkets, who live a ten-minute walk from our home in North Carolina; and our granddaughters, Isabel and Chloe (and their little stepbrother, Sebastian), who live in Yorkshire, in England.

In part, this book is the story of our grandchildren's maternal family's heritage and the history and blood of Jamaica and Scotland in their genes. They are all my inspiration.

Acknowledgments

The author is grateful to many fellow biographical and historical authors over countless decades and centuries, ancient chroniclers, and published works by historians and genealogists. He extends the same thanks to several DNA projects and research centers whose papers on the Hamiltons, their ancestors, or historical events formed part of his research. All such research over several years enabled the author to create a linear story from the first traceable Hamilton ancestor to all those Hamiltons in which his DNA flows.

The "modern-day" Alexander Hamilton approved the author writing his biography as part of this series of Hamilton biographical and historical works. Facilitated by his wife, Erica, Alec gave the author unlimited access to himself and those in his life. He also made a treasure trove of Hamilton records, images, and written material available, which proved invaluable research material for the book. His wife, Erica, wished to honor her husband's memory by bringing such a book to life, and the author owes her deep gratitude for unbounding support as someone who has become a cherished friend.

Sincere gratitude goes to a litany of people. While impossible to thank each, the author would like to give special thanks to several prominent supporters and, extends his apologies and equal gratitude to anyone not included:

His Grace, the 16th Duke of Hamilton, Chief of the Hamilton Clan worldwide, generously wrote the foreword to this book. The book's ability to bring these collective Hamilton and ancestor stories to public knowledge, clan societies, and associations was seen of great value. Many Hamiltons are based in the UK and overseas, especially in the USA, Canada, Australia, and New Zealand. Caroline Cooper from the Duke's household sought to assist the author at every opportunity with the Duke. The author is indebted to them.

H.H. Princess Olga Andreevna Romanov, great-niece of the last Tsar of Russia, fellow biographical and historical author, earned the author's gratitude when writing a past book. He is most grateful to Her Highness for her kind quote on this book.

Basia Kaczmarowska-Hamilton, the extraordinary portrait artist, allowed the author to reproduce several of her portraits or photos in this book, including that of Alex Hamilton on the front cover. Beyond that, she became one of the author's most supportive people, encouraged him at every opportunity, and has put the London book launch together.

To the noted military historians and authors, Celia and John Lee, deep gratitude is extended for their quote on the book, Celia's highly valued mentoring of the author, and John's critical mid-point professional big-picture editing advice.

For her exceptional positiveness, the author's American agent, Linda Barksdale-Case-Broughton moves mountains to open doors for those she represents, as she has for the author and this book. Many of the extraordinary events surrounding the book's launch in America would not have happened without her. She has, in the author, made a friend for life.

Many thanks to George Frederick "Grandlad" Smyth, the early draft manuscripts helicopter-view Editologist, for his continuous upbeat guidance and encouragement to write this book - from its early days to completion.

Fellow author Peter Jarrette, an accomplished artist, and prolific author gave sound publishing advice early on; fellow author and Jamaican, Geoffrey Haddad, introduced his publisher to the author and has been very helpful.

Thanks to an old and dear friend of 42-years, Katie Benson, and her sister Paddy Challens, who became developmental editors of later working drafts before submission to the publisher. Many thanks go to both ladies for their candid remarks and for volunteering so much of their time to support the author.

Archie, Lord Hamilton, Baron of Epsom, led with his unanswered question to the author discovering by research another famous Hamilton on the other side of the American War of Independence. He tracked his life and wrote about that aristocrat in this book. What good fortune to have had that question from his Lordship.

The Gordon Highlander Trust and volunteer researchers, The Scottish Buildings Historic Trust, the volunteer historians of Strathleven House, The Scottish Government archives department, and the Jamaican Archive departments gave the researcher valuable time and guidance. Debretts Peerage & Baronetage and the proved valuable resources also.

The Hamilton DNA Project at Pennsylvania State University (PSU), linked with the Hamilton National Genealogical Society, Inc. and supported by DNA analysis by the 'Family Tree DNA' company. The PSU Hamilton DNA project has an extraordinary database of worldwide Hamilton DNA built up. They commenced tracing Hamilton's lineage through different branches back over the centuries, sought ought, any, one bloodline origin and discovered several new branches, and asked the question, was the Hamilton father of America a Hamilton by bloodline. Their database proved invaluable, and so much of their data was not available to earlier Hamilton biographers and historians. Go Pen State! The Court of Lord Lyon (the Lyon Court of Scotland) is a standing court of law regulating heraldry in Scotland. The Lyon Court maintains the register of grants of arms, known as the Public Register of all components and bearings in Scotland and records of genealogies.

The late chairman and publisher, Oliver Clarke of The Daily Gleaner, Jamaica's earliest national newspaper, together with his senior researcher and librarian, Sheree Rhoden, gave unlimited access to their archives back to the 1800s. Oliver also shared comments with the author for parts of this book. Oliver was a much admired and highly respected leading member of the media in Jamaica and had been a close friend of the author's wife's family all his life and was greatly loved by them.

Various national country, military and museum archives and records were accessed by the author, which all helped with his research.

Dawn Joseph, the owner of "Make an Impression" printers and designers in Holly Springs, North Carolina, turned pages of handwritten author scribbles of family trees, names, dates, and heraldry into the polished charts you see in the book. Dawn is the author's local book champion, who also showed incredible patience and enthusiasm for the book as the family trees evolved.

Huge thanks go to individual Hamilton friends and family who gave time to talk about the modern-day Hamilton, his life's stories, and his ancestors. Such people are an author's blessing and appear throughout this book by name – each has contributed beyond measure to make this book what it is.

Last but not least, the author thanks his Canadian publisher FriesenPress and their specialist teams, who crafted the final manuscript into a form of art. They delivered spot-on editing and proofreading, design, and layout over several structured rounds to produce the book you see today. A special mention to their superb editors for their work and direction. Their design and promotional teams all gave invaluable advice to the author. For the guidance of Jamie, who commenced my journey with the publisher, and the support from the publisher's appointed journey guide, who has been steadfast throughout, go the author final thank you.

Their book distribution network through Ingram Content Group, book sales and distribution, and publishing services of Tennessee, USA. They are one of the largest book distribution networks globally and also upload their author's books to 50,000 worldwide book retailers, both physical and online companies. Ingram has the industry's largest active book inventory with access to 7.5 million books. With multiple print on demand warehouse in multiple sites in North America, as well as the United Kingdom, France and Australia, each handling their regions of the world. What's not to like and say thank you to the author's book distribution company.

Validating Research Can Be An Interesting Dilemma

Over the last four years, the author has conducted exhaustive research into hundreds of Hamilton, de Beaumont, and Viking ancestors of Alexander Hamilton's of this book. He has evidenced their family histories, lineage, and connections; he came across much data written by eminent historians and genealogists and reviewed and assessed a mind-boggling array of material. He has accessed numerous well-evidenced genealogy data, historical records and printed materials, and several valuable DNA studies. Several distinguished historians and genealogists disagree with one and other, as many findings and papers the author read illuminated. They may not be disagreeing at all but merely seeing evidence from their perspective and blotting out information not relevant to them or their work. Often one line of inquiry is ruled out by another as impossible or unlikely. As for well-intending lay historians, the author has even seen scorn heaped on them rather than guidance and encouragement for their passion.

Naturally, new evidence will appear from time to time unavailable to earlier researchers, such as recent DNA studies and frequently more recently discovered documents that change an entire picture. The author chose to evidence the same names, dates, and stories wherever possible from three separate reliable, respected, and aligned sources before using that data or lineage in this book: including Historical, genealogical, and DNA evidence where available. He then felt comfortable that he would be doing justice with fair accuracy to all concerned with lineage and dates.

For any genealogist or historian to the dissenter, the author's interpreted position on anyone or anything different from yours does not imply any other person is wrong. For him, combined historical and genealogical research is a fantastic resource for an author, and he respects all who conduct research. The conjoined journey historians and genealogists took the author were delightful, and for their outstanding work, he thanks all those who follow these professions and committed lay devotees. He indeed could not have written this book without so many ardent and committed individuals and research centers, several he engaged with directly, each who was delighted to help put a passionate lifetime lay-historian onto the right path.

Illustration Permissions and copyright

The Books Illustrations

The copyright status of each is coded according to the below list. Each illustration confirms the artist or person, date, and provenance wherever possible of a painting, photograph, illustration, drawing, or map, and attributes, thanks to the owner of a work placed into the public domain for all. Every effort has been made to verify any current copyright and take the owner's permission to reproduce any such works in this book.

+ (WOP) = With Owners Permission (or copyright holder) to reproduce.
+ (NCA) = No Copyright Attributable could be found, despite research.
+ (PBA) = Photographed by Author and permitted to reproduce.
+ (PIA) = Photographs in Archives of Hamilton or other personal collections, who've permitted reproduction in this book.
+ (CE) = Copyright Expired 70-years after the owner's death by law in the USA, Canada, the EU, UK, Australia, and most countries, unless additional unique elements by a photographer for example were added to such an image.

The book's dust cover images:

The front cover images are of today's Alexander Hamilton, painted by Basia Kaczmarowska Hamilton, and a sketch of the Founding Father.

The painting on the spine of the book of the founding father is by John Turnbull, 1805, displayed in the New York City Hall. The photograph of Alec on the back cover is by the author.

Copyright

Robert Gary Dodds – Author™, has done its best to ensure that copyright laws of all countries are adhered to and complied with concerning all images in this book. They have not knowingly published any image in breach of anyone's copyright. It is not the intent of this book's copyright owner to breach anyone's in-date copyright. If any unintended infringement of copyright is evidenced and notified to Robert Gary Dodds – Author™, they would immediately seek permission or remove that image from all future print of demand books, with sincere apologies.

Alexander Vereker Hamilton.
A portrait of the stoical Alec, painted by his wife, Erica, just a couple of months before he died, from a
sketch of hers made in 2019 off the coast of Deception Island in Antarctica. He was ravaged by skin cancer
and facial reconstruction, but Erica captured his character brilliantly. Godspeed, Alec! (WOP).

CPSIA information can be obtained
at www.ICGtesting.com
Printed in the USA
LVHW070106170322
713570LV00010B/557